# DASH DIET
## COOKBOOK

*500 Low Sodium, High-Potassium Recipes
to Lower Blood Pressure and Quickly Lose Weight.
Including a 140-Day Meal Plan to Improve Your Health*

Lara Brandon

LARA BRANDON

© Copyright 2021 - All rights reserved.
Lara Brandon

The content contained within this book may not be reproduced, duplicated or transmitted without direct written permission from the author or the publisher.
Under no circumstances will any blame or legal responsibility be held against the publisher, or author, for any damages, reparation, or monetary loss due to the information contained within this book. Either directly or indirectly.

**Legal Notice:**
This book is copyright protected. This book is only for personal use. You cannot amend, distribute, sell, use, quote or paraphrase any part, or the content within this book, without the consent of the author or publisher.

**Disclaimer Notice:**
Please note the information contained within this document is for educational and entertainment purposes only. All effort has been executed to present accurate, up to date, and reliable, complete information. No warranties of any kind are declared or implied. Readers acknowledge that the author is not engaging in the rendering of legal, financial, medical or professional advice. The content within this book has been derived from various sources. Please consult a licensed professional before attempting any techniques outlined in this book.
By reading this document, the reader agrees that under no circumstances is the author responsible for any losses, direct or indirect, which are incurred as a result of the use of information contained within this document, including, but not limited to, errors, omissions, or inaccuracies.

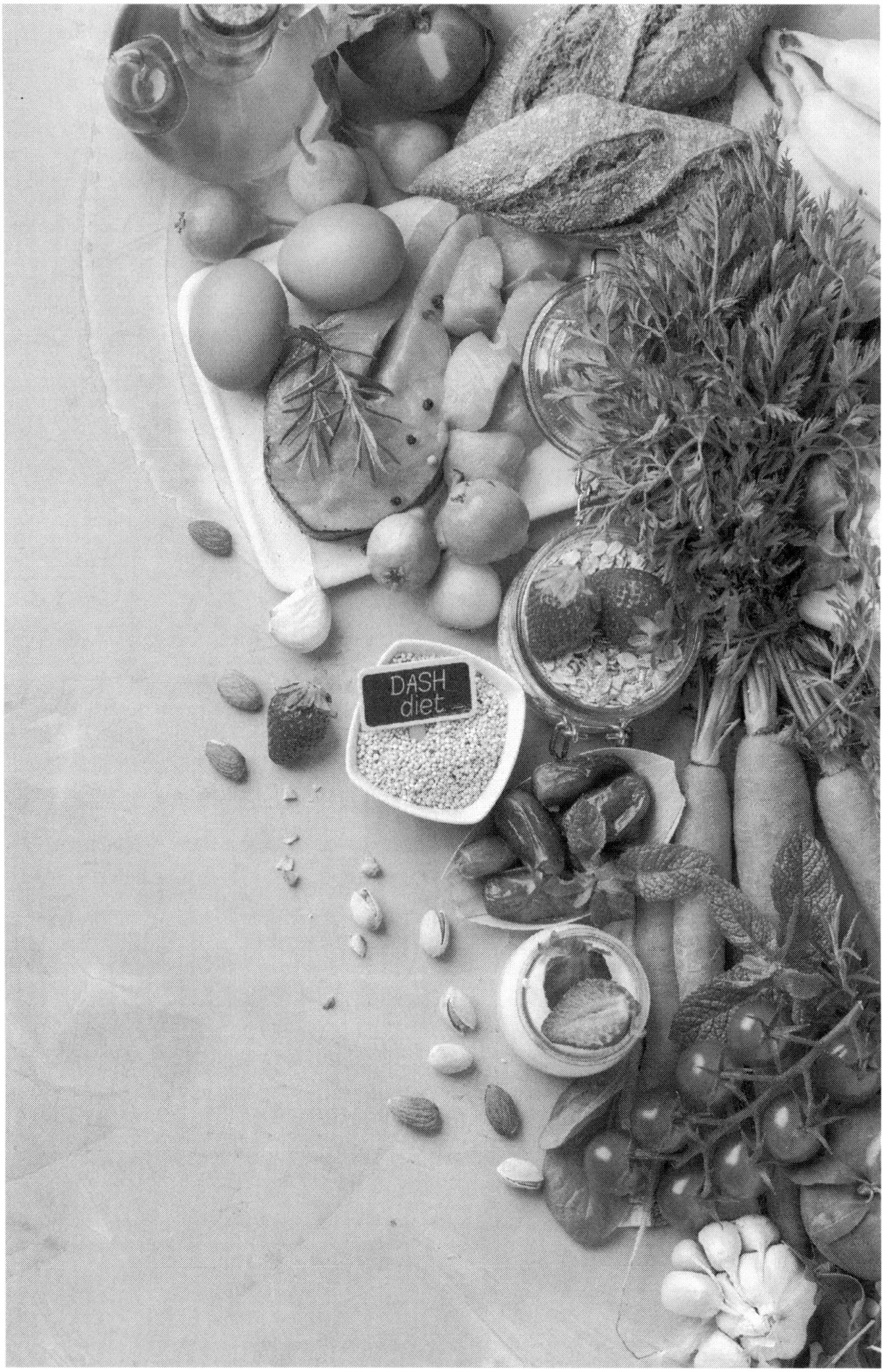
DASH
diet

# Table Of Contents

| | |
|---|---|
| INTRODUCTION .................................................. 11 | CHAPTER 3: FOOD PLAN FOR 140 DAYS ........................... 21 |
| MY STORY ......................................................... 13 | CHAPTER 4: THE IMPORTANCE OF REGULAR EXERCISE AND DEEP BREATHING BOTH FOR HYPERTENSION AND TO LOSE WEIGHT ...................... 27 |
| HOW I IMPROVED MY HEALTH AND REGAINED MY IDEAL WEIGHT .................................................... 13 | |
| THE ENCOUNTER THAT CHANGED MY LIFE! ............... 13 | |
| WHO FINDS A TRUE FRIEND FINDS A...TREASURE! ...... 13 | GRAPHS ON FOOD AND CALORIES, FOR EXAMPLE, FOR THOSE WHO WANT TO LOSE WEIGHT ............................ 28 |
| TAKE CARE OF YOUR BODY! ................................. 14 | |
| CHAPTER 1: UNDERSTANDING THE DASH DIET ......... 15 | CHAPTER 5: BREAKFAST RECIPES .................................. 29 |
| WHAT IS USED IN THIS DIET? ............................... 15 | 1. ENERGY SUNRISE MUFFINS ........................ 29 |
| ENHANCING HEALTHCARE TEAM OUTCOMES ........... 15 | 2. BLUEBERRY WAFFLES ............................... 30 |
| IS THE DASH DIET PRIMARILY PREFERRED FOR HYPERTENSION CARE ONLY? ................................. 16 | 3. APPLE PANCAKES .................................... 30 |
| | 4. SUPER-SIMPLE GRANOLA .......................... 31 |
| RESEARCH AND GENERAL ACCEPTANCE .................. 16 | 5. SAVORY YOGURT BOWLS .......................... 31 |
| PRECAUTIONS ..................................................... 16 | 6. SPINACH, EGG, AND CHEESE BREAKFAST QUESADILLAS 31 |
| IS IT HELPFUL IN WEIGHT LOSS? ............................. 17 | 7. SIMPLE CHEESE AND BROCCOLI OMELETS ...... 32 |
| HOW EFFECTIVE IS IT IN REDUCING BLOOD PRESSURE? ..... 17 | 8. CREAMY AVOCADO AND EGG SALAD SANDWICHES ...... 32 |
| CHAPTER 2: EVIDENCE THAT POTASSIUM IS EVEN MORE IMPORTANT THAN SODIUM REDUCTION FOR HYPERTENSION, HEART AND WEIGHT REDUCTION 18 | 9. BREAKFAST HASH .................................... 32 |
| | 10. HEARTY BREAKFAST CASSEROLE ................. 33 |
| | 11. CREAMY APPLE-AVOCADO SMOOTHIE .......... 33 |
| | 12. STRAWBERRY, ORANGE, AND BEET SMOOTHIE ..... 33 |
| DIABETICS WITH HIGH BLOOD PRESSURE TYPE 1 ACIDOSIS .... 19 | 13. BLUEBERRY-VANILLA YOGURT SMOOTHIE ...... 33 |
| POTASSIUM DEFICIENCY MAKES HYPERTENSION WORSE ........ 19 | 14. GREEK YOGURT OAT PANCAKES ................... 34 |
| POTASSIUM DEFICIENCY CAUSES INSULIN RESISTANCE ........... 19 | 15. SCRAMBLED EGG AND VEGGIE BREAKFAST QUESADILLAS ............................................ 34 |
| | 16. STUFFED BREAKFAST PEPPERS .................... 34 |

| #   | Recipe | Page |
|-----|--------|------|
| 17. | Sweet Potato Toast Three Ways | 34 |
| 18. | Apple-Apricot Brown Rice Breakfast Porridge | 35 |
| 19. | Carrot Cake Overnight Oats | 35 |
| 20. | Steel-Cut Oatmeal with Plums and Pear | 35 |
| 21. | French toast with Applesauce | 35 |
| 22. | Banana-Peanut Butter and Greens Smoothie | 36 |
| 23. | Baking Powder Biscuits | 36 |
| 24. | Oatmeal Banana Pancakes with Walnuts | 36 |
| 25. | Creamy Oats, Greens and Blueberry Smoothie | 36 |
| 26. | Banana and Cinnamon Oatmeal | 36 |
| 27. | Bagels Made Healthy | 37 |
| 28. | Cereal with Cranberry-Orange Twist | 37 |
| 29. | No-Cook Overnight Oats | 37 |
| 30. | Avocado Cup with Egg | 37 |
| 31. | Mediterranean Toast | 38 |
| 32. | Instant Banana Oatmeal | 38 |
| 33. | Almond Butter-Banana Smoothie | 38 |
| 34. | Brown Sugar Cinnamon Oatmeal | 38 |
| 35. | Buckwheat Pancakes with Vanilla Almond Milk | 38 |
| 36. | Salmon and Egg Scramble | 39 |
| 37. | Pumpkin Muffins | 39 |
| 38. | Sweet Berries Pancake | 39 |
| 39. | Zucchini Pancakes | 39 |
| 40. | Breakfast Banana Split | 40 |
| 41. | Easy Veggie Muffins | 40 |
| 42. | Carrot Muffins | 40 |
| 43. | Pineapple Oatmeal | 40 |
| 44. | Spinach Muffins | 41 |
| 45. | Chia Seeds Breakfast Mix | 41 |
| 46. | Breakfast Fruits Bowls | 41 |
| 47. | Pumpkin Cookies | 41 |
| 48. | Veggie Scramble | 41 |
| 49. | Mushrooms and Turkey Breakfast | 42 |
| 50. | Mushrooms and Cheese Omelet | 42 |
| 51. | Egg White Breakfast Mix | 42 |
| 52. | Pesto Omelet | 42 |
| 53. | Quinoa Bowls | 43 |
| 54. | Strawberry Sandwich | 43 |
| 55. | Apple Quinoa Muffins | 43 |
| 56. | Very Berry Muesli | 43 |
| 57. | Veggie Quiche Muffins | 44 |
| 58. | Turkey Sausage and Mushroom Strata | 44 |
| 59. | Bacon Bits | 44 |
| 60. | Steel Cut Oat Blueberry Pancakes | 44 |
| 61. | Spinach, Mushroom, and Feta Cheese Scramble | 45 |
| 62. | Red Velvet Pancakes with Cream Cheese Topping | 45 |
| 63. | Peanut Butter and Banana Breakfast Smoothie | 45 |
| 64. | No-Bake Breakfast Granola Bars | 46 |
| 65. | Mushroom Shallot Frittata | 46 |
| 66. | Jack-o-Lantern Pancakes | 46 |
| 67. | Fruit Pizza | 46 |
| 68. | Flax Banana Yogurt Muffins | 47 |
| 69. | Apple Oats | 47 |
| 70. | Buckwheat Crepes | 47 |
| 71. | Whole Grain Pancakes | 47 |
| 72. | Granola Parfait | 48 |
| 73. | Curry Tofu Scramble | 48 |
| 74. | Scallions Omelet | 48 |

## CHAPTER 6: SALADS .................................................................. 49

| #   | Recipe | Page |
|-----|--------|------|
| 75. | Tomato Salad | 49 |
| 76. | Feta Beet Salad | 49 |
| 77. | Cauliflower and Tomato Salad | 49 |
| 78. | Tahini Spinach | 50 |
| 79. | Pilaf with Cream Cheese | 50 |
| 80. | Easy Spaghetti Squash | 50 |
| 81. | Roasted Eggplant Salad | 51 |
| 82. | Penne with Tahini Sauce | 51 |
| 83. | Roasted Veggies | 51 |
| 84. | Zucchini Pasta | 51 |
| 85. | Asparagus Pasta | 52 |
| 86. | Feta and Spinach Pita Bake | 52 |
| 87. | Spelled Salad | 52 |
| 88. | Chickpea and Zucchini Salad | 53 |
| 89. | Provencal Artichoke Salad | 53 |
| 90. | Bulgarian Salad | 53 |
| 91. | Falafel Salad Bowl | 54 |
| 92. | Easy Greek Salad | 54 |
| 93. | Arugula Salad with Figs and Walnuts | 54 |
| 94. | Cauliflower Salad with Tahini Vinaigrette | 55 |
| 95. | Mediterranean Potato Salad | 55 |
| 96. | Quinoa and Pistachio Salad | 55 |
| 97. | Cucumber Chicken Salad with Spicy Peanut Dressing | 55 |
| 98. | German Hot Potato Salad | 56 |
| 99. | Chicken Fiesta Salad | 56 |
| 100. | Corn and Black Bean Salad | 56 |
| 101. | Awesome Pasta Salad | 57 |
| 102. | Tuna Salad | 57 |
| 103. | Southern Potato Salad | 57 |
| 104. | Seven-Layer Salad | 57 |
| 105. | Kale, Quinoa, and Avocado Salad | 58 |
| 106. | Chicken Salad | 58 |
| 107. | Cobb Salad | 58 |
| 108. | Broccoli Salad | 58 |
| 109. | Strawberry Spinach Salad | 59 |
| 110. | Pear Salad with Roquefort Cheese | 59 |
| 111. | Mexican Bean Salad | 59 |
| 112. | Melon-Mozzarella Salad | 60 |
| 113. | Citrus Celery Salad | 60 |
| 114. | Oven-Roasted Broccoli Salad | 60 |
| 115. | Sun-dried Tomato Salad | 60 |
| 116. | Feta Cheese and Beet Salad | 61 |
| 117. | Cauliflower-Tomato Salad | 61 |
| 118. | Cheesy and Spiced Pilaf | 61 |
| 119. | Oven-Roasted Vegetable Salad | 61 |
| 120. | Herb-Roasted Vegetables | 62 |
| 121. | Cheesy Pistachio Salad | 62 |
| 122. | Parmesan Barley Risotto | 62 |
| 123. | Seafood and Avocado Salad | 62 |
| 124. | Mediterranean Shrimp Salad | 63 |

## CHAPTER 7: LUNCH RECIPES .................................. 64

125. Zucchini Zoodles with Chicken and Basil..... 64
126. Parmesan Baked Chicken ........................................ 64
127. Crazy Japanese Potato and Beef Croquettes 65
128. Golden Eggplant Fries ............................................. 65
129. Very Wild Mushroom Pilaf....................................... 65
130. Sporty Baby Carrots ................................................. 66
131. Garden Salad............................................................. 66
132. Baked Smoky Broccoli and Garlic ...................... 66
133. Roasted Cauliflower and Lima Beans................. 67
134. Thai Roasted Spicy Black Beans and Choy Sum 67
135. Simple Roasted Broccoli and Cauliflower ... 67
136. Roasted Napa Cabbage and Turnips Extra .... 68
137. Simple Roasted Kale Artichoke Heart and Choy Sum Extra .............................................................. 68
138. Roasted Kale and Bok Choy Extra ................... 68
139. Roasted Soy Beans and Winter Squash .......... 68
140. Roasted Button Mushrooms and Squash........ 69
141. Roasted Tomatoes Rutabaga and Kohlrabi Main .............................................................................. 69
142. Roasted Brussels sprouts and Broccoli........... 70
143. Roasted Broccoli Sweet Potatoes and Bean Sprouts ........................................................................ 70
144. Roasted Sweet Potato and Red Beets ............. 70
145. Sichuan Style Baked Chioggia Beets and Broccoli Florets ......................................................... 71
146. Baked Enoki and Mini Cabbage ......................... 71
147. Roasted Triple Mushrooms .................................. 71
148. Roasted Mini Cabbage and Sweet Potato ...... 71
149. Tofu and Green Bean Stir-Fry................................ 72
150. Peanut Vegetable Pad Thai ................................... 72
151. Spicy Tofu Burrito Bowls with Cilantro Avocado Sauce ......................................................... 73
152. Sweet Potato Cakes with Classic Guacamole 73
153. Chickpea Cauliflower Tikka Masala ................... 73
154. Eggplant Parmesan Stacks...................................... 74
155. Roasted Vegetable Enchiladas ............................ 74
156. Lentil Avocado Tacos .............................................. 75
157. Tomato and Olive Orecchiette with Basil Pesto ............................................................................ 75
158. Italian Stuffed Portobello Mushroom Burgers ........................................................................ 75
159. Gnocchi with Tomato Basil Sauce ..................... 76
160. Creamy Pumpkin Pasta ......................................... 76
161. Mexican-Style Potato Casserole.......................... 77
162. Black Bean Stew with Cornbread ....................... 77
163. Mushroom Florentine ............................................ 78
164. Hassel back Eggplant ............................................. 78
165. Vegetarian Kebabs .................................................. 78
166. White Beans Stew .................................................... 78
167. Vegetarian Lasagna ................................................ 79
168. Pan-Fried Salmon with Salad .............................. 79
169. Veggie Variety .......................................................... 79
170. Vegetable Pasta........................................................ 79
171. Vegetable Noodles with Bolognese................. 80
172. Harissa Bolognese with Vegetable Noodles 80
173. Curry Vegetable Noodles with Chicken........ 81

## CHAPTER 8: DINNER RECIPES ............................... 82

174. Shrimp Cocktail ....................................................... 82
175. Squid and Shrimp Salad........................................ 82
176. Parsley Seafood Cocktail ..................................... 83
177. Shrimp and Onion Ginger Dressing ................. 83
178. Fruit Shrimp Soup ................................................... 84
179. Mussels and Chickpea Soup ............................... 84
180. Fish Stew .................................................................... 84
181. Shrimp and Broccoli Soup ................................... 85
182. Coconut Turkey Mix ............................................... 85
183. Lime Shrimp and Kale ........................................... 85
184. Parsley Cod Mix ....................................................... 85
185. Salmon and Cabbage Mix .................................... 86
186. Decent Beef and Onion Stew .............................. 86
187. Clean Parsley and Chicken Breast ..................... 86
188. Zucchini Beef Sauté with Coriander Greens 86
189. Hearty Lemon and Pepper Chicken................. 87
190. Walnuts and Asparagus Delight ........................ 87
191. Healthy Carrot Chips ............................................. 87
192. Beef Soup .................................................................. 87
193. Amazing Grilled Chicken and Blueberry Salad 88
194. Clean Chicken and Mushroom Stew................. 88
195. Elegant Pumpkin Chili Dish ................................. 88
196. Tasty Roasted Broccoli .......................................... 88
197. The Almond Breaded Chicken Goodness...... 89
198. South-Western Pork Chops ................................. 89
199. Almond butter Pork Chops ................................. 89
200. Chicken Salsa ........................................................... 89
201. Healthy Mediterranean Lamb Chops ............... 90
202. Amazing Sesame Breadsticks.............................. 90
203. Brown Butter Duck Breast ................................... 90
204. Generous Garlic Bread Stick ............................... 91
205. Cauliflower Bread Stick ........................................ 91
206. Bacon and Chicken Garlic Wrap ........................ 91
207. Chipotle Lettuce Chicken .................................... 92
208. Balsamic Chicken and Vegetables ..................... 92
209. Exuberant Sweet Potatoes ................................... 92
210. The Vegan Lovers Refried Beans........................ 92
211. Cool Apple and Carrot Harmony ....................... 93
212. Mac and Chokes ...................................................... 93
213. Black Eyed Peas and Spinach Platter ............... 93
214. Humble Mushroom Rice ....................................... 94
215. Sweet and Sour Cabbage and Apples ............. 94
216. Delicious Aloo Palak .............................................. 94
217. Orange and Chili Garlic Sauce ............................ 94
218. Tantalizing Mushroom Gravy .............................. 94
219. Everyday Vegetable Stock ................................... 95
220. Grilled Chicken with Lemon and Fennel ...... 95

| # | | Page |
|---|---|---|
| 221. | Caramelized Pork Chops and Onion | 95 |
| 222. | Hearty Pork Belly Casserole | 96 |
| 223. | Apple Pie Crackers | 96 |

## CHAPTER 9: POULTRY .................................. 97

| # | | Page |
|---|---|---|
| 224. | Lemon Garlic Chicken | 97 |
| 225. | Simple Mediterranean Chicken | 97 |
| 226. | Roasted Chicken Thighs | 98 |
| 227. | Mediterranean Turkey Breast | 98 |
| 228. | Olive Capers Chicken | 98 |
| 229. | Chicken with Mushrooms | 98 |
| 230. | Baked Chicken | 99 |
| 231. | Garlic Pepper Chicken | 99 |
| 232. | Mustard Chicken tenders | 99 |
| 233. | Salsa Chicken Chili | 99 |
| 234. | Honey Crusted Chicken | 100 |
| 235. | Paella with Chicken, Leeks, and Tarragon | 100 |
| 236. | Southwestern Chicken and Pasta | 100 |
| 237. | Stuffed Chicken Breasts | 100 |
| 238. | Buffalo Chicken Salad Wrap | 101 |
| 239. | Chicken Sliders | 101 |
| 240. | White Chicken Chili | 101 |
| 241. | Sweet Potato-Turkey Meatloaf | 102 |
| 242. | Oaxacan Chicken | 102 |
| 243. | Spicy Chicken with Minty Couscous | 103 |
| 244. | Chicken, Pasta and Snow Peas | 103 |
| 245. | Chicken with Noodles | 103 |
| 246. | Teriyaki Chicken Wings | 104 |
| 247. | Hot Chicken Wings | 104 |
| 248. | Crispy Cashew Chicken | 104 |
| 249. | Chicken Tortellini Soup | 104 |
| 250. | Chicken Divan | 105 |
| 251. | Creamy Chicken Fried Rice | 105 |
| 252. | Chicken Tikka | 105 |
| 253. | Honey Spiced Cajun Chicken | 106 |
| 254. | Italian Chicken | 106 |
| 255. | Lemon-Parsley Chicken Breast | 106 |
| 256. | Parmesan and Chicken Spaghetti Squash | 107 |
| 257. | Apricot Chicken | 107 |
| 258. | Oven-Fried Chicken Breasts | 107 |
| 259. | Rosemary Roasted Chicken | 107 |
| 260. | Artichoke and Spinach Chicken | 107 |
| 261. | Pumpkin and Black Beans Chicken | 108 |
| 262. | Chicken Thighs and Apples Mix | 108 |
| 263. | Thai Chicken Thighs | 108 |
| 264. | Falling "Off" The Bone Chicken | 108 |
| 265. | Feisty Chicken Porridge | 109 |
| 266. | The Ultimate Faux-Tisserie Chicken | 109 |
| 267. | Oregano Chicken Thighs | 109 |
| 268. | Pesto Chicken Breasts with Summer Squash | 109 |
| 269. | Chicken, Tomato and Green Beans | 110 |
| 270. | Chicken Tortillas | 110 |
| 271. | Chicken with Potatoes Olives and Sprouts | 110 |
| 272. | Garlic Mushroom Chicken | 110 |
| 273. | Grilled Chicken | 111 |
| 274. | Delicious Lemon Chicken Salad | 111 |

## CHAPTER 10: SEAFOOD .................................. 112

| # | | Page |
|---|---|---|
| 275. | Balsamic Salmon and Peaches Mix | 112 |
| 276. | Salmon and Beans Mix | 112 |
| 277. | Lemony Salmon and Pomegranate Mix | 113 |
| 278. | Salmon and Veggie Mix | 113 |
| 279. | Greek Salmon with Yogurt | 114 |
| 280. | Creamy Salmon and Asparagus Mix | 114 |
| 281. | Salmon and Brussels sprouts | 114 |
| 282. | Salmon and Beets Mix | 114 |
| 283. | Garlic Shrimp Mix | 115 |
| 284. | Salmon and Potatoes Mix | 115 |
| 285. | Cod Salad with Mustard | 115 |
| 286. | Broccoli and Cod Mash | 115 |
| 287. | Greek Style Salmon | 116 |
| 288. | Spicy Ginger Sea bass | 116 |
| 289. | Yogurt Shrimps | 116 |
| 290. | Aromatic Salmon with Fennel Seeds | 116 |
| 291. | Shrimp Quesadillas | 117 |
| 292. | The OG Tuna Sandwich | 117 |
| 293. | Easy to Understand Mussels | 117 |
| 294. | Citrus-Glazed Salmon with Zucchini Noodles | 117 |
| 295. | Salmon Cakes with Bell Pepper plus Lemon Yogurt | 118 |
| 296. | Halibut in Parchment with Zucchini, Shallots, and Herbs | 118 |
| 297. | Flounder with Tomatoes and Basil | 118 |
| 298. | Grilled Mahi-Mahi with Artichoke Caponata | 119 |
| 299. | Cod and Cauliflower Chowder | 119 |
| 300. | Sardine Bruschetta with Fennel and Lemon Cream | 119 |
| 301. | Chopped Tuna Salad | 120 |
| 302. | Monkfish with Sautéed Leeks, Fennel, and Tomatoes | 120 |
| 303. | Caramelized Fennel and Sardines with Penne | 120 |
| 304. | Coppin | 121 |
| 305. | Green Goddess Crab Salad with Endive | 121 |
| 306. | Seared Scallops with Blood Orange Glaze | 122 |
| 307. | Lemon Garlic Shrimp | 122 |
| 308. | Shrimp Fra Diavolo | 122 |
| 309. | Fish Amandine | 123 |
| 310. | Air-Fryer Fish Cakes | 123 |
| 311. | Pesto Shrimp Pasta | 123 |
| 312. | Easy Shrimp and Mango | 124 |
| 313. | Spring Salmon Mix | 124 |
| 314. | Smoked Salmon and Green Beans | 124 |
| 315. | Saffron Shrimp | 124 |
| 316. | Crab, Zucchini and Watermelon Soup | 125 |
| 317. | Shrimp and Orzo | 125 |
| 318. | Lemon and Garlic Scallops | 125 |
| 319. | Walnut Encrusted Salmon | 125 |
| 320. | Roasted Lemon Swordfish | 126 |
| 321. | Especial Glazed Salmon | 126 |

| # | | Page |
|---|---|---|
| 322. | Generous Stuffed Salmon Avocado | 126 |
| 323. | Spanish Mussels | 126 |
| 324. | Tilapia Broccoli Platter | 127 |
| 325. | Salmon with Peas and Parsley Dressing | 127 |
| 326. | Mackerel and Orange Medley | 127 |
| 327. | Spicy Chili Salmon | 128 |
| 328. | Simple One-Pot Mussels | 128 |
| 329. | Lemon Pepper and Salmon | 128 |
| 330. | Simple Sautéed Garlic and Parsley Scallops 128 | |
| 331. | Salmon and Cucumber Platter | 129 |

## CHAPTER 11: MEAT DISHES ................................ 130

| # | | Page |
|---|---|---|
| 332. | Tarragon Pork Steak with Tomatoes | 130 |
| 333. | Pork Meatballs | 130 |
| 334. | Lamb Chops with Rosemary | 131 |
| 335. | Cane Wrapped Around In Prosciutto | 131 |
| 336. | Beef Veggie Pot Meal | 131 |
| 337. | Braised Beef Shanks | 132 |
| 338. | Beef with Mushrooms | 132 |
| 339. | Lemony Braised Beef Roast | 132 |
| 340. | Grilled Fennel-Cumin Lamb Chops | 132 |
| 341. | Beef Heart | 132 |
| 342. | Jerk Beef and Plantain Kabobs | 133 |
| 343. | Beef Pot | 133 |
| 344. | Beef with Cucumber Raito | 133 |
| 345. | Bistro Beef tenderloin | 133 |
| 346. | The Surprising No "Noodle" Lasagna | 134 |
| 347. | Lamb Chops with Kale | 134 |
| 348. | Beef and Vegetable Stir-Fry | 134 |
| 349. | Simple Veal Chops | 135 |
| 350. | Beef and Barley Farmers Soup | 135 |
| 351. | Simple Pork and Capers | 135 |
| 352. | A "Boney" Pork Chop | 136 |
| 353. | Roast and Mushrooms | 136 |
| 354. | Pork and Celery Mix | 136 |
| 355. | Pork and Dates Sauce | 136 |
| 356. | Pork Roast and Cranberry Roast | 137 |
| 357. | Easy Pork Chops | 137 |
| 358. | Pork and Roasted Tomatoes Mix | 137 |
| 359. | Provence Pork Medallions | 137 |
| 360. | Garlic Pork Shoulder | 138 |
| 361. | Grilled Flank Steak with Lime Vinaigrette | 138 |
| 362. | Asian Pork tenderloin | 138 |
| 363. | Simple Beef Brisket and Tomato Soup | 138 |
| 364. | Beef Stew with Fennel and Shallots | 139 |
| 365. | Rustic Beef and Barley Soup | 139 |
| 366. | Beef Stroganoff | 140 |
| 367. | Curried Pork tenderloin in Apple Cider | 140 |
| 368. | Pork Medallions with 5 Spice Powder | 140 |
| 369. | Grilled Pork Fajitas | 141 |
| 370. | New York Strip Steak with Mushroom Sauce 141 | |
| 371. | Pork Chops with Black Currant Jam | 141 |
| 372. | Pork Medallion with Herbes de Provence | 141 |
| 373. | Pork tenderloin with Apples and Balsamic Vinegar | 142 |
| 374. | Pork with Apples and Blue Cheese | 142 |
| 375. | Pork tenderloin with Fennel Sauce | 142 |
| 376. | Spicy Beef Kebabs | 143 |
| 377. | Spicy Beef Curry | 143 |

## CHAPTER 12: STEWS AND SOUPS ........................ 144

| # | | Page |
|---|---|---|
| 378. | Chicken Wild Rice Soup | 144 |
| 379. | Classic Chicken Soup | 145 |
| 380. | Cucumber Soup | 145 |
| 381. | Squash and Turmeric Soup | 145 |
| 382. | Leek, Potato, and Carrot Soup | 146 |
| 383. | Bell Pepper Soup | 146 |
| 384. | Yucatan Soup | 146 |
| 385. | Zesty Taco Soup | 147 |
| 386. | Southwestern Posole | 147 |
| 387. | Spring Vegetable Soup | 147 |
| 388. | Seafood Corn Chowder | 148 |
| 389. | Beef Sage Soup | 148 |
| 390. | Cabbage Borscht | 148 |
| 391. | Ground Beef Soup | 148 |
| 392. | Mexican Tortilla Soup | 149 |
| 393. | Chicken Noodle Soup | 149 |
| 394. | Cheesy Broccoli Soup | 149 |
| 395. | Rich Potato Soup | 150 |
| 396. | Mediterranean Lentil Soup | 150 |
| 397. | Sausage Kale Soup with Mushrooms | 150 |
| 398. | Classic Minestrone | 151 |
| 399. | Turkey Meatball and Ditalini Soup | 151 |
| 400. | Mint Avocado Chilled Soup | 151 |

## CHAPTER 13: VEGETARIAN ................................ 152

| # | | Page |
|---|---|---|
| 401. | Lentil-Stuffed Zucchini Boats | 152 |
| 402. | Baked Eggplant Parmesan | 153 |
| 403. | Sweet Potato Rice with Spicy Peanut Sauce | 153 |
| 404. | Vegetable Red Curry | 154 |
| 405. | Black Bean Burgers | 154 |
| 406. | Summer Barley Pilaf with Yogurt Dill Sauce 154 | |
| 407. | Lentil Quinoa Gratin with Butternut Squash 155 | |
| 408. | Brown Rice Casserole with Cottage Cheese 155 | |
| 409. | Quinoa-Stuffed Peppers | 156 |
| 410. | Greek Flatbread with Spinach, Tomatoes, and Feta | 156 |
| 411. | Mushroom Risotto with Peas | 156 |
| 412. | Loaded Tofu Burrito with Black Beans | 157 |
| 413. | Southwest Tofu Scramble | 157 |
| 414. | Black-Bean and Vegetable Burrito | 157 |
| 415. | Baked Eggs in Avocado | 158 |
| 416. | Red Beans and Rice | 158 |
| 417. | Hearty Lentil Soup | 158 |
| 418. | Black-Bean Soup | 159 |
| 419. | Loaded Baked Sweet Potatoes | 159 |
| 420. | White Beans with Spinach and Pan-Roasted Tomatoes | 159 |
| 421. | Black-Eyed Peas and Greens Power Salad | 159 |
| 422. | Butternut-Squash Macaroni and Cheese | 160 |

| 423. | Pasta with Tomatoes and Peas | 160 |
| 424. | Healthy Vegetable Fried Rice | 160 |
| 425. | Portobello-Mushroom Cheeseburgers | 161 |
| 426. | And-Rosemary Omelet | 161 |
| 427. | Chilled Cucumber-And-Avocado Soup with Dill | 161 |
| 428. | Southwestern Bean-And-Pepper Salad | 162 |
| 429. | Cauliflower Mashed Potatoes | 162 |

## CHAPTER 14: SIDE DISHES AND APPETIZER ... 163

| 430. | Turmeric Endives | 163 |
| 431. | Parmesan Endives | 163 |
| 432. | Lemon Asparagus | 164 |
| 433. | Lime Carrots | 164 |
| 434. | Garlic Potato Pan | 164 |
| 435. | Balsamic Cabbage | 165 |
| 436. | Chili Broccoli | 165 |
| 437. | Hot Brussels sprouts | 165 |
| 438. | Paprika Brussels sprouts | 165 |
| 439. | Creamy Cauliflower Mash | 165 |
| 440. | Avocado, Tomato, and Olives Salad | 166 |
| 441. | Radish and Olives Salad | 166 |
| 442. | Spinach and Endives Salad | 166 |
| 443. | Basil Olives Mix | 166 |
| 444. | Arugula Salad | 166 |
| 445. | Spanish rice | 167 |
| 446. | Sweet Potatoes and Apples | 167 |
| 447. | Roasted Turnips | 167 |
| 448. | No-Mayo Potato Salad | 168 |
| 449. | Zucchini Tomato Bake | 168 |
| 450. | Creamy Broccoli Cheddar Rice | 168 |
| 451. | Smashed Brussels sprouts | 168 |
| 452. | Cilantro Lime Rice | 169 |

## CHAPTER 15: DESSERT ... 170

| 453. | Cheesecake Made Easy! | 170 |
| 454. | Grapefruit Compote | 170 |
| 455. | Instant Pot Applesauce | 171 |
| 456. | Plum Cake | 171 |
| 457. | Dates Brownies | 171 |
| 458. | Rose Lentils Ice Cream | 171 |
| 459. | Mandarin Almond Pudding | 172 |
| 460. | Cherry Stew | 172 |
| 461. | Rice Pudding | 172 |
| 462. | Apple Loaf | 172 |
| 463. | Cauliflower Cinnamon Pudding | 173 |
| 464. | Rhubarb Stew | 173 |
| 465. | Pumpkin Pudding | 173 |
| 466. | Cashew Lemon Fudge | 173 |
| 467. | Brown Cake | 173 |
| 468. | Delicious Berry Pie | 174 |
| 469. | Cinnamon Peach Cobbler | 174 |
| 470. | Resilient Chocolate Cream | 174 |
| 471. | Vanilla Poached Strawberries | 174 |
| 472. | Lemon Bananas | 175 |
| 473. | Pecans Cake | 175 |
| 474. | Coconut Cream and Plums Cake | 175 |
| 475. | Maple Syrup Poached Pears | 175 |
| 476. | Ginger and Pumpkin Pie | 176 |
| 477. | Cashew and Carrot Muffins | 176 |
| 478. | Lemon Custard | 176 |
| 479. | Rhubarb Dip | 176 |
| 480. | Summer Jam | 176 |
| 481. | Cinnamon Pudding | 177 |
| 482. | Orange Compote | 177 |
| 483. | Chocolate Bars | 177 |
| 484. | Lemon Zest Pudding | 177 |
| 485. | Coconut Figs | 177 |
| 486. | Lemony Banana Mix | 178 |
| 487. | Cocoa Banana Dessert Smoothie | 178 |
| 488. | Kiwi Bars | 178 |
| 489. | Black Tea Bars | 178 |
| 490. | Green Pudding | 178 |
| 491. | Lemony Plum Cake | 179 |
| 492. | Lentils Sweet Bars | 179 |
| 493. | Lentils and Dates Brownies | 179 |
| 494. | Mandarin Pudding | 179 |
| 495. | Walnut Apple Mix | 180 |
| 496. | Vanilla and Grapes Compote | 180 |
| 497. | Soft Pudding | 180 |
| 498. | Ginger and Cinnamon Pudding | 180 |
| 499. | Honey Compote | 180 |

## CONCLUSION ... 182

## THIS MY EXPERIENCE IN A NUTSHELL MY EXPERIENCE ... 184

How did I lower my blood pressure? ... 184

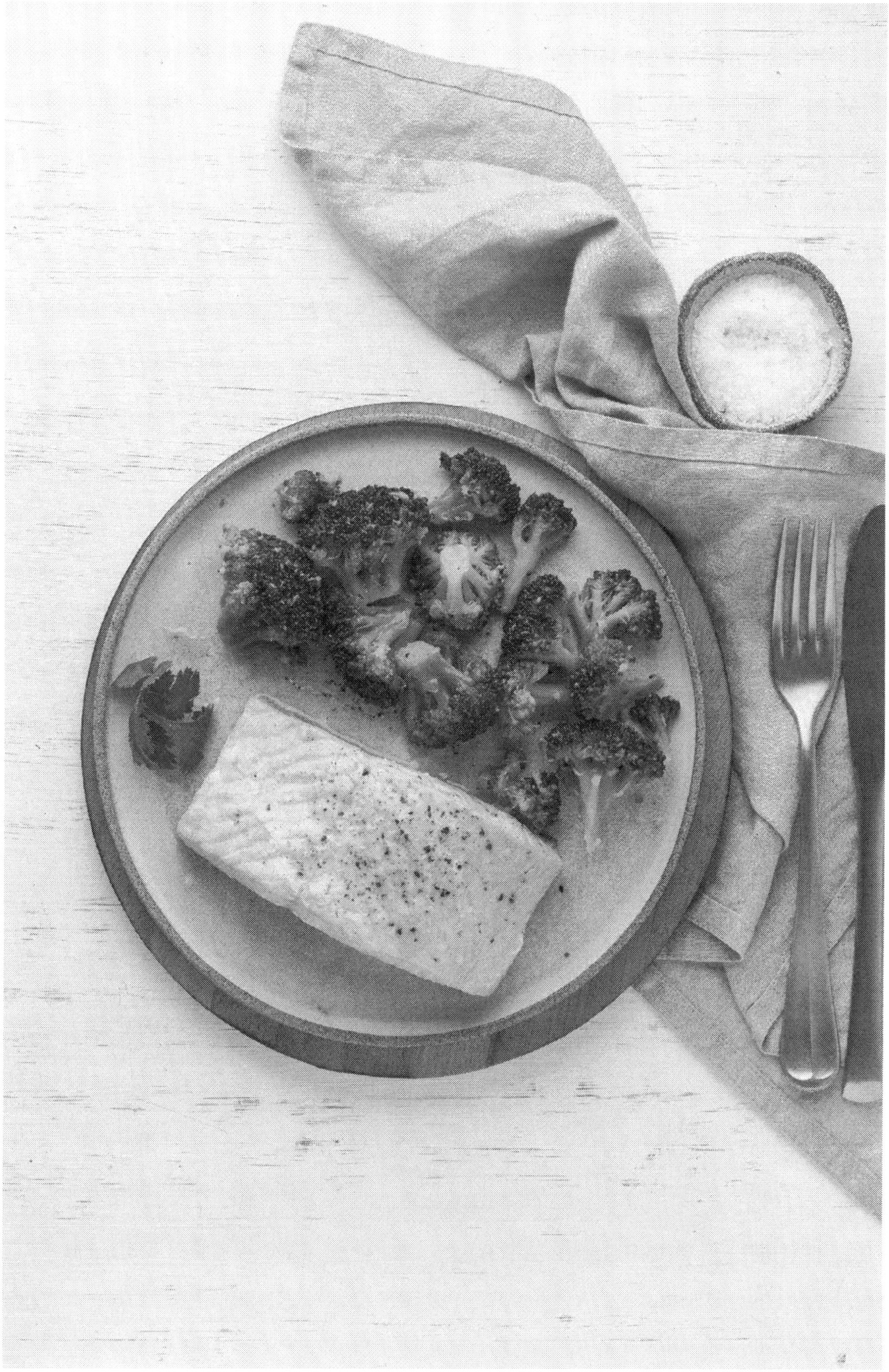

# Introduction

One of the most effective diets of the moment is the DASH diet, which stands for "Dietary Approaches to Stop Hypertension." It has been designed by The National Institutes of Health for people who suffer from hypertension and is based on reducing one's intake of salt, sugar, and fat. It turns out that this ancient concept is highly cost-effective—not only on your wallet (or purse), but on your health as well. There are many benefits of DASH diet, from weight loss to increased longevity. The main advantage of the DASH diet is that it is very affordable, while still being effective in its purpose. As a matter of fact, the diet will cost you less money than going out to a fast-food restaurant for a month!

Another helpful thing about the DASH diet is that it doesn't put your wallet at risk. Eating healthy may be more expensive than sticking to junk food, but not if you know how to shop in the right places. You can get everything you need for this diet in any supermarket, so if you are looking for healthy food recipes that won't break your bank, check out these 5 great recipes ideas! If you wish to get the best out of what you eat, it is important for you to know that this diet does not stop being effective after 6 months. Furthermore, this diet has been known to have many benefits even after several years of being used. If you wish for a healthy way to live your life, then stop considering other options that are basically "too good to be true" and give DASH diet a try!

We have to admit that this is one of the most important advantages you can get from this diet. It doesn't really matter if you are completely new to healthy diets, because this diet has been created by the National Institutes of Health—a prestigious organization that is recognized worldwide for its efforts in health care. If it's good enough for them, then it's definitely good enough for you!

Even if you are not used to healthy diets, it will not take too long until you can see positive results. In fact, many people who have been using this diet have reported losing weight in a few weeks. However, make sure you don't rush it too much, because you might put your health at risk!

If you are searching for a way to lose weight fast and then go back to your favorite junk food afterward, this is not the right diet for you. The DASH diet is completely different from other diets out there in the sense that it will keep your body functioning at its best for a longer period of time. You won't put on the weight back on after using this diet - if you do, then you are doing it wrong!

If you are well concerned about your health and want to prevent yourself from getting any health problems in the future, then this diet may be exactly what you need. It is not only efficient in losing weight fast, but it will also help you if you have hypertension.

LARA BRANDON

# My story

## How I improved my health and regained my ideal weight

Since I was 20 years old, I have often suffered from periodic peaks of high blood pressure, certainly due to my emotionality as a sensitive girl and a diet very rich in salt, various condiments, and animal fats. Later I discovered the harmful effects of this diet, combined with my agitated behavior in situations of fear and stress. In fact, within a few years, my weight increased by 44 lbs, and my cholesterol skyrocketed! The panic was total, especially when I had to go out with my friends and start an intimate relationship with a handsome guy, to feel emotionally more secure and accepted. Every time I had to wear a dress, it became torture to look at myself in the mirror; I tried to use mostly black colors to reduce the impression of being overweight, especially around my hips and thighs. In short, I didn't like myself, I didn't accept myself, and this was reflected in my love relationships, which failed miserably within a short time. The accumulation of negative emotions always kept me anxious. Any diet I did at that time was a guaranteed failure! The most troubled and depressive period lasted six years, from 20 to 26.

## The encounter that changed my life!

My life suddenly changed when I was 26 years old, after meeting "by chance" at a nutrition seminar, a coach I didn't know, who had experienced a similar situation to mine and successfully resolved it. Her name is Amanda.
This amazing woman, who was 47 at the time, revealed to me how her success was due to balancing emotions and food. Besides being a Life Coach very knowledgeable in different types of diets and recipes, Amanda was also an expert in yoga, meditation, and conscious breathing; she recommended the DASH Diet, thanks to which she had solved her problems, combined with a healthy lifestyle! She often told me that conflicting emotions such as fear and conflict are "food" that we unconsciously create and hurt our choice of junk food and, therefore, our health, including high blood pressure, cholesterol, overweight, and obesity. Rebalancing the emotional state, coupled with healthy, masterfully prepared foods, is the key to optimal health that lasts.

## Who finds a true friend finds a...Treasure!

In short, a true friendship was born with Amanda; we hung out often, spending several hours together, both at her place and mine. And it was on these occasions, Amanda revealed to me the principles on how to create extraordinary DASH recipes that have a beneficial impact on both the body and the emotional sphere. I thank God for allowing me to meet a true friend who has become a true treasure of knowledge, professionalism, and love over the years! Thanks to this meeting, I began to apply the DASH Diet principles. All the blood pressure values, including cholesterol and body weight, returned to normal within five months. Shortly after realizing my dream, I met my husband Richard, from whose relationship my two children, Deborah, 18, and Robert, 16, were born. They, too, follow the principles of the DASH Diet, which is not just a diet to reduce high blood pressure and lose weight, but a smart way to eat to be healthy, both when you are young and in old age.
I am 165 tall, and now my body weight varies from 123 to 127 lbs, while in the past, I weighed 172! I felt happy and confident for the first time in my life; I wanted to share this success with my family and friends, who saw me flourishing day by day! Many of my friends and family have successfully taken the same path that I report in my book! Many of them were in a state of high blood pressure, cholesterol, overweight, and obesity that they resolved with patience, following the indications that I suggest in my book. Because of this beginning, I felt the urge to turn my experience into a profession. Amanda pointed me to some schools and seminars in the USA and Europe. I drew lessons that I then shared with numerous clients, helping them improve their health and their lives.
Now I'm 49 years old and in my path as an independent researcher; in addition to the DASH diet, I have specialized in several truly healthy diets such as the Anti-Inflammatory Diet and the Mediterranean Diet. I will soon be publishing several books on such diets.

## Take care of your body!

Mens sana in corpore sano! This statement of the ancient Latins shows us how to take care of the body well. We must also take care of the mind. This path of mine with the DASH Diet, thanks to Amanda, has also fortified my mind. The body is the mirror of the mind and vice versa. Both produce healthy emotions when they are in balance. And emotions are "food" for the body and the mind. And that's why I introduced meditation and conscious breathing in my lifestyle and a moderate but constant physical activity, such as long walks in contact with nature, in parks, in the hills, in the mountains, at the beach to feel connected with Mother Nature!

# CHAPTER 1:
# Understanding The Dash Diet

**The DASH Diet**
DIETARY APPROACHES TO STOP HYPERTENSION

Dietary Methods to avoid Hypertension (DASH) emerged in the 1990s. The National Institute of Health (NIH) began funding a variety of research studies in 1992 to see whether particular dietary approaches are effective in the treatment of hypertension or not. To prevent any potential factors, the study participants were recommended to follow only the dietary treatments and not include any other lifestyle changes.

They observed that systolic blood pressure could only be lowered by around 6 to 11 mmHg by dietary activity alone. This influence was shown in persons with both hypertension and normotension. In several cases, the DASH diet centered upon these findings has been advised as the first-line therapy with a lifestyle change.

## What Is Used In This Diet?

DASH encourages the intake of fruits, vegetables, lean meat, and milk items and the use of micronutrients in the menu. The lowering of sodium in the diet to around 1500 mg/day is often advocated. DASH focuses on the consumption of food that is minimally refined and fresh.

There are also similarities between the DASH diet and some of the other nutricional strategies advocated for cardiovascular fitness. The DASH diet is an apogee of the modern world, as well as ancient times. Scientists have mined it on the basis of some ancient culinary principles, and it has been adapted to target some of the leading causes of mortality and morbidity in the modern world.

## Enhancing Healthcare Team Outcomes

For controlling hypertension, the DASH diet is a nutricionally balanced approach. In many clinical trials, the diet has been studied and found to reduce saturated fats, blood pressure, and cholesterol. DASH diet has been prescribed as the safest diet for those who wish to lose weight and reduce blood pressure. The real criterion is that the patients must be encouraged to this diet. Both nurses and pharmacists play a vital role in teaching the patients about the effects of this diet in addition to doctors. Nurses are in a perfect role . They can teach both patients and family members more about the DASH diet and its advantages right before discharge.

Similarly, the pharmacist should teach the customer about the DASH diet while patients visit a pharmacy. The DASH diet's most critical features are that it needs a lifestyle transition and a healthier way to eat. In conjunction, patients should be advised to avoid smoking, refrain from alcohol, and actively engage in any physical exercise.

## Is The DASH Diet Primarily Preferred For Hypertension Care Only?

It has been researched thoroughly to check the DASH diet's treatment paradigm and its effects on several other diseases. Several studies have found that the DASH diet improves by reducing triglycerides, LDL-C, blood glucose levels, as well as insulin tolerance. Such behavior allows the DASH diet to significantly contribute to metabolic syndrome's pharmacological treatment (a major epidemic in this region). It has also become a powerful element for weight control. Complying some populations with the DASH diet has demonstrated substantial changes in type 2 diabetes treatment. Its focus is on lowering dietary sodium and promoting the consumption of calcium, potassium, and magnesium, which is a recommended diet in patients with heart disease.

## Research And General Acceptance

Reports have indicated that excessive salt consumption plays a role in high blood pressure progression over the years. Dietary recommendations for the avoidance and control of hypertension have mostly centered on reducing sodium or salt consumption. In 1989, a study scrutinized the reaction of 3 to 12 g of salt consumption per day to blood pressure. This study showed that a small decrease in salt, i.e., 5–6 g of salt a day, allows the blood pressure to decrease in patients with hypertension. The better result was shown with just 3 g of salt a day intake, with a mean drop in blood pressure of systolic (11 mmHg) and diastolic (6 mmHg), respectively. More notably, the low-salt diets used for high blood pressure reduction or recovery have been questioned. The Phase II Hypertension Prevention Trials in 1997 suggested that energy consumption and weight loss in the prevention of hypertension were more significant than limiting dietary salt. A 2006 Cochrane study (which investigated the effect of a longer-term moderate reduction in salt on blood pressure) observed that a modest decrease in salt consumption could substantially influence blood pressure in individuals with hypertension but a smaller impact on those without blood pressure. It was decided that the 2007 public health guidelines would have a positive impact on blood pressure and cardiovascular disease by reducing salt consumption from 9–12 g / day to a modest level, i.e., 5–6 g /day. The potency of a DASH diet is well known for controlling blood pressure. As an example of a healthy eating schedule (compatible with the 2015 Dietary Guidelines' current recommendations for Americans), proposed the DASH Eating Plan, which constitutes the foundation for USDA MyPlate and their recommendations, such as those promoted by a British Nutrition Foundation, American Society for Hypertension and the American Heart Association also prescribe the DASH. While lowering sodium and increasing the consumption of potassium, calcium, and magnesium play a crucial role in decreasing blood pressure, but the reasons for the beneficial effects of the DASH eating plan remain unclear. The researchers say that it may be that whole food ingests potassium, calcium, and magnesium, or it may be due to the combined effect of consuming those nutrients collectively rather than the specific nutrients individually. It is also suspected that the link between diet and blood pressure could be another anonymous factor present in fruits, vegetables, and low-fat dairy products.

The Salt Institute encourages the DASH diet but without limiting the salt. They assert that a DASH diet alone would produce the necessary decrease in blood pressure without the decreased sodium consumption from packaged foods. Their suggestion is focused on the reality that no evidence-based findings justify a need for the whole population to limit dietary salt. The 2006 Cochrane review found that a small decrease in salt consumption dramatically reduced blood pressure in hypertension patients but had little impact on average blood pressure. The salt limitation is not advised for people without hypertension.

## Precautions

To prevent side effects such as gas, bloating, and diarrhea, the addition of high-fiber foods to the diet should be achieved progressively. Increasing fluid at the same time is necessary since fiber pulls water into the intestine. High fibers consumption can induce hard stools and constipation with insufficient fluid.

The rise in fruits and vegetables improves the diet's potassium content. A higher intake of potassium from foods presents little risk for healthy people with proper kidney function because extra potassium is excreted in the urine. However, there may be a chance of hyperkalemia (high potassium levels in the blood) in people whose urinary potassium excretion is compromised, such as patients with end-stage renal disease, significant cardiac failure, or adrenal insufficiency. Hyperkalemia can lead to an erratic heartbeat (cardiac arrhythmia), which can be dangerous. Also, some popular medications may minimize the excretion of potassium. Before beginning the DASH diet, patients at risk should contact a doctor since a higher intake of potassium in the form of fruit and vegetables might not be sufficient. For the substitution of potassium-containing salt, caution should also be taken.

**Foods To Eat**
Here are some foods that you should have, but remember that nothing is good in excess:
- Vegetables
- Fruits
- Poultry
- Seafood
- Seeds
- Pork
- Beef
- No Fat Dairy Products
- Low-fat Dairy Products
- Nuts
- Grains

**Foods to Avoid**
These foods you should try to limit as much as possible, and it would be better if you could cut them out of your diet all-together.
- Salt
- High Fat Dairy Products
- Salted Nuts
- Sugary Beverages
- Processed Food
- Animal Based Fats (In Excess)

## Is it helpful in weight loss?

The Dash diet is a safe, effective and healthy way to lose weight. Combining the food pyramid with an exercise plan and the Dash diet's meal plan will help you achieve your weight loss goals.

The Dash diet is not just about eating less fat or carbs, but by combining the food pyramid basics with an exercise plan and a healthy, balanced lifestyle, losing weight becomes easier.

The Dash diet does more than provide fast results for weight loss. It can improve your health overall. As you lose weight, you may feel more energetic and may have more confidence as well. Eating for your health may also improve your quality of life as you age.

## How effective is it in reducing blood pressure?

**When you have high blood pressure, it can be hard to feel like yourself.**

**The Dash Diet is an effective way of reducing your blood pressure naturally without the side effects of drugs.**

According to the Center for Disease Control and Prevention, it is highly important to get a good night's sleep. When you get enough sleep, your body produces a hormone that relaxes blood vessels. This helps to reduce your blood pressure naturally.

Getting 30 minutes of exercise every day also helps your body to produce a powerful mind-body connection. Physical activity has many benefits, including improving your circulation and immune system. This is why you should make the time to exercise every day. Don't miss out on these natural ways of lowering your blood pressure and feel healthier again!

# CHAPTER 2:
# Evidence That Potassium Is Even More Important Than Sodium Reduction For Hypertension, Heart And Weight Reduction

A large body of evidence reveals that potassium is an essential nutrient for heart health, hypertension, weight loss, and reducing the risk of diabetes. Potassium has been known to regulate blood pressure in the long term. However, most studies are focused on older populations.

Luckily, recent research suggests that there are specific ways to reduce both sodium and potassium in your diet for better health in general, regardless of whether you're over 60 or not! Believe it or not, foods like kale have a lot more potassium than sodium per serving! You can also use supplements like Natural Calm Muscle Care with magnesium chloride, which contains 82 mg of well-absorbed potassium chloride versus just 10 mg in a teaspoonful of salt.

Start eating more potassium, and you'll see your blood pressure drop and your health improve in many ways. Luckily, sodium has also been figured out in recent years. It's in most processed foods, so it's in your best interest to cut back on sodium. But you can as well feed your body with potassium-rich foods like kale! It really is great for lowering blood pressure.

Within the last 2 decades, there has been a tremendous increase in the amount of research identifying the importance of potassium and potassium-rich foods for heart health. Many studies have shown that potassium is essential for normal heart function.

Potassium essentially helps arterial walls relax and dilate (opening), which lowers blood pressure. To this end, a large body of evidence reveals that potassium is essential for normal heart function. Potassium keeps your heart beating and healthy many other things.

Even if you don't have high blood pressure, there are still billions of dollars being wasted each year on treating conditions that could have been prevented with potassium supplementation.

Take a look at the following 2 real-life examples where potassium could have helped both diabetics and high blood pressure patients:

## Diabetics With High Blood Pressure Type 1 Acidosis

In 1958 Prof. Waldo Stern of McGill University Nutrition Research Unit studied these diabetic patients and found out that just a few grams of potassium chloride kept their blood pressure down for 90 minutes straight.

The diabetics who took in more than seven grams of potassium daily had a blood pressure drop of 40 mmHg, while those who didn't take in enough potassium had a blood pressure rise while the potassium levels were only up by 15 mmHg.

Professor Stern and his team concluded: "One would say that these observations indicate that the action of insulin on the vascular wall is dependent upon the serum [blood] potassium level."

When you consume food rich in potassium, your body is able to process insulin easier and therefore, can control your blood sugar levels. Diabetics with high blood pressure don't absorb glucose properly, and their cells get damaged over time. Potassium deficiency definitely makes diabetes worse.

A study made at the Department of Medicine, Beth Israel Deaconess Medical Center, Boston, Massachusetts found that low potassium intake increases the risk of kidney damage in diabetics.

## Potassium Deficiency Makes Hypertension Worse

The Journal of Hypertension published a study in October 2003 where potassium was given to rats with high blood pressure. The researchers wanted to see if potassium would help with hypertension, and it did. The rats with hypertension were fed a diet that was very low in potassium, but after just four weeks of the treatment, their blood pressure came down dramatically. The researchers concluded that "treatment with potassium chloride decreased arterial pressure, normalized hemodynamics, and improved left ventricular function in spontaneously hypertensive rats."

## Potassium Deficiency Causes Insulin Resistance

High blood pressure is the #1 risk factor for heart attack, heart failure, and kidney failure. More than half of all men and one-third of all women have high blood pressure. Your risk of developing these conditions increases if you have diabetes. Researchers at Beth Israel Deaconess Medical Center were successful in lowering blood sugar levels by feeding patients absorbed potassium chloride. The people who took the potassium supplement gained more weight over time, but their waistlines had shrunk by 4% on average

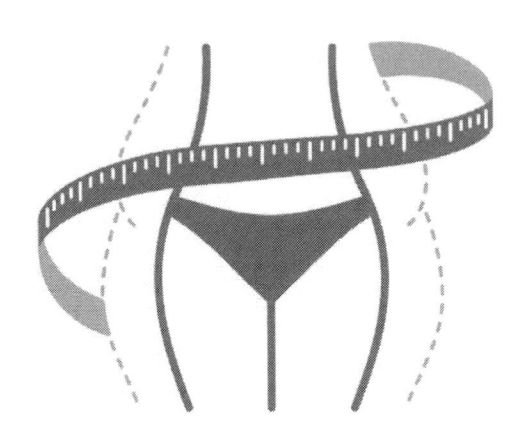

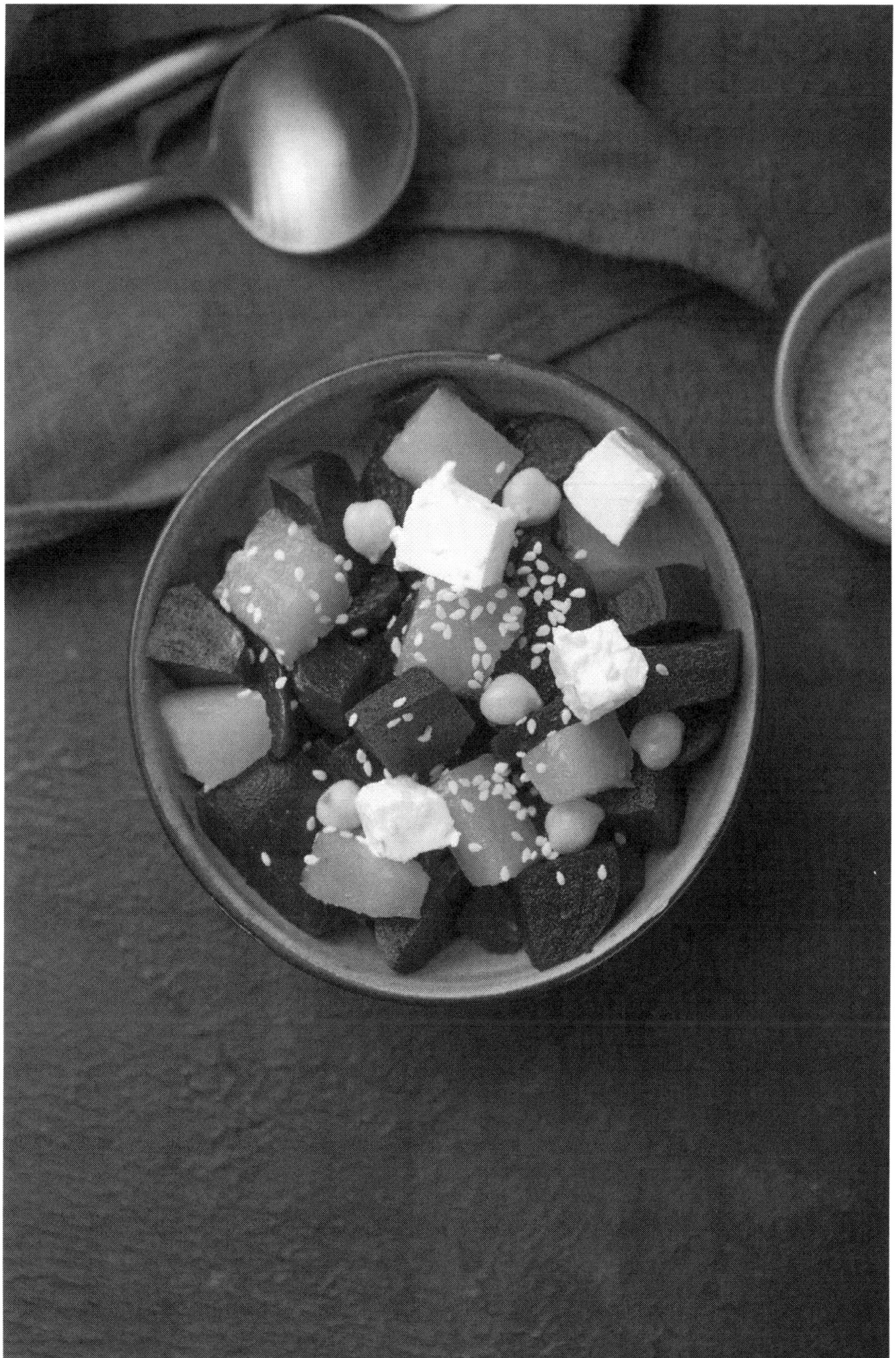

# CHAPTER 3:
# Food Plan For 140 Days

| Days | Breakfast | Lunch | Dinner | Dessert |
|---|---|---|---|---|
| 1 | Energy Sunrise Muffins | Zucchini Zoodles With Chicken And Basil | Shrimp Cocktail | Cheesecake Made Easy! |
| 2 | Blueberry Waffles | Parmesan Baked Chicken | Squid And Shrimp Salad | Grapefruit Compote |
| 3 | Apple Pancakes | Crazy Japanese Potato And Beef Croquettes | Parsley Seafood Cocktail | Instant Pot Applesauce |
| 4 | Super-Simple Granola | Golden Eggplant Fries | Shrimp And Onion Ginger Dressing | Plum Cake |
| 5 | Savory Yogurt Bowls | Very Wild Mushroom Pilaf | Fruit Shrimp Soup | Dates Brownies |
| 6 | Spinach, Egg, And Cheese Breakfast Quesadillas | Sporty Baby Carrots | Mussels And Chickpea Soup | Rose Lentils Ice Cream |
| 7 | Simple Cheese And Broccoli Omelets | Garden Salad | Fish Stew | Mandarin Almond Pudding |
| 8 | Creamy Avocado And Egg Salad Sandwiches | Baked Smoky Broccoli And Garlic | Shrimp And Broccoli Soup | Cherry Stew |
| 9 | Breakfast Hash | Roasted Cauliflower And Lima Beans | Coconut Turkey Mix | Rice Pudding |
| 10 | Hearty Breakfast Casserole | Thai Roasted Spicy Black Beans And Choy Sum | Lime Shrimp And Kale | Apple Loaf |
| 11 | Creamy Apple-Avocado Smoothie | Simple Roasted Broccoli And Cauliflower | Parsley Cod Mix | Cauliflower Cinnamon Pudding |
| 12 | Strawberry, Orange, And Beet Smoothie | Roasted Napa Cabbage And Turnips Extra | Salmon And Cabbage Mix | Rhubarb Stew |
| 13 | Blueberry-Vanilla Yogurt Smoothie | Simple Roasted Kale Artichoke Heart And Choy Sum Extra | Decent Beef And Onion Stew | Pumpkin Pudding |
| 14 | Greek Yogurt Oat Pancakes | Roasted Kale And Bok Choy Extra | Clean Parsley And Chicken Breast | Cashew Lemon Fudge |
| 15 | Scrambled Egg And Veggie Breakfast Quesadillas | Roasted Soy Beans And Winter Squash | Zucchini Beef Sauté With Coriander Greens | Brown Cake |
| 16 | Stuffed Breakfast Peppers | Roasted Button Mushrooms And Squash | Hearty Lemon And Pepper Chicken | Delicious Berry Pie |
| 17 | Sweet Potato Toast Three Ways | Roasted Tomatoes Rutabaga And Kohlrabi Main | Walnuts And Asparagus Delight | Cinnamon Peach Cobbler |
| 18 | Apple-Apricot Brown Rice Breakfast Porridge | Roasted Brussels Sprouts And Broccoli | Healthy Carrot Chips | Resilient Chocolate Cream |
| 19 | Carrot Cake Overnight Oats | Roasted Broccoli Sweet Potatoes And Bean Sprouts | Beef Soup | Vanilla Poached Strawberries |
| 20 | Steel-Cut Oatmeal With Plums And Pear | Roasted Sweet Potato And Red Beets | Amazing Grilled Chicken And Blueberry Salad | Lemon Bananas |
| 21 | French Toast With Applesauce | Sichuan Style Baked Chioggia Beets And Broccoli Florets | Clean Chicken And Mushroom Stew | Pecans Cake |

|  |  |  |  |  |
|---|---|---|---|---|
| 22 | Banana-Peanut Butter And Greens Smoothie | Baked Enoki And Mini Cabbage | Elegant Pumpkin Chili Dish | Coconut Cream And Plums Cake |
| 23 | Baking Powder Biscuits | Roasted Triple Mushrooms | Tasty Roasted Broccoli | Maple Syrup Poached Pears |
| 24 | Oatmeal Banana Pancakes With Walnuts | Roasted Mini Cabbage And Sweet Potato | The Almond Breaded Chicken Goodness | Ginger And Pumpkin Pie |
| 25 | Creamy Oats, Greens And Blueberry Smoothie | Tofu And Green Bean Stir-Fry | South-Western Pork Chops | Cashew And Carrot Muffins |
| 26 | Banana And Cinnamon Oatmeal | Peanut Vegetable Pad Thai | Almond Butter Pork Chops | Lemon Custard |
| 27 | Bagels Made Healthy | Spicy Tofu Burrito Bowls With Cilantro Avocado Sauce | Chicken Salsa | Rhubarb Dip |
| 28 | Cereal With Cranberry-Orange Twist | Sweet Potato Cakes With Classic Guacamole | Healthy Mediterranean Lamb Chops | Summer Jam |
| 29 | No Cook Overnight Oats | Chickpea Cauliflower Tikka Masala | Amazing Sesame Breadsticks | Cinnamon Pudding |
| 30 | Avocado Cup With Egg | Eggplant Parmesan Stacks | Brown Butter Duck Breast | Orange Compote |
| 31 | Mediterranean Toast | Roasted Vegetable Enchiladas | Generous Garlic Bread Stick | Chocolate Bars |
| 32 | Instant Banana Oatmeal | Lentil Avocado Tacos | Cauliflower Bread Stick | Lemon Zest Pudding |
| 33 | Almond Butter-Banana Smoothie | Tomato And Olive Orecchiette With Basil Pesto | Bacon And Chicken Garlic Wrap | Coconut Figs |
| 34 | Brown Sugar Cinnamon Oatmeal | Italian Stuffed Portobello Mushroom Burgers | Chipotle Lettuce Chicken | Lemony Banana Mix |
| 35 | Buckwheat Pancakes With Vanilla Almond Milk | Gnocchi With Tomato Basil Sauce | Balsamic Chicken And Vegetables | Cocoa Banana Dessert Smoothie |
| 36 | Salmon And Egg Scramble | Creamy Pumpkin Pasta | Exuberant Sweet Potatoes | Kiwi Bars |
| 37 | Pumpkin Muffins | Mexican-Style Potato Casserole | The Vegan Lovers Refried Beans | Black Tea Bars |
| 38 | Sweet Berries Pancake | Black Bean Stew With Cornbread | Cool Apple And Carrot Harmony | Green Pudding |
| 39 | Zucchini Pancakes | Mushroom Florentine | Mac And Chokes | Lemony Plum Cake |
| 40 | Breakfast Banana Split | Hassel Back Eggplant | Black Eyed Peas And Spinach Platter | Lentils Sweet Bars |
| 41 | Easy Veggie Muffins | Vegetarian Kebabs | Humble Mushroom Rice | Lentils And Dates Brownies |
| 42 | Carrot Muffins | White Beans Stew | Sweet And Sour Cabbage And Apples | Mandarin Pudding |
| 43 | Pineapple Oatmeal | Vegetarian Lasagna | Delicious Aloo Palak | Walnut Apple Mix |
| 44 | Spinach Muffins | Pan-Fried Salmon With Salad | Orange And Chili Garlic Sauce | Vanilla And Grapes Compote |
| 45 | Chia Seeds Breakfast Mix | Veggie Variety | Tantalizing Mushroom Gravy | Soft Pudding |
| 46 | Breakfast Fruits Bowls | Vegetable Pasta | Everyday Vegetable Stock | Ginger And Cinnamon Pudding |
| 47 | Pumpkin Cookies | Vegetable Noodles With Bolognese | Grilled Chicken With Lemon And Fennel | Honey Compote |
| 48 | Veggie Scramble | Harissa Bolognese With Vegetable Noodles | Caramelized Pork Chops And Onion | Dark Cherry And Stevia Compote |
| 49 | Mushrooms And Turkey Breakfast | Curry Vegetable Noodles With Chicken | Hearty Pork Belly Casserole | Vanilla Grapes Bowls |
| 50 | Mushrooms And Cheese Omelet | Sweet And Sour Vegetable Noodles | Apple Pie Crackers | Pears Mix |

| | | | | |
|---|---|---|---|---|
| 51 | Egg White Breakfast Mix | Zucchini Zoodles With Chicken And Basil | Paprika Lamb Chops | Pork Beef Bean Nachos |
| 52 | Pesto Omelet | Parmesan Baked Chicken | Lemon Garlic Chicken | Pressure Cooker Cranberry Hot Wings |
| 53 | Quinoa Bowls | Crazy Japanese Potato And Beef Croquettes | Simple Mediterranean Chicken | Cheesecake Made Easy! |
| 54 | Strawberry Sandwich | Golden Eggplant Fries | Roasted Chicken Thighs | Grapefruit Compote |
| 55 | Apple Quinoa Muffins | Very Wild Mushroom Pilaf | Mediterranean Turkey Breast | Instant Pot Applesauce |
| 56 | Very Berry Muesli | Sporty Baby Carrots | Olive Capers Chicken | Plum Cake |
| 57 | Veggie Quiche Muffins | Garden Salad | Chicken With Mushrooms | Dates Brownies |
| 58 | Turkey Sausage And Mushroom Strata | Baked Smoky Broccoli And Garlic | Baked Chicken | Rose Lentils Ice Cream |
| 59 | Bacon Bits | Roasted Cauliflower And Lima Beans | Garlic Pepper Chicken | Mandarin Almond Pudding |
| 60 | Steel Cut Oat Blueberry Pancakes | Thai Roasted Spicy Black Beans And Choy Sum | Mustard Chicken Tenders | Cherry Stew |
| 61 | Spinach, Mushroom, And Feta Cheese Scramble | Simple Roasted Broccoli And Cauliflower | Salsa Chicken Chili | Rice Pudding |
| 62 | Red Velvet Pancakes With Cream Cheese Topping | Roasted Napa Cabbage And Turnips Extra | Honey Crusted Chicken | Apple Loaf |
| 63 | Peanut Butter And Banana Breakfast Smoothie | Simple Roasted Kale Artichoke Heart And Choy Sum Extra | Shrimp Cocktail | Cauliflower Cinnamon Pudding |
| 64 | No-Bake Breakfast Granola Bars | Roasted Kale And Bok Choy Extra | Squid And Shrimp Salad | Rhubarb Stew |
| 65 | Mushroom Shallot Frittata | Roasted Soy Beans And Winter Squash | Parsley Seafood Cocktail | Pumpkin Pudding |
| 66 | Jack-O-Lantern Pancakes | Roasted Button Mushrooms And Squash | Shrimp And Onion Ginger Dressing | Cashew Lemon Fudge |
| 67 | Fruit Pizza | Roasted Tomatoes Rutabaga And Kohlrabi Main | Fruit Shrimp Soup | Brown Cake |
| 68 | Flax Banana Yogurt Muffins | Roasted Brussels Sprouts And Broccoli | Mussels And Chickpea Soup | Delicious Berry Pie |
| 69 | Apple Oats | Roasted Broccoli Sweet Potatoes And Bean Sprouts | Fish Stew | Cinnamon Peach Cobbler |
| 70 | Buckwheat Crepes | Roasted Sweet Potato And Red Beets | Shrimp And Broccoli Soup | Resilient Chocolate Cream |
| 71 | Whole Grain Pancakes | Sichuan Style Baked Chioggia Beets And Broccoli Florets | Coconut Turkey Mix | Vanilla Poached Strawberries |
| 72 | Granola Parfait | Baked Enoki And Mini Cabbage | Lime Shrimp And Kale | Lemon Bananas |
| 73 | Curry Tofu Scramble | Roasted Triple Mushrooms | Parsley Cod Mix | Pecans Cake |
| 74 | Scallions Omelet | Roasted Mini Cabbage And Sweet Potato | Salmon And Cabbage Mix | Coconut Cream And Plums Cake |
| 75 | Breakfast Almond Smoothie | Tofu And Green Bean Stir-Fry | Decent Beef And Onion Stew | Maple Syrup Poached Pears |
| 76 | Tomato Salad | Peanut Vegetable Pad Thai | Clean Parsley And Chicken Breast | Ginger And Pumpkin Pie |
| 77 | Feta Beet Salad | Spicy Tofu Burrito Bowls With Cilantro Avocado Sauce | Zucchini Beef Sauté With Coriander Greens | Cashew And Carrot Muffins |
| 78 | Cauliflower And Tomato Salad | Sweet Potato Cakes With Classic Guacamole | Hearty Lemon And Pepper Chicken | Lemon Custard |
| 79 | Tahini Spinach | Chickpea Cauliflower Tikka Masala | Walnuts And Asparagus Delight | Rhubarb Dip |

| | | | | |
|---|---|---|---|---|
| 80 | Pilaf With Cream Cheese | Eggplant Parmesan Stacks | Healthy Carrot Chips | Summer Jam |
| 81 | Easy Spaghetti Squash | Roasted Vegetable Enchiladas | Beef Soup | Cinnamon Pudding |
| 82 | Roasted Eggplant Salad | Lentil Avocado Tacos | Amazing Grilled Chicken And Blueberry Salad | Orange Compote |
| 83 | Penne With Tahini Sauce | Tomato And Olive Orecchiette With Basil Pesto | Clean Chicken And Mushroom Stew | Chocolate Bars |
| 84 | Roasted Veggies | Italian Stuffed Portobello Mushroom Burgers | Elegant Pumpkin Chili Dish | Lemon Zest Pudding |
| 85 | Zucchini Pasta | Gnocchi With Tomato Basil Sauce | Tasty Roasted Broccoli | Coconut Figs |
| 86 | Asparagus Pasta | Creamy Pumpkin Pasta | The Almond Breaded Chicken Goodness | Lemony Banana Mix |
| 87 | Energy Sunrise Muffins | Mexican-Style Potato Casserole | South-Western Pork Chops | Cocoa Banana Dessert Smoothie |
| 88 | Blueberry Waffles | Black Bean Stew With Cornbread | Almond Butter Pork Chops | Kiwi Bars |
| 89 | Apple Pancakes | Mushroom Florentine | Chicken Salsa | Black Tea Bars |
| 90 | Super-Simple Granola | Hassel Back Eggplant | Healthy Mediterranean Lamb Chops | Green Pudding |
| 91 | Savory Yogurt Bowls | Vegetarian Kebabs | Amazing Sesame Breadsticks | Lemony Plum Cake |
| 92 | Spinach, Egg, And Cheese Breakfast Quesadillas | White Beans Stew | Brown Butter Duck Breast | Lentils Sweet Bars |
| 93 | Simple Cheese And Broccoli Omelets | Vegetarian Lasagna | Generous Garlic Bread Stick | Lentils And Dates Brownies |
| 94 | Creamy Avocado And Egg Salad Sandwiches | Pan-Fried Salmon With Salad | Cauliflower Bread Stick | Mandarin Pudding |
| 95 | Breakfast Hash | Veggie Variety | Bacon And Chicken Garlic Wrap | Walnut Apple Mix |
| 96 | Hearty Breakfast Casserole | Vegetable Pasta | Chipotle Lettuce Chicken | Vanilla And Grapes Compote |
| 97 | Creamy Apple-Avocado Smoothie | Vegetable Noodles With Bolognese | Balsamic Chicken And Vegetables | Soft Pudding |
| 98 | Strawberry, Orange, And Beet Smoothie | Harissa Bolognese With Vegetable Noodles | Exuberant Sweet Potatoes | Ginger And Cinnamon Pudding |
| 99 | Blueberry-Vanilla Yogurt Smoothie | Curry Vegetable Noodles With Chicken | The Vegan Lovers Refried Beans | Honey Compote |
| 100 | Greek Yogurt Oat Pancakes | Sweet And Sour Vegetable Noodles | Cool Apple And Carrot Harmony | Dark Cherry And Stevia Compote |
| 101 | Scrambled Egg And Veggie Breakfast Quesadillas | Zucchini Zoodles With Chicken And Basil | Mac And Chokes | Vanilla Grapes Bowls |
| 102 | Stuffed Breakfast Peppers | Parmesan Baked Chicken | Black Eyed Peas And Spinach Platter | Pears Mix |
| 103 | Sweet Potato Toast Three Ways | Crazy Japanese Potato And Beef Croquettes | Humble Mushroom Rice | Pork Beef Bean Nachos |
| 104 | Apple-Apricot Brown Rice Breakfast Porridge | Golden Eggplant Fries | Sweet And Sour Cabbage And Apples | Pressure Cooker Cranberry Hot Wings |
| 105 | Carrot Cake Overnight Oats | Very Wild Mushroom Pilaf | Delicious Aloo Palak | Cheesecake Made Easy! |
| 106 | Steel-Cut Oatmeal With Plums And Pear | Sporty Baby Carrots | Orange And Chili Garlic Sauce | Grapefruit Compote |
| 107 | French Toast With Applesauce | Garden Salad | Tantalizing Mushroom Gravy | Instant Pot Applesauce |
| 108 | Banana-Peanut Butter And Greens Smoothie | Baked Smoky Broccoli And Garlic | Everyday Vegetable Stock | Plum Cake |

| | | | | |
|---|---|---|---|---|
| 109 | Baking Powder Biscuits | Roasted Cauliflower And Lima Beans | Grilled Chicken With Lemon And Fennel | Dates Brownies |
| 110 | Oatmeal Banana Pancakes With Walnuts | Thai Roasted Spicy Black Beans And Choy Sum | Caramelized Pork Chops And Onion | Rose Lentils Ice Cream |
| 111 | Creamy Oats, Greens And Blueberry Smoothie | Simple Roasted Broccoli And Cauliflower | Hearty Pork Belly Casserole | Mandarin Almond Pudding |
| 112 | Banana And Cinnamon Oatmeal | Roasted Napa Cabbage And Turnips Extra | Apple Pie Crackers | Cherry Stew |
| 113 | Bagels Made Healthy | Simple Roasted Kale Artichoke Heart And Choy Sum Extra | Paprika Lamb Chops | Rice Pudding |
| 114 | Cereal With Cranberry-Orange Twist | Roasted Kale And Bok Choy Extra | Lemon Garlic Chicken | Apple Loaf |
| 115 | No Cook Overnight Oats | Roasted Soy Beans And Winter Squash | Simple Mediterranean Chicken | Cauliflower Cinnamon Pudding |
| 116 | Avocado Cup With Egg | Roasted Button Mushrooms And Squash | Roasted Chicken Thighs | Rhubarb Stew |
| 117 | Mediterranean Toast | Roasted Tomatoes Rutabaga And Kohlrabi Main | Mediterranean Turkey Breast | Pumpkin Pudding |
| 118 | Instant Banana Oatmeal | Roasted Brussels Sprouts And Broccoli | Olive Capers Chicken | Cashew Lemon Fudge |
| 119 | Almond Butter-Banana Smoothie | Roasted Broccoli Sweet Potatoes And Bean Sprouts | Chicken With Mushrooms | Brown Cake |
| 110 | Brown Sugar Cinnamon Oatmeal | Roasted Sweet Potato And Red Beets | Baked Chicken | Delicious Berry Pie |
| 111 | Buckwheat Pancakes With Vanilla Almond Milk | Sichuan Style Baked Chioggia Beets And Broccoli Florets | Garlic Pepper Chicken | Cinnamon Peach Cobbler |
| 112 | Salmon And Egg Scramble | Baked Enoki And Mini Cabbage | Mustard Chicken Tenders | Resilient Chocolate Cream |
| 113 | Pumpkin Muffins | Roasted Triple Mushrooms | Salsa Chicken Chili | Vanilla Poached Strawberries |
| 114 | Sweet Berries Pancake | Roasted Mini Cabbage And Sweet Potato | Honey Crusted Chicken | Lemon Bananas |
| 115 | Zucchini Pancakes | Tofu And Green Bean Stir-Fry | Shrimp Cocktail | Pecans Cake |
| 116 | Breakfast Banana Split | Peanut Vegetable Pad Thai | Squid And Shrimp Salad | Coconut Cream And Plums Cake |
| 117 | Easy Veggie Muffins | Spicy Tofu Burrito Bowls With Cilantro Avocado Sauce | Parsley Seafood Cocktail | Maple Syrup Poached Pears |
| 118 | Carrot Muffins | Sweet Potato Cakes With Classic Guacamole | Shrimp And Onion Ginger Dressing | Ginger And Pumpkin Pie |
| 119 | Pineapple Oatmeal | Chickpea Cauliflower Tikka Masala | Fruit Shrimp Soup | Cashew And Carrot Muffins |
| 120 | Spinach Muffins | Eggplant Parmesan Stacks | Mussels And Chickpea Soup | Lemon Custard |
| 121 | Chia Seeds Breakfast Mix | Roasted Vegetable Enchiladas | Fish Stew | Rhubarb Dip |
| 122 | Breakfast Fruits Bowls | Lentil Avocado Tacos | Shrimp And Broccoli Soup | Summer Jam |
| 123 | Pumpkin Cookies | Tomato And Olive Orecchiette With Basil Pesto | Coconut Turkey Mix | Cinnamon Pudding |
| 124 | Veggie Scramble | Italian Stuffed Portobello Mushroom Burgers | Lime Shrimp And Kale | Orange Compote |
| 125 | Mushrooms And Turkey Breakfast | Gnocchi With Tomato Basil Sauce | Parsley Cod Mix | Chocolate Bars |

| | | | | |
|---|---|---|---|---|
| 126 | Mushrooms And Cheese Omelet | Creamy Pumpkin Pasta | Salmon And Cabbage Mix | Lemon Zest Pudding |
| 127 | Egg White Breakfast Mix | Mexican-Style Potato Casserole | Decent Beef And Onion Stew | Coconut Figs |
| 128 | Pesto Omelet | Black Bean Stew With Cornbread | Clean Parsley And Chicken Breast | Lemony Banana Mix |
| 129 | Quinoa Bowls | Mushroom Florentine | Zucchini Beef Sauté With Coriander Greens | Cocoa Banana Dessert Smoothie |
| 130 | Strawberry Sandwich | Hassel Back Eggplant | Hearty Lemon And Pepper Chicken | Kiwi Bars |
| 131 | Apple Quinoa Muffins | Vegetarian Kebabs | Walnuts And Asparagus Delight | Black Tea Bars |
| 132 | Very Berry Muesli | White Beans Stew | Healthy Carrot Chips | Green Pudding |
| 133 | Veggie Quiche Muffins | Vegetarian Lasagna | Beef Soup | Lemony Plum Cake |
| 134 | Turkey Sausage And Mushroom Strata | Pan-Fried Salmon With Salad | Amazing Grilled Chicken And Blueberry Salad | Lentils Sweet Bars |
| 135 | Bacon Bits | Veggie Variety | Clean Chicken And Mushroom Stew | Lentils And Dates Brownies |
| 136 | Steel Cut Oat Blueberry Pancakes | Vegetable Pasta | Elegant Pumpkin Chili Dish | Mandarin Pudding |
| 137 | Spinach, Mushroom, And Feta Cheese Scramble | Vegetable Noodles With Bolognese | Tasty Roasted Broccoli | Walnut Apple Mix |
| 138 | Red Velvet Pancakes With Cream Cheese Topping | Harissa Bolognese With Vegetable Noodles | The Almond Breaded Chicken Goodness | Vanilla And Grapes Compote |
| 139 | Peanut Butter And Banana Breakfast Smoothie | Curry Vegetable Noodles With Chicken | South-Western Pork Chops | Soft Pudding |
| 140 | No-Bake Breakfast Granola Bars | Sweet And Sour Vegetable Noodles | Almond Butter Pork Chops | Ginger And Cinnamon Pudding |

# CHAPTER 4:
# The Importance Of Regular Exercise And Deep Breathing Both For Hypertension And To Lose Weight

People who do regular physical activity, especially those who exercise intensely, tend to be healthier and live longer. Research shows that people who exercise four or more times a week have a lower risk of high blood pressure than those who do not. Exercise is also a great stress reliever and can decrease blood pressure.

If you have high blood pressure, start by including moderate physical activity in your daily routine – say 30 minutes of walking – for at least 5 days a week. In addition to helping with hypertension, aerobic exercise helps control weight. Studies show that the more time people spend being active, the more lb. they lose from their body weights each year.

When you're exercising, be sure to breathe deeply and talk out loud in a relaxed manner. Deep breathing and relaxation techniques can lower blood pressure, improve your mood and ease anxiety. In addition, the more physical activity you do, the better your body is able to deal with stress and remain healthy.

There are many different types of activities you can do as part of a healthy lifestyle. Exercise doesn't have to be strenuous. In fact, there are some things you can do to stay fit that don't involve going for a run or hitting the gym. During a workout, try going for a walk instead of running or riding a bike. A 45-minute walk per day is just as effective as a 30 minute run in weight loss and cardiovascular benefits.

If you don't have a gym near you, look into an exercise that your body can do in a small space, such as yoga or stretching. You can even do exercises in the comfort of your own home using items from around the house, such as water bottles filled with sand, soup cans, or magazines.

In addition to fighting high blood pressure, regular exercise will also help lower cholesterol and improve your mood. In addition to aerobic exercises, strength training is also important for its ability to improve muscle strength and joint range of motion.

The bottom line is that exercise has several positive effects on our health. It increases our endurance and allows us to fit more physically demanding activities into our daily lives. It as well reduces the risk of developing a number of health problems, such as type 2 diabetes and certain types of heart disease. And it decreases the risk of death from all causes – including cardiovascular disease – among those with high blood pressure. If you have some questions or concerns about exercise and your blood pressure, talk to your doctor. He or she might be able to give you useful suggestions on what to do. In addition, many health clubs offer free fitness assessments for their members. If you want to get started exercising right away, it's always a good idea to speak with a doctor before starting an intense or physically demanding exercise regimen. Remember that if you make regular physical activity a part of your daily life, the positive effects will last a lifetime.

Exercise can also help you sleep better. People who are physically active have longer periods of deep sleep each night, which reduces stress and helps you cope with stress during the day. It can also improve your mood and reduce anxiety. however, if you exercise too intensely or for too long at a time, you can increase your blood pressure. So if you possess high blood pressure, don't overdo it. And pay attention to how you feel when you exercise – if your BP is rising or falling around the time of your workouts, make adjustments to your activities to help keep it under control.

## Graphs on food and calories, for example, for those who want to lose weight

**Activity level**

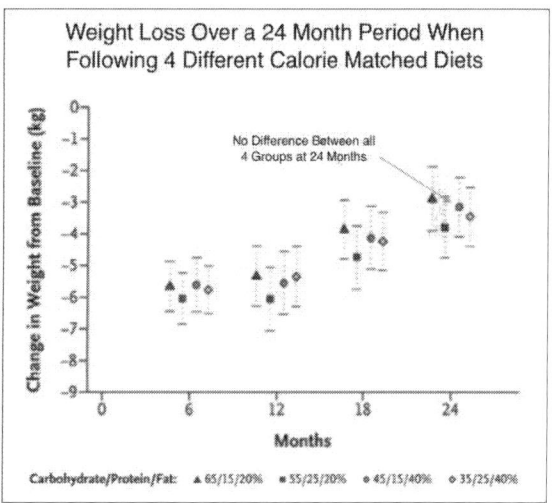

# CHAPTER 5:
# Breakfast Recipes

## 1. Energy Sunrise Muffins

**Preparation time:** 15 minutes
**Cooking time:** 25 minutes
**Servings:** 16
**Ingredients:**

- Nonstick cooking spray
- 2 cups whole wheat flour
- 2 tsp. baking soda
- 2 tsp. cinnamon, ground
- 1 tsp. ginger, ground
- ¼ tsp. salt
- 3 large eggs
- ½ cup brown sugar, packed
- ⅓ cup applesauce, unsweetened
- ¼ cup honey
- ¼ cup vegetable or canola oil
- 1 tsp. orange zest, grated
- Juice of 1 medium orange
- 2 tsp. vanilla extract
- 2 cups carrots, shredded
- 1 large apple, peeled and grated
- ½ cup golden raisins
- ½ cup pecans, chopped
- ½ cup coconut flakes, unsweetened

**Directions:**

1. If you can fit 2 12-cup muffin tins side by side in your oven, then leave a rack in the middle then preheat the oven to 350°F.
2. Coat 16 cups of the muffin tins with cooking spray or line with paper liners. Mix the flour, baking soda, cinnamon, ginger, and salt in a large bowl. Set aside.
3. Mix the eggs, brown sugar, applesauce, honey, oil, orange zest, orange juice, and vanilla until combined in a medium bowl. Add the carrots and apple and whisk again.

4. Mix the dry and wet ingredients with a spatula. Fold in the raisins, pecans, and coconut.
5. Mix everything once again, just until well combined. Put the batter into the prepared muffin cups, filling them to the top.
6. Bake within 20 to 25 minutes, or until a wooden toothpick inserted into the middle of the center muffin comes out clean (switching racks halfway through if baking on 2 racks). Cool for 5 minutes in the tins, then transfer to a wire rack to cool for an additional 5 minutes. Cool completely before storing in containers.

**Nutrition: Calories:** 292 kcal; **Fat:** 14 g; **Carbohydrates:** 42 g; **Protein:** 5g; **Sodium:** 84 mg

## 2. Blueberry Waffles

**Preparation time:** 15 minutes
**Cooking time:** 15 minutes
**Servings:** 8
**Ingredients:**
- 2 cups whole wheat flour
- 1 tbsp. baking powder
- 1 tsp. cinnamon, ground
- 2 tbsp. sugar
- 2 large eggs
- 3 tbsp. butter, unsalted and melted
- 3 tbsp. nonfat plain Greek yogurt
- 1½ cups 1% milk
- 2 tsp. vanilla extract
- 4 oz. blueberries
- Nonstick cooking spray
- ½ cup maple almond butter

**Directions:**
1. Preheat waffle iron. Mix the flour, baking powder, cinnamon, plus sugar in a large bowl. Mix the eggs, melted butter, yogurt, milk, and vanilla in a small bowl. Combine well.
2. Put the wet fixing to the dry mix and whisk until well combined. Do not over whisk; it's okay if the mixture has some lumps. Fold in the blueberries.
3. Oiled the waffle iron with cooking spray, then cook ⅓ cup of the batter until the waffles are lightly browned and slightly crisp.
4. Repeat with the rest of the batter. Place 2 waffles in each of 4 storage containers. Store the almond butter in 4 condiment cups.
5. To serve, top each warm waffle with 1 tbsp. of maple almond butter.

**Nutrition: Calories:** 647 kcal; **Fat:** 37 g; **Carbohydrates:** 67 g; **Protein:** 22 g; **Sodium:** 156 mg

## 3. Apple Pancakes

**Preparation time:** 15 minutes
**Cooking time:** 5 minutes
**Servings:** 16
**Ingredients:**
- ¼ cup extra-virgin olive oil, divided
- 1 cup whole wheat flour
- 2 tsp. baking powder
- 1 tsp. baking soda
- 1 tsp. cinnamon, ground
- 1 cup 1% milk
- 2 large eggs
- 1 medium Gala apple, diced
- 2 tbsp. maple syrup
- ¼ cup walnuts, chopped

**Directions:**
1. Set aside 1 tsp. of oil to use for greasing a griddle or skillet. In a large bowl, stir the flour, baking powder, baking soda, cinnamon, milk, eggs, apple, and the remaining oil.
2. Warm a griddle or skillet on medium-high heat, and coat with the reserved oil. Working in batches, pour in about ¼ cup of the batter for each pancake. Cook until browned on both sides. Place 4 pancakes into each of 4 medium storage containers and the maple syrup in 4 small containers. Put each serving with 1 tbsp. of walnuts and drizzle with ½ tbsp. of maple syrup.

**Nutrition: Calories:** 378 kcal; **Fat:** 22 g; **Carbohydrates:** 39 g; **Protein:** 10 g; **Sodium:** 65 mg

## 4. Super-Simple Granola

**Preparation time:** 15 minutes
**Cooking time:** 25 minutes
**Servings:** 8
**Ingredients:**
- ¼ cup extra-virgin olive oil
- ¼ cup honey
- ½ tsp. cinnamon, ground
- ½ tsp. vanilla extract
- ¼ tsp. salt
- 2 cups oats, rolled
- ½ cup walnuts, chopped
- ½ cup almonds, slivered

**Directions:**
1. Preheat the oven to 350°F. Mix the oil, honey, cinnamon, vanilla, and salt in a large bowl. Add the oats, walnuts, and almonds. Stir to coat. Put the batter out onto the prepared sheet pan. Bake for 20 minutes. Let cool.

**Nutrition: Calories:** 254 kcal; **Fat:** 16 g; **Carbohydrates:** 25 g; **Fiber:** 3.5 g; **Protein:** 5 g; **Potassium:** 163 mg; **Sodium:** 73 mg

## 5. Savory Yogurt Bowls

**Preparation time:** 15 minutes
**Cooking time:** 0 minutes
**Servings:** 4
**Ingredients:**
- 1 medium cucumber, diced
- ½ cup Kalamata olives, pitted and halved
- 2 tbsp. fresh lemon juice
- 1 tbsp. extra-virgin olive oil
- 1 tsp. oregano, dried
- ¼ tsp. black pepper, freshly ground
- 2 cups nonfat plain Greek yogurt
- ½ cup almonds, slivered

**Directions:**
1. In a small bowl, mix the cucumber, olives, lemon juice, oil, oregano, and pepper. Divide the yogurt evenly among 4 storage containers. Top with the cucumber-olive mix and almonds.

**Nutrition: Calories:** 240 kcal; **Fat:** 16 g; **Carbohydrates:** 10 mg; **Protein:** 16 g; **Potassium:** 353 mg, **Sodium:** 350 mg

## 6. Spinach, Egg, and Cheese Breakfast Quesadillas

**Preparation time:** 15 minutes
**Cooking time:** 15 minutes
**Servings:** 4
**Ingredients:**
- 1½ tbsp. extra-virgin olive oil
- ½ medium onion, diced
- 1 medium red bell pepper, diced
- 4 large eggs
- ⅛ tsp. salt
- ⅛ tsp. black pepper, freshly ground
- 4 cups baby spinach
- ½ cup feta cheese, crumbled
- Nonstick cooking spray
- 4 (6-inch) whole-wheat tortillas, divided
- 1 cup low-moisture mozzarella cheese, shredded part-skim, and divided

**Directions:**
1. Warm up the oil over medium heat in a large skillet. Add the onion and bell pepper and sauté for about 5 minutes, or until soft.
2. Mix the eggs, salt, and black pepper in a medium bowl. Stir in the spinach and feta cheese. Put the egg batter in the skillet and scramble for about 2 minutes, or until the eggs are cooked. Remove from the heat.
3. Coat a clean skillet with cooking spray and add 2 tortillas. Place ¼ of the spinach-egg mixture on one side of each tortilla. Sprinkle each with ¼ cup of mozzarella cheese. Fold the other halves of the tortillas down to close the quesadillas and brown for about 1 minute.
4. Turn over and cook again in a minute on the other side. Repeat with the remaining 2 tortillas and ½ cup of mozzarella cheese. Cut each quesadilla in half or wedges.
5. Divide among 4 storage containers or reusable bags.

**Nutrition: Calories:** 453 kcal; **Fat:** 28 g; **Carbohydrates:** 28 g; **Fiber:** 4.5 g; **Protein:** 23 g; **Potassium:** 205 mg; **Sodium:** 837 mg

## 7. Simple Cheese and Broccoli Omelets

**Preparation time:** 15 minutes
**Cooking time:** 10 minutes
**Servings:** 4
**Ingredients:**

- 3 tbsp. extra-virgin olive oil, divided
- 2 cups broccoli, chopped
- 8 large eggs
- ¼ cup 1% milk
- ½ tsp. black pepper, freshly ground
- 8 tbsp. reduced-fat Monterey Jack cheese, shredded, divided

**Directions:**

1. In a nonstick skillet, heat 1 tbsp. of oil over medium-high heat. Add the broccoli and sauté, occasionally stirring, for 3 to 5 minutes, or until the broccoli turns bright green. Scrape into a bowl.
2. Mix the eggs, milk, plus pepper in a small bowl. Wipe out the skillet and heat ½ tbsp. of oil. Add ¼ of the egg mixture and tilt the skillet to ensure an even layer. Cook for 2 minutes and then add 2 tbsp. of cheese and ¼ of the broccoli. Use a spatula to fold into an omelet.
3. Repeat step 3 with the remaining 1½ tbsp. of oil, remaining egg mixture, 6 tbsp. of cheese, and remaining broccoli to make a total of 4 omelets. Divide into 4 storage containers.

**Nutrition: Calories:** 292 kcal; **Fat:** 23 g; **Carbohydrates:** 4 g; **Fiber:** 1 g; **Protein:** 18 g; **Potassium:** 308 mg; **Sodium:** 282 mg

## 8. Creamy Avocado and Egg Salad Sandwiches

**Preparation time:** 15 minutes
**Cooking time:** 15 minutes
**Servings:** 4
**Ingredients:**

- 2 small avocados, halved and pitted
- 2 tbsp. nonfat plain Greek yogurt
- Juice of 1 large lemon
- ¼ tsp. salt
- ½ tsp. black pepper, freshly ground
- 8 large eggs, hardboiled, peeled, and chopped
- 3 tbsp. fresh dill, finely chopped
- 3 tbsp. fresh parsley, finely chopped
- 8 whole-wheat bread slices (or your choice)

**Directions:**

1. Scoop the avocados into a large bowl and mash. Mix in the yogurt, lemon juice, salt, and pepper.
2. Add the eggs, dill, and parsley and combine. Store the bread and salad separately in 4 reusable storage bags and 4 containers and assemble the night before or serving. To serve, divide the mixture evenly among 4 of the bread slices and top with the other slices to make sandwiches.

**Nutrition: Calories:** 488 kcal; **Fat:** 22 g; **Carbohydrates:** 48 g; **Fiber:** 8 g; **Protein:** 23 g; **Potassium:** 469 mg; **Sodium:** 597 mg

## 9. Breakfast Hash

**Preparation time:** 15 minutes
**Cooking time:** 25 minutes
**Servings:** 4
**Ingredients:**

- Nonstick cooking spray
- 2 large sweet potatoes, ½-inch cubes
- 1 scallion, finely chopped
- ¼ tsp. salt
- ½ tsp. black pepper, freshly ground
- 8 oz. extra-lean beef, ground (96% or leaner)
- 1 medium onion, diced
- 2 garlic cloves, minced
- 1 red bell pepper, diced
- ¼ tsp. cumin, ground
- ¼ tsp. paprika
- 2 cups kale leaves, coarsely chopped
- ¾ cup reduced-fat Cheddar cheese, shredded
- 4 large eggs

**Directions:**

1. Oil a large skillet with cooking spray and heat over medium heat. Add the sweet potatoes, scallion, salt, and pepper. Sauté for 10 minutes, stirring often.
2. Add the beef, onion, garlic, bell pepper, cumin, and paprika. Sauté, frequently stirring, for about 4 minutes, or until the meat browns.
3. Add the kale to the skillet and stir until wilted. Sprinkle with the Cheddar cheese.
4. Make four wells in the hash batter and crack an egg into each. Cover and let the eggs cook until the white is fully cooked and the yolk is to your liking. Divide into 4 storage containers.

**Nutrition: Calories:** 323 kcal; **Fat:** 15 g; **Carbohydrates:** 23 g; **Fiber:** 4 g; **Protein:** 25 g; **Potassium:** 676 mg; **Sodium:** 587 mg

## 10. Hearty Breakfast Casserole

**Preparation time:** 15 minutes
**Cooking time:** 30 minutes
**Servings:** 4
**Ingredients:**
- Nonstick cooking spray
- 1 large green bell pepper, diced
- 8 oz. Cremini mushrooms, diced
- ½ medium onion, diced
- 3 garlic cloves, minced
- 1 large sweet potato, grated
- 1 cup baby spinach
- 12 large eggs
- 3 tbsp. 1% milk
- 1 tsp. mustard powder
- 1 tsp. paprika
- 1 tsp. black pepper, freshly ground
- ½ tsp. salt
- ½ cup reduced-fat Colby-Jack cheese, shredded

**Directions:**
1. Preheat the oven to 350°F. Oil at a 9-x-13-inch baking dish with cooking spray. Coat a large skillet with cooking spray and heat over medium heat. Add the bell pepper, mushrooms, onion, garlic, and sweet potato.
2. Sauté, frequently stirring, for 3 to 4 minutes, or until the onion is translucent. Add the spinach and continue to sauté while stirring, until the spinach has wilted. Remove, and then set aside to cool slightly.
3. Mix the eggs, milk, mustard powder, paprika, black pepper, and salt in a large bowl. Add the sautéed vegetables. Put the batter into the prepared baking dish.
4. Bake for 30 minutes. Remove from the oven, sprinkle with the Colby-Jack cheese, return to the oven, and bake again within 5 minutes to melt the cheese. Divide into 4 storage containers.

**Nutrition: Calories:** 378 kcal; **Fat:** 25 g; **Carbohydrates:** 17 g; **Fiber:** 3 g; **Protein:** 26 g; **Potassium:** 717 mg; **Sodium:** 658 mg

## 11. Creamy Apple-Avocado Smoothie

**Preparation time:** 15 minutes
**Cooking time:** 0 minutes
**Servings:** 2
**Ingredients:**
- ½ medium avocado, peeled and pitted
- 1 medium apple, chopped
- 1 cup baby spinach leaves
- 1 cup nonfat vanilla Greek yogurt
- ½ to 1 cup water
- 1 cup ice
- lemon juice, freshly squeezed (optional)

**Directions:**
1. Blend all of the fixing using a blender, and blend until smooth and creamy.
2. Put a squeeze of lemon juice on top if desired, and serve immediately.

**Nutrition: Calories:** 200 kcal; **Fat:** 7 g; **Sodium:** 56 mg; **Potassium:** 378 mg; **Carbohydrates:** 27 g; **Fiber:** 5 g; **Sugars:** 20 g; **Protein:** 10 g

## 12. Strawberry, Orange, and Beet Smoothie

**Preparation time:** 5 minutes
**Cooking time:** 0 minutes
**Servings:** 2
**Ingredients:**
- 1 cup nonfat milk
- 1 cup strawberries, frozen
- 1 medium beet, cooked, peeled, and cubed
- 1 orange, peeled and quartered
- 1 banana frozen, peeled, and chopped
- 1 cup nonfat vanilla Greek yogurt
- 1 cup ice

**Directions:**
1. In a blender, combine all of the fixings, and blend until smooth.
2. Serve immediately.

**Nutrition: Calories:** 266 kcal; **Fat:** 0 g; **Cholesterol:** 7 mg, **Sodium:** 104 mg, **Carbohydrates:** 51 g; **Fiber:** 6 g; **Sugars:** 34 g; **Protein:** 15 g

## 13. Blueberry-Vanilla Yogurt Smoothie

**Preparation time:** 5 minutes
**Cooking time:** 0 minutes
**Servings:** 2
**Ingredients:**
- 1½ cups blueberries, frozen
- 1 cup nonfat vanilla Greek yogurt
- 1 banana frozen, peeled, and sliced
- ½ cup nonfat or low-fat milk
- 1 cup ice

**Directions:**
1. In a blender, combine all of the fixing listed, and blend until smooth and creamy.
2. Serve immediately.

**Nutrition: Calories:** 228 kcal; **Fat:** 1 g; **Sodium:** 63 mg; **Potassium:** 470 mg; **Carbohydrates:** 45 g; **Fiber:** 5 g; **Sugars:** 34 g; **Protein:** 12 g

## 14. Greek Yogurt Oat Pancakes

**Preparation time:** 15 minutes
**Cooking time:** 10 minutes
**Servings:** 2
**Ingredients:**

- 6 egg whites (or ¾ cup liquid egg whites)
- 1 cup oats, rolled
- 1 cup plain nonfat Greek yogurt
- 1 medium banana, peeled and sliced
- 1 tsp. cinnamon, ground
- 1 tsp. baking powder

**Directions:**

1. Blend all of the listed fixing using a blender. Warm a griddle over medium heat. Spray the skillet with nonstick cooking spray.
2. Put ⅓ cup of the mixture or batter onto the griddle. Allow to cook and flip when bubbles on the top burst, about 5 minutes. Cook again within a minute until golden brown. Repeat with the remaining batter. Divide between 2 serving plates and enjoy.

**Nutrition: Calories:** 318 kcal; **Fat:** 4 g; **Sodium:** 467 mg; **Potassium:** 634 mg; **Carbohydrates:** 47 g; **Fiber:** 6 g; **Sugars:** 13 g; **Protein:** 28 g

## 15. Scrambled Egg and Veggie Breakfast Quesadillas

**Preparation time:** 15 minutes
**Cooking time:** 15 minutes
**Servings:** 2
**Ingredients:**

- 2 eggs
- 2 egg whites
- 2 to 4 tbsp. nonfat or low-fat milk
- ¼ tsp. black pepper, freshly ground
- 1 large tomato, chopped
- 2 tbsp. cilantro, chopped
- ½ cup black beans canned, rinsed, and drained
- 1½ tbsp. olive oil, divided
- 4 corn tortillas
- ½ avocado, peeled, pitted, and thinly sliced

**Directions:**

1. Mix the eggs, egg whites, milk, and black pepper in a bowl. Using an electric mixer beat until smooth. To the same bowl, add the tomato, cilantro, and black beans, and fold into the eggs with a spoon.
2. Warm-up half of the olive oil in a medium pan over medium heat. Add the scrambled egg mixture and cook for a few minutes, stirring, until cooked through. Remove from the pan.
3. Divide the scrambled-egg mixture between the tortillas, layering only on one half of the tortilla. Top with avocado slices and fold the tortillas in half.
4. Heat the remaining oil over medium heat, and add one of the folded tortillas to the pan. Cook within 1 to 2 minutes on each side or until browned. Repeat with remaining tortillas. Serve immediately.

**Nutrition: Calories:** 445 kcal; **Fat:** 24 g; **Sodium:** 228 mg; **Potassium:** 614 mg; **Carbohydrates:** 42 g; **Fiber:** 11 g; **Sugars:** 2 g; **Protein:** 19 g

## 16. Stuffed Breakfast Peppers

**Preparation time:** 15 minutes
**Cooking time:** 45 minutes
**Servings:** 4
**Ingredients:**

- 4 bell peppers (any color)
- 1 (16-oz.) bag spinach, frozen
- 4 eggs
- ¼ cup low-fat cheese, shredded (optional)
- Black pepper, freshly ground

**Directions:**

1. Preheat the oven to 400°F. Line a baking dish with aluminum foil. Cut the tops off the pepper then discard the seeds. Discard the tops and seeds. Put the peppers in the baking dish, and bake for about 15 minutes.
2. While the peppers bake, defrost the spinach and drain off the excess moisture. Remove the peppers, and stuff the bottoms evenly with the defrosted spinach.
3. Crack an egg over the spinach inside each pepper. Top each egg with a tbsp. of the cheese (if using) and season with black pepper to taste. Bake within 15 to 20 minutes, or until the egg whites are set and opaque.

**Nutrition:**
**Calories:** 136 kcal; **Fat:** 5 g; **Sodium:** 131 mg; **Potassium:** 576 mg; **Carbohydrates:** 15 g; **Protein:** 11 g

## 17. Sweet Potato Toast Three Ways

**Preparation time:** 15 minutes
**Cooking time:** 25 minutes
**Servings:**
**Ingredients:**

- 1 large sweet potato, unpeeled

**Topping Choice #1:**

- 4 tbsp. peanut butter
- 1 ripe banana, sliced

- Dash cinnamon ground

**Topping Choice #2:**
- ½ avocado, peeled, pitted, and mashed
- 2 eggs (1 per slice)

**Topping Choice #3:**
- 4 tbsp. nonfat or low-fat ricotta cheese
- 1 tomato, sliced
- Dash black pepper

**Directions:**
1. Slice the sweet potato lengthwise into ¼-inch thick slices. Place the sweet potato slices in a toaster on high for about 5 minutes or until cooked through.
2. Repeat multiple times, if necessary, depending on your toaster settings.
3. Top with your desired topping choices and enjoy.

**Nutrition: Calories:** 137 kcal; **Fat:** 0 g; **Sodium:** 17 mg; **Potassium:** 265 mg; **Carbohydrates:** 32 g; **Fiber:** 4 g; **Sugars:** 0 g; **Protein:** 2 g

## 18. Apple-Apricot Brown Rice Breakfast Porridge

**Preparation time:** 15 minutes
**Cooking time:** 8 minutes
**Servings:** 4
**Ingredients:**
- 3 cups brown rice, cooked
- 1¾ cups nonfat or low-fat milk
- 2 tbsp. brown sugar, lightly packed
- 4 dried apricots, chopped
- 1 medium apple, cored and diced
- ¾ tsp. cinnamon, ground
- ¾ tsp. vanilla extract

**Directions:**
1. Combine the rice, milk, sugar, apricots, apple, and cinnamon in a medium saucepan. Boil it on medium heat, lower the heat down slightly and cook within 2 to 3 minutes. Turn it off, and then stir in the vanilla extract. Serve warm.

**Nutrition: Calories:** 260 kcal; **Fat:** 2 g; **Sodium:** 50 mg; **Potassium:** 421 mg; **Carbohydrates:** 57 g; **Fiber:** 4 g; **Sugars:** 22 g; **Protein:** 7 g

## 19. Carrot Cake Overnight Oats

**Preparation time:** overnight
**Cooking time:** 2 minutes
**Servings:** 1
**Ingredients:**
- ½ cup oats, rolled
- ½ cup plain nonfat or low-fat Greek yogurt - ½ cup nonfat or low-fat milk
- ¼ cup carrot, shredded
- 2 tbsp. raisins
- ½ tsp. cinnamon, ground
- 1 to 2 tbsp. walnuts, chopped (optional)

**Directions:**
1. Mix all of the fixings in a lidded jar, shake well, and refrigerate overnight. Serve.

**Nutrition: Calories:** 331 kcal; **Fat:** 3 g; **Sodium:** 141 mg; **Carbohydrates:** 59 g; **Fiber:** 8 g; **Sugars:** 26 g; **Protein:** 22 g

## 20. Steel-Cut Oatmeal with Plums and Pear

**Preparation time:** 15 minutes
**Cooking time:** 25 minutes
**Servings:** 4
**Ingredients:**
- 2 cups water
- 1 cup nonfat or low-fat milk
- 1 cup steel-cut oats
- 1 cup plums, dried and chopped
- 1 medium pear, cored, and skin removed, diced
- 4 tbsp. almonds, roughly chopped

**Directions:**
1. Mix the water, milk, plus oats in a medium pot and bring to a boil over high heat. Reduce the heat and cover. Simmer for about 10 minutes, stirring occasionally.
2. Add the plums and pear, and cover. Simmer for another 10 minutes. Turn off the heat and let stand within 5 minutes until all of the liquid is absorbed. To serve, top each portion with a sprinkling of almonds.

**Nutrition: Calories:** 307 kcal; **Fat:** 6 g; **Sodium:** 132 mg; **Potassium:** 640 mg; **Carbohydrates:** 58 g; **Fiber:** 9 g; **Sugars:** 24 g; **Protein:** 9 g

## 21. French toast with Applesauce

**Preparation time:** 5 minutes
**Cooking time:** 5 minutes
**Servings:** 6
**Ingredients:**
- ¼ cup applesauce, unsweetened
- ½ cup skim milk
- 2 packets Stevia
- 2 eggs
- 6 slices whole-wheat bread
- 1 tsp. cinnamon, ground

**Directions**:
1. Mix well applesauce, sugar, cinnamon, milk, and eggs in a mixing bowl. Soak the bread into the applesauce mixture until wet. On medium fire, heat a large nonstick skillet.
2. Add soaked bread on one side and another on the other side. Cook in a single layer within 2–3 minutes per side on medium-low fire or until lightly browned.
3. Serve and enjoy.

**Nutrition:** **Calories:** 122.6 kcal; **Fat:** 2.6 g; **Carbs:** 18.3 g; **Protein:** 6.5 g; **Sugars:** 14.8 g; **Sodium:** 11 mg

## 22. Banana-Peanut Butter and Greens Smoothie

**Preparation time:** 5 minutes
**Cooking time:** 0 minutes
**Servings:** 1
**Ingredients:**
- 1 cup Romaine lettuce, chopped and packed
- 1 medium banana, frozen
- 1 tbsp. all-natural peanut butter
- 1 cup cold almond milk

**Directions**:
1. In a heavy-duty blender, add all ingredients. Puree until smooth and creamy. Serve and enjoy.

**Nutrition:** **Calories:** 349.3 kcal; **Fat:** 9.7 g; **Carbs:** 57.4 g; **Protein:** 8.1 g; **Sugars:** 4.3 g; **Sodium:** 18 mg

## 23. Baking Powder Biscuits

**Preparation time:** 5 minutes
**Cooking time:** 5 minutes
**Servings:** 1
**Ingredients:**
- 1 egg white
- 1 cup white whole-wheat flour
- 4 tbsp. Non-hydrogenated vegetable shortening
- 1 tbsp. sugar
- ⅔ cup low-fat milk
- 1 cup all-purpose flour, unbleached
- 4 tsp.
- Sodium-free baking powder

**Directions**:
1. Warm oven to 450°F. Put the flour, sugar, plus baking powder into a mixing bowl and mix. Split the shortening into the batter using your fingers until it resembles coarse crumbs. Put the egg white plus milk and stir to combine.
2. Put the dough out onto a lightly floured surface and knead 1 minute.
3. Roll dough to ¾ inch thickness and cut into 12 rounds. Place rounds on the baking sheet.
4. Bake 10 minutes, then remove the baking sheet and place biscuits on a wire rack to cool.

**Nutrition:** **Calories:** 118 kcal; **Fat:** 4 g; **Carbs:** 16 g; **Protein:** 3 g; **Sugars:** 0.2 g; **Sodium:** 6 mg

## 24. Oatmeal Banana Pancakes with Walnuts

**Preparation time:** 15 minutes
**Cooking time:** 5 minutes
**Servings:** 8
**Ingredients:**
- 1 banana, finely firm, diced
- 1 cup whole-wheat pancake mix
- ⅛ cup walnuts, chopped
- ¼ cup old-fashioned oats

**Directions**:
1. Make the pancake mix, as stated in the directions on the package. Add walnuts, oats, and chopped bananas. Coat a griddle with cooking spray. Add about ¼ cup of the pancake batter onto the griddle when hot.
2. Turn pancake over when bubbles form on top. Cook until golden brown. Serve immediately.

**Nutrition:** **Calories:** 155 kcal; **Fat:** 4 g; **Carbs:** 28 g; **Protein:** 7 g; **Sugars:** 2.2 g; **Sodium:** 16 mg

## 25. Creamy Oats, Greens and Blueberry Smoothie

**Preparation time:** 4 minutes
**Cooking time:** 0 minutes
**Servings:** 1
**Ingredients:**
- 1 cup cold
- Fat-free milk
- 1 cup salad greens
- ½ cup fresh blueberries, frozen
- ½ cup oatmeal, cooked and frozen
- 1 tbsp. sunflower seeds

**Directions**:
1. Blend all ingredients using a powerful blender until smooth and creamy. Serve and enjoy.

**Nutrition:** **Calories:** 280 kcal; **Fat:** 6.8 g; **Carbs:** 44.0 g; **Protein:** 14.0 g; **Sugars:** 32 g; **Sodium:** 141 mg

## 26. Banana and Cinnamon Oatmeal

**Preparation time:** 5 minutes
**Cooking time:** 0 minutes
**Servings:** 6
**Ingredients:**
- 2 cup quick-cooking oats

- 4 cup Fat-free milk
- 1 tsp. cinnamon, ground
- 2 large ripe bananas, chopped
- 4 tsp. brown sugar
- Extra cinnamon, ground

**Directions:**
1. Place milk in a skillet and bring to boil. Add oats and cook over medium heat until thickened, for 2 to four minutes.
2. Stir intermittently. Add cinnamon, brown sugar, and banana and stir to combine. If you want, serve with the extra cinnamon and milk. Enjoy!

**Nutrition: Calories:** 215 kcal; **Fat:** 2 g; **Carbs:** 42 g; **Protein:** 10 g; **Sugars:** 1 g; **Sodium:** 40 mg

## 27. Bagels Made Healthy

**Preparation time:** 5 minutes
**Cooking time:** 40 minutes
**Servings:** 8
**Ingredients:**
- 1 ½ cup warm water
- 1 ¼ cup bread flour
- 2 tbsp. honey
- 2 cup whole-wheat flour
- 2 tsp. yeast
- 1 ½ tbsp. olive oil
- 1 tbsp. vinegar

**Directions:**
1. In a bread machine, mix all ingredients, and then process on dough cycle. Once done, create 8 pieces shaped like a flattened ball. Create a donut shape using your thumb to make a hole at the center of each ball.
2. Place donut-shaped dough on a greased baking sheet, then covers and let it rise for about ½ hour. Prepare about 2 inches of water to boil in a large pan. In boiling water, drop one at a time the bagels and boil for 1 minute, then turn them once. Remove them and return to the baking sheet and bake at 350°F for about 20 to 25 minutes until golden brown.

**Nutrition: Calories:** 228 kcal; **Fat:** 3.7 g; **Carbs:** 41.8 g; **Protein:** 6.9 g; **Sugars:** 0 g; **Sodium:** 15 mg

## 28. Cereal with Cranberry-Orange Twist

**Preparation time:** 5 minutes
**Cooking time:** 0 minutes
**Servings:** 1
**Ingredients:**
- ½ cup water
- ½ cup orange juice
- ⅓ cup oat bran
- ¼ cup cranberries, dried
- Sugar
- Milk

**Directions:**
1. In a bowl, combine all ingredients. For about 2 minutes, microwave the bowl, then serve with sugar and milk. Enjoy!

**Nutrition: Calories:** 220 kcal; **Fat:** 2.4 g; **Carbs:** 43.5 g; **Protein:** 6.2 g; **Sugars:** 8 g; **Sodium:** 1 mg

## 29. No-Cook Overnight Oats

**Preparation time:** 5 minutes
**Cooking time:** 0 minutes
**Servings:** 1
**Ingredients:**
- 1 ½ cup low-fat milk
- 5 whole almond pieces
- 1 tsp. chia seeds
- 2 tbsp. oats
- 1 tsp. sunflower seeds
- 1 tbsp. craisins

**Directions:**
1. In a jar or mason bottle with a cap, mix all ingredients. Refrigerate overnight. Enjoy for breakfast.

**Nutrition: Calories:** 271 kcal; **Fat:** 9.8 g; **Carbs:** 35.4 g; **Protein:** 16.7 g; **Sugars:** 9 g; **Sodium:** 103 mg

## 30. Avocado Cup with Egg

**Preparation time:** 5 minutes
**Cooking time:** 0 minutes
**Servings:** 4
**Ingredients:**
- 4 tsp. parmesan cheese
- 1 stalk scallion, chopped
- 4 dashes pepper
- 4 dashes paprika
- 2 ripe avocados
- 4 medium eggs

**Directions:**
1. Preheat oven to 375°F. Slice avocadoes in half and discard the seed.

2. Slice the rounded portions of the avocado to make it level and sit well on a baking sheet.
3. Place avocadoes on a baking sheet and crack one egg in each hole of the avocado. Season each egg evenly with pepper and paprika. Bake within 25 minutes or until eggs is cooked to your liking. Serve with a sprinkle of parmesan.

**Nutrition: Calories:** 206 kcal; **Fat:** 15.4 g; **Carbs:** 11.3 g; **Protein:** 8.5 g; **Sugars:** 0.4 g; **Sodium:** 21 mg

## 31. Mediterranean Toast

**Preparation time:** 10 minutes
**Cooking time:** 0 minutes
**Servings:** 2
**Ingredients:**
- 1 ½ tsp. reduced-fat feta cheese, crumbled
- 3 Greek olives, sliced
- ¼ avocado, mashed
- 1 slice good whole-wheat bread
- 1 tbsp. red pepper hummus, roasted
- 3 cherry tomatoes, sliced
- 1 hardboiled egg, sliced

**Directions:**
1. First, toast the bread and top it with ¼ mashed avocado and 1 tbsp. hummus. Add the cherry tomatoes, olives, hardboiled egg, and feta.

2. To taste, season with salt and pepper.

**Nutrition: Calories:** 333.7kcal; **Fat:** 17 g; **Carbs:** 33.3 g; **Protein:** 16.3 g; **Sugars:** 1 g; **Sodium:** 19 mg

## 32. Instant Banana Oatmeal

**Preparation time:** 1 minute
**Cooking time:** 2 minutes
**Servings:** 1
**Ingredients:**
- 1 ripe banana, mashed
- ½ cup water
- ½ cup quick oats

**Directions:**
1. Measure the oats and water into a microwave-safe bowl and stir to combine. Place bowl in microwave and heat on high for 2 minutes. Remove the bowl, then stir in the mashed banana and serve.

**Nutrition: Calories:** 243 kcal; **Fat:** 3 g; **Carbs:** 50 g; **Protein:** 6 g; **Sugars:** 20 g; **Sodium:** 30 mg

## 33. Almond Butter-Banana Smoothie

**Preparation time:** 5 minutes
**Cooking time:** 0 minutes
**Servings:** 1
**Ingredients:**
- 1 tbsp. almond butter
- ½ cup ice cubes
- ½ cup spinach, packed
- 1 medium banana, peeled and frozen
- 1 cup fat-free milk

**Directions:**
1. Blend all the listed fixing above in a powerful blender until smooth and creamy. Serve and enjoy.

**Nutrition: Calories:** 293 kcal; **Fat:** 9.8 g; **Carbs:** 42.5 g; **Protein:** 13.5 g; **Sugars:** 12 g; **Sodium:** 40 mg

## 34. Brown Sugar Cinnamon Oatmeal

**Preparation time:** 1 minute
**Cooking time:** 3 minutes
**Servings:** 4
**Ingredients:**
- ½ tsp. cinnamon, ground
- 1 ½ tsp. pure vanilla extract
- ¼ cup light brown sugar
- 2 cup low-fat milk
- 1 ⅓ cup quick oats

**Directions:**
1. Put the milk plus vanilla into a medium saucepan and boil over medium-high heat.
2. Lower the heat to medium once it boils. Mix in oats, brown sugar, plus cinnamon, and cook, stirring 2–3 minutes. Serve immediately.

**Nutrition: Calories:** 208 kcal; **Fat:** 3 g; **Carbs:** 38 g; **Protein:** 8 g; **Sugars:** 15 g; **Sodium:** 33 mg

## 35. Buckwheat Pancakes with Vanilla Almond Milk

**Preparation time:** 10 minutes
**Cooking time:** 10 minutes
**Servings:** 1
**Ingredients:**
- ½ cup vanilla almond milk, unsweetened
- 2-4 packets natural sweetener
- ⅛ tsp. salt
- ½ cup buckwheat flour
- ½ tsp. double-acting baking powder

Directions:
1. Prepare a nonstick pancake griddle and spray with the cooking spray, place over medium heat. Whisk the buckwheat flour, salt, baking powder, and stevia in a small bowl and stir in the almond milk after.
2. Onto the pan, scoop a large spoonful of batter, cook until bubbles no longer pop on the surface and the entire surface looks dry and (2-4 minutes). Flip and cook for another 2-4 minutes. Repeat with all the remaining batter.

**Nutrition: Calories:** 240 kcal; **Fat:** 4.5 g; **Carbs:** 2 g; **Protein:** 11 g; **Sugars:** 17 g; **Sodium:** 38 mg

## 36. Salmon and Egg Scramble

**Preparation time:** 15 minutes
**Cooking time:** 4 minutes
**Servings:** 4
**Ingredients:**
- 1 tsp. olive oil
- 3 organic whole eggs
- 3 tbsp. water
- 1 garlic, minced
- 6 oz. salmon, smoked, sliced
- 2 avocados, sliced
- Black pepper to taste
- 1 green onion, chopped

Directions:
1. Warm-up olive oil in a large skillet and sauté onion in it. Take a medium bowl and whisk eggs in it, add water and make a scramble with the help of a fork. Add to the skillet the smoked salmon along with garlic and black pepper.
2. Stir for about 4 minutes until all ingredients get fluffy. At this stage, add the egg mixture. Once the eggs get firm, serve on a plate with a garnish of avocados.

**Nutrition: Calories:** 120 kcal; **Carbs:** 3 g; **Fat:** 4 g; **Protein:** 19 g; **Sodium:** 898 mg; **Potassium:** 129mg

## 37. Pumpkin Muffins

**Preparation time:** 15 minutes
**Cooking time:** 20 minutes
**Servings:** 4
**Ingredients:**
- 4 cups almond flour
- 2 cups pumpkin, cooked and pureed
- 2 large whole organic eggs
- 3 tsp. baking powder
- 2 tsp. cinnamon, ground
- ½ cup raw honey
- 4 tsp. almond butter

Directions:
1. Preheat the oven to 400°F. Line the muffin paper on the muffin tray. Mix almond flour, pumpkin puree, eggs, baking powder, cinnamon, almond butter, and honey in a large bowl.
2. Put the prepared batter into a muffin tray and bake within 20 minutes. Once golden-brown, serve, and enjoy.

**Nutrition: Calories:** 136 kcal; **Carbs:** 22 g; **Fat:** 5 g; **Protein:** 2 g; **Sodium:** 11 mg; **Potassium:** 699 mg

## 38. Sweet Berries Pancake

**Preparation time:** 15 minutes
**Cooking time:** 15 minutes
**Servings:** 4
**Ingredients:**
- 4 cups almond flour
- Pinch sea salt - 2 organic eggs
- 4 tsp. walnut oil
- 1 cup strawberries, mashed
- 1 cup blueberries, mashed
- 1 tsp. baking powder
- Honey for topping, optional

Directions:
1. Take a bowl and add almond flour, baking powder, and sea salt. Take another bowl and add eggs, walnut oil, strawberries, and blueberries mash. Combine ingredients of both bowls.
2. Heat a bit of walnut oil in a cooking pan and pour the spoonful mixture to make pancakes. Once the bubble comes on the top, flip the pancake to cook from the other side. Once done, serve with the glaze of honey on top.

**Nutrition: Calories:** 161 kcal; **Carbs:** 23 g; **Fat:** 6 g; **Protein:** 3 g; **Cholesterol:** 82 mg; **Sodium:** 91 mg; **Potassium:** 252 mg

## 39. Zucchini Pancakes

**Preparation time:** 15 minutes
**Cooking time:** 10 minutes
**Servings:** 4
**Ingredients:**
- 4 large zucchinis
- 4 green onions, diced

- ⅓ cup milk - 1 organic egg
- Sea Salt, just a pinch
- Black pepper, grated
- 2 tbsp. olive oil

**Directions**:
1. First, wash the zucchinis and grate it with a cheese grater. Mix the egg and add in the grated zucchinis and milk in a large bowl. Warm oil in a skillet and sauté onions in it.
2. Put the egg batter into the skillet and make pancakes. Once cooked from both sides. Serve by sprinkling salt and pepper on top.

**Nutrition: Calories:** 70 kcal; **Carbs:** 8 g; **Fat:** 3 g; **Protein:** 2 g; **Cholesterol:** 43 mg; **Sodium:** 60 mg; **Potassium:** 914 mg

### 40. Breakfast Banana Split

**Preparation time:** 15 minutes
**Cooking time:** 0 minutes
**Servings:** 3
**Ingredients:**
- 2 bananas, peeled - 1 cup oats, cooked
- ½ cup low-fat strawberry yogurt
- ⅓ tsp. honey, optional
- ½ cup pineapple, chunks

**Directions**:
1. Peel the bananas and cut lengthwise. Place half of the banana in each separate bowl. Spoon strawberry yogurt on top and pour cooked oats with pineapple chunks on each banana. Serve immediately with a glaze of honey of liked.

**Nutrition: Calories:** 145 kcal; **Carbs:** 18 g; **Fat:** 7 g; **Protein:** 3 g; **Sodium:** 2 mg; **Potassium:** 380 mg

### 41. Easy Veggie Muffins

**Preparation time:** 10 minutes
**Cooking time:** 40 minutes
**Servings:** 4
**Ingredients:**
- ¾ cup cheddar cheese, shredded
- 1 cup green onion, chopped
- 1 cup tomatoes, chopped
- 1 cup broccoli, chopped
- 2 cups non-fat milk
- 1 cup biscuit mix
- 4 eggs
- Cooking spray
- 1 tsp. Italian seasoning
- A pinch black pepper

**Directions**:
1. Grease a muffin tray with cooking spray and divide broccoli, tomatoes, cheese, and onions in each muffin cup.
2. In a bowl, combine green onions with milk, biscuit mix, eggs, pepper, and Italian seasoning, whisk well and pour into the muffin tray as well.
3. Cook the muffins in the oven at 375°F for 40 minutes, divide them between plates, and serve.

**Nutrition: Calories:** 80 kcal; **Carbs:** 3 g; **Fat:** 5 g; **Protein:** 7 g; **Sodium:** 25 mg

### 42. Carrot Muffins

**Preparation time:** 10 minutes
**Cooking time:** 30 minutes
**Servings:** 5
**Ingredients:**
- 1 and ½ cups whole wheat flour
- ½ cup stevia
- 1 tsp. baking powder
- ½ tsp. cinnamon powder
- ½ tsp. baking soda
- ¼ cup natural apple juice
- ¼ cup olive oil
- 1 egg
- 1 cup fresh cranberries
- 2 carrots, grated
- 2 tsp. ginger, grated
- ¼ cup pecans, chopped
- Cooking spray

**Directions**:
1. Mix the flour with the stevia, baking powder, cinnamon, and baking soda in a large bowl. Add apple juice, oil, egg, cranberries, carrots, ginger, and pecans and stir well.
2. Oil a muffin tray with cooking spray, divide the muffin mix, put in the oven, and cook at 375°F within 30 minutes. Divide the muffins between plates and serve for breakfast.

**Nutrition: Calories:** 34 kcal; **Carbs:** 6 g; **Fat:** 1 g; **Protein:** 0 g; **Sodium:** 52 mg

### 43. Pineapple Oatmeal

**Preparation time:** 10 minutes
**Cooking time:** 25 minutes
**Servings:** 4
**Ingredients:**
- 2 cups old-fashioned oats
- 1 cup walnuts, chopped
- 2 cups pineapple, cubed
- 1 tbsp. ginger, grated

- 2 cups non-fat milk
- 2 eggs - 2 tbsp. stevia
- 2 tsp. vanilla extract

**Directions:**
1. In a bowl, combine the oats with the pineapple, walnuts, and ginger, stir and divide into 4 ramekins.
2. Mix the milk with the eggs, stevia, and vanilla in a bowl and pour over the oats mix. Bake at 400°F within 25 minutes. Serve for breakfast.

**Nutrition: Calories:** 200 kcal; **Carbs:** 40 g; **Fat:** 1 g; **Protein:** 3 g; **Sodium:** 275 mg

### 44. Spinach Muffins

**Preparation time:** 10 minutes
**Cooking time:** 30 minutes
**Servings:** 6
**Ingredients:**
- 6 eggs
- ½ cup non-fat milk
- 1 cup low-fat cheese, crumbled
- 4 oz. spinach
- ½ cup red pepper, roasted and chopped
- 2 oz. prosciutto, chopped
- Cooking spray

**Directions:**
1. Mix the eggs with the milk, cheese, spinach, red pepper, and prosciutto in a bowl. Grease a muffin tray with cooking spray, divide the muffin mix, introduce in the oven, and bake at 350°F within 30 minutes. Divide between plates and serve for breakfast.

**Nutrition: Calories:** 112 kcal; **Carbs:** 19 g; **Fat:** 3 g; **Protein:** 2 g; **Sodium:** 274 mg

### 45. Chia Seeds Breakfast Mix

**Preparation time:** 8 hours
**Cooking time:** 0 minutes
**Servings:** 4
**Ingredients:**
- 2 cups oats, old-fashioned
- 4 tbsp. chia seeds - 4 tbsp. coconut sugar
- 3 cups coconut milk
- 1 tsp. lemon zest, grated
- 1 cup blueberries

**Directions:**
1. In a bowl, combine the oats with chia seeds, sugar, milk, lemon zest, and blueberries, stir, divide into cups and keep in the fridge for 8 hours. 2. Serve for breakfast.

**Nutrition: Calories:** 69 kcal; **Carbs:** 0 g; **Fat:** 5 g; **Protein:** 3 g; **Sodium:** 0 mg

### 46. Breakfast Fruits Bowls

**Preparation time:** 10 minutes
**Cooking time:** 0 minutes
**Servings:** 2
**Ingredients:**
- 1 cup mango, chopped
- 1 banana, sliced
- 1 cup pineapple, chopped
- 1 cup almond milk

**Directions:**
1. Mix the mango with the banana, pineapple, and almond milk in a bowl, stir, divide into smaller bowls, and serve.

**Nutrition: Calories:** 10 kcal; **Carbs:** 0 g; **Fat:** 1 g; **Protein:** 0 g; **Sodium:** 0mg

### 47. Pumpkin Cookies

**Preparation time:** 10 minutes
**Cooking time:** 25 minutes
**Servings:** 6
**Ingredients:**
- 2 cups whole wheat flour
- 1 cup oats, old-fashioned
- 1 tsp. baking soda
- 1 tsp. pumpkin pie spice
- 15 oz. pumpkin puree
- 1 cup coconut oil, melted
- 1 cup coconut sugar
- 1 egg
- ½ cup pepitas, roasted
- ½ cup cherries, dried

**Directions:**
1. Mix the flour the oats, baking soda, pumpkin spice, pumpkin puree, oil, sugar, egg, pepitas, and cherries in a bowl, stir well, shape medium cookies out of this mix, arrange them all on a baking sheet, then bake within 25 minutes at 350°F. Serve the cookies for breakfast.

**Nutrition: Calories:** 150 kcal; **Carbs:** 24 g; **Fat:** 8 g; **Protein:** 1 g; **Sodium:** 220 mg

### 48. Veggie Scramble

**Preparation time:** 10 minutes
**Cooking time:** 2 minutes
**Servings:** 1
**Ingredients:**
- 1 egg
- 1 tbsp. water
- ¼ cup broccoli, chopped
- ¼ cup mushrooms, chopped
- A pinch black pepper

- 1 tbsp. low-fat mozzarella, shredded
- 1 tbsp. walnuts, chopped
- Cooking spray

**Directions:**
1. Grease a ramekin with cooking spray, add the egg, water, pepper, mushrooms, and broccoli, and whisk well. Introduce in the microwave and cook for 2 minutes. Add mozzarella and walnuts on top and serve for breakfast.

**Nutrition: Calories:** 128 kcal; **Carbs:** 24 g; **Fat:** 0 g; **Protein:** 9 g; **Sodium:** 86 mg

## 49. Mushrooms and Turkey Breakfast

**Preparation time:** 10 minutes
**Cooking time:** 1 hour and 5 minutes
**Servings:** 12
**Ingredients:**
- 8 oz. whole-wheat bread, cubed
- 12 oz. turkey sausage, chopped
- 2 cups fat-free milk
- 5 oz. low-fat cheddar, shredded
- 3 eggs
- ½ cup green onions, chopped
- 1 cup mushrooms, chopped
- ½ tsp. sweet paprika
- A pinch black pepper
- 2 tbsp. low-fat parmesan, grated

**Directions:**
1. Put the bread cubes on a prepared lined baking sheet, bake at 400°F for 8 minutes. Meanwhile, heat a pan over medium-high heat, add turkey sausage, stir, and brown for 7 minutes.
2. In a bowl, combine the milk with the cheddar, eggs, parmesan, black pepper, and paprika, and whisk well.
3. Add mushrooms, sausage, bread cubes, and green onions, stir, pour into a baking dish, and bake at 350°F within 50 minutes. 5. Slice, divide between plates and serve for breakfast.

**Nutrition: Calories:** 88 kcal; **Carbs:** 1 g; **Fat:** 9 g; **Protein:** 1 g; **Sodium:** 74 mg

## 50. Mushrooms and Cheese Omelet

**Preparation time:** 10 minutes
**Cooking time:** 15 minutes
**Servings:** 4
**Ingredients:**
- 2 tbsp. olive oil
- A pinch black pepper
- 3 oz. mushrooms, sliced
- 1 cup baby spinach, chopped
- 3 eggs, whisked
- 2 tbsp. low-fat cheese, grated
- 1 small avocado, peeled, pitted, and cubed
- 1 tbsp. parsley, chopped

**Directions:**
1. Add mushrooms, stir, cook them for 5 minutes and transfer to a bowl on a heated pan with the oil over medium-high heat.
2. Heat up the same pan over medium-high heat, add eggs and black pepper, spread into the pan, cook within 7 minutes, and transfer to a plate.
3. Spread mushrooms, spinach, avocado, and cheese on half of the omelet, fold the other half over this mix, sprinkle parsley on top, and serve.

**Nutrition: Calories:** 136 kcal; **Carbs:** 5 g; **Fat:** 5 g; **Protein:** 16 g; **Sodium:** 192 mg

## 51. Egg White Breakfast Mix

**Preparation time:** 10 minutes
**Cooking time:** 10 minutes
**Servings:** 4
**Ingredients:**
- 1 yellow onion, chopped
- 3 plum tomatoes, chopped
- 10 oz. spinach, chopped
- A pinch black pepper
- 2 tbsp. water
- 12 egg whites
- Cooking spray

**Directions:**
1. Mix the egg whites with water and pepper in a bowl. Grease a pan with cooking spray, heat up over medium heat, add ¼ of the egg whites, spread into the pan, and cook for 2 minutes.
2. Spoon ¼ of the spinach, tomatoes, and onion, fold, and add to a plate. Serve for breakfast. Enjoy!

**Nutrition: Calories:** 31 kcal; **Carbs:** 0 g; **Fat:** 2 g; **Protein:** 3 g; **Sodium:** 55 mg

## 52. Pesto Omelet

**Preparation time:** 10 minutes
**Cooking time:** 6 minutes
**Servings:** 2
**Ingredients:**
- 2 tsp. olive oil
- Handful cherry tomatoes, chopped
- 3 tbsp. pistachio pesto
- A pinch black pepper
- 4 eggs

Directions:
1. In a bowl, combine the eggs with cherry tomatoes, black pepper, and pistachio pesto and whisk well. Add eggs, mix, spread into the pan, cook for 3 minutes, flip, cook for 3 minutes more, divide between 2 plates, and serve on a heated pan with the oil over medium-high heat.

**Nutrition: Calories:** 240 kcal; **Carbs:** 23 g; **Fat:** 9 g; **Protein:** 17 g; **Sodium:** 292 mg

## 53. Quinoa Bowls
**Preparation time:** 10 minutes
**Cooking time:** 20 minutes
**Servings:** 2
**Ingredients:**
- 1 peach, sliced
- ⅓ cup quinoa, rinsed
- ⅔ cup low-fat milk
- ½ tsp. vanilla extract
- 2 tsp. brown sugar
- 12 raspberries
- 14 blueberries

**Directions:**
1. Mix the quinoa with the milk, sugar, and vanilla in a small pan, simmer over medium heat, cover the pan, cook for 20 minutes and flip with a fork. Divide this mix into 2 bowls, top each with raspberries and blueberries and serve for breakfast.

**Nutrition: Calories:** 170 kcal; **Carbs:** 31 g; **Fat:** 3 g; **Protein:** 6 g; **Sodium:** 120 mg

## 54. Strawberry Sandwich

**Preparation time:** 10 minutes
**Cooking time:** 0 minutes
**Servings:** 4
**Ingredients:**
- 8 oz. low-fat cream cheese, soft
- 1 tbsp. stevia
- 1 tsp. lemon zest, grated
- 4 whole-wheat English muffins, toasted
- 2 cups strawberries, sliced

Directions:
1. In your food processor, combine the cream cheese with the stevia and lemon zest and pulse well. Spread 1 tbsp. of this mix on 1 muffin half and top with some of the sliced strawberries. Repeat with the rest of the muffin halves and serve for breakfast. Enjoy!

**Nutrition: Calories:** 150 kcal; **Carbs:** 23 g; **Fat:** 7 g; **Protein:** 2 g; **Sodium:** 70 mg

## 55. Apple Quinoa Muffins
**Preparation time:** 10 minutes
**Cooking time:** 35 minutes
**Servings:** 4
**Ingredients:**
- ½ cup natural, unsweetened applesauce
- 1 cup banana, peeled and mashed
- 1 cup quinoa
- 2 and ½ cups old-fashioned oats
- ½ cup almond milk
- 2 tbsp. stevia
- 1 tsp. vanilla extract
- 1 cup water
- Cooking spray
- 1 tsp. cinnamon powder
- 1 apple, cored, peeled, and chopped

**Directions:**
1. Put the water in a small pan, bring to a simmer over medium heat, add quinoa, cook within 15 minutes, and fluff with a fork, and transfer to a bowl.
2. Add all ingredients, stir, divide into a muffin pan, greases with cooking spray, introduce in the oven, and bake within 20 minutes at 375°F. Serve for breakfast.

**Nutrition: Calories:** 241 kcal, **Carbs:** 31 g; **Fat:** 11 g; **Protein:** 5 g; **Sodium:** 251 mg

## 56. Very Berry Muesli
**Preparation time:** 15 minutes
**Cooking time:** 0 minutes
**Servings:** 2
**Ingredients:**
- 1 cup oats
- 1 cup fruit-flavored yogurt
- ½ cup milk
- ⅛ tsp. salt
- ½ cup raisins, dried
- ½ cup apple, chopped
- ½ cup blueberries, frozen
- ¼ cup walnuts, chopped

**Directions:**
1. Combine your yogurt, salt, and oats in a medium bowl, mix well, and then cover it tightly.
2. Fridge for at least 6 hours. Add your raisins and apples the gently fold. Top with walnuts and serve. Enjoy!

**Nutrition: Calories:** 195 kcal, **Protein:** 6 g; **Carbs:** 31 g; **Fat:** 4 g; **Sodium:** 0 mg

---

### 57. Veggie Quiche Muffins

**Preparation time:** 15 minutes
**Cooking time:** 40 minutes
**Servings:** 12
**Ingredients:**
- ¾ cup cheddar, shredded
- 1 cup green onion, chopped
- 1 cup broccoli, chopped
- 1 cup tomatoes, diced
- 2 cup milk - 4 eggs
- 1 cup pancake mix
- 1 tsp. oregano
- ½ tsp. salt
- ½ tsp. pepper

**Directions:**
1. Preheat your oven to 375°F, and lightly grease a 12-cup muffin tin with oil. Sprinkle your tomatoes, broccoli, onions, and cheddar into your muffin cups.
2. Combine your remaining ingredients in a medium, whisk to combine, then pour evenly on top of your veggies.
3. Set to bake in your preheated oven for about 40 minutes or until golden brown. Allow to cool slightly (about 5 minutes), then serve. Enjoy!

**Nutrition: Calories:** 58.5 kcal; **Protein:** 5.1 g; **Carbs:** 2.9 g; **Fat:** 3.2 g; **Sodium:** 340 mg

---

### 58. Turkey Sausage and Mushroom Strata

**Preparation time:** 15 minutes
**Cooking time:** 8 minutes
**Servings:** 12
**Ingredients:**
- 8 oz. ciabatta bread, cubed
- 12 oz. turkey sausage, chopped
- 2 cup milk
- 4 oz. cheddar, shredded
- 3 large eggs - 12 oz. egg substitute
- ½ cup green onion, chopped
- 1 cup mushroom, diced
- ½ tsp. paprika
- ½ tsp. pepper
- 2 tbsp. parmesan cheese, grated

**Directions:**
1. Set oven to preheat to 400°F. Lay your bread cubes flat on a baking tray and set it to toast for about 8 min. Meanwhile, add a skillet over medium heat with sausage and cook while stirring, until fully brown and crumbled.
2. Mix salt, pepper, paprika, parmesan cheese, egg substitute, eggs, cheddar cheese, and milk in a large bowl. Add in your remaining ingredients and toss well to incorporate.
3. Transfer mixture to a large baking dish (preferably a 9x13-inch), then tightly cover and allow to rest in the refrigerator overnight. Set your oven to preheat to 350°F, remove the cover from your casserole, and set to bake until golden brown and cooked through. Slice and serve.

**Nutrition: Calories:** 288.2 kcal; **Protein:** 24.3 g; **Carbs:** 18.2 g; **Fat:** 12.4 g; **Sodium** 355 mg

---

### 59. Bacon Bits

**Preparation time:** 15 minutes
**Cooking time:** 60 minutes
**Servings:** 4
**Ingredients:**
- 1 cup Millet - 5 cup water
- 1 cup sweet potato, diced
- 1 tsp. cinnamon, ground
- 2 tbsp. brown sugar
- 1 medium apple, diced
- ¼ cup honey

**Directions:**
1. In a deep pot, add your sugar, sweet potato, cinnamon, water, and millet, then stir to combine, then boil on high heat. After that, simmer on low.
2. Cook like this for about an hour, until your water is fully absorbed and millet is cooked. Stir in your remaining ingredients and serve.

**Nutrition: Calories:** 136 kcal; **Protein:** 3.1 g; **Carbs:** 28.5 g; **Fat:** 1.0 g; **Sodium:** 120 mg

---

### 60. Steel Cut Oat Blueberry Pancakes

**Preparation time:** 15 minutes
**Cooking time:** 15 minutes
**Servings:** 4
**Ingredients:**
- 1½ cup water
- ½ cup steel-cut oats

- ⅛ tsp. salt
- 1 cup whole-wheat flour
- ½ tsp. baking powder
- ½ tsp. baking soda
- 1 egg
- 1 cup milk
- ½ cup Greek yogurt
- 1 cup blueberries, frozen
- ¾ cup agave nectar

**Directions:**
1. Combine your oats, salt, and water in a medium saucepan, stir, and allow to come to a boil over high heat. Adjust the heat to low, and allow to simmer for about 10 min, or until oats get tender. Set aside.
2. Combine all your remaining ingredients, except agave nectar, in a medium bowl, then fold in oats.
3. Preheat your skillet, and lightly grease it. Cook ¼ cup of milk batter at a time for about 3 minutes per side. Garnish with Agave Nectar.

**Nutrition: Calories:** 257 kcal; **Protein:** 14 g; **Carbs:** 46 g; **Fat:** 7 g; **Sodium:** 123 mg

## 61. Spinach, Mushroom, and Feta Cheese Scramble

**Preparation time:** 15 minutes
**Cooking time:** 4 minutes
**Servings:** 1
**Ingredients:**
- Olive oil cooking spray
- ½ cup mushroom, sliced
- 1 cup spinach, chopped
- 3 eggs
- 2 tbsp. Feta cheese
- Pepper

**Directions:**
1. Set a lightly greased, medium skillet over medium heat. Add spinach and mushrooms, and cook until spinach wilts.
2. Combine egg whites, cheese, pepper, and whole egg in a medium bowl, whisk to combine. Pour into your skillet and cook, while stirring, until set (about 4 minutes). Serve.

**Nutrition: Calories:** 236.5 kcal; **Protein:** 22.2 g; **Carbs:** 12.9 g; **Fat:** 11. 4g; **Sodium:** 405 mg

## 62. Red Velvet Pancakes with Cream Cheese Topping

**Preparation time:** 15 minutes
**Cooking time:** 10 minutes
**Servings:** 2
**Ingredients:**
**Cream Cheese Topping:**
- 2 oz. cream cheese
- 3 tbsp. yogurt
- 3 tbsp. honey
- 1 tbsp. milk

**Pancakes:**
- ½ cup whole wheat flour
- ½ cup all-purpose flour
- 2 ¼ tsps. baking powder
- ½ tsp. cocoa powder, unsweetened
- ¼ tsp. salt - ¼ cup sugar
- 1 large egg - 1 cup + 2 tbsp. Milk
- 1 tsp. vanilla
- 1 tsp. red paste food coloring

**Directions:**
1. Combine all your topping ingredients in a medium bowl, and set aside. Add all your pancake ingredients to a large bowl and fold until combined. Set a greased skillet over medium heat to get hot.
2. Add ¼ cup of pancake batter onto the hot skillet and cook until bubbles begin to form on the top. Flip and cook until set. Repeat until your batter is done well. Add your toppings and serve.

**Nutrition: Calories:** 231 kcal; **Protein:** 7 g; **Carbs:** 43 g; **Fat:** 4 g; **Sodium:** 0mg

## 63. Peanut Butter and Banana Breakfast Smoothie

**Preparation time:** 15 minutes
**Cooking time:** 0 minutes
**Servings:** 1
**Ingredients:**
- 1 cup non-fat milk
- 1 tbsp. peanut butter
- 1 banana
- ½ tsp. vanilla

**Directions:**
1. Place non-fat milk, peanut butter, and banana in a blender. Blend until smooth.

**Nutrition: Calories:** 295 kcal; **Protein:** 133 g; **Carbs:** 42 g; **Fat:** 8.4 g; **Sodium:** 100 mg

## 64. No-Bake Breakfast Granola Bars

**Preparation time:** 15 minutes
**Cooking time:** 0 minutes
**Servings:** 18
**Ingredients:**
- 2 cup oatmeal, old fashioned
- ½ cup raisins
- ½ cup brown sugar
- 2 ½ cup corn rice cereal
- ½ cup syrup
- ½ cup peanut butter
- ½ tsp. vanilla

**Directions:**
1. In a suitable size mixing bowl, mix using a wooden spoon, rice cereal, oatmeal, and raisins. In a saucepan, combine corn syrup and brown sugar. On a medium-high flame, continuously stir the mixture and bring to a boil.
2. On boiling, take away from heat. In a saucepan, stir vanilla and peanut into the sugar mixture. Stir until very smooth.
3. Spoon peanut butter mixture on the cereal and raisins into the mixing bowl and combine — shape mixture into a 9 x 13 baking tin. Allow to cool properly, then cut into bars (18 pcs).

**Nutrition: Calories:** 152 kcal; **Protein:** 4 g; **Carbs:** 26 g; **Fat:** 4.3 g; **Sodium:** 160 mg

## 65. Mushroom Shallot Frittata

**Preparation time:** 15 minutes
**Cooking time:** 25 minutes
**Servings:** 4
**Ingredients:**
- 1 tsp. butter
- 4 shallots, chopped
- ½ lb. mushrooms, chopped
- 2 tsp. parsley, chopped
- 1 tsp. thyme, dried
- Black pepper
- 3 medium eggs
- 5 large egg whites
- 1 tbsp. milk
- ¼ cup parmesan cheese, grated

**Directions:**
1. Heat oven to 350°F. In a suitable size oven-proof skillet, heat butter over medium flame. Add shallots and sauté for about 5 mins. Or until golden brown. Add to pot, thyme, parsley, chopped mushroom, and black pepper to taste.
2. Whisk milk, egg whites, parmesan, and eggs into a bowl. Pour the mixture into the skillet, ensuring the mushroom is covered completely. Transfer the skillet to the oven as soon as the edges begin to set.
3. Bake until frittata is cooked (15–20 min). Should be served warm, cut into equal wedges (4 pcs).

**Nutrition: Calories:** 346 kcal; **Protein:** 19.1 g; **Carbs:** 48.3 g; **Fat:** 12 g; **Sodium:** 218 mg

## 66. Jack-o-Lantern Pancakes

**Preparation time:** 15 minutes
**Cooking time:** 5 minutes
**Servings:** 8
**Ingredients:**
- 1 egg
- ½ cup pumpkin, canned
- 1 ¾ cup low-fat milk
- 2 tbsp. vegetable oil
- 2 cup flour
- 2 tbsp. brown sugar
- 1 tbsp. baking powder
- 1 tsp. pumpkin pie spice
- 1 tsp. Salt

**Directions:**
1. In a mixing bowl, mix milk, pumpkin, eggs, and oil. Add dry ingredients to the egg mixture. Stir gently. Coat skillet lightly with cooking spray and heat on medium.
2. When the skillet is hot, spoon (using a dessert spoon) batter onto the skillet. When bubbles start bursting, flip pancakes over and cook until it's a nice golden-brown color.

**Nutrition: Calories:** 313 kcal; **Protein:** 15 g; **Carbs:** 28 g; **Fat:** 16 g; **Sodium:** 1 mg

## 67. Fruit Pizza

**Preparation time:** 15 minutes
**Cooking time:** 0 minutes
**Servings:** 2
**Ingredients:**
- 1 English muffin
- 2 tbsp. fat-free cream cheese
- 2 tbsp. strawberries, sliced
- 2 tbsp. blueberries
- 2 tbsp. pineapple, crushed

**Directions:**
1. Cut English muffin in half and toast halves until slightly browned. Coat both halves with cream cheese. Arrange fruits atop cream cheese on muffin halves. Serve soon after preparation.

2. Any leftovers refrigerate within 2 hours.

**Nutrition: Calories:** 119 kcal; **Protein:** 6 g; **Carbs:** 23 g; **Fat:** 1 g; **Sodium:** 288 mg

## 68. Flax Banana Yogurt Muffins

**Preparation time:** 15 minutes
**Cooking time:** 20 minutes
**Servings:** 12
**Ingredients:**
- 1 cup whole wheat flour
- 1 cup old-fashioned oats, rolled
- 1 tsp. baking soda
- 2 tbsp. flaxseed, ground
- 3 large ripe bananas
- ½ cup Greek yogurt
- ¼ cup applesauce, unsweetened
- ¼ cup brown sugar
- 2 tsp. vanilla extract

**Directions:**
1. Set oven at 355°F and preheat. Prepare muffin tin, or you can use cooking spray or cupcake liners. Combine dry ingredients in a mixing bowl. In a separate bowl, mix yogurt, banana, sugar, vanilla, and applesauce. Combine both mixtures and mix. Do not over mix. The batter should not be smooth but lumpy. Bake for 20 min., or when inserted, toothpick comes out clean.

**Nutrition: Calories:** 136 kcal; **Protein:** 4 g; **Carbs:** 30 g; **Fat:** 2 g; **Sodium:** 242 mg

## 69. Apple Oats

**Preparation time:** 5 minutes
**Cooking time:** 5 minutes
**Servings:** 2
**Ingredients:**
- ½ cup oats
- 1 cup water
- 1 apple, chopped
- 1 tsp. olive oil
- ½ tsp. vanilla extract

**Directions:**
1. Pour olive oil in the saucepan and add oats. Cook them for 2 minutes, stir constantly.
2. After this, add water and mix up.
3. Close the lid and cook oats on low heat for 5 minutes.
4. After this, add chopped apples and vanilla extract. Stir the meal.

**Nutrition: Calories:** 159 kcal; **Protein:** 3 g; **Carbohydrates:** 29.4 g; **Fat:** 3.9 g; **Fiber:** 4.8 g; **Cholesterol:** 0 mg; **Sodium:** 6 mg; **Potassium:** 196 mg

## 70. Buckwheat Crepes

**Preparation time:** 8 minutes
**Cooking time:** 15 minutes
**Servings:** 6
**Ingredients:**
- 1 cup buckwheat flour
- ⅓ cup whole grain flour
- 1 egg, beaten
- 1 cup skim milk
- 1 tsp. olive oil
- ½ tsp. cinnamon, ground

**Directions:**
1. In the mixing bowl, mix up all ingredients and whisk until you get a smooth batter.
2. Heat up the non-stick skillet on high heat for 3 minutes.
3. With the help of the ladle, pour the small amount of batter into the skillet and flatten it in the shape of the crepe.
4. Cook it for 1 minute and flip on another side. Cook it for 30 seconds more.
5. Repeat the same steps with the remaining batter.

**Nutrition: Calories:** 122 kcal; **Protein:** 5.7 g; **Carbohydrates:** 211 g; **Fat:** 2.2 g; **Fiber:** 2 g; **Cholesterol:** 28 mg; **Sodium:** 34 mg; **Potassium:** 216 mg

## 71. Whole Grain Pancakes

**Preparation time:** 10 minutes
**Cooking time:** 5 minutes
**Servings:** 4
**Ingredients:**
- ½ tsp. baking powder
- ¼ cup skim milk
- 1 cup whole-grain wheat flour
- 2 tsp. liquid honey
- 1 tsp. olive oil

**Directions:**
1. Mix up baking powder and flour in the bowl.
2. Add skim milk and olive oil. Whisk the mixture well.

3. Preheat the non-stick skillet and pour the small amount of dough inside in the shape of the pancake. Cook it for 2 minutes from each side or until the pancake is golden brown.
4. Top the cooked pancakes with liquid honey.

**Nutrition: Calories:** 129 kcal; **Protein:** 4.6 g; **Carbohydrates:** 25.7 g; **Fat:** 1.7 g; **Fiber:** 3.7 g; **Cholesterol:** 0 mg; **Sodium:** 10 mg; **Potassium:** 211 mg

## 72. Granola Parfait

**Preparation time:** 10 minutes
**Cooking time:** 0 minutes
**Servings:** 2
**Ingredients:**

- ½ cup low-fat yogurt
- 4 tbsp. granola

**Directions:**

1. Put ½ tbsp. of granola in every glass.
2. Then add 2 tbsp. of low-fat yogurt.
3. Repeat the steps till you use all ingredients.
4. Store the parfait in the fridge for up to 2 hours.

**Nutrition: Calories:** 79 kcal; **Protein:** 8 g; **Carbohydrates:** 20.6 g; **Fat:** 8.1 g; **Fiber:** 2.8 g; **Cholesterol:** 4 mg; **Sodium:** 51 mg; **Potassium:** 308mg

## 73. Curry Tofu Scramble

**Preparation time:** 10 minutes
**Cooking time:** 5 minutes
**Servings:** 3
**Ingredients:**

- 12 oz. tofu, crumbled
- 1 tsp. curry powder
- ¼ cup skim milk
- 1 tsp. olive oil
- ¼ tsp. chili flakes

**Directions:**

1. Heat up olive oil in the skillet.
2. Add crumbled tofu and chili flakes.
3. In the bowl, mix up curry powder and skim milk.
4. Pour the liquid over the crumbled tofu and stir well.
5. Cook the scrambled tofu for 3 minutes on medium-high heat.

**Nutrition: Calories:** 102 kcal; **Protein:** 10 g; **Carbohydrates:** 3.3 g; **Fat:** 6.4 g; **Fiber:** 1.2 g; **Cholesterol:** 0 mg; **Sodium:** 25 mg; **Potassium:** 210 mg

## 74. Scallions Omelet

**Preparation time:** 10 minutes
**Cooking time:** 10 minutes
**Servings:** 2
**Ingredients:**

- 1 oz. scallions, chopped
- 2 eggs, beaten
- 1 tbsp. low-fat sour cream
- ¼ tsp. black pepper, ground
- 1 tsp. olive oil

**Directions:**

1. Heat up olive oil in the skillet.
2. Meanwhile, in the mixing bowl, mix up all remaining ingredients.
3. Pour the egg mixture into the hot skillet, flatten well and cook for 7 minutes over medium-low heat.
4. The omelet is cooked when it is set.

**Nutrition: Calories:** 101 kcal; **Protein:** 6 g; **Carbohydrates:** 1.8 g; **Fat:** 8 g; **Fiber:** 0.4 g; **Cholesterol:** 166 mg; **Sodium:** 67 mg; **Potassium:** 110 mg

# CHAPTER 6:
# Salads

## 75. Tomato Salad

**Preparation time:** 22 minutes
**Cooking time:** 0 minute
**Servings:** 4
**Ingredients:**

- 1 cucumber, sliced
- ¼ cup sun-dried tomatoes, chopped
- 1 lb. tomatoes, cubed
- ½ cup black olives - 1 red onion, sliced
- 1 tbsp. balsamic vinegar
- ¼ cup parsley, fresh and chopped
- 2 tbsp. olive oil

**Directions:**
1. Get out a bowl and combine all of your vegetables together. To make your dressing, mix all your seasoning, olive oil, and vinegar.
2. Toss with your salad and serve fresh.

**Nutrition: Calories:** 126 kcal; **Protein:** 2.1 g; **Fat:** 9.2 g

## 76. Feta Beet Salad

**Preparation time:** 16 minutes
**Cooking time:** 0 minute
**Servings:** 4
**Ingredients:**

- 6 red beets, cooked and peeled
- 3 oz. feta cheese, cubed
- 2 tbsp. olive oil - 2 tbsp. balsamic vinegar

**Directions:**
1. Combine everything together, and then serve.

**Nutrition: Calories:** 230 kcal; **Protein:** 7.3 g; **Fat:** 12 g

## 77. Cauliflower and Tomato Salad

**Preparation time:** 17 minutes
**Cooking time:** 0 minute
**Servings:** 4
**Ingredients:**

- 1 head cauliflower, chopped
- 2 tbsp. parsley, fresh and chopped
- 2 cups cherry tomatoes, halved
- 2 tbsp. lemon juice, fresh
- 2 tbsp. pine nuts

Directions:
1. Incorporate lemon juice, cherry tomatoes, cauliflower, and parsley and season well. Sprinkle the pine nuts, and mix.

**Nutrition: Calories:** 64 kcal; **Protein:** 2.8 g; **Fat:** 3.3 g

## 78. Tahini Spinach

**Preparation time:** 11 minutes
**Cooking time:** 6 minutes
**Servings:** 3
**Ingredients:**
- 10 spinach, chopped
- ½ cup water
- 1 tbsp. tahini
- 2 cloves garlic, minced
- ¼ tsp. cumin
- ¼ tsp. paprika
- ¼ tsp. cayenne pepper
- ⅓ cup red wine vinegar

**Directions:**
1. Add your spinach and water to the saucepan, and then boil it on high heat. Once boiling, reduce to low, and cover. Allow it to cook on simmer for 5 minutes.
2. Add in your garlic, cumin, cayenne, red wine vinegar, paprika, and tahini. Whisk well, and season with salt and pepper.
3. Drain your spinach and top with tahini sauce to serve.

**Nutrition: Calories:** 69 kcal; **Protein:** 5 g; **Fat:** 3 g

## 79. Pilaf with Cream Cheese

**Preparation time:** 11 minutes
**Cooking time:** 34 minutes
**Servings:** 6
**Ingredients:**
- 2 cups yellow long grain rice, parboiled
- 1 cup onion
- 4 green onions
- 3 tbsp. butter
- 3 tbsp. vegetable broth
- 2 tsp. cayenne pepper
- 1 tsp. paprika - ½ tsp. cloves, minced
- 2 tbsp. mint leaves
- 1 bunch fresh mint leaves to garnish
- 1 tbsp. olive oil

**Cheese Cream:**
- 3 tbsp. olive oil
- Sea salt and black pepper to taste
- 9 oz. cream cheese

**Directions:**
1. Start by heating your oven to 360°F, and then get out a pan. Heat your butter and olive oil together, and cook your onions and spring onions for 2 minutes.
2. Add in your salt, pepper, paprika, cloves, vegetable broth, rice, and remaining seasoning. Sauté for 3 minutes.
3. Wrap with foil, and bake for another half hour. Allow it to cool.
4. Mix in the cream cheese, cheese, olive oil, salt, and pepper. Serve your pilaf garnished with fresh mint leaves.

**Nutrition: Calories:** 364 kcal; **Protein:** 5 g; **Fat:** 30 g

## 80. Easy Spaghetti Squash

**Preparation time:** 13 minutes
**Cooking time:** 45 minutes
**Servings:** 6
**Ingredients:**
- 2 spring onions, chopped fine
- 3 cloves garlic, minced
- 1 zucchini, diced
- 1 red bell pepper, diced
- 1 tbsp. Italian seasoning
- 1 tomato, small and chopped fine
- 1 tbsp. parsley, fresh and chopped
- pinch lemon pepper
- dash sea salt, fine
- 4 oz. feta cheese, crumbled
- 3 Italian sausage links, casing removed
- 2 tbsp. olive oil
- 1 spaghetti sauce, halved lengthwise

**Directions:**
1. Prep oven to 350°F, and get out a large baking sheet. Coat it with cooking spray, and then put your squash on it with the cut side down.
2. Bake at 350°F for 45 minutes. It should be tender. Turn the squash over, and bake for 5 more minutes. Scrape the strands into a larger bowl. Cook tbsp. of olive oil in a skillet, and then add in your Italian sausage. Cook at 8 minutes before removing it and placing it in a bowl.

3. Pour in an additional tbsp. of olive oil into the skillet and cook your garlic and onions until softened. This will take 5 minutes. Throw in your Italian seasoning, red peppers, and zucchini. Cook for another 5 minutes. Your vegetables should be softened.
4. Mix in your feta cheese and squash, cooking until the cheese has melted.
5. Stir in your sausage, and then season with lemon pepper and salt. Serve with parsley and tomato.

**Nutrition: Calories:** 423 kcal; **Protein:** 18 g; **Fat:** 30 g

## 81. Roasted Eggplant Salad

**Preparation time:** 14 minutes
**Cooking time:** 36 minutes
**Servings:** 6
**Ingredients:**
- 1 red onion, sliced
- 2 tbsp. parsley
- 1 tsp. thyme
- 2 cups cherry tomatoes
- 1 tsp. oregano
- 3 tbsp. olive oil
- 1 tsp. basil
- 3 eggplants, peeled and cubed

**Directions:**
1. Start by heating your oven to 350°F.
2. Season your eggplant with basil, salt, pepper, oregano, thyme, and olive oil.
3. Arrange it on a baking tray, and bake for a half-hour.
4. Toss with your remaining ingredients before serving.

**Nutrition: Calories:** 148 kcal; **Protein:** 3.5 g; **Fat:** 7.7 g

## 82. Penne with Tahini Sauce

**Preparation time:** 16 minutes
**Cooking time:** 22 minutes
**Servings:** 8
**Ingredients:**
- ⅓ cup water
- 1 cup yogurt, plain
- ⅛ cup lemon juice
- 3 tbsp. tahini
- 3 cloves garlic
- 1 onion, chopped
- ¼ cup olive oil
- 2 Portobello mushrooms, large and sliced
- ½ red bell pepper, diced
- 16 oz. penne pasta
- ½ cup parsley, fresh and chopped

**Directions:**
1. Start by getting out a pot and bringing a pot of salted water to a boil. Cook your pasta al dente per package instructions.
2. Mix your lemon juice and tahini together, and then place them in a food processor. Process with garlic, water, and yogurt.
3. Situate pan over medium heat. Heat up your oil, and cook your onions until soft.
4. Add in your mushroom and continue to cook until softened.
5. Add in your bell pepper, and cook until crispy.
6. Drain your pasta then toss with your tahini sauce, top with parsley and pepper, and serve with vegetables.

**Nutrition: Calories:** 332 kcal; **Protein:** 11 g; **Fat:** 12 g

## 83. Roasted Veggies

**Preparation time:** 14 minutes
**Cooking time:** 26 minutes
**Servings:** 12
**Ingredients:**
- 6 cloves garlic
- 6 tbsp. olive oil
- 1 fennel bulb, diced
- 1 zucchini, diced
- 2 red bell peppers, diced
- 6 potatoes, large and diced
- 2 tsp. sea salt
- ½ cup balsamic vinegar
- ¼ cup rosemary, chopped and fresh
- 2 tsp. vegetable bouillon powder

**Directions:**
1. Start by heating your oven to 400°F.
2. Get out a baking dish and place your potatoes, fennel, zucchini, garlic on a baking dish, drizzling with olive oil. Sprinkle with salt, bouillon powder, and rosemary. Mix well, and then bake at 450°F for 30 to 40 minutes.
3. Mix your vinegar into the vegetables before serving.

**Nutrition: Calories:** 675 kcal; **Protein:** 13 g; **Fat:** 21 g

## 84. Zucchini Pasta

**Preparation time:** 9 minutes
**Cooking time:** 32 minutes
**Servings:** 4
**Ingredients:**
- 3 tbsp. olive oil
- 2 cloves garlic, minced
- 3 zucchinis, large and diced
- sea salt and black pepper to taste

- ½ cup milk, 2%
- ¼ tsp. nutmeg
- 1 tbsp. lemon juice, fresh
- ½ cup parmesan, grated
- 8 oz. farfalle pasta, uncooked

**Directions:**
1. Get out a skillet and place it over medium heat, and then heat up the oil. Stir in your garlic and cook for a minute. Stir often so that it doesn't burn. Add in your salt, pepper, and zucchini. Stir well, and cook covered for 15 minutes. During this time, you'll want to stir the mixture twice.
2. Get out a microwave-safe bowl, and heat the milk for 30 seconds. Stir in your nutmeg, and then pour it into the skillet. Cook uncovered for 5 minutes. Stir occasionally to keep from burning.
3. Get out a stockpot and cook your pasta per package instructions. Drain the pasta, and then save 2 tbsp. of pasta water.
4. Stir everything together, and add in the cheese and lemon juice, and pasta water.

**Nutrition: Calories:** 410 kcal; **Protein:** 15 g; **Fat:** 17 g

## 85. Asparagus Pasta

**Preparation time:** 8 minutes
**Cooking time:** 33 minutes
**Servings:** 6
**Ingredients:**
- 8 oz. farfalle pasta, uncooked
- 1 ½ cups asparagus
- 1-pint grape tomatoes, halved
- 2 tbsp. olive oil
- 2 cups mozzarella, fresh and drained
- ⅓ cup basil leaves, fresh and torn
- 2 tbsp. balsamic vinegar

**Directions:**
1. Start by heating the oven to 400°F, and then get out a stockpot. Cook your pasta per package instructions, and reserve ¼ cup of pasta water.
2. Get out a bowl and toss the tomatoes, oil, asparagus, and season with salt and pepper. Spread this mixture on a baking sheet, and bake for 15 minutes. Stir twice in this time.
3. Remove your vegetables from the oven, and then add the cooked pasta to your baking sheet. Mix with a few tbsp. of pasta water so that your sauce becomes smoother.
4. Mix in your basil and mozzarella, drizzling with balsamic vinegar. Serve warm.

**Nutrition: Calories:** 307 kcal; **Protein:** 18 g; **Fat:** 14 g

## 86. Feta and Spinach Pita Bake

**Preparation time:** 11 minutes
**Cooking time:** 36 minutes
**Servings:** 6
**Ingredients:**
- 2 Roma tomatoes
- 6 whole-wheat pita bread
- 1 jar sun-dried tomato pesto
- 4 mushrooms, fresh and sliced
- 1 bunch spinach
- 2 tbsp. parmesan cheese
- 3 tbsp. olive oil
- ½ cup feta cheese

**Directions:**
1. Start by heating the oven to 350°F, and get to your pita bread. Spread the tomato pesto on the side of each one. Put them in a baking pan with the tomato side up.
2. Top with tomatoes, spinach, mushrooms, parmesan, and feta. Pour in olive oil and season with pepper.
3. Bake for twelve minutes, and then serve cut into quarters.

**Nutrition: Calories:** 350 kcal; **Protein:** 12 g; **Fat:** 17 g

## 87. Spelled Salad

**Preparation time:** 15 minutes
**Cooking time:** 30 minutes
**Servings:** 4
**Ingredients:**
**Salad:**
- 2 ½ cups vegetable broth
- ¾ cup feta cheese, crumbled
- 1 can chickpeas, drained
- 1 cucumber, chopped
- 1 ½ cup pearl spelled
- 1 tbsp. olive oil
- ½ onion, sliced
- 2 cups baby spinach, chopped
- 1-pint cherry tomatoes
- 1 ¼ cups water

**Dressing:**
- 2 tbsp. lemon juice
- 1 tbsp. honey

- ¼ cup olive oil
- ¼ tsp. oregano
- 1 pinch red pepper flakes
- ¼ tsp. salt
- 1 tbsp. red wine vinegar

**Directions**:
1. Heat the oil in a skillet. Add the spelled and cook for a minute. Be sure to stir it regularly during cooking. Fill in water and broth, then bring to a boil. Reduce the heat and simmer until the spelled is tender, about 30 minutes. Drain the water and transfer the spelled to a bowl.
2. Add the spinach and mix. Let cool for about 20 minutes. Add the cucumber, onions, tomatoes, peppers, chickpeas, and feta. Mix well to get a good mixture. Step back and prepare the dressing.
3. Mix all the dressing ingredients and mix well until smooth. Pour it into the bowl and mix it well. Season well to taste.

**Nutrition: Calories:** 365 kcal; **Fat:** 10 g; **Carbohydrates:** 43 g; **Protein:** 13 g

## 88. Chickpea and Zucchini Salad

**Preparation time:** 10 minutes
**Cooking time:** 0 minute
**Servings:** 3
**Ingredients:**

- ¼ cup balsamic vinegar
- ⅓ cup basil leaves, chopped
- 1 tbsp. capers, drained and chopped
- ½ cup feta cheese, crumbled
- 1 can chickpeas, drained
- 1 garlic clove, chopped
- ½ cup Kalamata olives, chopped
- ⅓ cup olive oil
- ½ cup sweet onion, chopped
- ½ tsp. oregano
- 1 pinch red pepper flakes, crushed
- ¾ cup red bell pepper, chopped
- 1 tbsp. rosemary, chopped
- 2 cups zucchini, diced
- salt and pepper, to taste

**Directions**:
1. Combine the vegetables in a bowl and cover well. Serve at room temperature. But for best results, refrigerate the bowl for a few hours before serving, to allow the flavors to blend.

**Nutrition: Calories:** 258 kcal; **Fat:** 12 g; **Carbohydrates:** 19 g; **Protein:** 5.6 g

## 89. Provencal Artichoke Salad

**Preparation time:** 15 minutes
**Cooking time:** 5 minutes
**Servings:** 3
**Ingredients:**

- 9 oz. artichoke hearts
- 1 tsp. basil, chopped
- 2 garlic cloves, chopped
- 1 lemon zest
- 1 tbsp. olives, chopped
- 1 tbsp. olive oil
- ½ onion, chopped
- 1 pinch or ½ tsp. salt
- 2 tomatoes, chopped
- 3 tbsp. water
- ½ glass white wine
- Salt and pepper, to taste

**Directions**:
1. Heat the oil in a skillet. Sauté the onion and garlic. Cook until the onions are translucent and season with a pinch of salt. Pour in the white wine and simmer until the wine is reduced by half. Add the chopped tomatoes, artichoke hearts, and water. Simmer, then add the lemon zest and about ½ tsp. of salt. Cover and cook for about 6 minutes.
2. Add the olives and basil. Season well and enjoy!

**Nutrition: Calories:** 147 kcal; **Fat:** 13 g; **Carbohydrates:** 18 g; **Protein:** 4 g

## 90. Bulgarian Salad

**Preparation time:** 10 minutes
**Cooking time:** 20 minutes
**Servings:** 2
**Ingredients:**

- 2 cups bulgur
- 1 tbsp. butter
- 1 cucumber, cut into pieces
- ¼ cup dill
- ¼ cup black olives, cut in half
- 2 tsp. olive oil
- 4 cups water
- 2 tsp. red wine vinegar
- salt, to taste

**Directions**:
1. In a saucepan, toast the bulgur on a mixture of butter and olive oil. Leave to cook until the bulgur is golden brown and begins to crack.

2. Add water and season with salt. Wrap everything and simmer for about 20 minutes or until the bulgur is tender.
3. In a bowl, mix the cucumber pieces with the olive oil, dill, red wine vinegar, and black olives. Mix everything well.
4. It combines cucumber and bulgur.

**Nutrition: Calories:** 386 kcal; **Fat:** 14 g; **Carbohydrates:** 55 g; **Protein:** 9 g

## 91. Falafel Salad Bowl

**Preparation time:** 15 minutes
**Cooking time:** 5 minutes
**Servings:** 2
**Ingredients:**
- 1 tbsp. chili garlic sauce
- 1 tbsp. garlic and dill sauce
- 1 pack vegetarian falafels
- 1 box hummus
- 2 tbsp. lemon juice
- 1 tbsp. Kalamata olives, pitted
- 1 tbsp. extra virgin olive oil
- ¼ cup onion, diced
- 2 cups parsley, chopped
- 2 cups crisp pita
- 1 pinch salt
- 1 tbsp. tahini sauce
- ½ cup tomato, diced

**Directions:**
1. Cook the prepared falafels. Put it aside. Prepare the salad. Mix the parsley, onion, tomato, lemon juice, olive oil, and salt. Throw it all out and put everything aside.
2. Transfer everything to the serving bowls. Add the parsley and cover with hummus and falafel. Sprinkle bowl with tahini sauce, chili garlic sauce, and dill sauce. Upon serving, add the lemon juice and mix the salad well. Serve with pita bread on the side.

**Nutrition: Calories:** 561 kcal; **Fat:** 11 g; **Carbohydrates:** 60.1 g; **Protein:** 18.5 g

## 92. Easy Greek Salad

**Preparation time:** 15 minutes
**Cooking time:** 0 minute
**Servings:** 2
**Ingredients:**
- 4 oz. Greek feta cheese, cubed
- 5 cucumbers, cut lengthwise
- 1 tsp. honey
- 1 lemon, chewed and grated
- 1 cup Kalamata olives, pitted and halved
- ¼ cup extra virgin olive oil
- 1 onion, sliced
- 1 tsp. oregano
- 1 pinch fresh oregano (for garnish)
- 12 tomatoes, quartered
- ¼ cup red wine vinegar
- salt and pepper, to taste

**Directions:**
1. In a bowl, soak the onions in salted water for 15 minutes. In a large bowl, combine the honey, lemon juice, lemon peel, oregano, salt, and pepper. Mix everything. Gradually add the olive oil, beating as you do, until the oil emulsifies. Add the olives and tomatoes. Put it right. Add the cucumbers Drain the onions soaked in salted water and add them to the salad mixture. Top the salad with fresh oregano and feta. Dash with olive oil and season with pepper, to taste.

**Nutrition: Calories:** 292 kcal; **Fat:** 17 g; **Carbohydrates:** 12 g **Protein:** 6 g

## 93. Arugula Salad with Figs and Walnuts

**Preparation time:** 15 minutes
**Cooking time:** 10 minutes
**Servings:** 2
**Ingredients:**
- 5 oz. arugula
- 1 carrot, scraped
- ⅛ tsp. cayenne pepper
- 3 oz. goat cheese, crumbled
- 1 can salt-free chickpeas, drained
- ½ cup figs, dried, cut into wedges
- 1 tsp. honey
- 3 tbsp. olive oil
- 2 tsp. balsamic vinegar
- ½ walnuts cut in half
- salt, to taste

**Directions:**
1. Preheat the oven to 175°F. In a baking dish, combine the nuts, 1 tbsp. of olive oil, cayenne pepper, and ⅛ tsp. of salt. Transfer the baking sheet to the oven and bake it until the nuts are golden. Set it aside when you are done.
2. In a bowl, incorporate the honey, balsamic vinegar, 2 tbsp. of oil, and ¾ tsp. of salt.
3. In a large bowl, combine the arugula, carrot, and figs. Add nuts and goat cheese and drizzle with balsamic honey vinaigrette.

4. Make sure you cover everything.

**Nutrition: Calories:** 403 kcal; **Fat:** 9 g; carbohydrates: 3 5g; **Protein:** 13 g

## 94. Cauliflower Salad with Tahini Vinaigrette

**Preparation time:** 15 minutes
**Cooking time:** 5 minutes
**Servings:** 2
**Ingredients:**

- 1 ½ lb. cauliflower
- ¼ cup cherries, dried
- 3 tbsp. lemon juice
- 1 tbsp. fresh mint, chopped
- 1 tsp. olive oil
- ½ cup parsley, chopped
- 3 tbsp. pistachios, roasted, salted, and chopped
- ½ tsp. salt
- ¼ cup shallot, chopped
- 2 tbsp. tahini

**Directions:**

1. Grate the cauliflower in a microwave-safe container. Add olive oil and ¼ salt. Be sure to cover and season the cauliflower evenly. Wrap the bowl with plastic wrap and heat it in the microwave for about 3 minutes. Put the rice with the cauliflower on a baking sheet and let cool for about 10 minutes. Add the lemon juice and the shallots. Let it rest to allow the cauliflower to absorb the flavor.
2. Add the mixture of tahini, cherries, parsley, mint, and salt. Mix everything well. Sprinkle with roasted pistachios before serving.

**Nutrition: Calories:** 165 kcal; **Fat:** 10 g; **Carbohydrates:** 20 g; **Protein:** 6 g

## 95. Mediterranean Potato Salad

**Preparation time:** 15 minutes
**Cooking time:** 10 minutes
**Servings:** 2
**Ingredients:**

- 1 bunch basil leaves, torn
- 1 garlic clove, crushed
- 1 tbsp. olive oil
- 1 onion, sliced
- 1 tsp. oregano
- 100 g red pepper, roasted.
- 300 g potatoes, cut in half
- 1 can cherry tomatoes
- salt and pepper, to taste

**Directions:**

1. Sauté the onions in a saucepan. Add oregano and garlic. Cook everything for a minute. Add the pepper and tomatoes. Season well, then simmer for about 10 minutes. Put that aside.
2. In a saucepan, boil the potatoes in salted water. Cook until tender, about 15 minutes. Drain well. Mix the potatoes with the sauce and add the basil and olives. Finally, throw everything away before serving.

**Nutrition: Calories:** 111 kcal; **Fat:** 9 g; **Carbohydrates:** 16 g; **Protein:** 3 g

## 96. Quinoa and Pistachio Salad

**Preparation time:** 10 minutes
**Cooking time:** 15 minutes
**Servings:** 2
**Ingredients:**

- ¼ tsp. cumin
- ½ cup currants, dried
- 1 tsp. lemon zest, grated
- 2 tbsp. lemon juice
- ½ cup green onions, chopped
- 1 tbsp. mint, chopped
- 2 tbsp. extra virgin olive oil
- ¼ cup parsley, chopped
- ¼ tsp. pepper, ground
- ⅓ cup pistachios, chopped
- 1 ¼ cups quinoa, uncooked
- 1 ⅔ cup water

**Directions:**

1. In a saucepan, combine 1 ⅔ cups of water, raisins, and quinoa. Cook everything until boiling then reduce the heat. Simmer everything for about 10 minutes and let the quinoa become frothy.
2. Set it aside for about 5 minutes. In a container, transfer the quinoa mixture. Add the nuts, mint, onions, and parsley. Mix everything. In a separate bowl, incorporate the lemon zest, lemon juice, currants, cumin, and oil. Beat them together. Mix the dry and wet ingredients.

**Nutrition: Calories:** 248 kcal; **Fat:** 8 g; **Carbohydrates:** 35 g; **Protein:** 7 g

## 97. Cucumber Chicken Salad with Spicy Peanut Dressing

**Preparation time:** 15 minutes
**Cooking time:** 0 minute
**Servings:** 2
**Ingredients:**

- ½ cup peanut butter

- 1 tbsp. Sambal Oelek (chili paste)
- 1 tbsp. low-sodium soy sauce
- 1 tsp. sesame oil, grilled
- 4 tbsp. of water, or more if necessary
- 1 cucumber, peeled and cut into thin strips
- 1 chicken fillet, cooked and grated into thin strips
- 2 tbsp. peanuts, chopped

**Directions**:
1. Combine peanut butter, soy sauce, sesame oil, sambal oelek, and water in a bowl. Place the cucumber slices on a dish. Garnish with grated chicken and sprinkle with sauce. Sprinkle the chopped peanuts.

**Nutrition: Calories:** 720 kcal; **Fat:** 54 g; **Carbohydrates:** 8.9 g; **Protein:** 45.9 g

## 98. German Hot Potato Salad

**Preparation time:** 10 minutes
**Cooking time:** 30 minutes
**Servings:** 12
**Ingredients:**
- 9 potatoes, peeled
- 6 slices bacon
- ⅛ tsp. black pepper, ground
- ½ tsp. celery seed
- 2 tbsp. white sugar
- 2 tsp. salt
- ¾ cup water
- ⅓ cup white vinegar, distilled
- 2 tbsp. all-purpose flour
- ¾ cup onions, chopped

**Directions**:
1. Boil salted water in a large pot. Put in the potatoes and cook until soft but still firm, about 30 minutes. Drain, let cool, and cut finely. Over medium heat, cook bacon in a pan. Drain, crumble, and set aside. Save the cooking juices. Cook onions in bacon grease until golden brown.
2. Combine flour, sugar, salt, celery seed, and pepper in a small bowl. Add sautéed onions and cook, stirring until bubbling, and remove from heat. Stir in the water and vinegar, then bring back to the fire and bring to a boil, stirring constantly. Boil and stir. Slowly add bacon and potato slices to the vinegar/water mixture, stirring gently until the potatoes are warmed up.

**Nutrition: Calories:** 205 kcal; **Fat:** 6.5 g; **Carbohydrates:** 32.9 g; **Protein:** 4.3 g

## 99. Chicken Fiesta Salad

**Preparation time:** 20 minutes
**Cooking time:** 20 minutes
**Servings:** 4
**Ingredients:**
- 2 halves chicken fillet without skin or bones
- 1 packet herbs for fajitas, divided
- 1 tbsp. vegetable oil
- 1 can black beans, rinsed and drained
- 1 box Mexican-style corn
- ½ cup salsa
- 1 packet green salad
- 1 onion, minced
- 1 tomato, quartered

**Directions**:
1. Rub the chicken evenly with ½ of the herbs for fajitas. Cook the oil in a frying pan over medium heat and cook the chicken for 8 minutes on the side by side or until the juice is clear; put aside.
2. Combine beans, corn, salsa, and other ½ fajita spices in a large pan. Heat over medium heat until lukewarm. Prepare the salad by mixing green vegetables, onion, and tomato.
3. Cover the chicken salad and dress the beans and corn mixture.

**Nutrition: Calories:** 311 kcal; **Fat:** 6.4 g; **Carbohydrates:** 42.2 g; **Protein:** 23 g

## 100. Corn and Black Bean Salad

**Preparation time:** 10 minutes
**Cooking time:** 0 minute
**Servings:** 4
**Ingredients:**
- 2 tbsp. vegetable oil
- ¼ cup balsamic vinegar - ½ tsp. salt
- ½ tsp. white sugar
- ½ tsp. cumin, ground
- ½ tsp. black pepper, ground
- ½ tsp. chili powder
- 3 tbsp. fresh coriander, chopped
- 1 can black beans (15 oz.)
- 1 can sweetened corn (8.75 oz.) drained

**Directions**:
1. Combine balsamic vinegar, oil, salt, sugar, black pepper, cumin, and chili powder in a small bowl. Combine black corn and beans in a medium bowl.
2. Mix with vinegar and oil vinaigrette and garnish with coriander. Cover and refrigerate overnight.

**Nutrition: Calories:** 214 kcal; **Fat:** 8.4 g; **Carbohydrates:** 28.6 g; **Protein:** 7.5 g

## 101. Awesome Pasta Salad

**Preparation time:** 30 minutes
**Cooking time:** 10 minutes
**Servings:** 16
**Ingredients:**
- 1 (16-oz) fusilli pasta package
- 3 cups cherry tomatoes
- ½ lb. provolone, diced
- ½ lb. sausage, diced
- ¼ lb. pepperoni, cut in half
- 1 large green pepper
- 1 can of black olives, drained
- 1 chili jar, drained
- 1 bottle (8 oz.) Italian vinaigrette

**Directions:**
1. Boil lightly salted water in a pot. Stir in the pasta and cook for about 8 to 10 minutes or until al dente. Drain and rinse with cold water.
2. Combine pasta with tomatoes, cheese, salami, pepperoni, green pepper, olives, and peppers in a large bowl. Pour the vinaigrette and mix well.

**Nutrition: Calories:** 310 kcal; **Fat:** 17.7 g; **Carbohydrates:** 25.9 g; **Protein:** 12.9 g

## 102. Tuna Salad

**Preparation time:** 20 minutes
**Cooking time:** 0 minute
**Servings:** 4
**Ingredients:**
- 1 (19 oz.) can garbanzo beans
- 2 tbsp. mayonnaise
- 2 tsp. spicy brown mustard
- 1 tbsp. sweet pickle
- Salt and pepper to taste
- 2 green onions, chopped

**Directions:**
1. Combine green beans, mayonnaise, mustard, sauce, chopped green onions, salt, and pepper in a medium bowl. Mix well.

**Nutrition: Calories:** 220 kcal; **Fat:** 7.2 g; **Carbohydrates:** 32.7 g; **Protein:** 7 g

## 103. Southern Potato Salad

**Preparation time:** 15 minutes
**Cooking time:** 15 minutes
**Servings:** 4
**Ingredients:**
- 4 potatoes
- 4 eggs
- ½ stalk celery, finely chopped
- ¼ cup sweet taste
- 1 garlic clove, minced
- 2 tbsp. mustard - ½ cup mayonnaise
- Salt and pepper to taste

**Directions:**
1. Boil water in a pot, then situate the potatoes and cook until soft but still firm, about 15 minutes; drain and chop. Transfer the eggs to a pan and cover with cold water.
2. Boil the water; cover, remove from heat, and let the eggs soak in hot water for 10 minutes. Remove, then shell, and chop.
3. Combine potatoes, eggs, celery, sweet sauce, garlic, mustard, mayonnaise, salt, and pepper in a large bowl. Mix and serve hot.

**Nutrition: Calories:** 460 kcal; **Fat:** 27.4 g; **Carbohydrates:** 44.6 g; **Protein:** 11.3 g

## 104. Seven-Layer Salad

**Preparation time:** 15 minutes
**Cooking time:** 5 minutes
**Servings:** 10
**Ingredients:**
- 1-lb. bacon - 1 head iceberg lettuce
- 1 red onion, minced
- 1 pack 10 peas, frozen and thawed
- 10 oz. cheddar cheese, grated
- 1 cup cauliflower, chopped
- 1 ¼ cup mayonnaise
- 2 tbsp. white sugar
- ⅔ cup Parmesan cheese, grated

**Directions:**
1. Put the bacon in a huge, shallow frying pan. Bake over medium heat until smooth. Crumble and set aside. Situate the chopped lettuce in a large bowl and cover with a layer of onion, peas, grated cheese, cauliflower, and bacon.
2. Prepare the vinaigrette by mixing the mayonnaise, sugar, and parmesan cheese. Pour over the salad and cool to cool.

**Nutrition: Calories:** 387 kcal; **Fat:** 32.7 g; **Carbohydrates:** 9.9 g; **Protein:** 14.5 g

## 105. Kale, Quinoa, and Avocado Salad

**Preparation time:** 5 minutes
**Cooking time:** 25 minutes
**Servings:** 4
**Ingredients:**
- ⅔ cup quinoa
- 1 ⅓ cup water
- 1 bunch kale, torn into bite-sized pieces
- ½ avocado, peeled, diced, and pitted
- ½ cup cucumber, chopped
- ⅓ cup red pepper, chopped
- 2 tbsp. red onion, chopped
- 1 tbsp. feta cheese, crumbled

**Directions:**
1. Boil the quinoa and 1 ⅓ cup of water in a pan. Adjust heat and simmer until quinoa is tender and water is absorbed for about 15 to 20 minutes. Set aside to cool.
2. Place the cabbage in a steam basket over more than an inch of boiling water in a pan. Seal the pan with a lid and steam until hot, about 45 seconds; transfer to a large plate. Garnish with cabbage, quinoa, avocado, cucumber, pepper, red onion, and feta cheese.
3. Combine olive oil, lemon juice, Dijon mustard, sea salt, and black pepper in a bowl until the oil is emulsified in the dressing; pour over the salad.

**Nutrition: Calories:** 342 kcal; **Fat:** 20.3 g; **Carbohydrates:** 35.4 g; **Protein:** 8.9 g

## 106. Chicken Salad

**Preparation time:** 20 minutes
**Cooking time:** 0 minute
**Servings:** 9
**Ingredients:**
- ½ cup mayonnaise
- ½ tsp. salt
- ¾ tsp. poultry herbs
- 1 tbsp. lemon juice
- 3 cups chicken breast, cooked and diced
- ¼ tsp. black pepper, ground
- ¼ tsp. garlic powder
- ¼ tsp. onion powder
- ½ cup celery, finely chopped
- 1 (8 oz.) box water chestnuts, drained and chopped
- ½ cup green onions, chopped
- 1 ½ cups green grapes cut in half
- 1 ½ cups Swiss cheese, diced

**Directions:**
1. Combine mayonnaise, salt, chicken spices, onion powder, garlic powder, pepper, and lemon juice in a medium bowl.
2. Combine chicken, celery, green onions, water chestnuts, Swiss cheese, and raisins in a big bowl. Stir in the mayonnaise mixture and coat. Cool until ready to serve.

**Nutrition: Calories:** 293 kcal; **Fat:** 19.5 g; **Carbohydrates:** 10.3 g; **Protein:** 19.4 g

## 107. Cobb Salad

**Preparation time:** 5 minutes
**Cooking time:** 15 minutes
**Servings:** 6
**Ingredients:**
- 6 slices bacon
- 3 eggs
- 1 cup Iceberg lettuce, grated
- 3 cups chicken meat, cooked and minced
- 2 tomatoes, seeded and minced
- ¾ cup blue cheese, crumbled
- 1 avocado, peeled, pitted, and diced
- 3 green onions, minced
- 1 bottle (8 oz.) Ranch Vinagrette

**Directions:**
1. Situate the eggs in a pan and soak them completely with cold water. Boil the water. Cover and remove from heat and let the eggs rest in hot water for 10 to 12 minutes. Remove from hot water, let cool, peel, and chop. Situate the bacon in a big, deep frying pan. Bake over medium heat until smooth. Set aside.
2. Divide the grated lettuce into separate plates. Spread the chicken, eggs, tomatoes, blue cheese, bacon, avocado, and green onions in rows on lettuce. Sprinkle with your favorite vinaigrette and enjoy.

**Nutrition: Calories:** 525 kcal; **Fat:** 39.9 g; **Carbohydrates:** 10.2 g; **Protein:** 31.7 g

## 108. Broccoli Salad

**Preparation time:** 10 minutes
**Cooking time:** 15 minutes
**Servings:** 6
**Ingredients:**
- 10 slices bacon
- 1 cup fresh broccoli
- ¼ cup red onion, minced
- ½ cup raisins
- 3 tbsp. white wine vinegar

- 2 tbsp. white sugar
- 1 cup mayonnaise
- 1 cup sunflower seeds

**Directions:**
1. Cook the bacon in a deep-frying pan over medium heat. Drain, crumble, and set aside. Combine broccoli, onion, and raisins in a medium bowl. Mix vinegar, sugar, and mayonnaise in a small bowl. Pour over the broccoli mixture and mix. Cool for at least 2 hours.
2. Before serving, mix the salad with crumbled bacon and sunflower seeds.

**Nutrition: Calories:** 559 kcal; **Fat:** 48.1 g; **Carbohydrates:** 31 g; **Protein:** 18 g

## 109. Strawberry Spinach Salad

**Preparation time:** 10 minutes
**Cooking time:** 0 minute
**Servings:** 4
**Ingredients:**
- 2 tbsp. sesame seeds
- 1 tbsp. poppy seeds
- ½ cup white sugar
- ½ cup olive oil
- ¼ cup distilled white vinegar
- ¼ tsp. paprika
- ¼ tsp. Worcestershire sauce
- 1 tbsp. onion, minced
- 10 oz. fresh spinach
- 1-quart strawberries, cleaned, hulled, and sliced
- ¼ cup almonds, blanched and slivered

**Directions:**
1. In a medium bowl, whisk together the same seeds, poppy seeds, sugar, olive oil, vinegar, paprika, Worcestershire sauce, and onion. Cover, and chill for one hour.
2. In a large bowl, incorporate spinach, strawberries, and almonds. Drizzle the dressing over salad and toss. Refrigerate 10 to 15 minutes before serving.

**Nutrition: Calories:** 491 kcal; **Fat:** 35.2 g; **Carbohydrates:** 42.9 g; **Protein:** 6 g

## 110. Pear Salad with Roquefort Cheese

**Preparation time:** 20 minutes
**Cooking time:** 10 minutes
**Servings:** 2
**Ingredients:**
- 1 leaf lettuce, torn into bite-sized pieces
- 3 pears, peeled, cored, and diced
- 5 oz. Roquefort, crumbled
- 1 avocado, peeled, seeded, and diced
- ½ cup green onions, chopped
- ¼ cup white sugar
- ½ cup pecan nuts
- ⅓ cup olive oil
- 3 tbsp. red wine vinegar
- 1 ½ tsp. white sugar
- 1 ½ tsp. prepared mustard
- ½ tsp. black pepper, salted
- 1 garlic clove

**Directions:**
1. Stir in ¼ cup of sugar with the pecans in a pan over medium heat. Continue to stir gently until the sugar is caramelized with pecans. Cautiously transfer the nuts to wax paper. Let it chill and break into pieces. Mix for vinaigrette oil, marinade, 1 ½ tsp. of sugar, mustard, chopped garlic, salt, and pepper. In a deep bowl, combine lettuce, pears, blue cheese, avocado, and green onions. Put vinaigrette over salad, sprinkle with pecans and serve.

**Nutrition: Calories:** 426 kcal; **Fat:** 31.6 g; **Carbohydrates:** 33.1 g; **Protein:** 8 g

## 111. Mexican Bean Salad

**Preparation time:** 15 minutes
**Cooking time:** 0 minute
**Servings:** 6
**Ingredients:**
- 1 can black beans (15 oz.), drained
- 1 can red beans (15 oz.), drained
- 1 can white beans (15 oz.), drained
- 1 green pepper, minced
- 1 red pepper, minced
- 1 pack corn kernels, frozen
- 1 red onion, minced
- 2 tbsp. fresh lime juice
- ½ cup olive oil
- ½ cup red wine vinegar
- 1 tbsp. lemon juice
- 1 tbsp. salt
- 2 tbsp. white sugar
- 1 garlic clove, crushed
- ¼ cup coriander, chopped
- ½ tbsp. cumin, ground
- ½ tbsp. black pepper, ground

- 1 dash hot pepper sauce
- ½ tsp. chili powder

**Directions:**
1. Combine beans, peppers, frozen corn, and red onion in a large bowl. Combine olive oil, lime juice, red wine vinegar, lemon juice, sugar, salt, garlic, coriander, cumin, and black pepper in a small bowl — season with hot sauce and chili powder.
2. Pour the vinaigrette with olive oil over the vegetables; mix well. Cool well and serve cold.

**Nutrition: Calories:** 334 kcal; **Fat:** 8 g; **Carbohydrates:** 41.7 g; **Protein:** 11.2 g

## 112. Melon-Mozzarella Salad

**Preparation time:** 20 minutes
**Cooking time:** 0 minute
**Servings:** 6
**Ingredients:**

- ¼ tsp. sea salt - ¼ tsp. black pepper
- 1 tbsp. balsamic vinegar
- 1 cantaloupe, quartered and seeded
- 1/2 watermelon, small and seedless
- 2 cups mozzarella balls, fresh
- ⅓ cup basil, fresh and torn
- 2 tbsp. olive oil

**Directions:**
1. Scrape out balls of cantaloupe, and place them in a colander over a serving bowl. Use your melon baller to cut the watermelon as well, and then put them in with your cantaloupe.
2. Allow your fruit to drain for 10 minutes, and then refrigerate the juice for another recipe. It can even be added to smoothies. Wipe the bowl dry, and then place your fruit in it.
3. Add in your basil, oil, vinegar, mozzarella, and tomatoes before seasoning with salt and pepper. Gently mix and serve immediately or chilled.

**Nutrition: Calories:** 218 kcal; **Fat:** 13 g; **Carbohydrates:** 9 g; **Protein:** 10 g

## 113. Citrus Celery Salad

**Preparation time:** 15 minutes
**Cooking time:** 0 minute
**Servings:** 6
**Ingredients:**

- 1 tbsp. lemon juice, fresh
- ¼ tsp. sea salt, fine
- ¼ tsp. black pepper
- 1 tbsp. olive brine
- 1 tbsp. olive oil
- ¼ cup red onion, sliced
- ½ cup green olives
- 2 oranges, peeled and sliced
- 3 celery stalks, sliced diagonally in ½ inch slices

**Directions:**
1. Put your oranges, olives, onion, and celery in a shallow bowl. In a different bowl, whisk your oil, olive brine, and lemon juice; pour this over your salad. Season with salt and pepper before serving.

**Nutrition: Calories:** 65 kcal; **Fat:** 7 g; **Carbohydrates:** 9 g; **Protein:** 2 g

## 114. Oven-Roasted Broccoli Salad

**Preparation time:** 20 minutes
**Cooking time:** 10 minutes
**Servings:** 4
**Ingredients:**

- 1 lb. broccoli, cut into florets and stem sliced
- 3 tbsp. olive oil, divided
- 1-pint cherry tomatoes
- 1 ½ tsp. honey, raw and divided
- 3 cups bread, cubed whole grain
- 1 tbsp. balsamic vinegar
- ½ tsp. black pepper
- ¼ tsp. sea salt, fine
- Parmesan, grated, for serving

**Directions:**
1. Prepare oven at 450°F, and then get out a rimmed baking sheet. Place it in the oven to heat up. Drizzle your broccoli with a tbsp. of oil, and toss to coat.
2. Remove the baking sheet from the oven, and spoon the broccoli on it. Leave oil at the bottom of the bowl and add in your tomatoes, toss to coat, and then toss your tomatoes with a tbsp. of honey. Pour them on the same baking sheet as your broccoli. Roast for 15 minutes, and stir halfway through your cooking time. Add in your bread, and then roast for 3 more minutes. Whisk 2 tbsp. of oil, vinegar, and remaining honey. Season with salt and pepper. Pour this over your broccoli mix to serve.

**Nutrition: Calories:** 226 kcal; **Fat:** 12 g; **Carbohydrates:** 26 g; **Protein:** 7 g

## 115. Sun-dried Tomato Salad

**Preparation time:** 20 minutes
**Cooking time:** 0 minute
**Servings:** 4
**Ingredients:**

- 1 cucumber, sliced

- ¼ cup sun-dried tomatoes, chopped
- 1 lb. tomatoes, cubed
- ½ cup black olives
- 1 red onion, sliced
- 1 tbsp. balsamic vinegar
- ¼ cup parsley, fresh and chopped
- 2 tbsp. olive oil
- Sea salt and black pepper to taste

**Directions:**
1. Get out a bowl and combine all of your vegetables together. To make your dressing, mix all your seasoning, olive oil, and vinegar. Toss with your salad and serve fresh.

**Nutrition: Calories:** 126 kcal; **Fat:** 9.2 g; **Carbohydrates:** 11.5 g; **Protein:** 2.1 g

## 116. Feta Cheese and Beet Salad

**Preparation time:** 15 minutes
**Cooking time:** 0 minute
**Servings:** 4
**Ingredients:**
- 6 red beets, cooked and peeled
- 3 oz. Feta cheese, cubed
- 2 tbsp. olive oil
- 2 tbsp. balsamic vinegar

**Directions:**
1. Combine everything together, and then serve.

**Nutrition: Calories:** 230 kcal; **Fat:** 12 g; **Carbohydrates:** 26.3 g; **Protein:** 7.3 g

## 117. Cauliflower-Tomato Salad

**Preparation time:** 15 minutes
**Cooking time:** 0 minute
**Servings:** 4
**Ingredients:**
- 1 head cauliflower, chopped
- 2 tbsp. parsley, fresh and chopped
- 2 cups cherry tomatoes, halved
- 2 tbsp. lemon juice, fresh
- 2 tbsp. pine nuts
- Sea salt and black pepper to taste

**Directions:**
1. Mix your lemon juice, cherry tomatoes, cauliflower, and parsley together, and then season. Top with pine nuts, and mix well before serving.

**Nutrition: Calories:** 64 kcal; **Fat:** 3.3 g; **Carbohydrates:** 7.9 g; **Protein:** 2.8 g

## 118. Cheesy and Spiced Pilaf

**Preparation time:** 20 minutes
**Cooking time:** 10 minutes
**Servings:** 6
**Ingredients:**
- 2 cups yellow long grain rice, parboiled
- 1 cup onion
- 4 green onions
- 3 tbsp. butter
- 3 tbsp. vegetable broth
- 2 tsp. cayenne pepper
- 1 tsp. paprika
- ½ tsp. cloves, minced
- 2 tbsp. mint leaves, fresh and chopped
- 1 bunch fresh mint leaves to garnish
- 1 tbsp. olive oil
- Sea salt and black pepper to taste

**Cheese Cream:**
- 3 tbsp. olive oil
- Sea salt and black pepper to taste
- 9 oz. cream cheese

**Directions:**
1. Ready the oven at 360°F, and then pull out a pan. Heat your butter and olive oil together, and cook your onions and spring onions for 2 minutes. Add in your salt, pepper, paprika, cloves, vegetable broth, rice, and remaining seasoning. Sauté for 3 minutes. Wrap with foil, and bake for another half hour. Allow it to cool.
2. Mix in the cream cheese, cheese, olive oil, salt, and pepper. Serve your pilaf garnished with fresh mint leaves.

**Nutrition: Calories:** 364 kcal; **Fat:** 30 g; **Carbohydrates:** 20 g; **Protein:** 5 g

## 119. Oven-Roasted Vegetable Salad

**Preparation time:** 10 minutes
**Cooking time:** 20 minutes
**Servings:** 6
**Ingredients:**
- 1 red onion, sliced
- 2 tbsp. parsley, fresh and chopped
- 1 tsp. thyme
- 2 cups cherry tomatoes, halved
- Sea salt and black pepper to taste
- 1 tsp. oregano
- 3 tbsp. olive oil
- 1 tsp. basil
- 3 eggplants, peeled and cubed

**Directions**:
1. Start by heating your oven to 350°F. Season your eggplant with basil, salt, pepper, oregano, thyme, and olive oil. Situate it on a baking tray, and bake for a half-hour. Toss with your remaining ingredients before serving.

**Nutrition**: **Calories**: 148 kcal; **Fat**: 20.5 g; **Carbohydrates**: 3.5 g; **Protein**: 7.7 g

## 120. Herb-Roasted Vegetables

**Preparation time**: 5 minutes
**Cooking time**: 15 minutes
**Servings**: 12
**Ingredients**:
- 6 cloves garlic
- 6 tbsp. olive oil
- 1 fennel bulb, diced
- 1 zucchini, diced
- 2 red bell peppers, diced
- 6 potatoes, large and diced
- 2 tsp. sea salt
- ½ cup balsamic vinegar
- ¼ cup rosemary, chopped and fresh
- 2 tsp. vegetable bouillon powder

**Directions**:
1. Start by heating your oven to 400°F. Put your potatoes, fennel, zucchini, garlic, and fennel on a baking dish, drizzling with olive oil. Sprinkle with salt, bouillon powder, and rosemary. Mix well, and then bake at 450 F for 30 to forty minutes. Mix your vinegar into the vegetables before serving.

**Nutrition**: **Calories**: 675 kcal; **Fat**: 21 g; **Carbohydrates**: 112 g; **Protein**: 13 g

## 121. Cheesy Pistachio Salad

**Preparation time**: 20 minutes
**Cooking time**: 0 minute
**Servings**: 6
**Ingredients**:
- 6 cups kale, chopped
- ¼ cup olive oil
- 2 tbsp. lemon juice, fresh
- ½ tsp. paprika, smoked
- 2 cups arugula
- ⅓ cup pistachios, unsalted and shelled
- 6 tbsp. parmesan cheese, grated

**Directions**:
1. Get out a salad bowl and combine your oil, lemon, smoked paprika, and kale. Gently massage the leaves for half a minute.
2. Your kale should be coated well. Gently mix your arugula and pistachios when ready to serve.

**Nutrition**: **Calories**: 150 kcal; **Fat**: 12 g; **Carbohydrates**: 8 g; **Protein**: 5 g

## 122. Parmesan Barley Risotto

**Preparation time**: 10 minutes
**Cooking time**: 20 minutes
**Servings**: 6
**Ingredients**:
- 1 cup yellow onion, chopped
- 1 tbsp. olive oil
- 4 cups vegetable broth, low-sodium
- 2 cups pearl barley, uncooked
- ½ cup dry white wine
- 1 cup parmesan cheese, grated fine and divided
- Sea salt and black pepper to taste
- fresh chives, chopped for serving
- lemon wedges, for serving

**Directions**:
1. Add your broth into a saucepan and bring it to a simmer over medium-high heat. Get out a stock pot and put it over medium-high heat as well. Heat up your oil before adding in your onion. Cook for eight minutes and stir occasionally. Add in your barley and cook for 2 minutes more. Stir in your barley, cooking until it's toasted.
2. Pour in the wine, cooking for a minute more. Most of the liquid should have evaporated before adding in a cup of warm broth. Cook and stir for 2 minutes. Your liquid should be absorbed. Add in the remaining broth by the cup, and cook until each cup is absorbed fore adding more. It should take about 2 minutes each time.
3. Pull out from the heat, and add in half a cup of cheese, and top with remaining cheese, chives, and lemon wedges.

**Nutrition**: **Calories**: 345 kcal; **Fat**: 7 g; **Carbohydrates**: 56 g; **Protein**: 14 g

## 123. Seafood and Avocado Salad

**Preparation time**: 10 minutes
**Cooking time**: 0 minute
**Servings**: 4
**Ingredients**:
- 2 lb. salmon, cooked and chopped
- 2 lb. shrimp, cooked and chopped
- 1 cup avocado, chopped
- 1 cup mayonnaise

- 4 tbsp. lime juice, fresh
- 2 garlic cloves
- 1 cup sour cream
- Sea salt and black pepper to taste
- ½ red onion, minced
- 1 cup cucumber, chopped

**Directions:**
1. Start by getting out a bowl and combine your garlic, salt, pepper, onion, mayonnaise, sour cream, and lime juice,
2. Get out a different bowl and mix together your salmon, shrimp, cucumber, and avocado.
3. Add the mayonnaise mixture to your shrimp, and then allow it to sit for 20 minutes in the fridge before serving.

**Nutrition: Calories:** 394 kcal; **Fat:** 30 g; **Carbohydrates:** 3 g; **Protein:** 27 g

## 124. Mediterranean Shrimp Salad

**Preparation time:** 40 minutes
**Cooking time:** 0 minute
**Servings:** 6
**Ingredients:**
- 1 ½ lb. shrimp, cleaned and cooked
- 2 celery stalks, fresh
- 1 onion
- 2 green onions
- 4 eggs, boiled
- 3 potatoes, cooked
- 3 tbsp. mayonnaise
- sea salt and black pepper to taste

**Directions:**
1. Start by slicing your potatoes and chopping your celery. Slice your eggs, and season. Mix everything together. Put your shrimp over the eggs, and then serve with onion and green onions.

**Nutrition: Calories:** 207 kcal; **Fat:** 6 g; **Carbohydrates:** 15 g; **Protein:** 17 g

# CHAPTER 7:
# Lunch Recipes

## 125. Zucchini Zoodles with Chicken and Basil

**Preparation time:** 10 minutes
**Cooking time:** 10 minutes
**Servings:** 3
**Ingredients:**
- 2 chicken fillets, cubed
- 2 tbsp. ghee
- 1 lb. tomatoes, diced
- ½ cup basil, chopped
- ¼ cup almond milk
- 1 garlic clove, peeled, minced
- 1 zucchini, shredded

**Directions:**
1. Sauté cubed chicken in ghee until no longer pink.
2. Add tomatoes and season with sunflower seeds.
3. Simmer and reduce the liquid.
4. Prepare your zucchini Zoodles by shredding zucchini in a food processor.
5. Add basil, garlic, coconut almond milk to the chicken and cook for a few minutes. Add half of the zucchini Zoodles to a bowl and top with creamy tomato basil chicken. Enjoy!

**Nutrition: Calories:** 156 kcal; **Protein:** 9.4 g; **Carbohydrates:** 12.2 g; **Fat:** 7.1 g; **Fiber:** 0.8 g; **Cholesterol:** 7 mg; **Sodium:** 86 mg; **Potassium:** 365 mg

## 126. Parmesan Baked Chicken

**Preparation time:** 5 minutes
**Cooking time:** 20 minutes
**Servings:** 2
**Ingredients:**
- 2 tbsp. ghee
- 2 chicken breasts, boneless and skinless

- Pink sunflower seeds
- Black pepper, freshly ground
- ½ cup mayonnaise, low-fat
- ¼ cup parmesan cheese, grated
- 1 tbsp. Italian seasoning, dried, low-fat, low-sodium
- ¼ cup pork rinds, crushed

**Directions:**
1. Preheat your oven to 425°F.
2. Take a large baking dish and coat with ghee.
3. Pat chicken breasts dry and wrap with a towel.
4. Season with sunflower seeds and pepper.
5. Place in baking dish.
6. Take a small bowl and add mayonnaise, parmesan cheese, Italian seasoning.
7. Slather mayo mix evenly over chicken breast.
8. Sprinkle crushed pork rinds on top.
9. Bake for 20 minutes until topping is browned.
10. Serve and enjoy!

**Nutrition: Calories:** 156 kcal; **Protein:** 9.4 g; **Carbohydrates:** 12.2 g; **Fat:** 7.1 g; **Fiber:** 0.8 g; **Cholesterol:** 7 mg; **Sodium:** 86 mg; **Potassium:** 365 mg

## 127. Crazy Japanese Potato and Beef Croquettes

**Preparation time:** 10 minutes
**Cooking time:** 20 minutes
**Servings:** 10
**Ingredients:**
- 3 medium russet potatoes, peeled and chopped
- 1 tbsp. almond butter
- 1 tbsp. vegetable oil
- 3 onions, diced
- ¾ lb. beef, ground
- 4 tsp. light coconut aminos
- All-purpose flour for coating
- 2 eggs, beaten
- Panko bread crumbs for coating
- ½ cup oil, frying

**Directions:**
1. Take a saucepan and place it over medium-high heat; add potatoes and sunflower seeds water, boil for 16 minutes.
2. Remove water and put potatoes in another bowl, add almond butter and mash the potatoes.
3. Take a frying pan and place it over medium heat, add 1 tbsp. oil and let it heat up. Add onions and stir fry until tender.
4. Add coconut amino to beef to onions.
5. Keep frying until beef is browned.
6. Mix the beef with the potatoes evenly.
7. Take another frying pan and place it over medium heat; add half a cup of oil.
8. Form croquettes using the mashed potato mixture and coat them with flour, then eggs, and finally breadcrumbs.
9. Fry patties until golden on all sides.
10. Enjoy!

**Nutrition: Calories:** 156 kcal; **Protein:** 9.4 g; **Carbohydrates:** 12.2 g; **Fat:** 7.1 g; **Fiber:** 0.8 g; **Cholesterol:** 7 mg; **Sodium:** 86 mg; **Potassium:** 365 mg

## 128. Golden Eggplant Fries

**Preparation time:** 10 minutes
**Cooking time:** 15 minutes
**Servings:** 8
**Ingredients:**
- 2 eggs
- 2 cups almond flour
- 2 tbsp. coconut oil, spray
- 2 eggplants, peeled and cut thinly
- Sunflower seeds and pepper

**Directions:**
1. Preheat your oven to 400°F.
2. Take a bowl and mix with sunflower seeds and black pepper.
3. Take another bowl and beat eggs until frothy.
4. Dip the eggplant pieces into the eggs.
5. Then coat them with the flour mixture.
6. Add another layer of flour and egg.
7. Then, take a baking sheet and grease with coconut oil on top.
8. Bake for about 15 minutes.
9. Serve and enjoy!

**Nutrition: Calories:** 156 kcal; **Protein:** 9.4 g; **Carbohydrates:** 12.2 g; **Fat:** 7.1 g; **Fiber:** 0.8 g; **Cholesterol:** 7 mg; **Sodium:** 86 mg; **Potassium:** 365 mg

## 129. Very Wild Mushroom Pilaf

**Preparation time:** 10 minutes
**Cooking time:** 3 hours
**Servings:** 4
**Ingredients:**
- 1 cup wild rice
- 2 garlic cloves, minced
- 6 green onions, chopped
- 2 tbsp. olive oil
- ½ lb. baby Bella mushrooms
- 2 cups water

**Directions:**
1. Add rice, garlic, onion, oil, mushrooms, and water to your Slow Cooker.

2. Stir well until mixed.
   3. Place lid and cook on LOW for 3 hours.
   4. Stir pilaf and divide between serving platters. Enjoy!

**Nutrition: Calories:** 156 kcal; **Protein:** 9.4 g; **Carbohydrates:** 12.2 g; **Fat:** 7.1 g; **Fiber:** 0.8 g; **Cholesterol:** 7 mg; **Sodium:** 86 mg; **Potassium:** 365 mg

## 130. Sporty Baby Carrots

**Preparation time:** 5 minutes
**Cooking time:** 5 minutes
**Servings:** 4
**Ingredients:**

- 1 lb. baby carrots
- 1 cup water
- 1 tbsp. ghee, clarified
- 1 tbsp. fresh mint leaves, chopped up
- Sea flavored vinegar, as needed

**Directions:**
1. Place a steamer rack on top of your pot and add the carrots.
2. Add water.
3. Lock the lid and cook at HIGH pressure for 2 minutes.
4. Do a quick release.
5. Pass the carrots through a strainer and drain them.
6. Wipe the insert clean.
7. Return the insert to the pot and set the pot to Sauté mode.
8. Add clarified butter and allow it to melt.
9. Add mint and sauté for 30 seconds.
10. Add carrots to the insert and sauté well.
11. Remove them and sprinkle with a bit of flavored vinegar on top. Enjoy

**Nutrition: Calories:** 156 kcal; **Protein:** 9.4 g; **Carbohydrates:** 12.2 g; **Fat:** 7.1 g; **Fiber:** 0.8 g; **Cholesterol:** 7 mg; **Sodium:** 86 mg; **Potassium:** 365 mg

## 131. Garden Salad

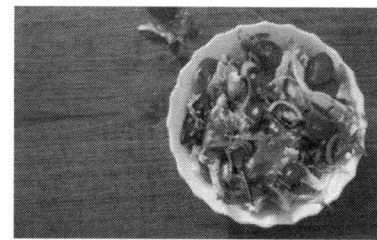

**Preparation time:** 5 minutes
**Cooking time:** 20 minutes
**Servings:** 6
**Ingredients:**

- 1 lb. raw peanuts in the shell
- 1 bay leaf
- 2 medium-sized tomatoes, chopped up
- ½ cup green pepper, diced up
- ½ cup sweet onion, diced up
- ¼ cup hot pepper, finely diced
- ¼ cup celery, diced up
- 2 tbsp. olive oil
- ¾ tsp. flavored vinegar
- ¼ tsp. black pepper, freshly ground

**Directions:**
1. Boil your peanuts for 1 minute and rinse them.
2. The skin will be soft, so discard the skin.
3. Add 2 cups of water to the Instant Pot.
4. Add bay leaf and peanuts.
5. Lock the lid and cook on HIGH pressure for 20 minutes.
6. Drain the water.
7. Take a large bowl and add the peanuts, diced vegetables.
8. Whisk in olive oil, lemon juice, pepper in another bowl.
9. Pour the mixture over the salad and mix. Enjoy!

**Nutrition: Calories:** 156 kcal; **Protein:** 9.4 g; **Carbohydrates:** 12.2 g; **Fat:** 7.1 g; **Fiber:** 0.8 g; **Cholesterol:** 7 mg; **Sodium:** 86 mg; **Potassium:** 365 mg

## 132. Baked Smoky Broccoli and Garlic

**Preparation time:** 5 minutes
**Cooking time:** 20 minutes
**Servings:** 6
**Ingredients:**

- Cooking spray
- 1 tbsp. extra-virgin olive oil
- 3 cloves garlic, minced
- ½ tsp. sea salt
- ¼ tsp. black pepper, ground
- ½ tsp. cumin
- ½ tsp. annatto seeds
- 3 ½ cups broccoli, sliced
- 1 lime, cut into wedges
- 1 tbsp. fresh cilantro, chopped

**Directions:**
1. Preheat your oven to 450°F.
2. Line a baking sheet with foil and grease with olive oil. Mix the olive oil, garlic, cumin, annatto seeds, salt, and pepper in a bowl. Add in the cauliflower, carrots, and broccoli.

3. Combine until well coated. Spread them out in a single layer on the baking sheet. Add the lime wedges.
4. Roast in the oven until vegetables become caramelized, for about 25 minutes.
5. Take out the lime wedges and top with the cilantro.

**Nutrition: Calories:** 156 kcal; **Protein:** 9.4 g; **Carbohydrates:** 12.2 g; **Fat:** 7.1 g; **Fiber:** 0.8 g; **Cholesterol:** 7 mg; **Sodium:** 86 mg; **Potassium:** 365 mg

## 133. Roasted Cauliflower and Lima Beans

**Preparation time:** 5 minutes
**Cooking time:** 20 minutes
**Servings:** 6
**Ingredients:**

- Cooking spray
- 1 tbsp. vegan butter/margarine, melted
- 9 cloves garlic, minced
- ½ tsp. sea salt
- ¼ tsp. black pepper, ground
- 1 ½ cups cauliflower, sliced
- 3 ½ cups cherry tomatoes
- 1 (15 oz.) can lima beans, drained
- 1 lemon, cut into wedges

**Directions:**

1. Preheat your oven to 450°F.
2. Line a baking sheet with foil and grease with melted vegan butter or margarine.
3. Mix the olive oil, garlic, salt, and pepper in a bowl.
4. Add in the cauliflower, tomatoes, and lima beans.
5. Combine until well coated.
6. Spread them out in a single layer on the baking sheet. Add the lemon wedges.
7. Roast in the oven until vegetables become caramelized, for about 25 minutes.
8. Take out the lemon wedges.

**Nutrition: Calories:** 156 kcal; **Protein:** 9.4 g; **Carbohydrates:** 12.2 g; **Fat:** 7.1 g; **Fiber:** 0.8 g; **Cholesterol:** 7 mg; **Sodium:** 86 mg; **Potassium:** 365 mg

## 134. Thai Roasted Spicy Black Beans and Choy Sum

**Preparation time:** 5 minutes
**Cooking time:** 20 minutes
**Servings:** 6
**Ingredients:**

- Cooking spray
- 1 tbsp. sesame oil
- 3 garlic cloves, minced
- ½ tsp. sea salt
- 1 tbsp. Thai chili paste
- ¼ tsp. black pepper, ground
- 3 ½ cups Choy Sum, coarsely chopped
- 2 ½ cups cherry tomatoes
- 1 (15 oz.) can black beans, drained
- 1 lime, cut into wedges
- 1 tbsp. chopped fresh cilantro

**Directions:**

1. Preheat your oven to 450°F.
2. Line a baking sheet with foil and grease with sesame oil. Mix the olive oil, garlic, salt, Thai chili paste, and pepper in a bowl. Add in the Choy sum, tomatoes, and black beans. Combine until well coated. Spread them out in a single layer on the baking sheet. Add the lime wedges. Roast in the oven until vegetables become caramelized, for about 25 minutes.
3. Take out the lime wedges and top with the cilantro.

**Nutrition: Calories:** 156 kcal; **Protein:** 9.4 g; **Carbohydrates:** 12.2 g; **Fat:** 7.1 g; **Fiber:** 0.8 g; **Cholesterol:** 7 mg; **Sodium:** 86 mg; **Potassium:** 365 mg

## 135. Simple Roasted Broccoli and Cauliflower

**Preparation time:** 5 minutes
**Cooking time:** 20 minutes
**Servings:** 6
**Ingredients:**

- Cooking spray
- 1 tbsp. extra-virgin olive oil
- 3 garlic cloves, minced - ½ tsp. sea salt
- ¼ tsp. black pepper, ground
- 3 ½ cups broccoli florets
- 2 ½ cups cauliflower florets
- 1 tbsp. fresh thyme, chopped

**Directions:**

1. Preheat your oven to 450°F.
2. Line a baking sheet with foil and grease with olive oil. Mix the olive oil, garlic, salt, and pepper in a bowl. Add in the cauliflower and tomatoes. Combine until well coated.
3. Spread them out in a single layer on the baking sheet. Roast in the oven until vegetables become caramelized, for about 25 minutes. Top with the thyme. Simple

**Nutrition: Calories:** 156 kcal; **Protein:** 9.4 g; **Carbohydrates:** 12.2 g; **Fat:** 7.1 g; **Fiber:** 0.8 g; **Cholesterol:** 7 mg; **Sodium:** 86 mg; **Potassium:** 365 mg

## 136. Roasted Napa Cabbage and Turnips Extra

**Preparation time:** 5 minutes
**Cooking time:** 20 minutes
**Servings:** 6
**Ingredients:**
- Cooking spray
- 1 tbsp. extra-virgin olive oil
- ½ tsp. sea salt
- ¼ tsp. black pepper, ground
- ½ medium Napa cabbage, sliced thinly
- 1 medium turnip, sliced thinly

**Directions:**
1. Preheat your oven to 450°F. Line a baking sheet with foil and grease with olive oil. Mix the extra ingredients thoroughly. Add in the main ingredients Combine until well coated. Spread them out in a single layer on the baking sheet. Roast in the oven until vegetables become caramelized, for about 25 minutes.

**Nutrition: Calories:** 156 kcal; **Protein:** 9.4 g; **Carbohydrates:** 12.2 g; **Fat:** 7.1 g; **Fiber:** 0.8 g; **Cholesterol:** 7 mg; **Sodium:** 86 mg; **Potassium:** 365 mg

## 137. Simple Roasted Kale Artichoke Heart and Choy Sum Extra

**Preparation time:** 5 minutes
**Cooking time:** 20 minutes
**Servings:** 6
**Ingredients:**
- Cooking spray
- 1 tbsp. extra-virgin olive oil
- ½ tsp. sea salt
- ¼ tsp. black pepper, ground
- 1 bunch kale, rinsed and drained
- 1 cup artichoke hearts, canned
- ½ medium Chinese flowery cabbage (Choy sum), coarsely chopped

**Directions:**
1. Preheat your oven to 450°F. Line a baking sheet with foil and grease with olive oil. Mix the extra ingredients thoroughly. Add in the main ingredients Combine until well coated. Spread them out in a single layer on the baking sheet.
2. Roast in the oven until vegetables become caramelized, for about 25 minutes.

**Nutrition: Calories:** 156 kcal; **Protein:** 9.4 g; **Carbohydrates:** 12.2 g; **Fat:** 7.1 g; **Fiber:** 0.8 g; **Cholesterol:** 7 mg; **Sodium:** 86 mg; **Potassium:** 365 mg

## 138. Roasted Kale and Bok Choy Extra

**Preparation time:** 5 minutes
**Cooking time:** 20 minutes
**Servings:** 6
**Ingredients:**
- Cooking spray
- 1 tbsp. extra-virgin olive oil
- ½ tsp. sea salt
- ¼ tsp. black pepper, ground
- 1 bunch kale, rinsed and drained
- 1 bunch Bok Choy, rinsed, drained, and coarsely chopped

**Directions:**
1. Preheat your oven to 450°F. Line a baking sheet with foil and grease with olive oil.
2. Mix the extra ingredients thoroughly. Add in the main ingredients
3. Combine until well coated. Spread them out in a single layer on the baking sheet.
4. Roast in the oven until vegetables become caramelized, for about 25 minutes.

**Nutrition: Calories:** 156 kcal; **Protein:** 9.4 g; **Carbohydrates:** 12.2 g; **Fat:** 7.1 g; **Fiber:** 0.8 g; **Cholesterol:** 7 mg; **Sodium:** 86 mg; **Potassium:** 365 mg

## 139. Roasted Soy Beans and Winter Squash

**Preparation time:** 5 minutes
**Cooking time:** 20 minutes
**Servings:** 6
**Ingredients:**
- 2 (15 oz.) cans soy beans, rinsed and drained
- ½ winter squash - peeled, seeded, and cut into 1-inch pieces
- 1 red onion, diced 1 sweet potato, peeled, and cut into 1-inch cubes
- 2 large carrots, cut into 1-inch pieces
- 3 medium potatoes, cut into 1-inch pieces - 4 tbsp. extra virgin oil

**Seasoning Ingredients:**
- 1 tsp. salt
- ½ tsp. black pepper, ground
- 1 tsp. onion powder - 1 tsp. basil, dried
- 1 tsp. Italian seasoning

**Garnishing Ingredients:**
- 2 green onions, chopped (optional)

**Directions:**
1. Preheat your oven to 350°F. Grease your baking pan.

2. Combine the beans, squash, onion, sweet potato, carrots, and russet potatoes on the prepared sheet pan. Drizzle with the oil and toss to coat.
3. Combine the seasoning ingredients in a bowl. Sprinkle them over the vegetables on the pan and toss to coat with seasonings. Bake in the oven for 25 minutes.
4. Stir frequently until vegetables are soft and lightly browned and beans are crisp, for about 20 to 25 minutes more. Season with more salt and black pepper to taste, top with the green onion before serving.

**Nutrition: Calories:** 156 kcal; **Protein:** 9.4 g; **Carbohydrates:** 12.2 g; **Fat:** 7.1 g; **Fiber:** 0.8 g; **Cholesterol:** 7 mg; **Sodium:** 86 mg; **Potassium:** 365 mg

## 140. Roasted Button Mushrooms and Squash

**Preparation time:** 5 minutes
**Cooking time:** 20 minutes
**Servings:** 6
**Ingredients:**
- 2 (15 oz.) cans button mushrooms, rinsed and drained
- ½ summer squash, peeled, seeded, and cut into 1-inch pieces
- 1 red onion, diced
- 2 large turnips, cut into 1-inch pieces
- 2 large parsnips, cut into 1-inch pieces
- 1 medium potato, cut into 1-inch pieces
- 3 tbsp. butter

**Seasoning Ingredients:**
- 1 tsp. salt
- ½ tsp. black pepper, ground
- 1 tsp. onion powder
- 2 tsp. garlic powder
- 1 tsp. herbs de Provence

**Garnishing Ingredients:**
- 2 sprigs thyme, chopped (optional)

**Directions:**
1. Preheat your oven to 350°F. Grease your baking pan.
2. Combine the main ingredients on the prepared sheet pan. Drizzle with the melted butter or margarine and toss to coat.
3. Combine the seasoning ingredients in a bowl. Sprinkle them over the vegetables on the pan and toss to coat with seasonings.
4. Bake in the oven for 25 minutes. Stir frequently until vegetables are soft and lightly browned and chickpeas are crisp, for about 20 to 25 minutes more.
5. Season with more salt and black pepper to taste, top with thyme before serving.

**Nutrition: Calories:** 156 kcal; **Protein:** 9.4 g; **Carbohydrates:** 12.2 g; **Fat:** 7.1 g; **Fiber:** 0.8 g; **Cholesterol:** 7 mg; **Sodium:** 86 mg; **Potassium:** 365 mg

## 141. Roasted Tomatoes Rutabaga and Kohlrabi Main

**Preparation time:** 5 minutes
**Cooking time:** 20 minutes
**Servings:** 6
**Ingredients:**
- 3 large tomatoes, cut into 1-inch pieces
- 3 red onions, diced
- 1 rutabaga, peeled and cut into 1-inch cubes
- 2 large carrots, cut into 1-inch pieces
- 3 medium kohlrabi, cut into 1-inch pieces
- 3 tbsp. extra virgin olive oil

**Seasoning Ingredients:**
- 1 tsp. salt
- ½ tsp. black pepper, ground
- 1 tsp. onion powder
- 2 tsp. garlic powder
- 1 tsp. Spanish paprika
- 1 tsp. cumin

**Garnishing Ingredients:**
- 2 sprigs parsley, chopped (optional)

**Directions:**
1. Preheat your oven to 350°F. Grease your baking pan.
2. Combine the main ingredients on the prepared sheet pan. Drizzle with the oil and toss to coat.
3. Combine the seasoning ingredients in a bowl. Sprinkle them over the vegetables on the pan and toss to coat with seasonings.
4. Bake in the oven for 25 minutes. Stir frequently until vegetables are soft, for about 20 to 25 minutes more. Season with more salt and black pepper to taste, top with the parsley before serving.

**Nutrition: Calories:** 156 kcal; **Protein:** 9.4 g; **Carbohydrates:** 12.2 g; **Fat:** 7.1 g; **Fiber:** 0.8 g; **Cholesterol:** 7 mg; **Sodium:** 86 mg; **Potassium:** 365 mg

## 142. Roasted Brussels sprouts and Broccoli

**Preparation time:** 5 minutes
**Cooking time:** 20 minutes
**Servings:** 6
**Ingredients:**
- 1 large broccoli, sliced
- 1 cup bean sprouts
- 1 red onion, diced
- 3 large kohlrabies, cut into 1-inch pieces
- 2 large carrots, cut into 1-inch pieces
- 3 medium potatoes, cut into 1-inch pieces
- 3 tbsp. extra virgin olive oil

**Seasoning Ingredients:**
- 1 tsp. salt - ½ tsp. black pepper, ground
- 1 tsp. onion powder
- 2 tsp. garlic powder
- 1 tsp. fennel seeds, ground
- 1 tsp. rubbed sage, dried

**Garnishing Ingredients:**
- 2 green onions, chopped (optional)

**Directions:**
1. Preheat your oven to 350°F. Grease your baking pan.
2. Combine the main ingredients on the prepared sheet pan. Drizzle with the oil and toss to coat.
3. Combine the seasoning ingredients in a bowl. Sprinkle them over the vegetables on the pan and toss to coat with seasonings.
4. Bake in the oven for 25 minutes. Stir frequently until vegetables are soft and lightly browned and chickpeas are crisp, for about 20 to 25 minutes more.
5. Season with more salt and black pepper to taste, top with the green onion before serving.

**Nutrition: Calories:** 156 kcal; **Protein:** 9.4 g; **Carbohydrates:** 12.2 g; **Fat:** 7.1 g; **Fiber:** 0.8 g; **Cholesterol:** 7 mg; **Sodium:** 86 mg; **Potassium:** 365 mg

## 143. Roasted Broccoli Sweet Potatoes and Bean Sprouts

**Preparation time:** 5 minutes
**Cooking time:** 20 minutes
**Servings:** 6
**Ingredients:**
- 1 large broccoli, sliced
- 1 cup bean sprouts
- 1 yellow onion, diced
- 1 sweet potato, peeled and cut into 1-inch cubes
- 2 large carrots, cut into 1-inch pieces
- 3 medium potatoes, cut into 1-inch pieces - 3 tbsp. canola oil

**Seasoning Ingredients:**
- 1 tsp. salt - ½ tsp. black pepper, ground
- 1 tsp. onion powder
- 2 tsp. garlic powder
- ½ cup gouda cheese, grated
- ¼ cup parmesan cheese

**Garnishing Ingredients:**
- 2 green onions, chopped (optional)

**Directions:**
1. Preheat your oven to 350°F. Grease your baking pan.
2. Combine the main ingredients on the prepared sheet pan.
3. Drizzle with the oil and toss to coat. Combine the seasoning ingredients in a bowl. Sprinkle them over the vegetables on the pan and toss to coat with seasonings. Bake in the oven for 25 minutes. Stir frequently until vegetables are soft and lightly browned and chickpeas are crisp, for about 20 to 25 minutes more. Season with more salt and black pepper to taste, top with the green onion before serving.

**Nutrition: Calories:** 156 kcal; **Protein:** 9.4 g; **Carbohydrates:** 12.2 g; **Fat:** 7.1 g; **Fiber:** 0.8 g; **Cholesterol:** 7 mg; **Sodium:** 86 mg; **Potassium:** 365 mg

## 144. Roasted Sweet Potato and Red Beets

**Preparation time:** 5 minutes
**Cooking time:** 20 minutes
**Servings:** 6
**Ingredients:**
- 1 ½ cups Brussels sprouts, trimmed
- 1 cup large sweet potato chunks
- 1 cup large carrot chunks
- 1 ½ cup broccoli florets
- 1 cup red beets, cubed
- ½ cup yellow onion chunks
- 2 tbsp. sesame seed oil
- salt and black pepper, ground, to taste

**Directions:**
1. Preheat your oven to 425°F (220°C). Set the rack to the second-lowest level in the oven.
2. Pour some lightly salted water in a bowl. Submerge the Brussels sprouts in salted water for 15 minutes and drain.
3. Place the rest of the ingredients together in a bowl. Spread the vegetables in a single layer onto a baking pan.

4. Roast in the oven until the vegetables start to brown and cook through, for about 45 minutes.

**Nutrition: Calories:** 156 kcal; **Protein:** 9.4 g; **Carbohydrates:** 12.2 g; **Fat:** 7.1 g; **Fiber:** 0.8 g; **Cholesterol:** 7 mg; **Sodium:** 86 mg; **Potassium:** 365 mg

## 145. Sichuan Style Baked Chioggia Beets and Broccoli Florets

**Preparation time:** 5 minutes
**Cooking time:** 20 minutes
**Servings:** 6
**Ingredients:**
- 1 ½ cups Brussels sprouts, trimmed
- 1 cup broccoli florets
- 1 cup Chioggia beets, cut into chunks
- 1 ½ cup cauliflower florets
- 1 cup button mushrooms, sliced
- ½ cup red onion chunks
- 2 tbsp. sesame oil
- ½ tsp. Sichuan peppercorns
- salt ground black pepper to taste

**Directions:**
1. Preheat your oven to 425°F (220°C). Set the rack to the second-lowest level in the oven. Pour some lightly salted water in a bowl. Submerge the Brussels sprouts in salted water for 15 minutes and drain.
2. Place the rest of the ingredients together in a bowl. Spread the vegetables in a single layer onto a baking pan. Roast in the oven until the vegetables start to brown and cook through, for about 45 minutes.

**Nutrition: Calories:** 156 kcal; **Protein:** 9.4 g; **Carbohydrates:** 12.2 g; **Fat:** 7.1 g; **Fiber:** 0.8 g; **Cholesterol:** 7 mg; **Sodium:** 86 mg; **Potassium:** 365 mg

## 146. Baked Enoki and Mini Cabbage

**Preparation time:** 5 minutes
**Cooking time:** 20 minutes
**Servings:** 6
**Ingredients:**
- 1 ½ cups mini cabbage, trimmed
- 1 cup broccoli florets
- 1 cup Enoki mushrooms, sliced
- 1 ½ cup cauliflower florets
- 1 cup oyster mushrooms
- ½ cup red onion chunks - 2 tbsp. olive oil
- Salt and black pepper, ground, to taste

**Directions:**
1. Preheat your oven to 425°F (220°C). Set the rack to the second-lowest level in the oven.
2. Pour some lightly salted water into a bowl. Submerge the Brussels sprouts in salted water for 15 minutes and drain.
3. Place the rest of the ingredients together in a bowl. Spread the vegetables in a single layer onto a baking pan.
4. Roast in the oven until the vegetables start to brown and cook through, for about 45 minutes.

**Nutrition: Calories:** 156 kcal; **Protein:** 9.4 g; **Carbohydrates:** 12.2 g; **Fat:** 7.1 g; **Fiber:** 0.8 g; **Cholesterol:** 7 mg; **Sodium:** 86 mg; **Potassium:** 365 mg

## 147. Roasted Triple Mushrooms

**Preparation time:** 5 minutes
**Cooking time:** 20 minutes
**Servings:** 6
**Ingredients:**
- 2 cups Spinach, rinsed
- 1 cup oyster mushrooms
- 1 cup button mushrooms, sliced
- 1 ½ cup Enoki mushrooms
- ½ cup red onion chunks
- 2 tbsp. extra-virgin olive oil
- Salt and black pepper, ground, to taste
- ¼ cup Ricotta cheese

**Directions:**
1. Preheat your oven to 425°F (220°C). Set the rack to the second-lowest level in the oven.
2. Pour some lightly salted water into a bowl. Submerge the spinach in salted water for 15 minutes and drain.
3. Place the rest of the ingredients together in a bowl. Spread the vegetables in a single layer onto a baking pan.
4. Roast in the oven until the vegetables start to brown and cook through, for about 45 minutes.

**Nutrition: Calories:** 156 kcal; **Protein:** 9.4 g; **Carbohydrates:** 12.2 g; **Fat:** 7.1 g; **Fiber:** 0.8 g; **Cholesterol:** 7 mg; **Sodium:** 86 mg; **Potassium:** 365 mg

## 148. Roasted Mini Cabbage and Sweet Potato

**Preparation time:** 5 minutes
**Cooking time:** 20 minutes
**Servings:** 6
**Ingredients:**
- 1 ½ cups mini cabbage, trimmed

- 1 cup large potato chunks
- 1 cup large rainbow carrot chunks
- 1 ½ cup potato chunks
- 1 cup parsnips
- ½ cup red onion chunks
- 2 tbsp. extra-virgin olive oil
- Sea salt
- Rainbow peppercorns to taste
- ¼ cup cottage cheese

**Directions:**
1. Preheat your oven to 425°F (220°C). Set the rack to the second-lowest level in the oven.
2. Pour some lightly salted water into a bowl. Submerge the mini cabbage in salted water for 15 minutes and drain.
3. Place the rest of the ingredients together in a bowl. Spread the vegetables in a single layer onto a baking pan.
4. Roast in the oven until the vegetables start to brown and cook through, for about 45 minutes.

**Nutrition: Calories:** 156 kcal; **Protein:** 9.4 g; **Carbohydrates:** 12.2 g; **Fat:** 7.1 g; **Fiber:** 0.8 g; **Cholesterol:** 7 mg; **Sodium:** 86 mg; **Potassium:** 365 mg

## 149. Tofu and Green Bean Stir-Fry

**Preparation time:** 15 minutes
**Cooking time:** 20 minutes
**Servings:** 4
**Ingredients:**

- 1 (14-oz.) package extra-firm tofu
- 2 tbsp. canola oil
- 1-lb. green beans, chopped
- 2 carrots, peeled and thinly sliced
- ½ cup Stir-Fry Sauce or store-bought lower-sodium Stir-Fry Sauce
- 2 cups Fluffy Brown Rice
- 2 scallions, thinly sliced
- 2 tbsp. sesame seeds

**Directions:**
1. Put the tofu on your plate lined with a kitchen towel, put a separate kitchen towel over the tofu, and place a heavy pot on top, changing towels every time they become soaked. Let sit within 15 minutes to remove the moisture. Cut the tofu into 1-inch cubes.
2. Heat the canola oil in a large wok or skillet to medium-high heat. Add the tofu cubes and cook, flipping every 1 to 2 minutes, so all sides become browned.
3. Remove from the skillet and place the green beans and carrots in the hot oil. Stir-fry for 4 to 5 minutes, occasionally tossing, until crisp and slightly tender.
4. While the vegetables are cooking, prepare the Stir-Fry Sauce (if using homemade). Place the tofu back in the skillet. Put the sauce over the tofu and vegetables and let simmer for 2 to 3 minutes. Serve over rice then top with scallions and sesame seeds.

**Nutrition: Calories:** 380 kcal; **Fat:** 15 g; **Sodium:** 440 mg; **Potassium:** 454 mg; **Carbohydrate:** 45 g; **Protein:** 16 g

## 150. Peanut Vegetable Pad Thai

**Preparation time:** 15 minutes
**Cooking time:** 20 minutes
**Servings:** 6
**Ingredients:**

- 8 oz. brown rice noodles
- ⅓ cup natural peanut butter
- 3 tbsp. vegetable broth, unsalted
- 1 tbsp. low-sodium soy sauce
- 2 tbsp. rice wine vinegar
- 1 tbsp. honey - 2 tsp. sesame oil
- 1 tsp. sriracha (optional)
- 1 tbsp. canola oil
- 1 red bell pepper, thinly sliced
- 1 zucchini, cut into matchsticks
- 2 large carrots, cut into matchsticks
- 3 large eggs, beaten
- ¾ tsp. Kosher or sea salt
- ½ cup peanuts, unsalted and chopped
- ½ cup cilantro leaves, chopped

**Directions:**
1. Boil a large pot of water. Cook the rice noodles as stated in package directions. Mix the peanut butter, vegetable broth, soy sauce, rice wine vinegar, honey, sesame oil, and sriracha in a bowl. Set aside.
2. Warm-up the canola oil over medium heat in a large nonstick skillet. Add the red bell pepper, zucchini, and carrots, and sauté for 2 to 3 minutes, until slightly soft. Stir in the eggs and fold with a spatula until scrambled. Add the cooked rice noodles, sauce, and salt. Toss to combine. Spoon into bowls and evenly top with the peanuts and cilantro.

**Nutrition: Calories:** 393 kcal; **Fat:** 19 g; **Sodium:** 561 mg; **Carbohydrate:** 45 g; **Protein:** 13 g

## 151. Spicy Tofu Burrito Bowls with Cilantro Avocado Sauce

**Preparation time:** 15 minutes
**Cooking time:** 15 minutes
**Servings:** 4
**Ingredients:**
For the sauce:
- ¼ cup plain nonfat Greek yogurt
- ½ cup fresh cilantro leaves
- ½ ripe avocado, peeled
- 1 lime, zest and juice
- 2 garlic cloves, peeled
- ¼ tsp. Kosher or sea salt
- 2 tbsp. water

For the burrito bowls:
- 1 (14-oz.) package extra-firm tofu
- 1 tbsp. canola oil
- 1 yellow or orange bell pepper, diced
- 2 tbsp. Taco Seasoning
- ¼ tsp. Kosher or sea salt
- 2 cups Fluffy Brown Rice
- 1 (15-oz.) can black beans, drained

**Directions:**
1. Place all the sauce ingredients in the bowl of a food processor or blender and purée until smooth. Taste and adjust the seasoning, if necessary. Refrigerate until ready for use.
2. Put the tofu on your plate lined with a kitchen towel. Put another kitchen towel over the tofu and place a heavy pot on top, changing towels if they become soaked. Let it stand within 15 minutes to remove the moisture. Cut the tofu into 1-inch cubes.
3. Warm-up the canola oil in a large skillet over medium heat. Add the tofu and bell pepper, and sauté, breaking up the tofu into smaller pieces for 4 to 5 minutes. Stir in the taco seasoning, salt, and ¼ cup of water. Evenly divide the rice and black beans among 4 bowls. Top with the tofu/bell pepper mixture and top with the cilantro avocado sauce.

**Nutrition: Calories:** 383 kcal; **Fat:** 13 g; **Sodium:** 438 mg; **Carbohydrate:** 48 g; **Protein:** 21 g

## 152. Sweet Potato Cakes with Classic Guacamole

**Preparation time:** 15 minutes
**Cooking time:** 20 minutes
**Servings:** 4
**Ingredients:**
For the guacamole:
- 2 ripe avocados, peeled and pitted
- ½ jalapeño, seeded and finely minced
- ¼ red onion, peeled and finely diced
- ¼ cup fresh cilantro leaves, chopped
- 1 lime, zest and juice
- ¼ tsp. Kosher or sea salt

For the cakes:
- 3 sweet potatoes, cooked and peeled
- ½ cup black beans, cooked
- 1 large egg - ½ cup panko bread crumbs
- 1 tsp. cumin, ground
- 1 tsp. chili powder
- ½ tsp. Kosher or sea salt
- ¼ tsp. black pepper, ground
- 2 tbsp. canola oil

**Directions:**
1. Mash the avocado, then stir in the jalapeño, red onion, cilantro, lime zest and juice, and salt in a bowl. Taste and adjust the seasoning, if necessary.
2. Put the cooked sweet potatoes plus black beans in a bowl and mash until a paste forms. Stir in the egg, bread crumbs, cumin, chili powder, salt, and black pepper until combined.
3. Warm-up the canola oil in a large skillet at medium heat. Form the sweet potato mixture into 4 patties, place them in the hot skillet, and cook within 3 to 4 minutes per side, until browned and crispy. Serve the sweet potato cakes with guacamole on top.

**Nutrition: Calories:** 369 kcal; **Fat:** 22 g; **Sodium:** 521 mg; **Carbohydrate:** 38 g; **Protein:** 8 g

## 153. Chickpea Cauliflower Tikka Masala

**Preparation time:** 15 minutes
**Cooking time:** 40 minutes
**Servings:** 6
**Ingredients:**
- 2 tbsp. olive oil
- 1 yellow onion, peeled and diced
- 4 garlic cloves, peeled and minced
- 1-inch piece fresh ginger, peeled and minced

- 2 tbsp. Garam Masala
- 1 tsp. Kosher or sea salt
- ½ tsp. black pepper, ground
- ¼ tsp. cayenne pepper, ground
- ½ small head cauliflower, small florets
- 2 (15-oz.) cans no-salt-added chickpeas, rinsed and drained
- 1 (15-oz.) can no-salt-added petite diced tomatoes, drained
- 1½ cups vegetable broth, unsalted
- ½ (15-oz.) can coconut milk
- Zest and juice of 1 lime
- ½ cup fresh cilantro leaves, chopped, divided
- 1½ cups Fluffy Brown Rice, divided and cooked

**Directions:**
1. Warm-up olive oil over medium heat, then put the onion and sauté within 4 to 5 minutes in a large Dutch oven or stockpot. Stir in the garlic, ginger, garam masala, salt, black pepper, and cayenne pepper and toast for 30 to 60 seconds, until fragrant.
2. Stir in the cauliflower florets, chickpeas, diced tomatoes, and vegetable broth and increase to medium-high. Simmer within 15 minutes, until the cauliflower is fork-tender.
3. Remove, then stir in the coconut milk, lime juice, lime zest, and half of the cilantro. Taste and adjust the seasoning, if necessary. Serve over the rice and the remaining chopped cilantro.

**Nutrition: Calories:** 323 kcal; **Fat:** 12 g; **Sodium:** 444 mg; **Carbohydrate:** 44 g; **Protein:** 11 g

## 154. Eggplant Parmesan Stacks

**Preparation time:** 15 minutes
**Cooking time:** 20 minutes
**Servings:** 4
**Ingredients:**
- 1 large eggplant, cut into thick slices
- 2 tbsp. olive oil, divided
- ¼ tsp. Kosher or sea salt
- ¼ tsp. black pepper, ground
- 1 cup panko bread crumbs
- ¼ cup Parmesan cheese, freshly grated
- 5 to 6 garlic cloves, minced
- ½ lb. fresh mozzarella, sliced
- 1½ cups lower-sodium marinara
- ½ cup fresh basil leaves, torn

**Directions:**
1. Preheat the oven to 425°F. Coat the eggplant slices in 1 tbsp. olive oil and sprinkle with salt and black pepper. Put on a large baking sheet, then roast for 10 to 12 minutes, until soft with crispy edges. Remove the eggplant and set the oven to a low boil.
2. In a bowl, stir the remaining tbsp. of olive oil, bread crumbs, Parmesan cheese, and garlic. Remove the cooled eggplant from the baking sheet and clean it.
3. Create layers on the same baking sheet by stacking a roasted eggplant slice with a slice of mozzarella, a tbsp. of marinara, and a tbsp. of the bread crumb mixture, repeating with 2 layers of each ingredient. Cook under the broiler within 3 to 4 minutes until the cheese is melted and bubbly.

**Nutrition: Calories:** 377 kcal; **Fat:** 22 g; **Sodium:** 509 mg; **Carbohydrate:** 29 g; **Protein:** 16 g

## 155. Roasted Vegetable Enchiladas

**Preparation time:** 15 minutes
**Cooking time:** 45 minutes
**Servings:** 8
**Ingredients:**
- 2 zucchinis, diced
- 1 red bell pepper, seeded and sliced
- 1 red onion, peeled and sliced
- 2 ears corn
- 2 tbsp. canola oil
- 1 can no-salt-added black beans, drained
- 1½ tbsp. chili powder
- 2 tsp. cumin, ground
- ⅛ tsp. Kosher or sea salt
- ½ tsp. black pepper, ground
- 8 (8-inch) whole-wheat tortillas
- 1 cup Enchilada Sauce or store-bought enchilada sauce
- ½ cup Mexican-style cheese, shredded
- ½ cup plain nonfat Greek yogurt
- ½ cup cilantro leaves, chopped

**Directions:**
1. Preheat oven to 400°F. Place the zucchini, red bell pepper, and red onion on a baking sheet. Place the ears of corn separately on the same baking sheet. Drizzle all with the canola oil and toss to coat. Roast for 10 to 12 minutes, until the vegetables are tender. Remove and reduce the temperature to 375°F.

2. Cut the corn from the cob. Transfer the corn kernels, zucchini, red bell pepper, and onion to a bowl and stir in the black beans, chili powder, cumin, salt, and black pepper until combined.
3. Oil a 9-x-13-inch baking dish with cooking spray. Line up the tortillas in the greased baking dish. Evenly distribute the vegetable bean filling into each tortilla. Pour half of the enchilada sauce and sprinkle half of the shredded cheese on top of the filling.
4. Roll each tortilla into an enchilada shape and place them seam-side down. Pour the remaining enchilada sauce and sprinkle the remaining cheese over the enchiladas. Bake for 25 minutes until the cheese is melted and bubbly. Serve the enchiladas with Greek yogurt and chopped cilantro.

**Nutrition: Calories:** 335 kcal; **Fat:** 15 g; **Sodium:** 557 mg; **Carbohydrate:** 42 g; **Protein:** 13 g

### 156. Lentil Avocado Tacos

**Preparation time:** 15 minutes
**Cooking time:** 35 minutes
**Servings:** 6
**Ingredients:**
- 1 tbsp. canola oil
- ½ yellow onion, peeled and diced
- 2-3 garlic cloves, minced
- 1½ cups lentils, dried
- ½ tsp. Kosher or sea salt
- 3 to 3½ cups vegetable or chicken stock, unsalted
- 2½ tbsp. Taco Seasoning or store-bought low-sodium taco seasoning
- 16 (6-inch) corn tortillas, toasted
- 2 ripe avocados, peeled and sliced

**Directions:**
1. Heat up the canola oil in a large skillet or Dutch oven over medium heat. Cook the onion within 4 to 5 minutes, until soft. Mix in the garlic and cook within 30 seconds until fragrant. Then add the lentils, salt, and stock. Bring to a simmer for 25 to 35 minutes, adding additional stock if needed.
2. When there's only a small amount of liquid left in the pan, and the lentils are al dente, stir in the taco seasoning and let simmer for 1 to 2 minutes. Taste and adjust the seasoning, if necessary. Spoon the lentil mixture into tortillas and serve with the avocado slices.

**Nutrition: Calories:** 400 kcal; **Fat:** 14 g; **Sodium:** 336 mg; **Carbohydrate:** 64 g; **Fiber:** 15 g; **Protein:** 16 g

### 157. Tomato and Olive Orecchiette with Basil Pesto

**Preparation time:** 15 minutes
**Cooking time:** 25 minutes
**Servings:** 6
**Ingredients:**
- 12 oz. Orecchiette pasta
- 2 tbsp. olive oil
- 1-pint cherry tomatoes, quartered
- ½ cup Basil Pesto or store-bought pesto
- ¼ cup Kalamata olives, sliced
- 1 tbsp. oregano leaves, dried
- ¼ tsp. Kosher or sea salt
- ½ tsp. black pepper, freshly cracked
- ¼ tsp. red pepper flakes, crushed
- 2 tbsp. Parmesan cheese, freshly grated

**Directions:**
1. Boil a large pot of water. Cook the Orecchiette, drain and transfer the pasta to a large nonstick skillet. Put the skillet over medium-low heat, then heat the olive oil. Stir in the cherry tomatoes, pesto, olives, oregano, salt, black pepper, and crushed red pepper flakes. Cook within 8 to 10 minutes, until heated throughout.
2. Serve the pasta with the freshly grated Parmesan cheese.

**Nutrition: Calories:** 332 kcal; **Fat:** 13 g; **Sodium:** 389 mg; **Carbohydrate:** 44 g; **Protein:** 9 g

### 158. Italian Stuffed Portobello Mushroom Burgers

**Preparation time:** 15 minutes
**Cooking time:** 25 minutes
**Servings:** 4
**Ingredients:**
- 1 tbsp. olive oil
- 4 large Portobello mushrooms, washed and dried
- ½ yellow onion, peeled and diced
- 4 garlic cloves, peeled and minced
- 1 can cannellini beans, drained

- ½ cup fresh basil leaves, torn
- ½ cup panko bread crumbs
- ⅛ tsp. Kosher or sea salt
- ¼ tsp. ground black pepper
- 1 cup lower-sodium marinara, divided
- ½ cup shredded mozzarella cheese
- 4 whole-wheat buns, toasted
- 1 cup fresh arugula

**Directions**:
1. Heat up the olive oil in a large skillet to medium-high heat. Sear the mushrooms for 4 to 5 minutes per side, until slightly soft. Place on a baking sheet. Preheat the oven to a low boil.
2. Put the onion in the skillet and cook for 4 to 5 minutes, until slightly soft. Mix in the garlic, then cooks within 30 to 60 seconds. Move the onions plus garlic to a bowl. Add the cannellini beans and smash with the back of a fork to form a chunky paste.
3. Stir in the basil, bread crumbs, salt, and black pepper, and half of the marinara. Cook for 5 minutes. Remove the bean mixture from the stove and divide among the mushroom caps. Spoon the remaining marinara over the stuffed mushrooms and top each with mozzarella cheese.
4. Broil within 3 to 4 minutes, until the cheese is melted and bubbly. Transfer the burgers to the toasted whole-wheat buns and top with the arugula.

**Nutrition: Calories:** 407 kcal; **Fat:** 9 g; **Sodium:** 575 mg; **Carbohydrate:** 63 g; **Protein:** 25 g

## 159. Gnocchi with Tomato Basil Sauce

**Preparation time:** 15 minutes
**Cooking time:** 25 minutes
**Servings:** 6
**Ingredients:**
- 2 tbsp. olive oil
- ½ yellow onion, peeled and diced
- 3 cloves garlic, peeled and minced
- 1 (32-oz.) can no-salt-added San Marzano tomatoes, crushed
- ¼ cup fresh basil leaves
- 2 tsp. Italian seasoning
- ½ tsp. Kosher or sea salt
- 1 tsp. sugar, granulated
- ½ tsp. black pepper, ground
- ⅛ tsp. red pepper flakes, crushed
- 1 tbsp. heavy cream (optional)
- 12 oz. gnocchi
- ¼ cup Parmesan cheese, freshly grated

**Directions**:
1. Heat up the olive oil in a Dutch oven or stockpot over medium heat. Add the onion and sauté for 5 to 6 minutes, until soft. Stir in the garlic and stir until fragrant, 30 to 60 seconds. Then stir in the tomatoes, basil, Italian seasoning, salt, sugar, black pepper, and crushed red pepper flakes.
2. Bring to a simmer for 15 minutes. Stir in the heavy cream, if desired. For a smooth, puréed sauce, use an immersion blender or transfer sauce to a blender and purée until smooth. Taste and adjust the seasoning, if necessary.
3. While the sauce simmers, cook the gnocchi according to the package instructions, remove with a slotted spoon, and transfer to 6 bowls.
4. Pour the sauce over the gnocchi and top with the Parmesan cheese.

**Nutrition: Calories:** 287 kcal; **Fat:** 7 g; **Sodium:** 527 mg; **Carbohydrate:** 41 g; **Protein:** 10 g

## 160. Creamy Pumpkin Pasta

**Preparation time:** 15 minutes
**Cooking time:** 30 minutes
**Servings:** 6
**Ingredients:**
- 1-lb. whole-grain linguine
- 1 tbsp. olive oil
- 3 garlic cloves, peeled and minced
- 2 tbsp. fresh sage, chopped
- 1½ cups pumpkin purée
- 1 cup vegetable stock, unsalted
- ½ cup low-fat evaporated milk
- ¾ tsp. Kosher or sea salt
- ½ tsp. black pepper, ground
- ½ tsp. nutmeg, ground
- ¼ tsp. cayenne pepper, ground
- ½ cup Parmesan cheese, divided and freshly grated

**Directions**:
1. Cook the whole-grain linguine in a large pot of boiled water. Reserve ½ cup of pasta water and drain the rest. Set the pasta aside.
2. Warm-up the olive oil over medium heat in a large skillet.

3. Add the garlic and sage and sauté for 1 to 2 minutes, until soft and fragrant. Whisk in the pumpkin purée, stock, milk, and reserved pasta water and simmer for 4 to 5 minutes, until thickened.
4. Whisk in the salt, black pepper, nutmeg, and cayenne pepper, and half of the Parmesan cheese. Stir in the cooked whole-grain linguine. Evenly divide the pasta among 6 bowls and top with the remaining Parmesan cheese.

**Nutrition: Calories:** 381 kcal; **Fat:** 8 g; **Sodium:** 175 mg; **Carbohydrate:** 63 g; **Protein:** 15 g

## 161. Mexican-Style Potato Casserole

**Preparation time:** 15 minutes
**Cooking time:** 60 minutes
**Servings:** 8
**Ingredients:**

- Cooking spray
- 2 tbsp. canola oil
- ½ yellow onion, peeled and diced
- 4 garlic cloves, peeled and minced
- 2 tbsp. all-purpose flour
- 1¼ cups milk
- 1 tbsp. chili powder
- ½ tbsp. cumin, ground
- 1 tsp. Kosher salt or sea salt
- ½ tsp. black pepper, ground
- ¼ tsp. cayenne pepper, ground
- 1½ cups Mexican-style cheese, shredded and divided
- 1 (4-oz.) can green chilies, drained
- 1½ lb. baby Yukon Gold or red potatoes, thinly sliced
- 1 red bell pepper, thinly sliced

**Directions:**

1. Preheat the oven to 400°F. Oil a 9-x-13-inch baking dish with cooking spray. In a large saucepan, warm canola oil on medium heat. Add the onion and sauté for 4 to 5 minutes, until soft. Mix in the garlic, then cook until fragrant, 30 to 60 seconds.
2. Mix in the flour, then put in the milk while whisking. Slow simmer for about 5 minutes, until thickened. Whisk in the chili powder, cumin, salt, black pepper, and cayenne pepper.
3. Remove from the heat and whisk in half of the shredded cheese and the green chilies.
4. Taste and adjust the seasoning, if necessary. Line up one-third of the sliced potatoes and sliced bell pepper in the baking dish and top with a quarter of the remaining shredded cheese.
5. Repeat with 2 more layers. Pour the cheese sauce over the top and sprinkle with the remaining shredded cheese. Cover it with aluminum foil and bake within 45 to 50 minutes, until the potatoes are tender.
6. Remove the foil and bake again within 5 to 10 minutes, until the topping is slightly browned. Let cool within 20 minutes before slicing into 8 pieces. Serve.

**Nutrition: Calories:** 195 kcal; **Fat:** 10 g; **Sodium:** 487 mg; **Carbohydrate:** 19 g; **Protein:** 8 g

## 162. Black Bean Stew with Cornbread

**Preparation time:** 15 minutes
**Cooking time:** 55 minutes
**Servings:** 6
**Ingredients:**
**For the black bean stew:**

- 2 tbsp. canola oil
- 1 yellow onion, peeled and diced
- 4 garlic cloves, peeled and minced
- 1 tbsp. chili powder
- 1 tbsp. cumin, ground
- ¼ tsp. Kosher or sea salt
- ½ tsp. black pepper, ground
- 2 cans no-salt-added black beans, drained
- 1 (10-oz.) can tomatoes, fire-roasted, diced
- ½ cup fresh cilantro leaves, chopped

**For the cornbread topping:**

- 1¼ cups cornmeal
- ½ cup all-purpose flour
- ½ tsp. baking powder
- ¼ tsp. baking soda
- ⅛ tsp. Kosher or sea salt
- 1 cup low-fat buttermilk
- 2 tbsp. honey
- 1 large egg

**Directions:**

1. Warm-up the canola oil over medium heat in a large Dutch oven or stockpot. Add the onion and sauté for 4 to 6 minutes, until the onion is soft. Stir in the garlic, chili powder, cumin, salt, and black pepper.

2. Cook within 1 to 2 minutes, until fragrant. Add the black beans and diced tomatoes. Bring to a simmer and cook for 15 minutes. Remove, then stir in the fresh cilantro. Taste and adjust the seasoning, if necessary.
3. Preheat the oven to 375°F. While the stew simmers, prepare the cornbread topping. Mix the cornmeal, baking soda, flour, baking powder, plus salt in a bowl. In a measuring cup, whisk the buttermilk, honey, and egg until combined. Put the batter into the dry fixing until just combined.
4. In oven-safe bowls or dishes, spoon out the black bean soup. Distribute dollops of the cornbread batter on top and then spread it out evenly with a spatula. Bake within 30 minutes, until the cornbread is just set.

**Nutrition: Calories:** 359 kcal; **Fat:** 7 g; **Sodium:** 409 mg; **Carbohydrate:** 61 g; **Protein:** 14 g

## 163. Mushroom Florentine

**Preparation time:** 15 minutes
**Cooking time:** 20 minutes
**Servings:** 4
**Ingredients:**

- 5 oz. whole-grain pasta
- ¼ cup low-sodium vegetable broth
- 1 cup mushrooms, sliced
- ¼ cup soy milk
- 1 tsp. olive oil
- ½ tsp. Italian seasonings

**Directions:**
1. Cook the pasta according to the direction of the manufacturer. Then pour olive oil into the saucepan and heat it. Add mushrooms and Italian seasonings. Stir the mushrooms well and cook for 10 minutes.
2. Then add soy milk and vegetable broth. Add cooked pasta and mix up the mixture well. Cook it for 5 minutes on low heat.

**Nutrition: Calories:** 287 kcal; **Protein:** 12.4 g; **Carbohydrates:** 50.4 g; **Fat:** 4.2 g; **Sodium:** 26 mg

## 164. Hassel back Eggplant

**Preparation time:** 15 minutes
**Cooking time:** 25 minutes
**Servings:** 2
**Ingredients:**

- 2 eggplants, trimmed
- 2 tomatoes, sliced
- 1 tbsp. low-fat yogurt
- 1 tsp. curry powder
- 1 tsp. olive oil

**Directions:**
1. Make the cuts in the eggplants in the shape of the Hassel back. Then rub the vegetables with curry powder and fill with sliced tomatoes. Sprinkle the eggplants with olive oil and yogurt and wrap in the foil (each Hassel back eggplant wrap separately). Bake the vegetables at 375°F for 25 minutes.

**Nutrition: Calories:** 188 kcal; **Protein:** 7 g; **Carbohydrates:** 38.1 g; **Fat:** 3 g; **Sodium:** 23 mg

## 165. Vegetarian Kebabs

**Preparation time:** 15 minutes
**Cooking time:** 6 minutes
**Servings:** 4
**Ingredients:**

- 2 tbsp. balsamic vinegar
- 1 tbsp. olive oil
- 1 tsp. parsley, dried
- 2 tbsp. water
- 2 sweet peppers
- 2 red onions, peeled
- 2 zucchinis, trimmed

**Directions:**
1. Cut the sweet peppers and onions into medium size squares. Then slice the zucchini. String all vegetables into the skewers.
2. After this, in the shallow bowl, mix up olive oil, dried parsley, water, and balsamic vinegar.
3. Sprinkle the vegetable skewers with olive oil mixture and transfer in the preheated to 390°F grill. Cook the kebabs within 3 minutes per side or until the vegetables are light brown.

**Nutrition: Calories:** 88 kcal; **Protein:** 2.4 g; **Carbohydrates:** 13 g; **Fat:** 3.9 g; **Sodium:** 14 mg

## 166. White Beans Stew

**Preparation time:** 15 minutes
**Cooking time:** 55 minutes
**Servings:** 4
**Ingredients:**

- 1 cup white beans, soaked
- 1 cup low-sodium vegetable broth
- 1 cup zucchini, chopped
- 1 tsp. tomato paste
- 1 tbsp. avocado oil - 4 cups water
- ½ tsp. peppercorns
- ½ tsp. black pepper, ground
- ¼ tsp. nutmeg, ground

**Directions:**
1. Heat avocado oil in the saucepan, add zucchinis, and roast them for 5 minutes. After this, add white beans, vegetable broth, tomato paste, water, peppercorns, ground black pepper, and ground nutmeg. Simmer the stew within 50 minutes on low heat.

**Nutrition: Calories:** 184 kcal; **Protein:** 12.3 g; **Carbohydrates:** 32.6 g; **Fat:** 1 g; **Sodium:** 55 mg

### 167. Vegetarian Lasagna
**Preparation time:** 15 minutes
**Cooking time:** 30 minutes
**Servings:** 6
**Ingredients:**
- 1 cup carrot, diced
- ½ cup bell pepper, diced
- 1 cup spinach, chopped
- 1 tbsp. olive oil - 1 tsp. chili powder
- 1 cup tomatoes, chopped
- 4 oz. low-fat cottage cheese
- 1 eggplant, sliced
- 1 cup low-sodium vegetable broth

**Directions:**
1. Put carrot, bell pepper, and spinach in the saucepan. Add olive oil and chili powder and stir the vegetables well. Cook them for 5 minutes.
2. Make the sliced eggplant layer in the casserole mold and top it with a vegetable mixture.
3. Add tomatoes, vegetable stock, and cottage cheese. Bake the lasagna for 30 minutes at 375°F.

**Nutrition: Calories:** 77 kcal; **Protein:** 4.1 g; **Carbohydrates:** 9.7 g; **Fat:** 3 g; **Sodium:** 124 mg

### 168. Pan-Fried Salmon with Salad
**Preparation time:** 15 minutes
**Cooking time:** 20 minutes
**Servings:** 4
**Ingredients:**
- Pinch salt and pepper
- 1 tbsp. extra-virgin olive oil
- 2 tbsp. butter, unsalted
- ½ tsp. fresh dill
- 1 tbsp. fresh lemon juice
- 100g salad leaves, or bag of mixed leaves

**Salad Dressing:**
- 3 tbsp. olive oil
- 2 tbsp. balsamic vinaigrette
- ½ tsp. maple syrup (honey)

**Directions:**
1. Pat-dry the salmon fillets with a paper towel and season with a pinch of salt and pepper. In a skillet, warm-up oil over medium-high heat and add fillets. Cook each side within 5 to 7 minutes until golden brown.
2. Dissolve butter, dill, and lemon juice in a small saucepan. Put the butter mixture onto the cooked salmon. Lastly, combine all the salad dressing ingredients and drizzle to mixed salad leaves in a large bowl. Toss to coat. Serve with fresh salads on the side. Enjoy!

**Nutrition: Calories:** 307 kcal; **Fat:** 22 g; **Protein:** 34.6 g; **Sodium:** 80 mg; **Carbohydrate:** 1.7 g

### 169. Veggie Variety
**Preparation time:** 15 minutes
**Cooking time:** 15 minutes
**Servings:** 2
**Ingredients:**
- ½ onion, diced
- 1 tsp. vegetable oil (corn or sunflower oil)
- 200 g Tofu/bean curd
- 4 cherry tomatoes, halved
- 30ml vegetable milk (soy or oat milk)
- ½ tsp. curry powder
- 0.25 tsp. paprika
- Pinch Salt and Pepper
- 2 slices Vegan protein bread/ Whole grain bread
- Chives, for garnish

**Directions:**
1. Dice the onion and fry in a frying pan with the oil. Break the tofu by hand into small pieces and put them in the pan. Sauté 7-8 min. Season with curry, paprika, salt, and pepper. The cherry tomatoes and milk and cook it all over roast a few minutes. Serve with bread as desired and sprinkle with chopped chives.

**Nutrition: Calories:** 216 kcal; **Fat:** 8.4 g; **Protein:** 14.1 g; **Sodium:** 140 mg; **Carbohydrate:** 24.8 g

### 170. Vegetable Pasta
**Preparation time:** 15 minutes
**Cooking time:** 15 minutes
**Servings:** 4
**Ingredients:**
- 1 kg thin zucchini
- 20 g fresh ginger
- 350g tofu, smoked
- 1 lime

- 2 cloves garlic
- 2 tbsp. sunflower oil
- 2 tbsp. sesame seeds
- Pinch salt and pepper
- 4 tbsp. onions, fried

**Directions:**
1. Wash and clean the zucchini and, using a julienne cutter, cut the pulp around the kernel into long thin strips (noodles). Ginger peel and finely chop. Crumble tofu. Halve lime, squeeze juice. Peel and chop garlic.
2. Warm-up 1 tbsp. of oil in a large pan and fry the tofu for about 5 minutes. After about 3 minutes, add ginger, garlic, and sesame. Season with soy sauce. Remove from the pan and keep warm. Wipe out the pan, then warm 2 tbsp. of oil in it.
3. Stir fry zucchini strips for about 4 minutes while turning. Season with salt, pepper, and lime juice. Arrange pasta and tofu. Sprinkle with fried onions.

**Nutrition: Calories:** 262 kcal; **Fat:** 17.7 g; **Protein:** 15.4 g; **Sodium:** 62 mg; **Carbohydrate:** 17.1 g

## 171. Vegetable Noodles with Bolognese

**Preparation time:** 15 minutes
**Cooking time:** 15 minutes
**Servings:** 4
**Ingredients:**
- 1 kg small zucchini (e.g., green and yellow)
- 600 g carrots
- 1 onion
- 1 tbsp. olive oil
- 250 g beef steak
- Pinch Salt and pepper
- 2 tbsp. tomato paste
- 1 tbsp. flour
- 1 tsp. vegetable broth (instant)
- 40 g pecorino or parmesan cheese
- 1 small potty of basil

**Directions:**
1. Clean and peel zucchini and carrots and wash. Using a sharp, long knife, cut first into thin slices, then into long, fine strips. Clean or peel the soup greens, wash and cut into tiny cubes. Peel the onion and chop finely. Heat the Bolognese oil in a large pan. Fry hack in it crumbly. Season with salt and pepper.
2. Briefly sauté the prepared vegetable and onion cubes. Stir in tomato paste. Dust the flour, sweat briefly. Pour in 400 ml of water and stir in the vegetable stock. Boil everything, simmer for 7-8 minutes.
3. Meanwhile, cook the vegetable strips in plenty of salted water for 3-5 minutes. Drain, collecting some cooking water. Add the vegetable strips to the pan and mix well. If the sauce is not liquid enough, stir in some vegetable cooking water and season everything again.
4. Slicing cheese into fine shavings. Wash the basil, shake dry, peel off the leaves, and cut roughly. Arrange vegetable noodles, sprinkle with parmesan and basil

**Nutrition: Calories:** 269 kcal; **Fat:** 9.7 g; **Protein:** 25.6 g; **Sodium:** 253 mg; **Carbohydrate:** 21.7 g

## 172. Harissa Bolognese with Vegetable Noodles

**Preparation time:** 15 minutes
**Cooking time:** 30 minutes
**Servings:** 4
**Ingredients:**
- 2 onions
- 1 garlic clove
- 3-4 tbsp. oil
- 400 g beef, ground
- Pinch salt, pepper, cinnamon
- 1 tsp. Harissa (Arabic seasoning paste, tube)
- 1 tbsp. tomato paste
- 2 sweet potatoes
- 2 medium Zucchini
- 3 stems/basil
- 100 g feta cheese

**Directions:**
1. Peel onions and garlic, finely dice. Warm-up 1 tbsp. of oil in a wide saucepan. Fry hack in it crumbly. Fry onions and garlic for a short time. Season with salt, pepper, and ½ tsp. cinnamon. Stir in harissa and tomato paste.
2. Add tomatoes and 200 ml of water, and bring to the boil and simmer for about 15 minutes with occasional stirring. Peel sweet potatoes and zucchini or clean and wash. Cut vegetables into spaghetti with a spiral cutter.
3. Warm-up 2-3 tbsp. of oil in a large pan. Braise sweet potato spaghetti in it for about 3 minutes. Add the zucchini spaghetti and continue to simmer for 3-4 minutes while turning.

4. Season with salt and pepper. Wash the basil, shake dry and peel off the leaves. Garnish vegetable spaghetti and Bolognese on plates. Feta crumbles over. Sprinkle with basil.

**Nutrition:**
**Calories:** 452 kcal; **Fat:** 22.3 g; **Protein:** 37.1 g; **Sodium:** 253 mg; **Carbohydrate:** 27.6 g

## 173. Curry Vegetable Noodles with Chicken

**Preparation time:** 15 minutes
**Cooking time:** 15 minutes
**Servings:** 2
**Ingredients:**
- 600g zucchini
- 500g chicken fillet
- Pinch salt and pepper
- 2 tbsp. oil
- 150 g red and yellow cherry tomatoes
- 1 tsp. curry powder
- 150g Fat-free cheese
- 200 ml vegetable broth
- 4 stalks fresh basil

**Directions:**
1. Wash the zucchini, clean, and cut into long thin strips with a spiral cutter. Wash meat, pat dry, and season with salt. Heat 1 tbsp. oil in a pan. Roast chicken in it for about 10 minutes until golden brown.
2. Wash cherry tomatoes and cut in half. Approximately 3 minutes before the end of the cooking time to the chicken in the pan. Heat 1 tbsp. oil in another pan. Sweat curry powder into it then stirs in cream cheese and broth. Flavor the sauce with salt plus pepper and simmer for about 4 minutes.
3. Wash the basil, shake it dry and pluck the leaves from the stems. Cut small leaves of 3 stems. Remove meat from the pan and cut it into strips. Add tomatoes, basil, and zucchini to the sauce and heat for 2–3 minutes. Serve vegetable noodles and meat on plates and garnish with basil.

**Nutrition: Calories:** 376 kcal; **Fat:** 17.2 g; **Protein:** 44.9 g; **Sodium:** 352 mg; **Carbohydrate:** 9.5 g; **Cholesterol:** 53 mg

# CHAPTER 8: Dinner Recipes

## 174. Shrimp Cocktail

**Preparation time:** 10 minutes
**Cooking time:** 5 minutes
**Servings:** 8
**Ingredients:**
- 2 lb. big shrimp, deveined
- 4 cups water
- 2 bay leaves
- 1 small lemon, halved
- Ice for cooling the shrimp
- Ice for serving
- 1 medium lemon sliced for serving
- ¾ cup tomato Passata
- 2 and ½ tbsp. horseradish, prepared
- ¼ tsp. chili powder
- 2 tbsp. lemon juice

**Directions:**
1. Pour the 4 cups water into a large pot, add lemon and bay leaves. Boil over medium-high heat, reduce temperature, and boil for 10 minutes. Put shrimp, stir and cook within 2 minutes. Move the shrimp to a bowl filled with ice and leave aside for 5 minutes.
2. In a bowl, mix tomato Passata with horseradish, chili powder, and lemon juice and stir well. Place shrimp in a serving bowl filled with ice, with lemon slices, and serve with the cocktail sauce you've prepared.

**Nutrition:** **Calories:** 276 kcal; **Carbs:** 0 g; **Fat:** 8 g; **Protein:** 25 g; **Sodium:** 182 mg

## 175. Squid and Shrimp Salad

**Preparation time:** 10 minutes
**Cooking time:** 15 minutes
**Servings:** 4
**Ingredients:**
- 8 oz. squid, cut into medium pieces

- 8 oz. shrimp, peeled and deveined
- 1 red onion, sliced
- 1 cucumber, chopped
- 2 tomatoes, cut into medium wedges
- 2 tbsp. cilantro, chopped
- 1 hot jalapeno pepper, cut in rounds
- 3 tbsp. rice vinegar
- 3 tbsp. dark sesame oil
- Black pepper, to the taste

**Directions:**
1. In a bowl, mix the onion with cucumber, tomatoes, pepper, cilantro, shrimp, and squid and stir well. Cut a big parchment paper in half, and fold it in half heart shape and open. Place the seafood mixture in this parchment piece, fold over, seal edges, place on a baking sheet, and introduce in the oven at 400°F for 15 minutes.
2. Meanwhile, in a small bowl, mix sesame oil with rice vinegar and black pepper and stir very well. Take the salad out of the oven, leave to cool down for a few minutes, and transfer to a serving plate. Put the dressing over the salad and serve right away.

**Nutrition:** **Calories:** 235 kcal; **Carbs:** 9 g; **Fat:** 8 g; **Protein:** 30 g; **Sodium:** 165 mg

## 176. Parsley Seafood Cocktail

**Preparation time:** 2 hours and 10 minutes
**Cooking time:** 1 hour and 30 minutes
**Servings:** 4
**Ingredients:**
- 1 big octopus, cleaned
- 1-lb. mussels
- 2 lb. clams
- 1 big squid cut in rings
- 3 garlic cloves, chopped
- 1 celery rib, cut crosswise into thirds
- ½ cup celery rib, sliced
- 1 carrot, cut crosswise into 3 pieces
- 1 small white onion, chopped
- 1 bay leaf
- ¾ cup white wine
- 2 cups radicchio, sliced
- 1 red onion, sliced
- 1 cup parsley, chopped
- 1 cup olive oil
- 1 cup red wine vinegar
- Black pepper, to the taste

**Directions:**
1. Put the octopus in a pot with celery rib cut in thirds, garlic, carrot, bay leaf, white onion, and white wine. Add water to cover the octopus, cover with a lid, bring to a boil over high heat, reduce to low, and simmer within 1 and ½ hours.
2. Drain octopus, reserve boiling liquid, and leave aside to cool down. Put ¼ cup octopus cooking liquid in another pot, add mussels, and heat up over medium-high heat, cook until they open, transfer to a bowl, and leave aside.
3. Add clams to the pan, cover, cook over medium-high heat until they open, transfer to the bowl with mussels, and leave aside. Add squid to the pan, cover and cook over medium-high heat for 3 minutes, transfer to the bowl with mussels and clams.
4. Meanwhile, slice octopus into small pieces and mix with the rest of the seafood. Add sliced celery, radicchio, red onion, vinegar, olive oil, parsley, salt, and pepper, stir gently, and leave aside in the fridge within 2 hours before serving.

**Nutrition:** **Calories:** 102 kcal; **Carbs:** 7 g; **Fat:** 1 g; **Protein:** 16 g; **Sodium:** 0 mg

## 177. Shrimp and Onion Ginger Dressing

**Preparation time:** 10 minutes
**Cooking time:** 5 minutes
**Servings:** 2
**Ingredients:**
- 8 medium shrimp, peeled and deveined
- 12 oz. package mixed salad leaves
- 10 cherry tomatoes, halved
- 2 green onions, sliced
- 2 medium mushrooms, sliced
- ⅓ cup rice vinegar
- ¼ cup sesame seeds, toasted

- 1 tbsp. low-sodium soy sauce
- 2 tsp. ginger, grated
- 2 tsp. garlic, minced
- ⅔ cup canola oil
- ⅓ cup sesame oil

**Directions:**
1. In a bowl, mix rice vinegar with sesame seeds, soy sauce, garlic, ginger, and stir well. Pour this into your kitchen blender, add canola oil and sesame oil, pulse very well, and leave aside. Brush shrimp with 3 tbsp. of the ginger dressing you've prepared.
2. Heat your kitchen grill over high heat, add shrimp and cook for 3 minutes, flipping once. In a salad bowl, mix salad leaves with grilled shrimp, mushrooms, green onions, and tomatoes. Drizzle ginger dressing on top and serve right away!

**Nutrition: Calories:** 360 kcal; **Carbs:** 14 g; **Fat:** 11 g; **Protein:** 49 g; **Sodium:** 469 mg

---

### 178. Fruit Shrimp Soup

**Preparation time:** 10 minutes
**Cooking time:** 25 minutes
**Servings:** 6
**Ingredients:**

- 8 oz. shrimp, peeled and deveined
- 1 stalk lemongrass, smashed
- 2 small ginger pieces, grated
- 6 cup chicken stock
- 2 jalapenos, chopped
- 4 lime leaves
- 1 and ½ cups pineapple, chopped
- 1 cup shiitake mushroom caps, chopped
- 1 tomato, chopped
- ½ bell pepper, cubed
- 2 tbsp. fish sauce
- 1 tsp. sugar
- ¼ cup lime juice
- ⅓ cup cilantro, chopped
- 2 scallions, sliced

**Directions:**
1. In a pot, mix ginger with lemongrass, stock, jalapenos, and lime leaves, stir, boil over medium heat, cook within 15 minutes. Strain liquid in a bowl and discard solids.
2. Return soup to the pot again, add pineapple, tomato, mushrooms, bell pepper, sugar, and fish sauce, stir, boil over medium heat, cook for 5 minutes, add shrimp and cook for 3 more minutes.

3. Remove from heat, and add lime juice, cilantro, and scallions, stir, ladle into soup bowls and serve.

**Nutrition: Calories:** 290 kcal; **Carbs:** 39 g; **Fat:** 12 g; **Protein:** 7 g; **Sodium:** 21 mg

---

### 179. Mussels and Chickpea Soup

**Preparation time:** 10 minutes
**Cooking time:** 10 minutes
**Servings:** 6
**Ingredients:**

- 3 garlic cloves, minced
- 2 tbsp. olive oil
- A pinch chili flakes
- 1 and ½ tbsp. fresh mussels, scrubbed
- 1 cup white wine
- 1 cup chickpeas, rinsed
- 1 small fennel bulb, sliced
- Black pepper to the taste
- Juice of 1 lemon
- 3 tbsp. parsley, chopped

**Directions:**
1. Heat a big saucepan with the olive oil over medium-high heat, add garlic and chili flakes, stir and cook within a couple of minutes. Add white wine and mussels, stir, cover, and cook for 3-4 minutes until mussels open.
2. Transfer mussels to a baking dish, add some of the cooking liquid over them, and fridge until they are cold enough. Take mussels out of the fridge and discard shells.
3. Heat another pan over medium-high heat, add mussels, reserved cooking liquid, chickpeas, and fennel, stir well, and heat them. Add black pepper to the taste, lemon juice, and parsley, stir again, divide between plates and serve.

**Nutrition: Calories:** 286 kcal; **Carbs:** 49 g; **Fat:** 4 g; **Protein:** 14 g; **Sodium:** 145 mg

---

### 180. Fish Stew

**Preparation time:** 10 minutes
**Cooking time:** 30 minutes
**Servings:** 4
**Ingredients:**

- 1 red onion, sliced
- 2 tbsp. olive oil
- 1-lb. white fish fillets, boneless, skinless, and cubed
- 1 avocado, pitted and chopped
- 1 tbsp. oregano, chopped
- 1 cup chicken stock

- 2 tomatoes, cubed
- 1 tsp. sweet paprika
- A pinch of salt and black pepper
- 1 tbsp. parsley, chopped
- Juice of 1 lime

**Directions:**
1. Warm-up oil in a pot over medium heat, add the onion, and sauté within 5 minutes. Add the fish, the avocado, and the other ingredients, toss, cook over medium heat for 25 minutes more, divide into bowls and serve for lunch.

**Nutrition:** **Calories:** 78 kcal; **Carbs:** 8 g; **Fat:** 1 g; **Protein:** 11 g; **Sodium:** 151 mg

## 181. Shrimp and Broccoli Soup

**Preparation time:** 5 minutes
**Cooking time:** 25 minutes
**Servings:** 4
**Ingredients:**
- 2 tbsp. olive oil
- 1 yellow onion, chopped
- 4 cups chicken stock
- Juice of 1 lime
- 1-lb. shrimp, peeled and deveined
- ½ cup coconut cream
- ½ lb. broccoli florets
- 1 tbsp. parsley, chopped

**Directions:**
1. Heat a pot with the oil over medium heat; add the onion and sauté for 5 minutes. Add the shrimp and the other ingredients; simmer over medium heat for 20 minutes more. Ladle the soup into bowls and serve.

**Nutrition:** **Calories:** 220 kcal; **Carbs:** 12 g; **Fat:** 7 g; **Protein:** 26 g; **Sodium:** 577 mg

## 182. Coconut Turkey Mix

**Preparation time:** 10 minutes
**Cooking time:** 30 minutes
**Servings:** 4
**Ingredients:**
- 1 yellow onion, chopped
- 1-lb. turkey breast, skinless, boneless, and cubed
- 2 tbsp. olive oil
- 2 garlic cloves, minced
- 1 zucchini, sliced
- 1 cup coconut cream
- A pinch sea salt
- black pepper

**Directions:**
1. Bring the pan to medium heat, add the onion and the garlic and sauté for 5 minutes. Put the meat and brown within 5 minutes more.
2. Add the rest of the ingredients, toss, bring to a simmer and cook over medium heat for 20 minutes more.
3. Serve for lunch.

**Nutrition:** **Calories:** 200 kcal; **Fat:** 4 g; **Fiber:** 2 g; **Carbs:** 14 g; **Protein:** 7 g; **Sodium:** 111 mg

## 183. Lime Shrimp and Kale

**Preparation time:** 10 minutes
**Cooking time:** 20 minutes
**Servings:** 4
**Ingredients:**
- 1-lb. shrimp, peeled and deveined
- 4 scallions, chopped
- 1 tsp. sweet paprika
- 1 tbsp. olive oil
- Juice of 1 lime
- Zest of 1 lime, grated
- A pinch of salt and black pepper
- 2 tbsp. parsley, chopped

**Directions:**
1. Bring the pan to medium heat; add the scallions and sauté for 5 minutes.
2. Add the shrimp and the other ingredients, toss, cook over medium heat for 15 minutes more, divide into bowls and serve.

**Nutrition:** **Calories:** 149; **Carbs:** 12g; **Fat:** 4g; **Protein:** 21g; **Sodium:** 250 mg

## 184. Parsley Cod Mix

**Preparation time:** 10 minutes
**Cooking time:** 20 minutes
**Servings:** 4
**Ingredients:**
- 1 tbsp. olive oil
- 2 shallots, chopped
- 4 cod fillets, boneless and skinless
- 2 garlic cloves, minced
- 2 tbsp. lemon juice
- 1 cup chicken stock
- A pinch salt and black pepper

**Directions:**
1. Bring the pan to medium heat -high heat, add the shallots and the garlic and sauté for 5 minutes.

2. Add the cod and the other ingredients, cook everything for 15 minutes more, divide between plates and serve for lunch.

**Nutrition: Calories:** 216 kcal; **Carbs:** 7 g; **Fat:** 5 g; **Protein:** 34 g; **Sodium:** 380 mg

## 185. Salmon and Cabbage Mix

**Preparation time:** 5 minutes
**Cooking time:** 25 minutes
**Servings:** 4
**Ingredients:**
- 4 salmon fillets, boneless
- 1 yellow onion, chopped
- 2 tbsp. olive oil
- 1 cup red cabbage, shredded
- 1 red bell pepper, chopped
- 1 tbsp. rosemary, chopped
- 1 tbsp. coriander, ground
- 1 cup tomato sauce
- A pinch sea salt
- Black pepper

**Directions:**
1. Bring the pan to medium heat; add the onion and sauté for 5 minutes. Put the fish and sear it within 2 minutes on each side. Add the cabbage and the remaining ingredients, toss, cook over medium heat for 20 minutes more, divide between plates and serve.

**Nutrition: Calories:** 130 kcal; **Carbs:** 8 g; **Fat:** 6 g; **Protein:** 12 g; **Sodium:** 345 mg

## 186. Decent Beef and Onion Stew

**Preparation time:** 10 minutes
**Cooking time:** 1-2 hours
**Servings:** 4
**Ingredients:**
- 2 lb. lean beef, cubed
- 3 lb. shallots, peeled
- 5 garlic cloves, peeled, whole
- 3 tbsp. tomato paste
- 1 bay leaves
- ¼ cup olive oil
- 3 tbsp. lemon juice

**Directions:**
1. Take a stew pot and place it over medium heat.
2. Add olive oil and let it heat up.
3. Add meat and brown.
4. Add remaining ingredients and cover with water.
5. Bring the whole mix to a boil.
6. Reduce heat to low and cover the pot.
7. Simmer for 1-2 hours until beef is cooked thoroughly. Serve hot!

**Nutrition: Calories:** 136 kcal; **Fat:** 3 g; **Carbohydrates:** 0.9 g; **Protein:** 24 g

## 187. Clean Parsley and Chicken Breast

**Preparation time:** 10 minutes
**Cooking time:** 40 minutes
**Servings:** 2
**Ingredients:**
- ½ tbsp. dry parsley
- ½ tbsp. dry basil
- 2 chicken breast halves, boneless and skinless
- ¼ tsp. sunflower seeds
- ¼ tsp. red pepper flakes, crushed
- 1 tomato, sliced

**Directions:**
1. Preheat your oven to 350°F.
2. Take a 9x13 inch baking dish and grease it up with cooking spray.
3. Sprinkle 1 tbsp. of parsley, 1 tsp. of basil and spread the mixture over your baking dish.
4. Arrange the chicken breast halves over the dish and sprinkle garlic slices on top.
5. Take a small bowl and add 1 tsp. parsley, 1 tsp. of basil, sunflower seeds, basil, and red pepper and mix well. Pour the mixture over the chicken breast.
6. Top with tomato slices and cover, bake for 25 minutes. Remove the cover and bake for 15 minutes more.
7. Serve and enjoy!

**Nutrition: Calories:** 150 kcal; **Fat:** 4 g; **Carbohydrates:** 4 g; **Protein:** 25 g

## 188. Zucchini Beef Sauté with Coriander Greens

**Preparation time:** 10 minutes
**Cooking time:** 10 minutes
**Servings:** 4
**Ingredients:**
- 10 oz. beef, sliced into 1-2 inch strips
- 1 zucchini, cut into 2-inch strips
- ¼ cup parsley, chopped
- 3 garlic cloves, minced
- 2 tbsp. tamari sauce
- 4 tbsp. avocado oil

**Directions:**
1. Add 2 tbsp. avocado oil in a frying pan over high heat.

2. Place strips of beef and brown for a few minutes on high heat.
3. Once the meat is brown, add zucchini strips and sauté until tender.
4. Once tender, add tamari sauce, garlic, parsley and let them sit for a few minutes more.
5. Serve immediately and enjoy!

**Nutrition: Calories:** 500 kcal; **Fat:** 40 g; **Carbohydrates:** 5 g; **Protein:** 31 g

### 189. Hearty Lemon and Pepper Chicken

**Preparation time:** 5 minutes
**Cooking time:** 15 minutes
**Servings:** 4
**Ingredients:**
- 2 tsp. olive oil
- 1 ¼ lb. chicken cutlets, skinless
- 2 whole eggs
- ¼ cup panko crumbs
- 1 tbsp. lemon pepper
- Sunflower seeds and pepper to taste
- 3 cups green beans
- ¼ cup parmesan cheese
- ¼ tsp. garlic powder

**Directions:**
1. Preheat your oven to 425°F.
2. Take a bowl and stir in seasoning, parmesan, lemon pepper, garlic powder, panko.
3. Whisk eggs in another bowl.
4. Coat cutlets in eggs and press into panko mix.
5. Transfer coated chicken to a parchment lined baking sheet.
6. Toss the beans in oil, pepper, add sunflower seeds, and lay them on the side of the baking sheet.
7. Bake for 15 minutes.
8. Enjoy!

**Nutrition:** Calorie: 299 kcal; **Fat:** 10 g; **Carbohydrates:** 10 g; **Protein:** 43 g

### 190. Walnuts and Asparagus Delight

**Preparation time:** 5 minutes
**Cooking time:** 5 minutes
**Servings:** 4
**Ingredients:**
- 1 ½ tbsp. olive oil
- ¾ lb. asparagus, trimmed
- ¼ cup walnuts, chopped
- Sunflower seeds and pepper to taste

**Directions:**
1. Place a skillet over medium heat, add olive oil and let it heat up.
2. Add asparagus, sauté for 5 minutes until browned.
3. Season with sunflower seeds and pepper.
4. Remove heat.
5. Add walnuts and toss.
6. Serve warm!

**Nutrition: Calories:** 124 kcal; **Fat:** 12 g; **Carbohydrates:** 2 g; **Protein:** 3 g

### 191. Healthy Carrot Chips

**Preparation time:** 10 minutes
**Cooking time:** 10 minutes
**Servings:** 4
**Ingredients:**
- 3 cups carrots, sliced paper-thin rounds
- 2 tbsp. olive oil
- 2 tsp. cumin, ground
- ½ tsp. paprika, smoked
- Pinch sunflower seeds

**Directions:**
1. Preheat your oven to 400°F.
2. Slice carrots into paper-thin shaped coins using a peeler.
3. Place slices in a bowl and toss with oil and spices.
4. Layout the slices on a parchment paper, lined baking sheet in a single layer.
5. Sprinkle sunflower seeds.
6. Transfer to oven and bake for 8-10 minutes.
7. Remove and serve.
8. Enjoy!

**Nutrition: Calories:** 434 kcal; **Fat:** 35 g; **Carbohydrates:** 31 g; **Protein:** 2 g

### 192. Beef Soup

**Preparation time:** 10 minutes
**Cooking time:** 40 minutes
**Servings:** 4
**Ingredients:**
- 1 lb. beef, lean, and ground
- 1 cup mixed vegetables, frozen
- 1 yellow onion, chopped
- 6 cups vegetable broth
- 1 cup low-fat cream
- Pepper, to taste

**Directions:**
1. Take a stockpot and add all the ingredients except heavy cream, salt, and black pepper.
2. Bring to a boil.

3. Reduce heat to simmer.
4. Cook for 40 minutes.
5. Once cooked, warm the heavy cream.
6. Then add once the soup is cooked.
7. Blend the soup till smooth by using an immersion blender.
8. Season with salt and black pepper.
9. Serve and enjoy!

**Nutrition: Calories:** 270 kcal; **Fat:** 14 g; **Carbohydrates:** 6 g; **Protein:** 29 g

## 193. Amazing Grilled Chicken and Blueberry Salad

**Preparation time:** 10 minutes
**Cooking time:** 25 minutes
**Servings:** 5
**Ingredients:**
- 5 cups mixed greens
- 1 cup blueberries
- ¼ cup almonds, slivered
- 2 cups chicken breasts, cooked and cubed

**For dressing:**
- ¼ cup olive oil
- ¼ cup apple cider vinegar
- ¼ cup blueberries
- 2 tbsp. honey
- Sunflower seeds and pepper to taste

**Directions:**
1. Take a bowl and add greens, berries, almonds, chicken cubes and mix well.
2. Take a bowl and mix the dressing ingredients, pour the mix into a blender, and blitz until smooth. Add dressing on top of the chicken cubes and toss well.
3. Season more and enjoy!

**Nutrition: Calories:** 266 kcal; **Fat:** 17 g; **Carbohydrates:** 18 g; **Protein:** 10 g

## 194. Clean Chicken and Mushroom Stew

**Preparation time:** 10 minutes
**Cooking time:** 35 minutes
**Servings:** 4
**Ingredients:**
- 4 chicken breast halves, cut into bite sized pieces
- 1 lb. mushrooms, sliced (5-6 cups)
- 1 bunch spring onion, chopped
- 4 tbsp. olive oil
- 1 tsp. thyme
- Sunflower seeds and pepper as needed

**Directions:**
1. Take a large deep frying pan and place it over medium-high heat.
2. Add oil and let it heat up.
3. Add chicken and cook for 4–5 minutes per side until slightly browned.
4. Add spring onions and mushrooms, season with sunflower seeds and pepper according to your taste.
5. Stir. Cover with lid and bring the mix to a boil. Reduce heat and simmer for 25 minutes. Serve!

**Nutrition: Calories:** 247 kcal; **Fat:** 12 g; **Carbohydrates:** 10 g; **Protein:** 23 g

## 195. Elegant Pumpkin Chili Dish

**Preparation time:** 10 minutes
**Cooking time:** 15 minutes
**Servings:** 4
**Ingredients:**
- 3 cups yellow onion, chopped
- 8 garlic cloves, chopped
- 1 lb. turkey, ground
- 2 cans (15 oz. each) fire-roasted tomatoes - 2 cups pumpkin puree
- 1 cup chicken broth
- 4 tsp. chili spice
- 1 tsp. cinnamon, ground
- 1 tsp. sea sunflower seeds

**Directions:**
1. Take a large-sized pot and place it over medium-high heat.
2. Add coconut oil and let the oil heat up.
3. Add onion and garlic, sauté for 5 minutes.
4. Add ground turkey and break it while cooking, cook for 5 minutes.
5. Add remaining ingredients and bring the mix to simmer.
6. Simmer for 15 minutes over low heat (lid off). Pour chicken broth.
7. Serve with desired salad. Enjoy!

**Nutrition: Calories:** 312 kcal; **Fat:** 16 g; **Carbohydrates:** 14 g; **Protein:** 27 g

## 196. Tasty Roasted Broccoli

**Preparation time:** 5 minutes
**Cooking time:** 20 minutes
**Servings:** 4
**Ingredients:**
- 4 cups broccoli florets
- 1 tbsp. olive oil
- Sunflower seeds and pepper to taste

**Directions:**
1. Preheat your oven to 400°F.
2. Add broccoli in a zip bag alongside oil and shake until coated.
3. Add seasoning and shake again.
4. Spread broccoli out on a baking sheet, bake for 20 minutes.
5. Let it cool and serve.
6. Enjoy!

**Nutrition: Calories:** 62 kcal; **Fat:** 4 g; **Carbohydrates:** 4 g; **Protein:** 4 g

### 197. The Almond Breaded Chicken Goodness

**Preparation time:** 15 minutes
**Cooking time:** 15 minutes
**Servings:** 3
**Ingredients:**
- 2 large chicken breasts, boneless and skinless
- ⅓ cup lemon juice
- 1 ½ cups seasoned almond meal
- 2 tbsp. coconut oil
- Lemon pepper, to taste
- Parsley, for decoration

**Directions:**
1. Slice chicken breast in half. Lb. out each half until ¼ inch thick. Take a pan and place it over medium heat, add oil, and heat it up.
2. Dip each chicken breast slice into lemon juice and let it sit for 2 minutes.
3. Turn over, and let the other side sit for 2 minutes as well.
4. Transfer to almond meal and coat both sides.
5. Add coated chicken to the oil and fry for 4 minutes per side, making sure to sprinkle lemon pepper liberally.
6. Transfer to a paper-lined sheet and repeat until all chicken is fried.
7. Garnish with parsley and enjoy!

**Nutrition: Calories:** 325 kcal; **Fat:** 24 g; **Carbohydrates:** 3 g; **Protein:** 16 g

### 198. South-Western Pork Chops

**Preparation time:** 10 minutes
**Cooking time:** 15 minutes
**Servings:** 4
**Ingredients:**
- Cooking spray as needed
- 4-oz. pork loin chop, boneless and fat rimmed
- ⅓ cup salsa
- 2 tbsp. fresh lime juice
- ¼ cup fresh cilantro, chopped

**Directions:**
1. Take a large-sized non-stick skillet and spray it with cooking spray.
2. Heat until hot over high heat.
3. Press the chops with your palm to flatten them slightly.
4. Add them to the skillet and cook for 1 minute for each side until they are nicely browned.
5. Lower the heat to medium-low.
6. Combine the salsa and lime juice.
7. Pour the mix over the chops.
8. Simmer uncovered for about 8 minutes until the chops are perfectly done.
9. If needed, sprinkle some cilantro on top.
10. Serve!

**Nutrition: Calories:** 184 kcal; **Fat:** 4 g; **Carbohydrates:** 4 g; **Protein:** 0.5 g

### 199. Almond butter Pork Chops

**Preparation time:** 5 minutes
**Cooking time:** 25 minutes
**Servings:** 2
**Ingredients:**
- 1 tbsp. almond butter, divided
- 2 pork chops, boneless
- Pepper to taste
- 1 tbsp. Italian seasoning, dried, low-fat, and low-sodium
- 1 tbsp. olive oil

**Directions:**
1. Preheat your oven to 350 °F.
2. Pat pork chops dry with a paper towel, and place them in a baking dish.
3. Season with pepper, and Italian seasoning.
4. Drizzle olive oil over pork chops.
5. Top each chop with ½ tbsp. almond butter.
6. Bake for 25 minutes.
7. Transfer pork chops on 2 plates and top with almond butter juice.
8. Serve and enjoy!

**Nutrition: Calories:** 333 kcal; **Fat:** 23 g; **Carbohydrates:** 1 g; **Protein:** 31 g

### 200. Chicken Salsa

**Preparation time:** 4 minutes
**Cooking time:** 14 minutes
**Servings:** 1
**Ingredients:**
- 2 chicken breasts
- 1 cup salsa
- 1 taco seasoning mix
- 1 cup plain Greek Yogurt

- ½ cup kite ricotta/cashew cheese, cubed

**Directions:**
1. Take a skillet and place over medium heat.
2. Add chicken breast, ½ cup of salsa, and taco seasoning.
3. Mix well and cook for 12-15 minutes until the chicken is done.
4. Take the chicken out and cube them.
5. Place the cubes on a toothpick and top with cheddar.
6. Place yogurt and remaining salsa in cups and use as dips.
7. Enjoy!

**Nutrition: Calories:** 359 kcal; **Fat:** 14 g; **Net Carbohydrates:** 14 g; **Protein:** 43 g

## 201. Healthy Mediterranean Lamb Chops

**Preparation time:** 10 minutes
**Cooking time:** 10 minutes
**Servings:** 4
**Ingredients:**

- 4 lamb shoulder chops (8 oz8. each)
- 2 tbsp. Dijon mustard
- 2 tbsp. Balsamic vinegar
- ½ cup olive oil
- 2 tbsp. fresh basil, shredded

**Directions:**
1. Pat your lamb chop dry using a kitchen towel and arrange them on a shallow glass baking dish.
2. Take a bowl and whisk in Dijon mustard, balsamic vinegar, pepper, and mix them well.
3. Whisk in the oil very slowly into the marinade until the mixture is smooth.
4. Stir in basil.
5. Pour the marinade over the lamb chops and stir to coat both sides well.
6. Cover the chops and allow them to marinate for 1-4 hours (chilled).
7. Take the chops out and leave them for 30 minutes to allow the temperature to reach a normal level.
8. Preheat your grill to medium heat and add oil to the grate.
9. Grill the lamb chops for 5-10 minutes per side until both sides are browned.
10. Once the center reads 145 °F, the chops are ready, serve and enjoy!

**Nutrition: Calories:** 521 kcal; **Fat:** 45 g; **Carbohydrates:** 3.5 g; **Protein:** 22 g

## 202. Amazing Sesame Breadsticks

**Preparation time:** 10 minutes
**Cooking time:** 20 minutes
**Servings:** 5
**Ingredients:**

- 1 egg white
- 2 tbsp. almond flour
- 1 tsp. Himalayan pink sunflower seeds
- 1 tbsp. extra-virgin olive oil
- ½ tsp. sesame seeds

**Directions:**
1. Preheat your oven to 320°F.
2. Line a baking sheet with parchment paper and keep it on the side.
3. Take a bowl and whisk in egg whites, add flour and half of sunflower seeds and olive oil.
4. Knead until you have a smooth dough.
5. Divide into 4 pieces and roll into breadsticks.
6. Place on prepared sheet and brush with olive oil, sprinkle sesame seeds and remaining sunflower seeds.
7. Bake for 20 minutes.
8. Serve and enjoy!

**Nutrition: Total Carbs:** 1.1 g; **Fiber:** 1 g; **Protein:** 1.6 g; **Fat:** 5 g

## 203. Brown Butter Duck Breast

**Preparation time:** 5 minutes
**Cooking time:** 25 minutes
**Servings:** 3
**Ingredients:**

- 1 whole duck breast (6 oz.), skin on
- Pepper to taste
- 1 head radicchio (4 oz.), core removed
- ¼ cup butter, unsalted
- 6 fresh sage leaves, sliced

**Directions:**
1. Preheat your oven to 400°F.
2. Pat duck breast dry with a paper towel.
3. Season with pepper.
4. Place duck breast in skillet and place it over medium heat; sear for 3-4 minutes on each side.
5. Turn the breast over and transfer the skillet to the oven.
6. Roast for 10 minutes (uncovered).
7. Cut radicchio in half.
8. Remove and discard the woody white core and thinly slice the leaves.
9. Keep them on the side.
10. Remove skillet from oven.

11. Transfer the duck breast, fat side up to the cutting board, and let it rest.
12. Re-heat your skillet over medium heat.
13. Add unsalted butter, sage and cook for 3-4 minutes.
14. Cut the duck into 6 equal slices.
15. Divide radicchio between 2 plates, top with slices of duck breast, and drizzle browned butter and sage. Enjoy!

**Nutrition:** Calories: 393 kcal; **Fat:** 33 g; Carbohydrates: 2 g; **Protein:** 22 g

## 204. Generous Garlic Bread Stick

**Preparation time:** 15 minutes
**Cooking time:** 15 minutes
**Servings:** 8
**Ingredients:**
- ¼ cup almond butter, softened
- 1 tsp. garlic powder
- 2 cups almond flour
- ½ tbsp. baking powder
- 1 tbsp. Psyllium husk powder
- ¼ tsp. sunflower seeds
- 3 tbsp. almond butter, melted
- 1 egg
- ¼ cup boiling water

**Directions:**
1. Preheat your oven to 400°F.
2. Line the baking sheet with parchment paper and keep it on the side.
3. Beat almond butter with garlic powder and keep it on the side.
4. Add almond flour, baking powder, husk, sunflower seeds in a bowl and mix in almond butter and egg, mix well.
5. Pour boiling water into the mix and stir until you have a nice dough.
6. Divide the dough into 8 balls and roll into breadsticks.
7. Place on a baking sheet and bake for 15 minutes. Brush each stick with garlic almond butter and bake for 5 minutes more. Serve and enjoy!

**Nutrition:** Total Carbs: 7 g; **Fiber:** 2 g; **Protein:** 7 g; **Fat:** 24 g

## 205. Cauliflower Bread Stick

**Preparation time:** 10 minutes
**Cooking time:** 48 minutes
**Servings:** 5
**Ingredients:**
- 1 cup cashew cheese/ kite ricotta cheese
- 1 tbsp. organic almond butter
- 1 whole egg
- ½ tsp. Italian seasoning
- ¼ tsp. red pepper flakes
- ⅛ tsp. Kosher sunflower seeds
- 2 cups cauliflower rice, cooked for 3 minutes in the microwave
- 3 tsp. garlic, minced
- Parmesan cheese, grated

**Directions:**
1. Preheat your oven to 350°F.
2. Add almond butter to a small pan and melt over low heat
3. Add red pepper flakes, garlic to the almond butter and cook for 2–3 minutes.
4. Add garlic and almond butter mix to the bowl with cooked cauliflower and add the Italian seasoning.
5. Season with sunflower seeds and mix; refrigerate for 10 minutes.
6. Add cheese and eggs to the bowl and mix.
7. Place a layer of parchment paper at the bottom of a 9x9 baking dish and grease with cooking spray; add egg and mozzarella cheese mix to the cauliflower mix.
8. Add mix to the pan and smooth to a thin layer with the palms of your hand.
9. Bake for 30 minutes, take out from the oven, and top with a few shakes of parmesan and mozzarella.
10. Cook for 8 minutes more.
11. Enjoy!

**Nutrition:** Total Carbs: 11.5 g; **Fiber:** 2 g; **Protein:** 10.7 g; **Fat:** 20 g

## 206. Bacon and Chicken Garlic Wrap

**Preparation time:** 15 minutes
**Cooking time:** 10 minutes
**Servings:** 4
**Ingredients:**
- 1 chicken fillet, cut into small cubes
- 8–9 thin slices bacon, cut to fit cubes
- 6 garlic cloves, minced

**Directions:**
1. Preheat your oven to 400°F.
2. Line a baking tray with aluminum foil.
3. Add minced garlic to a bowl and rub each chicken piece with it.
4. Wrap a bacon piece around each garlic chicken bite.
5. Secure with a toothpick.

6. Transfer bites to baking sheet, keeping a little bit of space between them.
7. Bake for about 15-20 minutes until crispy.
8. Serve and enjoy!

**Nutrition: Calories:** 260 kcal; **Fat:** 19 g; **Carbohydrates:** 5 g; **Protein:** 22 g

### 207. Chipotle Lettuce Chicken

**Preparation time:** 10 minutes
**Cooking time:** 25 minutes
**Servings:** 6
**Ingredients:**
- 1 lb. chicken breast, cut into strips
- Splash olive oil
- 1 red onion, finely sliced
- 14 oz. tomatoes
- 1 tsp. chipotle, chopped
- ½ tsp. cumin
- Lettuce as needed
- Fresh coriander leaves
- Jalapeno chilies, sliced
- Fresh tomato slices for garnish
- Lime wedges

**Directions:**
1. Take a non-stick frying pan and place it over medium heat.
2. Add oil and heat it up.
3. Add chicken and cook until brown.
4. Keep the chicken on the side.
5. Add tomatoes, sugar, chipotle, cumin to the same pan and simmer for 25 minutes until you have a nice sauce.
6. Add chicken into the sauce and cook for 5 minutes.
7. Transfer the mix to another place.
8. Use lettuce wraps to take a portion of the mixture and serve with a squeeze of lemon.
9. Enjoy!

**Nutrition: Calories:** 332 kcal; **Fat:** 15 g; **Carbohydrates:** 13 g; **Protein:** 34 g

### 208. Balsamic Chicken and Vegetables

**Preparation time:** 15 minutes
**Cooking time:** 25 minutes
**Servings:** 2
**Ingredients:**
- 4 chicken thigh, boneless and skinless
- 5 stalks asparagus, halved
- 1 pepper, cut in chunks
- ½ red onion, diced
- ½ cup carrots, sliced
- 1 garlic cloves, minced
- 2-oz. mushrooms, diced
- ¼ cup balsamic vinegar
- 1 tbsp. olive oil
- ½ tsp. stevia
- ½ tbsp. oregano
- Sunflower seeds and pepper as needed

**Directions:**
1. Preheat your oven to 425°F.
2. Take a bowl and add all of the vegetables, and mix.
3. Add spices and oil and mix.
4. Dip the chicken pieces into the spice mix and coat them well.
5. Place the veggies and chicken onto a pan in a single layer.
6. Cook for 25 minutes.
7. Serve and enjoy!

**Nutrition:**
**Calories:** 401 kcal; **Fat:** 17 g; **Net Carbohydrates:** 11 g; **Protein:** 48 g

### 209. Exuberant Sweet Potatoes

**Preparation time:** 5 minutes
**Cooking time:** 7-8 hours
**Servings:** 4
**Ingredients:**
- 6 sweet potatoes, washed and dried

**Directions:**
1. Loosely ball up 7-8 pieces of aluminum foil in the bottom of your Slow Cooker, covering about half of the surface area.
2. Prick each potato 6-8 times using a fork.
3. Wrap each potato with foil and seal them.
4. Place wrapped potatoes in the cooker on top of the foil bed.
5. Place lid and cook on LOW for 7-8 hours.
6. Use tongs to remove the potatoes and unwrap them.
7. Serve and enjoy!

**Nutrition: Calories:** 129 kcal; **Fat:** 0 g; **Carbohydrates:** 30 g; **Protein:** 2 g

### 210. The Vegan Lovers Refried Beans

**Preparation time:** 5 minutes
**Cooking time:** 10 hours
**Servings:** 12
**Ingredients:**
- 4 cups vegetable broth
- 4 cups water

- 3 cups pinto beans, dried
- 1 onion, chopped
- 2 jalapeno peppers, minced
- 4 garlic cloves, minced
- 1 tbsp. chili powder
- 2 tsp. cumin, ground
- 1 tsp. sweet paprika
- 1 tsp. salt
- ½ tsp. fresh black pepper, ground

**Directions**:
1. Add the listed ingredients to your Slow Cooker.
2. Cover and cook on HIGH for 10 hours.
3. If there's any extra liquid, ladle the liquid up and reserve it in a bowl.
4. Use an immersion blender to blend the mixture (in the Slow Cooker) until smooth.
5. Add the reserved liquid.
6. Serve hot and enjoy!

**Nutrition: Calories:** 91 kcal, **Fat:** 0 g; **Carbohydrates:** 16 g; **Protein:** 5 g

### 211. Cool Apple and Carrot Harmony

**Preparation time:** 10 minutes
**Cooking time:** 10 minutes
**Servings:** 6
**Ingredients:**

- 1 cup apple juice
- 1 lb. baby carrots
- 1 tbsp. cornstarch
- 1 tbsp. mint, chopped

**Directions**:
1. Add apple juice, carrots, cornstarch, and mint to your Instant Pot.
2. Stir and lock the lid.
3. Cook on HIGH pressure for 10 minutes.
4. Perform a quick release.
5. Divide the mix amongst plates and serve.
6. Enjoy!

**Nutrition: Calories:** 161 kcal; **Fat:** 2 g; **Carbohydrates:** 9 g; **Protein:** 8 g

### 212. Mac and Chokes

**Preparation time:** 5 minutes
**Cooking time:** 20 minutes
**Servings:** 6
**Ingredients:**

- 1 tbsp. olive oil
- 1 large-sized onion, diced
- 10 minced garlic cloves
- 1 can artichoke hearts
- 1 lb. macaroni shells, uncooked
- 12 oz. baby spinach
- 4 cups vegetable broth
- 1 tsp. red pepper flakes
- 4 oz. vegan cheese
- ¼ cup cashew cream

**Directions**:
1. Set the pot to Sauté mode and add oil, allow the oil to heat up, and add onions.
2. Cook for 2 minutes.
3. Add garlic and stir well.
4. Add artichoke hearts and sauté for 1 minute more.
5. Add uncooked pasta and 3 cups of broth alongside 2 cups of water.
6. Mix well.
7. Lock the lid and cook on HIGH pressure for 4 minutes.
8. Quick-release the pressure.
9. Open the pot and stir.
10. Add extra water, fold in spinach and cook on Sauté mode for a few minutes.
11. Add cashew cream and grated vegan cheese.
12. Add pepper flakes and mix well.
13. Enjoy!

**Nutrition: Calories:** 649 kcal; **Fat:** 29 g; **Carbohydrates:** 64 g; **Protein:** 34 g

### 213. Black Eyed Peas and Spinach Platter

**Preparation time:** 10 minutes
**Cooking time:** 8 hours
**Servings:** 4
**Ingredients:**

- 1 cup black-eyed peas, soaked overnight, and drained
- 2 cups low-sodium vegetable broth
- 1 can (15 oz.) tomatoes, diced with juice
- 8 oz. ham, chopped
- 1 onion, chopped
- 2 garlic cloves, minced
- 1 tsp. oregano, dried
- 1 tsp. salt
- ½ tsp. black pepper, freshly ground
- ½ tsp. mustard, ground
- 1 bay leaf

**Directions**:
1. Add the listed ingredients to your Slow Cooker and stir.
2. Place lid and cook on LOW for 8 hours.
3. Discard the bay leaf.

4. Serve and enjoy!

**Nutrition: Calories:** 209 kcal; **Fat:** 6 g; **Carbohydrates:** 22 g; **Protein:** 17 g

## 214. Humble Mushroom Rice

**Preparation time:** 10 minutes
**Cooking time:** 3 hours
**Servings:** 3
**Ingredients:**

- ½ cup rice
- 2 green onions chopped
- 1 garlic clove, minced
- ¼ lb. baby Portobello mushrooms, sliced
- 1 cup vegetable stock

**Directions:**

1. Add rice, onions, garlic, mushrooms, and stock to your Slow Cooker.
2. Stir well and place the lid.
3. Cook on LOW for 3 hours.
4. Stir and divide amongst serving platters.
5. Enjoy!

**Nutrition: Calories:** 200 kcal; **Fat:** 6 g; **Carbohydrates:** 28 g; **Protein:** 5 g

## 215. Sweet and Sour Cabbage and Apples

**Preparation time:** 15 minutes
**Cooking time:** 8 hours
**Servings:** 4
**Ingredients:**

- ¼ cup honey
- ¼ cup apple cider vinegar
- 2 tbsp. Orange Chili-Garlic Sauce
- 1 tsp. sea salt
- 3 sweet-tart apples, peeled, cored, and sliced
- 2 heads green cabbage, cored and shredded
- 1 sweet red onion, thinly sliced

**Directions:**

1. Take a small bowl and whisk in honey, orange-chili garlic sauce, vinegar. Stir well.
2. Add honey mix, apples, onion, and cabbage to your Slow Cooker and stir. Close the lid and cook on LOW for 8 hours. Serve and enjoy!

**Nutrition: Calories:** 164 kcal; **Fat:** 1 g; **Carbohydrates:** 41 g; **Protein:** 4 g

## 216. Delicious Aloo Palak

**Preparation time:** 10 minutes
**Cooking time:** 6-8 hours
**Servings:** 6
**Ingredients:**

- 2 lb. red potatoes, chopped
- 1 small onion, diced
- 1 red bell pepper, seeded and diced
- ¼ cup fresh cilantro, chopped
- ⅓ cup low-sodium veggie broth
- 1 tsp. salt
- ½ tsp. Garam masala
- ½ tsp. cumin, ground
- ¼ tsp. turmeric, ground
- ¼ tsp. coriander, ground
- ¼ tsp. black pepper, freshly ground
- 2 lb. fresh spinach, chopped

**Directions:**

1. Add potatoes, bell pepper, onion, cilantro, broth, and seasoning to your Slow Cooker.
2. Mix well. Add spinach on top.
3. Place lid and cook on LOW for 6-8 hours.
4. Stir and serve. Enjoy!

**Nutrition: Calories:** 205 kcal; **Fat:** 1 g; **Carbohydrates:** 44 g; **Protein:** 9 g

## 217. Orange and Chili Garlic Sauce

**Preparation time:** 15 minutes
**Cooking time:** 8 hours
**Servings:** 5
**Ingredients:**

- ½ cup apple cider vinegar
- 4 lb. red jalapeno peppers, stems, seeds, and ribs removed, chopped
- 10 garlic cloves, chopped
- ½ cup tomato paste
- Juice of 1 orange zest
- ½ cup honey
- 2 tbsp. soy sauce
- 2 tsp. salt

**Directions:**

1. Add vinegar, garlic, peppers, tomato paste, orange juice, honey, zest, soy sauce, and salt to your Slow Cooker.
2. Stir and close the lid. Cook on LOW for 8 hours. Use as needed!

**Nutrition: Calories:** 33 kcal; **Fat:** 1 g; **Carbohydrates:** 8 g; **Protein:** 1 g

## 218. Tantalizing Mushroom Gravy

**Preparation time:** 5 minutes
**Cooking time:** 5–8 hours
**Servings:** 2
**Ingredients:**

- 1 cup button mushrooms, sliced

- ¾ cup low-fat buttermilk
- ⅓ cup water
- 1 medium onion, finely diced
- 2 garlic cloves, minced
- 2 tbsp. extra virgin olive oil
- 2 tbsp. all-purpose flour
- 1 tbsp. fresh rosemary, minced
- Freshly ground black pepper

**Directions:**
1. Add the listed ingredients to your Slow Cooker.
2. Place the lid and cook on LOW for 5–8 hours.
3. Serve warm and use as needed!

**Nutrition: Calories:** 54 kcal; **Fat:** 4 g; **Carbohydrates:** 4 g; **Protein:** 2 g

---

## 219. Everyday Vegetable Stock

**Preparation time:** 5 minutes
**Cooking time:** 8–12 hours
**Servings:** 10
**Ingredients:**
- 2 celery stalks (with leaves), quartered
- 4 oz. mushrooms, with stems
- 2 carrots, unpeeled and quartered
- 1 onion, unpeeled, quartered from pole to pole
- 1 garlic head, unpeeled, halved across the middle
- 2 fresh thyme sprigs
- 10 peppercorns
- ½ tsp. salt
- Enough water to fill 3 quarters of Slow Cooker

**Directions:**
1. Add celery, mushrooms, onion, carrots, garlic, thyme, salt, peppercorn, and water to your Slow Cooker.
2. Stir and cover.
3. Cook on LOW for 8–12 hours.
4. Strain the stock through a fine-mesh cloth/metal mesh and discard solids.
5. Use as needed.

**Nutrition: Calories:** 38 kcal; **Fat:** 5 g; **Carbohydrates:** 1 g; **Protein:** 0 g

---

## 220. Grilled Chicken with Lemon and Fennel

**Preparation time:** 5 minutes
**Cooking time:** 25 minutes
**Servings:** 4
**Ingredients:**
- 2 cups chicken fillets, cut and skewed
- 1 large fennel bulb - 2 garlic cloves
- 1 jar green olives
- 1 lemon

**Directions:**
1. Preheat your grill to medium-high.
2. Crush garlic cloves.
3. Take a bowl and add olive oil, and season with sunflower seeds and pepper.
4. Coat chicken skewers with the marinade.
5. Transfer them under the grill and grill for 20 minutes, making sure to turn them halfway through until golden.
6. Zest half of the lemon and cut the other half into quarters.
7. Cut the fennel bulb into similarly sized segments.
8. Brush olive oil all over the garlic clove segments and cook for 3-5 minutes.
9. Chop them and add them to the bowl with the marinade.
10. Add lemon zest and olives.
11. Once the meat is ready, serve with the vegetable mix.
12. Enjoy!

**Nutrition: Calories:** 649 kcal; **Fat:** 16 g; **Carbohydrates:** 33 g; **Protein:** 18 g

---

## 221. Caramelized Pork Chops and Onion

**Preparation time:** 5 minutes
**Cooking time:** 40 minutes
**Servings:** 4
**Ingredients:**
- 4-lb. chuck roast
- 4 oz. green Chili, chopped
- 2 tbsp. chili powder
- ½ tsp. oregano, dried
- ½ tsp. cumin, ground
- 2 garlic cloves, minced

**Directions:**
1. Rub the chops with a seasoning of 1 tsp. of pepper and 2 tsp. of sunflower seeds.
2. Take a skillet and place it over medium heat, add oil and allow the oil to heat up
3. Brown the seasoned chop on both sides.
4. Add water and onion to the skillet and cover, lower the heat to low, and simmer for 20 minutes.
5. Turn the chops over and season with more sunflower seeds and pepper.
6. Cover and cook until the water fully evaporates and the beer shows a slightly brown texture.

7. Remove the chops and serve with a topping of the caramelized onion.
8. Serve and enjoy!

**Nutrition:** Calorie: 47 kcal; **Fat:** 4 g; **Carbohydrates:** 4 g; **Protein:** 0.5 g

## 222. Hearty Pork Belly Casserole

**Preparation time:** 5 minutes
**Cooking time:** 25 minutes
**Servings:** 4
**Ingredients:**

- 8 pork belly slices, cut into small pieces
- 3 large onions, chopped
- 4 tbsp. lemon
- Juice of 1 lemon
- Seasoning, as you needed

**Directions:**

1. Take a large pressure cooker and place it over medium heat.
2. Add onions and sweat them for 5 minutes.
3. Add pork belly slices and cook until the meat browns and onions become golden.
4. Cover with water and add honey, lemon zest, sunflower seeds, pepper, and close the pressure seal.
5. Pressure cook for 40 minutes.
6. Serve and enjoy with a garnish of fresh chopped parsley if you prefer.

**Nutrition: Calories:** 753 kcal; **Fat:** 41 g; **Carbohydrates:** 68 g; **Protein:** 30 g

## 223. Apple Pie Crackers

**Preparation time:** 10 minutes
**Cooking time:** 120 minutes
**Servings:** 100 crackers
**Ingredients:**

- 2 tbsp. + 2 tsp. avocado oil
- 1 medium Granny Smith apple, roughly chopped
- ¼ cup Erythritol
- ¼ cup sunflower seeds, ground
- 1 ¾ cups flax seeds, roughly ground
- ⅛ tsp. cloves, ground
- ⅛ tsp. cardamom, ground
- 3 tbsp. nutmeg
- ¼ tsp. ginger, ground

**Directions:**

1. Preheat your oven to 225°F.
2. Line 2 baking sheets with parchment paper and keep them on the side.
3. Add oil, apple, Erythritol to a bowl and mix.
4. Transfer to a food processor and add remaining ingredients, process until combined.
5. Transfer batter to baking sheets, spread evenly, and cut into crackers.
6. Bake for 1 hour, flip and bake for another hour.
7. Let them cool and serve.
8. Enjoy!

**Nutrition: Total Carbs:** 0.9 g (%); **Fiber:** 0.5 g; **Protein:** 0.4 g (%); **Fat:** 2.1 g (%)

# CHAPTER 9:
# Poultry

### 224. Lemon Garlic Chicken
**Preparation time:** 15 minutes
**Cooking time:** 12 minutes
**Servings:** 3
**Ingredients:**
- 3 chicken breasts, cut into thin slices
- 2 lemon zest, grated
- ¼ cup olive oil
- 4 garlic cloves, minced
- Pepper
- Salt

**Directions:**
1. Warm-up the olive oil in a pan over medium heat. Add garlic to the pan and sauté for 30 seconds.
2. Put the chicken in the pan and sauté within 10 minutes. Add lemon zest and lemon juice and bring to boil. Remove from heat and season with pepper and salt.
3. Serve and enjoy.

**Nutrition: Calories:** 439 kcal; **Fat:** 27.8 g; **Protein:** 42.9 g; **Carbs:** 4.9 g; **Sodium:** 306 mg

### 225. Simple Mediterranean Chicken
**Preparation time:** 15 minutes
**Cooking time:** 15 minutes
**Servings:** 12
**Ingredients:**
- 2 chicken breasts, skinless and boneless
- 1 ½ cup grape tomatoes, cut in half
- ½ cup olives
- 2 tbsp. olive oil
- 1 tsp. Italian seasoning
- ¼ tsp. pepper
- ¼ tsp. salt

**Directions:**
1. Season chicken with Italian seasoning, pepper, and salt. Warm-up olive oil in a pan over medium heat. Add season chicken to the pan and cook for 4-6 minutes on each side. Transfer chicken on a plate.
2. Put tomatoes plus olives in the pan and cook for 2-4 minutes. Pour olive and tomato mixture on top of the chicken and serve.

**Nutrition: Calories:** 468 kcal; **Fat:** 29.4 g; **Protein:** 43.8 g; **Carbs:** 7.8 g; **Sodium:** 410 mg

### 226. Roasted Chicken Thighs

**Preparation time:** 15 minutes
**Cooking time:** 55 minutes
**Servings:** 4
**Ingredients:**
- 8 chicken thighs
- 3 tbsp. fresh parsley, chopped
- 1 tsp. oregano, dried
- 6 garlic cloves, crushed
- ¼ cup capers, drained
- 10 oz. red peppers, roasted and sliced
- 2 cups grape tomatoes
- 1 ½ lb. potatoes, cut into small chunks
- 4 tbsp. olive oil - Pepper - Salt

**Directions:**
1. Warm oven to 200°/400°F. Season chicken with pepper and salt. Heat up 2 tbsp. of olive oil in a pan over medium heat. Add chicken to the pan and sear until lightly golden brown from all the sides.
2. Transfer chicken onto a baking tray. Add tomato, potatoes, capers, oregano, garlic, and red peppers around the chicken. Season with pepper and salt and drizzle with remaining olive oil. Bake in preheated oven for 45–55 minutes. Garnish with parsley and serve.

**Nutrition: Calories:** 848 kcal; **Fat:** 29.1 g; **Protein:** 91.3 g; **Carbs:** 45.2 g; **Sodium:** 110 mg

### 227. Mediterranean Turkey Breast

**Preparation time:** 15 minutes
**Cooking time:** 4 minutes and 30 minutes
**Servings:** 6
**Ingredients:**
- 4 lb. turkey breast
- 3 tbsp. flour
- ¾ cup chicken stock
- 4 garlic cloves, chopped
- 1 tsp. oregano, dried
- ½ fresh lemon juice
- ½ cup tomatoes, sun-dried and chopped
- ½ cup olives, chopped
- 1 onion, chopped
- ¼ tsp. pepper
- ½ tsp. salt

**Directions:**
1. Add turkey breast, garlic, oregano, lemon juice, sun-dried tomatoes, olives, onion, pepper, and salt to the slow cooker. Add half stock. Cook on high within 4 hours.
2. Whisk remaining stock and flour in a small bowl and add to slow cooker. Cover and cook for 30 minutes more. Serve and enjoy.

**Nutrition: Calories:** 537 kcal; **Fat:** 9.7 g; **Protein:** 79.1 g; **Carbs:** 29.6 g; **Sodium:** 330 mg

### 228. Olive Capers Chicken

**Preparation time:** 15 minutes
**Cooking time:** 16 minutes
**Servings:** 4
**Ingredients:**
- 2 lb. chicken
- ⅓ cup chicken stock
- oz. capers
- 6 oz. olives
- ¼ cup fresh basil
- 1 tbsp. olive oil
- 1 tsp. oregano
- 2 garlic cloves, minced
- 2 tbsp. red wine vinegar
- ⅛ tsp. pepper
- ¼ tsp. salt

**Directions:**
1. Put olive oil in your instant pot and set the pot on sauté mode. Add chicken to the pot and sauté for 3-4 minutes. Add remaining ingredients and stir well. Seal pot with the lid and select manual and set timer for 12 minutes. Serve and enjoy.

**Nutrition: Calories:** 433 kcal; **Fat:** 15.2 g; **Protein:** 66.9 g; **Carbs:** 4.8 g; **Sodium:** 244 mg

### 229. Chicken with Mushrooms

**Preparation time:** 15 minutes
**Cooking time:** 6 hours and 10 minutes
**Servings:** 2
**Ingredients:**
- 2 chicken breasts, skinless and boneless
- 1 cup mushrooms, sliced
- 1 onion, sliced
- 1 cup chicken stock
- ½ tsp. thyme, dried
- Pepper
- Salt

**Directions**:
1. Add all ingredients to the slow cooker. Cook on low within 6 hours. Serve and enjoy.

**Nutrition: Calories:** 313 kcal; **Fat:** 11.3 g; **Protein:** 44.3 g; **Carbs:** 6.9 g; **Sodium:** 541 mg

### 230. Baked Chicken

**Preparation time:** 15 minutes
**Cooking time:** 35 minutes
**Servings:** 4
**Ingredients:**
- 2 lb. chicken tenders
- 1 large zucchini
- 1 cup grape tomatoes
- 2 tbsp. olive oil
- 3 dill sprigs

**For topping:**
- 2 tbsp. feta cheese, crumbled
- 1 tbsp. olive oil
- 1 tbsp. fresh lemon juice
- 1 tbsp. fresh dill, chopped

**Directions**:
1. Warm oven to 200°C/400°F. Drizzle the olive oil on a baking tray, then place chicken, zucchini, dill, and tomatoes on the tray. Season with salt. Bake chicken within 30 minutes.
2. Meanwhile, in a small bowl, stir all topping ingredients. Place chicken on the serving tray, then top with veggies and discard dill sprigs. Sprinkle topping mixture on top of chicken and vegetables. Serve and enjoy.

**Nutrition: Calories:** 557 kcal; **Fat:** 28.6 g; **Protein:** 67.9 g; **Carbs:** 5.2 g; **Sodium:** 760 mg

### 231. Garlic Pepper Chicken

**Preparation time:** 15 minutes
**Cooking time:** 21 minutes
**Servings:** 2
**Ingredients:**
- 2 chicken breasts, cut into strips
- 2 bell peppers, cut into strips
- 5 garlic cloves, chopped
- 3 tbsp. water
- 2 tbsp. olive oil
- 1 tbsp. paprika
- 2 tsp. black pepper
- ½ tsp. salt

**Directions**:
1. Warm-up the olive oil in a large saucepan over medium heat. Add garlic and sauté for 2-3 minutes. Add peppers and cook for 3 minutes. Add chicken and spices and stir to coat. Add water and stir well. Bring to boil. Cover and simmer for 10-15 minutes. Serve and enjoy.

**Nutrition: Calories:** 462 kcal; **Fat:** 25.7 g; **Protein:** 44.7 g; **Carbs:** 14.8 g; **Sodium:** 720 mg

### 232. Mustard Chicken tenders

**Preparation time:** 15 minutes
**Cooking time:** 20 minutes
**Servings:** 4
**Ingredients:**
- 1 lb. chicken tenders
- 2 tbsp. fresh tarragon, chopped
- ½ cup whole grain mustard
- ½ tsp. paprika
- 1 garlic clove, minced
- ½ oz. fresh lemon juice
- ½ tsp. pepper
- ¼ tsp. Kosher salt

**Directions**:
1. Warm oven to 425°F. Add all ingredients except chicken to the large bowl and mix well. Put the chicken in the bowl, then stir until well coated. Place chicken on a baking dish and cover. Bake within 15-20 minutes. Serve and enjoy.

**Nutrition: Calories:** 242 kcal; **Fat:** 9.5 g; **Protein:** 33.2 g; **Carbs:** 3.1 g; **Sodium:** 240 mg

### 233. Salsa Chicken Chili

**Preparation time:** 15 minutes
**Cooking time:** 20 minutes
**Servings:** 8
**Ingredients:**
- 2 ½ lb. chicken breasts, skinless and boneless
- ½ tsp. cumin powder
- 3 garlic cloves, minced
- 1 onion, diced
- 16 oz. salsa
- 1 tsp. oregano
- 1 tbsp. olive oil

**Directions**:
1. Add oil into the instant pot and set the pot on sauté mode. Add onion to the pot and sauté until softened, about 3 minutes. Add garlic and sauté for a minute. Add oregano and cumin and sauté for a minute.

2. Add half salsa and stir well. Place chicken and pour remaining salsa over chicken.
3. Seal pot with the lid and select manual and set timer for 10 minutes. Remove chicken and shred. Move it back to the pot then stir well to combine. Serve and enjoy.

**Nutrition: Calories:** 308 kcal; **Fat:** 12.4 g; **Protein:** 42.1 g; **Carbs:** 5.4 g; **Sodium:** 656 mg

### 234. Honey Crusted Chicken

**Preparation time:** 10 minutes
**Cooking time:** 25 minutes
**Servings:** 2
**Ingredients:**
- 1 tsp. paprika
- 8 saltine crackers, 2 inches square
- 2 chicken breasts, each 4 oz.
- 4 tsp. honey

**Directions:**
1. Set the oven to heat at 375°F. Grease a baking dish with cooking oil. Smash the crackers in a Ziplock bag and toss them with paprika in a bowl. Brush chicken with honey and add it to the crackers.
2. Mix well and transfer the chicken to the baking dish. Bake the chicken for 25 minutes until golden brown. Serve.

**Nutrition: Calories:** 219 kcal; **Fat:** 17 g; **Sodium:** 456 mg; **Carbs:** 12.1 g; **Protein:** 31 g

### 235. Paella with Chicken, Leeks, and Tarragon

**Preparation time:** 10 minutes
**Cooking time:** 20 minutes
**Servings:** 2
**Ingredients:**
- 1 tsp. extra-virgin olive oil
- 1 small onion, sliced
- 2 leeks (whites only), thinly sliced
- 3 garlic cloves, minced
- 1-lb. chicken breast, boneless, skinless, cut into strips ½-inch-wide and 2 inches long
- 2 large tomatoes, chopped
- 1 red pepper, sliced
- ⅔ cup long-grain brown rice
- 1 tsp. tarragon, or to taste
- 2 cups fat-free, unsalted chicken broth
- 1 cup peas, frozen
- ¼ cup fresh parsley, chopped
- 1 lemon, cut into 4 wedges

**Directions:**
1. Preheat a nonstick pan with olive oil over medium heat. Toss in leeks, onions, chicken strips, and garlic. Sauté for 5 minutes. Stir in red pepper slices and tomatoes. Stir and cook for 5 minutes.
2. Add tarragon, broth, and rice. Let it boil, then reduce the heat to a simmer. Continue cooking for 10 minutes, then add peas and continue cooking until the liquid is thoroughly cooked. Garnish with parsley and lemon. Serve.

**Nutrition: Calories:** 388 kcal; **Fat:** 15.2 g; **Sodium:** 572 mg; **Carbs:** 5.4 g; **Protein:** 27 g

### 236. Southwestern Chicken and Pasta

**Preparation time:** 10 minutes
**Cooking time:** 10 minutes
**Servings:** 2
**Ingredients:**
- 1 cup whole-wheat rigatoni, uncooked
- 2 chicken breasts, cut into cubes
- ¼ cup salsa
- 1 ½ cups tomato sauce, canned and unsalted
- ⅛ tsp. garlic powder
- 1 tsp. cumin
- ½ tsp. chili powder
- ½ cup black beans, canned and drained
- ½ cup fresh corn
- ¼ cup Monterey Jack and Colby cheese, shredded

**Directions:**
1. Fill a pot with water up to ¾ full and boil it. Add pasta to cook until it is al dente, then drain the pasta while rinsing under cold water. Preheat a skillet with cooking oil, then cook the chicken for 10 minutes until golden from both sides.
2. Add tomato sauce, salsa, cumin, garlic powder, black beans, corn, and chili powder. Cook the mixture while stirring, then toss in the pasta. Serve with 2 tbsp. cheese on top. Enjoy.

**Nutrition: Calories:** 245 kcal; **Fat:** 16.3 g; **Sodium:** 515 mg; **Carbs:** 19.3 g; **Protein:** 33.3 g

### 237. Stuffed Chicken Breasts

**Preparation time:** 15 minutes
**Cooking time:** 30 minutes
**Servings:** 4
**Ingredients:**
- 3 tbsp. seedless raisins
- ½ cup onion, chopped

- ½ cup celery, chopped
- ¼ tsp. garlic, minced
- 1 bay leaf
- 1 cup apple with peel, chopped
- 2 tbsp. water chestnuts, chopped
- 4 large chicken breast halves, 5 oz. each
- 1 tbsp. olive oil
- 1 cup fat-free milk
- 1 tsp. curry powder
- 2 tbsp. all-purpose (plain) flour
- 1 lemon, cut into 4 wedges

**Directions:**
1. Set the oven to heat at 425°F. Grease a baking dish with cooking oil. Soak raisins in warm water until they swell. Grease a heated skillet with cooking spray.
2. Add celery, garlic, onions, and bay leaf. Sauté for 5 minutes. Discard the bay leaf, then toss in apples. Stir cook for 2 minutes. Drain the soaked raisin and pat them dry to remove excess water.
3. Add raisins and water chestnuts to the apple mixture. Pull apart the chicken's skin and stuff the apple raisin mixture between the skin and the chicken. Preheat olive oil in another skillet and sear the breasts for 5 minutes per side.
4. Place the chicken breasts in the baking dish and cover the dish. Bake for 15 minutes until temperature reaches 165°F. Prepare sauce by mixing milk, flour, and curry powder in a saucepan.
5. Stir cook until the mixture thickens, about 5 minutes. Pour this sauce over the baked chicken. Bake again in the covered dish for 10 minutes. Serve.

**Nutrition: Calories:** 357 kcal; **Fat:** 32.7 g; **Sodium:** 277 mg; **Carbs:** 17.7 g; **Protein:** 31.2 g

## 238. Buffalo Chicken Salad Wrap

**Preparation time:** 10 minutes
**Cooking time:** 10 minutes
**Servings:** 4
**Ingredients:**
- 3-4 oz. chicken breasts
- 2 whole chipotle peppers
- ¼ cup white wine vinegar
- ¼ cup low-calorie mayonnaise
- 2 stalks celery, diced
- 2 carrots, cut into matchsticks
- 1 small yellow onion, diced
- ½ cup rutabaga or another root vegetable, thinly sliced
- 4 oz. spinach, cut into strips
- 2 whole-grain tortillas (12-inch diameter)

**Directions:**
1. Set the oven or a grill to heat at 375°F. Bake the chicken first for 10 minutes per side. Blend chipotle peppers with mayonnaise and wine vinegar in the blender. Dice the baked chicken into cubes or small chunks.
2. Mix the chipotle mixture with all the ingredients except tortillas and spinach. Spread 2 oz. of spinach over the tortilla and scoop the stuffing on top. Wrap the tortilla and cut it into half. Serve.

**Nutrition: Calories:** 300 kcal; **Fat:** 16.4 g; **Sodium:** 471 mg; **Carbs:** 8.7 g; **Protein:** 38.5 g

## 239. Chicken Sliders

**Preparation time:** 10 minutes
**Cooking time:** 10 minutes
**Servings:** 4
**Ingredients:**
- 10 oz. chicken breast, ground
- 1 tbsp. black pepper
- 1 tbsp. garlic, minced
- 1 tbsp. balsamic vinegar
- ½ cup onion, minced
- 1 fresh chili pepper, minced
- 1 tbsp. fennel seed, crushed
- 4 whole-wheat mini buns
- 4 lettuce leaves
- 4 tomato slices

**Directions:**
1. Combine all the ingredients except the wheat buns, tomato, and lettuce. Mix well and refrigerate the mixture for 1 hour. Divide the mixture into 4 patties.
2. Broil these patties in a greased baking tray until golden brown. Place the chicken patties in the wheat buns along with lettuce and tomato. Serve.

**Nutrition: Calories:** 224 kcal; **Fat:** 4.5 g; **Sodium:** 212 mg; **Carbs:** 10.2 g; **Protein:** 67.4 g

## 240. White Chicken Chili

**Preparation time:** 20 minutes
**Cooking time:** 15 minutes
**Servings:** 4
**Ingredients:**
- 1 can white chunk chicken
- 2 cans low-sodium white beans, drained

- 1 can low-sodium tomatoes, diced
- 4 cups low-sodium chicken broth
- 1 medium onion, chopped
- ½ medium green pepper, chopped
- 1 medium red pepper, chopped
- 2 garlic cloves, minced
- 2 tsp. chili powder
- 1 tsp. cumin, ground
- 1 tsp. oregano, dried
- Cayenne pepper, to taste
- 8 tbsp. reduced-fat Monterey Jack cheese, shredded
- 3 tbsp. fresh cilantro, chopped

**Directions**:
1. In a soup pot, add beans, tomatoes, chicken, and chicken broth. Cover this soup pot and let it simmer over medium heat. Meanwhile, grease a nonstick pan with cooking spray. Add peppers, garlic, and onions. Sauté for 5 minutes until soft.
2. Transfer the mixture to the soup pot. Add cumin, chili powder, cayenne pepper, and oregano. Cook for 10 minutes, then garnish the chili with cilantro and 1 tbsp. cheese. Serve.

**Nutrition: Calories:** 225 kcal; **Fat:** 12.9 g; **Sodium:** 480 mg; **Carbs:** 24.7 g; **Protein:** 25.3g

## 241. Sweet Potato-Turkey Meatloaf

**Preparation time:** 15 minutes
**Cooking time:** 25 minutes
**Servings:** 4
**Ingredients:**
- 1 large sweet potato, peeled and cubed
- 1-lb. turkey (breast), ground
- 1 large egg
- 1 small sweet onion, finely chopped
- 2 cloves garlic, minced
- 2 slices whole-wheat bread, crumbs
- ¼ cup honey barbecue sauce
- ¼ cup ketchup
- 2 tbsp. Dijon mustard
- 1 tbsp. pepper, fresh ground
- ½ tbsp. salt

**Directions**:
1. Warm oven to 350°F. Grease a baking dish. In a large pot, boil a cup of lightly salted water, add the sweet potato. Cook until tender. Drain the water. Mash the potato.
2. Mix the honey barbecue sauce, ketchup, and Dijon mustard in a small bowl. Mix thoroughly. In a large bowl, mix the turkey and the egg. Add the sweet onion, garlic. Pour in the combined sauces. Add the bread crumbs. Season the mixture with salt and pepper.
3. Add the sweet potato. Combine thoroughly with your hands. If the mixture feels wet, add more bread crumbs. Shape the mixture into a loaf. Place in the loaf pan. Bake for 25–35 minutes until the meat is cooked through. Broil for 5 minutes. Slice and serve.

**Nutrition: Calories:** 133 kcal; **Protein:** 85 g; **Carbohydrates:** 50 g; **Fat:** 34 g; **Sodium:** 202 mg

## 242. Oaxacan Chicken

**Preparation time:** 15 minutes
**Cooking time:** 28 minutes
**Servings:** 2
**Ingredients:**
- 1 4-oz. chicken breast, skinned and halved
- ½ cup long-grain rice, uncooked
- 1 tsp. extra-virgin olive oil
- ½ cup low-sodium salsa
- ½ cup chicken stock, mixed with 2 tbsp. water
- ¾ cup baby carrots
- 2 tbsp. green olives, pitted and chopped
- 2 tbsp. dark raisins
- ½ tsp. Cinnamon, ground
- 2 tbsp. fresh cilantro or parsley, coarsely chopped

**Directions**:
1. Warm oven to 350°F. In a large saucepan that can go in the oven, heat the olive oil. Add the rice. Sauté the rice until it begins to pop, approximately 2 minutes.
2. Add the salsa, baby carrots, green olives, dark raisins, halved chicken breast, chicken stock, and ground cinnamon. Bring the mix to a simmer, stir once.
3. Cover the mixture tightly, bake in the oven until the chicken stock has been completely absorbed, approximately 25 minutes. Sprinkle fresh cilantro or parsley, mix. Serve immediately.

**Nutrition: Calories:** 143 kcal; **Protein:** 102 g; **Carbohydrates:** 66 g; **Fat:** 18 g; **Sodium:** 97 mg

## 243. Spicy Chicken with Minty Couscous

**Preparation time:** 15 minutes
**Cooking time:** 25 minutes
**Servings:** 2
**Ingredients:**
- 2 small chicken breasts, sliced
- 1 red chili pepper, finely chopped
- 1 garlic clove, crushed
- Ginger root, 2 cm long peeled and grated
- 1 tsp. cumin, ground
- ½ tsp. turmeric
- 2 tbsp. extra-virgin olive oil
- 1 pinch sea salt
- ¾ cup couscous
- Small bunch mint leaves, finely chopped
- 2 lemons, grate the rind and juice them

**Directions:**
1. In a large bowl, place the chicken breast slices and chopped chili pepper. Sprinkle with the crushed garlic, ginger, cumin, turmeric, and a pinch of salt. Add the grated rind of both lemons and the juice from 1 lemon. Pour 1 tbsp. of the olive oil over the chicken, coat evenly.
2. Cover the dish with plastic and refrigerate within 1 hour. After 1 hour, coat a skillet with olive oil and fry the chicken. As the chicken is cooking, pour the couscous into a bowl and pour hot water over it, let it absorb the water (approximately 5 minutes).
3. Fluff the couscous. Add some chopped mint, the other tbsp. of olive oil, and juice from the second lemon. Top the couscous with the chicken. Garnish with chopped mint. Serve immediately.

**Nutrition: Calories:** 166 kcal; **Protein:** 106 g; **Carbohydrates:** 52 g; **Sugars:** 0.1 g; **Fat:** 17 g; **Sodium:** 108 mg

## 244. Chicken, Pasta and Snow Peas

**Preparation time:** 15 minutes
**Cooking time:** 20 minutes
**Servings:** 2
**Ingredients:**
- 1-lb. chicken breasts
- 2 ½ cups penne pasta
- 1 cup snow peas, trimmed and halved
- 1 tsp. olive oil
- 1 standard jar Tomato and Basil pasta sauce
- Pepper, fresh ground

**Directions:**
1. In a medium frying pan, heat the olive oil. Flavor the chicken breasts with salt and pepper. Cook the chicken breasts until cooked through (approximately 5–7 minutes each side).
2. Cook the pasta, as stated in the instruction of the package. Cook the snow peas with the pasta. Scoop 1 cup of the pasta water. Drain the pasta and peas, set aside.
3. Once the chicken is cooked, slice diagonally. Return back the chicken in the frying pan. Add the pasta sauce. If the mixture seems dry, add some of the pasta water to the desired consistency. Heat, then divide into bowls. Serve immediately.

**Nutrition: Calories:** 140 kcal; **Protein:** 34 g; **Carbohydrates:** 52 g; **Fat:** 17 g; **Sodium:** 118 mg

## 245. Chicken with Noodles

**Preparation time:** 15 minutes
**Cooking time:** 30 minutes
**Servings:** 6
**Ingredients:**
- 4 chicken breasts, skinless, boneless
- 1-lb. pasta (angel hair, or linguine, or ramen)
- ½ tsp. sesame oil
- 1 tbsp. canola oil
- 2 tbsp. chili paste
- 1 onion, diced
- 2 garlic cloves, chopped coarsely
- ½ cup soy sauce
- ½ medium cabbage, sliced
- 2 carrots, chopped coarsely

**Directions:**
1. Cook your pasta in a large pot. Mix the canola oil, sesame oil, and chili paste and heat for 25 seconds in a large pot. Add the onion, cook for 2 minutes. Put the garlic and fry within 20 seconds. Add the chicken, cook on each side 5-7 minutes, until cooked through.
2. Remove the mix from the pan, set aside. Add the cabbage, carrots, cook until the vegetables are tender. Pour everything back into the pan. Add the noodles. Pour in the soy sauce and combine thoroughly. Heat for 5 minutes. Serve immediately.

**Nutrition: Calories:** 110 kcal; **Protein:** 30 g; **Carbohydrates:** 32 g; **Sugars:** 0.1 g; **Fat:** 18 g; **Sodium:** 121 mg

### 246. Teriyaki Chicken Wings

**Preparation time:** 15 minutes
**Cooking time:** 30 minutes
**Servings:** 6
**Ingredients:**
- 3 lb. chicken wings (15–20)
- ⅓ cup lemon juice
- ¼ cup soy sauce
- ¼ cup vegetable oil
- 3 tbsp. chili sauce
- 1 garlic clove, finely chopped
- ¼ tsp. fresh ground pepper
- ¼ tsp. celery seed
- Dash liquid mustard

**Directions:**
1. Prepare the marinade. Combine lemon juice, soy sauce, chili sauce, oil, celery seed, garlic, pepper, and mustard. Stir well, set aside. Rinse and dry the chicken wings.
2. Pour marinade over the chicken wings. Coat thoroughly. Refrigerate for 2 hours. After 2 hours. Preheat the broiler in the oven. Drain off the excess sauce.
3. Place the wings on a cookie sheet with parchment paper. Broil on each side for 10 minutes. Serve immediately.

**Nutrition: Calories:** 96 kcal; **Protein:** 15 g; **Carbohydrates:** 63 g; **Fat:** 15 g; **Sodium:** 145 mg;

### 247. Hot Chicken Wings

**Preparation time:** 15 minutes
**Cooking time:** 25 minutes
**Servings:** 4
**Ingredients:**
- 10–20 chicken wings
- ½ stick margarine
- 1 bottle Durkee hot sauce
- 2 tbsp. honey
- 10 shakes Tabasco sauce
- 2 tbsp. cayenne pepper

**Directions:**
1. Warm canola oil in a deep pot. Deep-fry the wings until cooked, approximately 20 minutes. Mix the hot sauce, honey, Tabasco, and cayenne pepper in a medium bowl. Mix well.
2. Place the cooked wings on paper towels. Drain the excess oil. Mix the chicken wings in the sauce until coated evenly.

**Nutrition: Calories:** 102 kcal; **Protein:** 23 g; **Carbohydrates:** 55 g; **Sugars:** 0.1 g; **Fat:** 14 g; **Sodium:** 140 mg

### 248. Crispy Cashew Chicken

**Preparation time:** 15 minutes
**Cooking time:** 30 minutes
**Servings:** 5
**Ingredients:**
- 2 chicken breasts, skinless, boneless
- 2 egg whites
- 1 cup cashew nuts
- ¼ cup bread crumbs
- 2 cups peanut oil or vegetable oil
- ¼ cup corn starch
- 1 tsp. brown sugar
- 2 tsp. salt
- 1 tsp. dry sherry

**Directions:**
1. Warm oven to 400°F. Put the cashews in a blender. Pulse until they are finely chopped. Place in a shallow bowl and stir in the bread crumbs. Wash the chicken breasts. Pat them dry. Cut into small cubes. In a separate shallow bowl, mix the salt, corn starch, brown sugar, and sherry. In a separate bowl, beat the egg white. Put the oil into a large, deep pot. Heat to high temp. Place the chicken pieces on a plate. Arrange the bowls in a row; flour, eggs, cashews and bread crumbs. Prepare a baking tray with parchment paper. Dunk the chicken pieces in the flour, then the egg, and then the cashew mixture. Shake off the excess mixture. Gently place the chicken in the oil. Fry on each side for 2 minutes. Place on the baking tray. Once done, slide the baking tray into the oven. Cook for an additional 4 minutes, flip, cook for an additional 4 minutes, until golden brown. Serve immediately, or cold, with your favorite low-fat dip.

**Nutrition: Calories:** 86 kcal; **Protein:** 21 g; **Carbohydrates:** 50 g; **Sugars:** 0.1 g; **Fat:** 16 g; **Sodium:** 139 mg

### 249. Chicken Tortellini Soup

**Preparation time:** 15 minutes
**Cooking time:** 30 minutes
**Servings:** 5
**Ingredients:**
- 2 chicken breasts, boneless, skinless; diced into cubes
- 1 tbsp. flavorless oil (olive oil, canola, sunflower)
- 1 tsp. butter
- 2 cups cheese tortellini

- 2 cups broccoli, frozen
- 2 cans cream chicken soup
- 4 cups water
- 1 large onion, diced
- 2 garlic cloves, minced
- 2 large carrots, sliced
- 1 celery stick, sliced
- 1 tsp. oregano
- ½ tsp. basil

**Directions**:
1. Pull the broccoli out of the freezer. Set in a bowl. Rinse and pat dry the chicken breasts. Dice into cubes. In a large pot, heat the oil. Fry the cubes of chicken breast. Pull from the pot, place on paper to drain off the oil.
2. Add the tsp. of butter to the hot pot. Sauté the onion, garlic, carrots, and celery, broccoli. Once the vegetable el dente, add the chicken soup and water. Stir the ingredients until they are combined. Bring it to a simmer.
3. Add the chicken and tortellini back to the pot. Cook on low within 10 minutes, or until the tortellini is cooked. Serve immediately.

**Nutrition: Calories:** 79 kcal; **Protein:** 15 g; **Carbohydrates:** 55 g; **Sugars:** 0 g; **Fat:** 13 g; **Sodium:** 179 mg

## 250. Chicken Divan

**Preparation time:** 15 minutes
**Cooking time:** 30 minutes
**Servings:** 4
**Ingredients:**
- ½-lb. chicken, cooked and boneless, skinless, diced in bite-size pieces
- 1 cup broccoli, cooked, diced into bite-size pieces
- 1 cup extra sharp cheddar cheese, grated
- 1 can mushroom soup
- ½ cup water
- 1 cup croutons

**Directions**:
1. Warm oven to 350°F. In a large pot, heat the soup and water. Add the chicken, broccoli, and cheese. Combine thoroughly. Pour into a greased baking dish. Place the croutons over the mixture. Bake within 30 minutes or until the casserole is bubbling, and the croutons are golden brown.
2. **Nutrition: Calories:** 380 kcal; **Protein:** 25 g; **Carbohydrates:** 10 g; **Sugars:** 1 g; **Fat:** 22 g; **Sodium:** 397 mg

## 251. Creamy Chicken Fried Rice

**Preparation time:** 15 minutes
**Cooking time:** 45 minutes
**Servings:** 4
**Ingredients:**
- 2 lb. chicken; white and dark meat (diced into cubes)
- 2 tbsp. butter or margarine
- 1 ½ cups instant rice
- 1 cup mixed vegetables, frozen
- 1 can condensed cream chicken soup
- 1 cup water
- 1 cube instant chicken bouillon
- Salt and pepper to taste

**Directions**:
1. Take the vegetables out of the freezer. Set aside. Warm large, deep skillet over medium heat, add the butter or margarine. Place the chicken in the skillet, season with salt and pepper. Fry until both sides are brown.
2. Remove the chicken, then adjust the heat and add the rice. Add the water and bouillon. Cook the rice, then add the chicken, the vegetables. Mix in the soup, then simmer until the vegetables are tender. Serve immediately.

**Nutrition: Calories:** 119 kcal **Protein:** 22 g; **Carbohydrates:** 63 g; **Fat:** 18 g; **Sodium:** 180 mg;

## 252. Chicken Tikka

**Preparation time:** 15 minutes
**Cooking time:** 20 minutes

**Ingredients:**
- 4 chicken breasts, skinless, boneless; cubed
- 2 large onions, cubed
- 10 Cherry tomatoes
- ⅓ cup plain non-fat yogurt
- 4 garlic cloves, crushed
- 1 ½ inch fresh ginger, peeled and chopped - 1 small onion, grated
- 1 ½ tsp. chili powder
- 1 tbsp. coriander, ground
- 1 tsp. salt
- 2 tbsp. coriander leaves

**Directions**:
1. In a large bowl, combine the non-fat yogurt, crushed garlic, ginger, chili powder, coriander, salt, and pepper. Add the cubed chicken, stir until the chicken is coated. Cover with plastic film, place in the fridge. Marinate 2–4 hours. Heat the broiler or barbecue.

2. After marinating the chicken, get some skewers ready. Alternate pieces of chicken cubes, cherry tomatoes, and cubed onions onto the skewers.
3. Grill within 6–8 minutes on each side. Once the chicken is cooked through, pull the meat and vegetables off the skewers onto plates. Garnish with coriander. Serve immediately.

**Nutrition:** **Calories:** 117 kcal; **Protein:** 19 g; **Carbohydrates:** 59 g; **Fat:** 19 g; **Sodium:** 203 mg

## 253. Honey Spiced Cajun Chicken

**Preparation time:** 15 minutes
**Cooking time:** 20 minutes
**Servings:** 4
**Ingredients:**
- 2 chicken breasts, skinless, boneless
- 1 tbsp. butter or margarine
- 1 lb. linguini
- 3 large mushrooms, sliced
- 1 large tomato, diced
- 2 tbsp. regular mustard
- 4 tbsp. honey
- 3 oz. low-fat table cream
- Parsley, roughly chopped

**Directions:**
1. Wash and dry the chicken breasts. Warm 1 tbsp. of butter or margarine in a large pan. Add the chicken breasts. Season with salt and pepper. Cook on each side 6–10 minutes, until cooked thoroughly. Pull the chicken breasts from the pan. Set aside.
2. Cook the linguine as stated to instructions on the package in a large pot. Save 1 cup of the pasta water. Drain the linguine. Add the mushrooms, tomatoes to the pan from cooking the chicken. Heat until they are tender.
3. Add the honey, mustard, and cream. Combine thoroughly. Add the chicken and linguine to the pan. Stir until coated. Garnish with parsley. Serve immediately.

**Nutrition:**
**Calories:** 112 kcal; **Protein:** 12 g; **Carbohydrates:** 56 g; **Fat:** 20 g; **Sodium:** 158 mg

## 254. Italian Chicken

**Preparation time:** 15 minutes
**Cooking time:** 35 minutes
**Servings:** 4
**Ingredients:**
- 4 chicken breasts, skinless boneless
- 1 large jar of pasta sauce, low-sodium
- 1 tbsp. flavorless oil (olive, canola, or sunflower)
- 1 large onion, diced
- 1 large green pepper, diced
- ½ tsp. garlic salt
- Salt and pepper to taste
- 1 cup low-fat mozzarella cheese, grated
- Spinach leaves, washed, dried, rough chop

**Directions:**
1. Wash the chicken breasts, pat dry. In a large pot, heat the oil. Add the onion, cook, until it sweats and becomes translucent. Add the chicken. Season with salt, pepper, and garlic salt. Cook the chicken. 6–10 minutes on each side.
2. Add the peppers. Cook for 2 minutes. Pour the pasta sauce over the chicken. Mix well. Simmer on low for 20 minutes. Serve on plates, sprinkle the cheese over each piece. Garnish with spinach.

**Nutrition:** **Calories:** 142 kcal; **Protein:** 17 g; **Carbohydrates:** 51 g; **Fat:** 15 g; **Sodium:** 225 mg

## 255. Lemon-Parsley Chicken Breast

**Preparation time:** 15 minutes
**Cooking time:** 15 minutes
**Servings:** 2
**Ingredients:**
- 2 chicken breasts, skinless, boneless
- ⅓ cup white wine
- ⅓ cup lemon juice
- 2 garlic cloves, minced
- 3 tbsp. bread crumbs
- 2 tbsp. flavorless oil (olive, canola, or sunflower)
- ¼ cup fresh parsley

**Directions:**
1. Mix the wine, lemon juice, plus garlic in a measuring cup. Pound each chicken breast until they are ¼ inch thick. Coat the chicken with bread crumbs, and heat the oil in a large skillet.
2. Fry the chicken within 6 minutes on each side, until they turn brown. Stir in the wine mixture over the chicken. Simmer for 5 minutes. Pour any extra juices over the chicken. Garnish with parsley.

**Nutrition:** **Calories:** 117 kcal; **Protein:** 14 g; **Carbohydrates:** 74 g; **Fat:** 12 g; **Sodium:** 189 mg

## 256. Parmesan and Chicken Spaghetti Squash

**Preparation time:** 15 minutes
**Cooking time:** 20 minutes
**Servings:** 6
**Ingredients:**
- 16 oz. mozzarella
- 1 spaghetti squash piece
- 1 lb. cube chicken, cooked
- 1 cup Marinara sauce

**Directions:**
1. Split up the squash in halves and remove the seeds. Arrange or put one cup of water in your pot, then put a trivet on top.
2. Add the squash halves to the trivet. Cook within 20 minutes at HIGH pressure. Remove the squashes and shred them using a fork into spaghetti portions
3. Pour sauce over the squash and give it a nice mix. Top them up with the cubed-up chicken and top with mozzarella. Broil for 1-2 minutes and broil until the cheese has melted

**Nutrition: Calories:** 237 kcal; **Fat:** 10 g; **Carbs:** 32 g; **Protein:** 11 g; **Sodium:** 500 mg

## 257. Apricot Chicken

**Preparation time:** 15 minutes
**Cooking time:** 6 minutes
**Servings:** 4
**Ingredients:**
- 1 bottle creamy French dressing
- ¼ cup flavorless oil
- White rice, cooked
- 1 large jar Apricot preserve
- 4 lb. chicken, boneless and skinless
- 1 package onion soup mix

**Directions:**
1. Rinse and pat dry the chicken. Dice into bite-size pieces. In a large bowl, mix the apricot preserve, creamy dressing, and onion soup mix. Stir until thoroughly combined. Place the chicken in the bowl. Mix until coated.
2. In a large skillet, heat the oil. Place the chicken in the oil gently. Cook 4 – 6 minutes on each side, until golden brown. Serve over rice.

**Nutrition: Calories:** 202 kcal; **Fat:** 12 g; **Carbs:** 75 g; **Protein:** 20 g; **Sugars:** 10 g; **Sodium:** 630 mg

## 258. Oven-Fried Chicken Breasts

**Preparation time:** 15 minutes
**Cooking time:** 30 minutes
**Servings:** 8
**Ingredients:**
- ½ pack Ritz crackers
- 1 cup plain non-fat yogurt
- 8 chicken breasts, boneless, skinless, and halved

**Directions:**
1. Preheat the oven to 350°F. Rinse and pat dry the chicken breasts. Pour the yogurt into a shallow bowl. Dip the chicken pieces in the yogurt, then roll in the cracker crumbs. Place the chicken in a single layer in a baking dish. Bake within 15 minutes per side Serve.

**Nutrition: Calories:** 200 kcal; **Fat:** 13 g; **Carbs:** 98 g; **Protein:** 19 g; **Sodium:** 217 mg

## 259. Rosemary Roasted Chicken

**Preparation time:** 15 minutes
**Cooking time:** 20 minutes
**Servings:** 8
**Ingredients:**
- 8 rosemary springs
- 1 garlic clove, minced
- Black pepper
- 1 tbsp. rosemary, chopped
- 1 chicken
- 1 tbsp. organic olive oil

**Directions:**
1. In a bowl, mix garlic with rosemary, rub the chicken with black pepper, the oil and rosemary mix, place it inside roasting pan, introduce inside the oven at 350°F, and roast for sixty minutes and 20 min. Carve chicken, divide between plates and serve using a side dish. Enjoy!

**Nutrition: Calories:** 325 kcal; **Fat:** 5 g; **Carbs:** 15 g; **Protein:** 14 g; **Sodium:** 950 mg

## 260. Artichoke and Spinach Chicken

**Preparation time:** 15 minutes
**Cooking time:** 5 minutes
**Servings:** 4
**Ingredients:**
- 10 oz. baby spinach
- ½ tsp. red pepper flake, crushed
- 14 oz. artichoke hearts, chopped
- 28 oz. no-salt-added tomato sauce

- 2 tbsp. essential olive oil
- 4 chicken breasts, boneless and skinless

**Directions:**
1. Heat up a pan with the oil over medium-high heat, add chicken and red pepper flakes and cook for 5 minutes on them. Add spinach, artichokes, and tomato sauce, toss, cook for 10 minutes more, divide between plates and serve. Enjoy!

**Nutrition: Calories:** 212 kcal; **Fat:** 3 g; **Carbs:** 16 g; **Protein:** 20 g; **Sugars:** 5 g; **Sodium:** 418 mg

### 261. Pumpkin and Black Beans Chicken

**Preparation time:** 15 minutes
**Cooking time:** 25 minutes
**Servings:** 4
**Ingredients:**
- 1 tbsp. essential olive oil
- 1 tbsp. cilantro, chopped
- 1 cup coconut milk
- 15 oz. black beans, canned and drained
- 1 lb. chicken breasts, skinless and boneless
- 2 cup water
- ½ cup pumpkin flesh

**Directions:**
1. Heat a pan when using oil over medium-high heat, add the chicken and cook for 5 minutes.
2. Add the river, milk, pumpkin, and black beans toss, cover the pan, reduce heat to medium and cook for 20 min. Add cilantro, toss, divide between plates and serve. Enjoy!

**Nutrition: Calories:** 254 kcal; **Fat:** 6 g; **Carbs:** 16 g; **Protein:** 22 g; **Sodium:** 92 mg

### 262. Chicken Thighs and Apples Mix

**Preparation time:** 15 minutes
**Cooking time:** 60 minutes
**Servings:** 4
**Ingredients:**
- 3 apples, cored and sliced
- 1 tbsp. apple cider vinegar treatment
- ¾ cup natural apple juice
- ¼ tsp. pepper and salt
- 1 tbsp. ginger, grated
- 8 chicken thighs
- 3 tbsp. onion, chopped

**Directions:**
1. In a bowl, mix chicken with salt, pepper, vinegar, onion, ginger, and apple juice, toss well, cover, keep within the fridge for 10 minutes, transfer with a baking dish, and include apples. Introduce inside the oven at 400°F for just 1 hour. Divide between plates and serve. Enjoy!

**Nutrition: Calories:** 214; **Fat:** 3 g; **Carbs:** 14 g; **Protein:** 15 g; **Sodium:** 405 mg

### 263. Thai Chicken Thighs

**Preparation time:** 15 minutes
**Cooking time:** 1 hour and 5minutes
**Servings:** 6
**Ingredients:**
- ½ cup Thai chili sauce
- 1 green onions bunch, chopped
- 4 lb. chicken thighs

**Directions:**
1. Heat a pan over medium-high heat. Add chicken thighs, brown them for 5 minutes on both sides Transfer to some baking dish then add chili sauce and green onions and toss.
2. Introduce within the oven and bake at 400°F for 60 minutes. Divide everything between plates and serve. Enjoy!

**Nutrition: Calories:** 220 kcal; **Fat:** 4 g; **Carbs:** 12 g; **Protein:** 10 g; **Sodium:** 870 mg

### 264. Falling "Off" The Bone Chicken

**Preparation time:** 15 minutes
**Cooking time:** 40 minutes
**Servings:** 4
**Ingredients:**
- 6 garlic cloves, peeled
- 1 tbsp. organic extra virgin coconut oil
- 2 tbsp. lemon juice
- 1 ½ cup pacific organic bone chicken broth - ¼ tsp. black pepper, freshly ground - ½ tsp. sea flavored vinegar
- 1 whole organic chicken piece
- 1 tsp. paprika - 1 tsp. thyme, dried

**Directions:**
1. Take a small bowl and toss in the thyme, paprika, pepper, and flavored vinegar and mix them. Use the mixture to season the chicken properly. Pour down the oil in your instant pot and heat it to shimmering; toss in the chicken with breast downward and let it cook for about 6-7 minutes

2. After 7 minutes, flip over the chicken pour down the broth, garlic cloves, and lemon juice. Cook within 25 minutes on a high setting. Remove the dish from the cooker and let it stand for about 5 minutes before serving.

**Nutrition: Calories:** 664 kcal; **Fat:** 44 g; **Carbs:** 44 g; **Protein:** 27 g; **Sugars:** 0.1 g; **Sodium:** 800 mg

### 265. Feisty Chicken Porridge

**Preparation time:** 15 minutes
**Cooking time:** 30 minutes
**Servings:** 4
**Ingredients:**
- 1 ½ cup fresh ginger
- 1 lb. chicken legs, cooked
- Green onions
- Cashew nuts, toasted
- 5 cup chicken broth
- 1 cup jasmine rice
- 4 cup water

**Directions:**
1. Place the rice in your fridge and allow it to chill 1 hour before cooking. Take the rice out and add them to your Instant Pot. Pour broth and water. Lock up the lid and cook on Porridge mode.
2. Separate the meat from the chicken legs and add the meat to your soup. Stir well over sauté mode. Season with a bit of flavored vinegar and enjoy with a garnish of nuts and onion

**Nutrition: Calories:** 206 kcal; **Fat:** 8 g; **Carbs:** 8 g; **Protein:** 23 g; **Sugars:** 0 g; **Sodium:** 950 mg

### 266. The Ultimate Faux-Tisserie Chicken

**Preparation time:** 15 minutes
**Cooking time:** 35 minutes
**Servings:** 5
**Ingredients:**
- 1 cup low-sodium broth
- 2 tbsp. olive oil
- ½ medium onion, quartered
- 2 tbsp. favorite seasoning
- 2 ½ lb. whole chicken
- Black pepper
- 5 large fresh garlic cloves

**Directions:**
1. Massage the chicken with 1 tbsp. of olive oil and sprinkle pepper on top. Place onion wedges and garlic cloves inside the chicken. Take a butcher's twin and secure the legs

2. Set your pot to Sauté mode. Put olive oil in your pan on medium heat, allow the oil to heat up. Add chicken and sear both sides for 4 minutes per side. Sprinkle your seasoning over the chicken, remove the chicken and place a trivet at the bottom of your pot
3. Sprinkle seasoning over the chicken, making sure to rub it. Transfer the chicken to the trivet with the breast side facing up, lock up the lid. Cook on HIGH pressure for 25 minutes. Allow it to rest and serve!

**Nutrition: Calories:** 1010 kcal; **Fat:** 64 g; **Carbs:** 47 g; **Protein:** 60 g; **Sodium:** 209 mg

### 267. Oregano Chicken Thighs

**Preparation time:** 15 minutes
**Cooking time:** 20 minutes
**Servings:** 6
**Ingredients:**
- 12 chicken thighs
- 1 tsp. parsley, dried
- ¼ tsp. pepper and salt.
- ½ cup extra virgin essential olive oil
- 4 garlic cloves, minced
- 1 cup oregano, chopped
- ¼ cup low-sodium veggie stock

**Directions:**
1. In your food processor, mix parsley with oregano, garlic, salt, pepper, and stock and pulse. Put chicken thighs within the bowl, add oregano paste, toss, cover, and then leave aside within the fridge for 10 minutes.
2. Heat the kitchen grill over medium heat, add chicken pieces, close the lid and cook for 20 or so minutes with them. Divide between plates and serve!

**Nutrition: Calories:** 254 kcal; **Fat:** 3 g; **Carbs:** 7 g; **Protein:** 17 g; **Sugars:** 0.9 g; **Sodium:** 730 mg

### 268. Pesto Chicken Breasts with Summer Squash

**Preparation time:** 15 minutes
**Cooking time:** 10 minutes
**Servings:** 4
**Ingredients:**
- 4 medium chicken breast, boneless, skinless halves
- 1 tbsp. olive oil
- 2 tbsp. Homemade pesto
- 2 cup zucchini, finely chopped
- 2 tbsp. Asiago, finely shredded

**Directions:**
1. Cook your chicken in hot oil on medium heat within 4 minutes in a large nonstick skillet. Flip the chicken then put the zucchini.
2. Cook within 4 to 6 minutes more or until the chicken is tender and no longer pink (170°F), and squash is crisp-tender, stirring squash gently once or twice. Transfer chicken and squash to 4 dinner plates. Spread pesto over chicken; sprinkle with Asiago.

**Nutrition: Calories:** 230 kcal; **Fat:** 9 g; **Carbs:** 8 g; **Protein:** 30 g; **Sodium:** 578 mg

## 269. Chicken, Tomato and Green Beans

**Preparation time:** 15 minutes
**Cooking time:** 25 minutes
**Servings:** 4
**Ingredients:**
- 6 oz. low-sodium canned tomato paste
- 2 tbsp. olive oil - ¼ tsp. black pepper
- 2 lb. green beans, trimmed
- 2 tbsp. parsley, chopped
- 1 ½ lb. chicken breasts, boneless, skinless, and cubed
- 25 oz. no-salt-added tomato sauce, canned

**Directions:**
1. Heat a pan with 50 % with the oil over medium heat, add chicken, stir, cover, and cook within 5 minutes on both sides and transfer to a bowl. Heat inside the same pan while using rest through the oil over medium heat, add green beans, stir and cook for 10 minutes.
2. Return chicken for that pan, add black pepper, tomato sauce, tomato paste, and parsley, stir, cover, cook for 10 minutes more, divide between plates and serve. Enjoy!

**Nutrition: Calories:** 190 kcal; **Fat:** 4 g; **Carbs:** 12 g; **Protein:** 9 g; **Sodium:** 168 mg

## 270. Chicken Tortillas

**Preparation time:** 15 minutes
**Cooking time:** 5 minutes
**Servings:** 4
**Ingredients:**
- 6 oz. chicken breasts, boneless, skinless, and cooked
- Black pepper
- ⅓ cup Fat-free yogurt
- 4 whole-wheat tortillas, heated up
- 2 tomatoes, chopped

**Directions:**
1. Heat-up a pan over medium heat, add one tortilla during those times, heat up, and hang them on the working surface. Spread yogurt on each tortilla, add chicken and tomatoes, roll, divide between plates and serve. Enjoy!

**Nutrition: Calories:** 190 kcal; **Fat:** 2 g; **Carbs:** 12 g; **Protein:** 6 g; **Sodium:** 300 mg

## 271. Chicken with Potatoes Olives and Sprouts

**Preparation time:** 15 minutes
**Cooking time:** 35 minutes
**Servings:** 4
**Ingredients:**
- 1 lb. chicken breasts, skinless, boneless, and cut into pieces
- ¼ cup olives, quartered
- 1 tsp. oregano
- 1 ½ tsp. Dijon mustard
- 1 lemon juice
- ⅓ cup vinaigrette dressing
- 1 medium onion, diced
- 3 cups potatoes cut into pieces
- 4 cups Brussels sprouts, trimmed and quartered
- ¼ tsp. pepper
- ¼ tsp. salt

**Directions:**
1. Warm-up oven to 400°F. Place chicken in the center of the baking tray, then place potatoes, sprouts, and onions around the chicken.
2. In a small bowl, mix vinaigrette, oregano, mustard, lemon juice, and salt and pour over chicken and veggies. Sprinkle olives and season with pepper.
3. Bake in preheated oven for 20 minutes. Transfer chicken to a plate. Stir the vegetables and roast for 15 minutes more. Serve and enjoy.

**Nutrition: Calories:** 397 kcal; **Fat:** 13g; **Protein:** 38.3g; **Carbs:** 31.4g; **Sodium:** 175 mg

## 272. Garlic Mushroom Chicken

**Preparation time:** 15 minutes
**Cooking time:** 15 minutes
**Servings:** 4
**Ingredients:**
- 4 chicken breasts, boneless and skinless
- 3 garlic cloves, minced
- 1 onion, chopped
- 2 cups mushrooms, sliced
- 1 tbsp. olive oil

- ½ cup chicken stock
- ¼ tsp. pepper
- ½ tsp. salt

**Directions**:
1. Season chicken with pepper and salt. Warm oil in a pan on medium heat, then put season chicken in the pan and cook for 5-6 minutes on each side. Remove and place on a plate.
2. Add onion and mushrooms to the pan and sauté until tender, about 2-3 minutes. Add garlic and sauté for a minute. Add stock and bring to boil. Stir well and cook for 1-2 minutes. Pour over chicken and serve.

**Nutrition: Calories:** 331 kcal; **Fat:** 14.5 g; **Protein:** 43.9 g; **Carbs:** 4.6 g; **Sodium:** 420 mg

## 273. Grilled Chicken

**Preparation time:** 15 minutes
**Cooking time:** 15 minutes
**Servings:** 4
**Ingredients:**
- 4 chicken breasts, skinless and boneless
- 1 ½ tsp. oregano, dried
- 1 tsp. paprika
- 5 garlic cloves, minced
- ½ cup fresh parsley, minced
- ½ cup olive oil
- ½ cup fresh lemon juice
- Pepper
- Salt

**Directions**:
1. Add lemon juice, oregano, paprika, garlic, parsley, and olive oil to a large zip-lock bag. Season chicken with pepper and salt and add to bag. Seal bag and shake well to coat chicken with marinade. Let sit chicken in the marinade for 20 minutes.
2. Remove chicken from marinade and grill over medium-high heat for 5–6 minutes on each side. Serve and enjoy.

**Nutrition: Calories:** 512 kcal; **Fat:** 36.5 g; **Protein:** 43.1 g; **Carbs:** 3 g; **Sodium:** 110 mg

## 274. Delicious Lemon Chicken Salad

**Preparation time:** 15 minutes
**Cooking time:** 5 minutes
**Servings:** 4
**Ingredients:**
- 1 lb. chicken breast, cooked and diced
- 1 tbsp. fresh dill, chopped
- 2 tsp. olive oil
- ¼ cup low-fat yogurt
- 1 tsp. lemon zest, grated
- 2 tbsp. onion, minced
- ¼ tsp. pepper
- ¼ tsp. salt

**Directions**:
1. Put all fixing into the large mixing bowl and toss well.
2. Season with pepper and salt. Cover and place in the refrigerator.
3. Serve chilled and enjoy.

**Nutrition: Calories:** 165 kcal; **Fat:** 5.4 g; **Protein:** 25.2 g; **Carbs:** 2.2 g; **Sodium:** 153 mg

# CHAPTER 10:
# Seafood

### 275. Balsamic Salmon and Peaches Mix

**Preparation time:** 10 minutes
**Cooking time:** 10 minutes
**Servings:** 4
**Ingredients:**
- 1 tbsp. balsamic vinegar
- 1 tsp. thyme, chopped
- 1 tbsp. ginger, grated
- 4 tbsp. olive oil
- Black pepper to the taste
- 2 red onions, cut into wedges
- 2 peaches cut into wedges
- 2 salmon steaks

**Directions:**
1. In a small bowl, combine vinegar with ginger, thyme, 3 tbsp. olive oil, and black pepper and whisk In another bowl, mix the onion with peaches, 1 tbsp. oil, and pepper, and toss.
2. Season salmon with black pepper, place on preheated grill over medium heat, cook for 5 minutes on each side, and divide between plates.
3. Put the peaches and onions on the same grill, cook for 4 minutes on each side, divide next to the salmon, drizzle the vinegar mix and serve.
4. Enjoy!

**Nutrition: Calories:** 200 kcal; **Fat:** 2 g; **Fiber:** 2 g; **Carbs:** 3 g; **Protein:** 2 g

### 276. Salmon and Beans Mix

**Preparation time:** 10 minutes
**Cooking time:** 20 minutes
**Servings:** 4
**Ingredients:**
- 2 tbsp. coconut aminos
- ½ cup olive oil
- ½ cup low-sodium chicken stock

- 6 oz. salmon fillets
- 2 Garlic cloves, minced
- 1 tbsp. ginger, grated
- 1 cup black beans, canned, no-salt-added, drained, and rinsed
- 1 tsp. balsamic vinegar
- ¼ cup radishes, grated
- ¼ cup carrots, grated
- ¼ cup scallions, chopped

**Directions**:
1. In a bowl, combine the aminos with half of the oil and whisk.
2. Put the salmon in a baking dish, add coconut aminos and the stock, toss a bit, leave aside in the fridge for 10 minutes, introduce in preheated broiler and cook over medium-high heat for 4 minutes on each side.
3. Heat up a pan with the rest of the oil over medium heat, add garlic, ginger, and black beans, stir and cook for 3 minutes.
4. Add vinegar, radishes, carrots, and scallions, toss and cook for 5 minutes more.
5. Divide fish and the black beans mix between plates and serve.
6. Enjoy!

**Nutrition: Calories:** 220 kcal; **Fat:** 4 g; **Fiber:** 2 g; **Carbs:** 12 g; **Protein:** 7 g

## 277. Lemony Salmon and Pomegranate Mix

**Preparation time:** 20 minutes
**Cooking time:** 10 minutes
**Servings:** 4
**Ingredients:**
- 2 tbsp. olive oil
- 4 salmon fillets, skinless and boneless
- 4 tbsp. sesame paste
- Juice of 1 lemon
- 2 lemon, cut into wedges
- ½ cucumber, chopped
- Seeds from 1 pomegranate
- A bunch parsley, chopped

**Directions**:
1. Heat up a pan with the oil over medium heat, add salmon, cook for 5 minutes on each side, and divide between plates
2. In a bowl, mix sesame paste and lemon juice and whisk.
3. Add cucumber, parsley, and pomegranate seeds and toss
4. Divide this over the salmon and serve.
5. Enjoy!

**Nutrition: Calories:** 254 kcal; **Fat:** 3 g; **Fiber:** 6 g; **Carbs:** 9 g; **Protein:** 14 g

## 278. Salmon and Veggie Mix

**Preparation time:** 10 minutes
**Cooking time:** 30 minutes
**Servings:** 6
**Ingredients:**
- 3 red onions, cut into wedges
- ¾ cup green olives, pitted
- 3 red bell peppers, cut into strips
- ½ tsp. paprika, smoked
- Black pepper, to the taste
- 5 tbsp. olive oil
- 6 salmon fillets, skinless and boneless
- 2 tbsp. parsley, chopped

**Directions**:
1. Spread bell peppers, onions, and olives on a lined baking sheet, add smoked paprika, black pepper, and 3 tbsp. olive oil, toss to coat, bake in the oven at 375°F for 15 minutes, and divide between plates.
2. Heat up a pan with the rest of the oil over medium-high heat, add the salmon, season with black pepper, cook for 5 minutes on each side, divide next to the bell peppers and olives mix, sprinkle parsley on top, and serve.
3. Enjoy!

**Nutrition: Calories:** 221 kcal; **Fat:** 2 g; **Fiber:** 3 g; **Carbs:** 8 g; **Protein:** 10 g

## 279. Greek Salmon with Yogurt

**Preparation time:** 10 minutes
**Cooking time:** 15 minutes
**Servings:** 4
**Ingredients:**

- 4 medium salmon fillets, skinless and boneless
- 2 fennel bulb, chopped
- Black pepper to the taste
- ¼ cup low-sodium veggie stock
- 1 cup non-fat yogurt
- ¼ cup green olives pitted and chopped
- ¼ cup chives, chopped
- 2 tbsp. olive oil
- 2 tbsp. lemon juice

**Directions:**
1. Arrange the fennel in a baking dish, add salmon fillets, season with black pepper, add stock, bake in the oven at 390°F for 10 minutes and divide everything between plates.
2. In a bowl, mix yogurt with chives, olives, lemon juice, olive oil, and black pepper and whisk well. Top the salmon with this mix and serve. Enjoy!

**Nutrition: Calories:** 252 kcal; **Fat:** 2 g; **Fiber:** 4 g; **Carbs:** 12 g; **Protein:** 9 g

## 280. Creamy Salmon and Asparagus Mix

**Preparation time:** 10 minutes
**Cooking time:** 10 minutes
**Servings:** 6
**Ingredients:**

- 1 tbsp. lemon zest, grated
- 2 tbsp. lemon juice
- Black pepper to the taste
- 1 cup coconut cream
- lb. asparagus, trimmed
- 20 oz. salmon, skinless and boneless
- 1-oz. parmesan cheese, grated

**Directions:**
1. Put some water in a pot, add a pinch of salt, bring to a boil over medium heat, add asparagus, cook for 1 minute, transfer to a bowl filled with ice water, drain and put in a bowl.
2. Heat up the pot with the water again over medium heat, add salmon, cook for 5 minutes and also drain.
3. In a bowl, mix lemon peel with cream and lemon juice and whisk
4. Heat up a pan over medium-high heat, asparagus, cream, and pepper, cook for 1 more minute, divide between plates, add salmon and serve with grated parmesan.
5. Enjoy!

**Nutrition: Calories:** 354 kcal; **Fat:** 2 g; **Fiber:** 2 g; **Carbs:** 2 g; **Protein:** 4 g

## 281. Salmon and Brussels sprouts

**Preparation time:** 10 minutes
**Cooking time:** 20 minutes
**Servings:** 6
**Ingredients:**

- 2 tbsp. brown sugar
- 1 tsp. onion powder
- 1 tsp. garlic powder
- 1 tsp. paprika, smoked
- 2 tbsp. olive oil
- ¼ lb. Brussels sprouts, halved
- 6 medium salmon fillets, boneless

**Directions:**
1. In a bowl, mix sugar with onion powder, garlic powder, smoked paprika, and 2 tbsp. olive oil and whisk well.
2. Spread Brussels sprouts on a lined baking sheet, drizzle the rest of the olive oil, toss to coat, introduce in the oven at 450°F and bake for 5 minutes.
3. Add salmon fillets brush with sugar mix you've prepared, introduce in the oven and bake for 15 minutes more.
4. Divide everything between plates and serve.
5. Enjoy!

**Nutrition: Calories:** 212 kcal; **Fat:** 5 g; **Fiber:** 3 g; **Carbs:** 12 g; **Protein:** 8 g

## 282. Salmon and Beets Mix

**Preparation time:** 10 minutes
**Cooking time:** 35 minutes
**Servings:** 4
**Ingredients:**

- 1-lb. medium beets, sliced
- 6 tbsp. olive oil
- ½ lb. salmon fillets, skinless and boneless
- Black pepper to the taste
- 1 tbsp. chives, chopped
- 1 tbsp. parsley, chopped

- 1 tbsp. shallots, chopped
- 2 tbsp. lemon zest, grated
- ¼ cup lemon juice

**Directions:**
1. In a bowl, mix beets with ½ tbsp. oil and toss to coat, season with black pepper, spread on a lined baking sheet, and bake in the oven at 450°F for 20 minutes.
2. Add salmon, brush it with the rest of the oil, introduce in the oven, and bake for 15 minutes more.
3. In a bowl, combine the chives with the parsley, shallots, lemon zest, and lemon juice and toss.
4. Divide the salmon and the beets between plates, drizzle the chives mix on top, and serve.
5. Enjoy!

**Nutrition: Calories:** 272 kcal; **Fat:** 6 g; **Fiber:** 2 g; **Carbs:** 12 g; **Protein:** 9 g

## 283. Garlic Shrimp Mix

**Preparation time:** 10 minutes
**Cooking time:** 10 minutes
**Servings:** 4
**Ingredients:**
- 2 lb. shrimp, deveined and peeled
- 2 tsp. olive oil
- 6 tbsp. lemon juice
- 2 tbsp. dill, chopped
- 3 tbsp. oregano, chopped
- 2 garlic cloves, chopped
- Black pepper to the taste
- ¾ cup non-fat yogurt
- ½ lb. cherry tomatoes, halved

**Directions:**
1. Heat up a pan with the oil over medium-high heat, add the shrimp and cook for 3 minutes.
2. Add lemon juice, dill, oregano, garlic, black pepper, yogurt, and tomatoes, toss, cook for 5 minutes more, divide into bowls and serve.
3. Enjoy!

**Nutrition: Calories:** 253 kcal; **Fat:** 6 g; **Fiber:** 6 g; **Carbs:** 10 g; **Protein:** 17 g

## 284. Salmon and Potatoes Mix

**Preparation time:** 10 minutes
**Cooking time:** 10 minutes
**Servings:** 4
**Ingredients:**
- ½ lb. potatoes, chopped
- 2 tbsp. olive oil
- 4 oz. salmon, smoked and chopped
- 2 tbsp. chives, chopped
- 1 tsp. prepared horseradish
- ¼ cup coconut cream
- Black pepper to the taste

**Directions:**
1. Heat up a pan with the oil over medium heat, add potatoes and cook for 10 minutes.
2. Add salmon, chives, horseradish, cream, and black pepper, toss, cook for 1 minute more, divide between plates and serve.
3. Enjoy!

**Nutrition: Calories:** 233 kcal; **Fat:** 6 g; **Fiber:** 5 g; **Carbs:** 9 g; **Protein:** 11 g

## 285. Cod Salad with Mustard

**Preparation time:** 12 minutes
**Cooking time:** 12 minutes
**Servings:** 4
**Ingredients:**
- 4 medium cod fillets, skinless and boneless - 2 tbsp. mustard
- 2 tbsp. tarragon, chopped
- 2 tbsp. capers, drained
- 4 tbsp. olive oil+ 1 tsp.
- Black pepper to the taste
- 2 cups baby arugula
- 2 small red onion, sliced
- 1 small cucumber, sliced
- 1 tbsp. lemon juice

**Directions:**
1. In a bowl, mix mustard with 2 tbsp. olive oil, tarragon, and capers, and whisk.
2. Heat up a pan with 1 tsp. oil over medium-high heat, add fish, season with black pepper to the taste, and cook for 6 minutes on each side and cut into medium cubes.
3. In a salad bowl, combine the arugula with onion, cucumber, lemon juice, cod, and mustard mix, toss, and serve.
4. Enjoy!

**Nutrition: Calories:** 258 kcal; **Fat:** 12 g; **Fiber:** 6 g; **Carbs:** 12 g; **Protein:** 18 g

## 286. Broccoli and Cod Mash

**Preparation time:** 10 minutes
**Cooking time:** 20 minutes
**Servings:** 1
**Ingredients:**
- 2 cups broccoli, chopped
- 4 cod fillets, boneless, chopped
- 2 white onion, chopped

- 2 tbsp. olive oil
- 1 cup water
- 1 tbsp. low-fat cream cheese
- ½ tsp. black pepper, ground

**Directions:**
1. Roast the cod in the saucepan with olive oil for 1 minute per side.
2. Then add all remaining ingredients except cream cheese and boil the meal for 18 minutes.
3. After this, drain water, add cream cheese, and stir the meal well.

**Nutrition: Calories:** 186 kcal; **Protein:** 21.8 g; **Carbohydrates:** 5.8 g; **Fat:** 9.1 g; **Fiber:** 1.8 g; **Cholesterol:** 43 mg; **Sodium:** 105 mg; **Potassium:** 191 mg

## 287. Greek Style Salmon

**Preparation time:** 10 minutes
**Cooking time:** 10 minutes
**Servings:** 2
**Ingredients:**
- 4 medium salmon fillets, skinless and boneless - 2 tbsp. lemon juice
- 1 tbsp. oregano, dried
- 1 tsp. thyme, dried
- ¼ tsp. onion powder
- 1 tbsp. olive oil

**Directions:**
1. Heat up olive oil in the skillet.
2. Sprinkle the salmon with dried oregano, thyme, onion powder, and lemon juice.
3. Put the fish in the skillet and cook for 4 minutes per side.

**Nutrition: Calories:** 271 kcal; **Protein:** 34.7 g; **Carbohydrates:** 1.1 g; **Fat:** 14.7 g; **Fiber:** 0.6 g; **Cholesterol:** 78 mg; **Sodium:** 80 mg; **Potassium:** 711 mg

## 288. Spicy Ginger Sea bass

**Preparation time:** 5 minutes
**Cooking time:** 10 minutes
**Servings:** 2
**Ingredients:**
- 1 tbsp. ginger, grated
- 1 tbsp. sesame oil - ¼ tsp. chili powder
- 1 lb. sea bass fillets, boneless
- 1 tbsp. margarine

**Directions:**
1. Heat up sesame oil and margarine in the skillet. Add chili powder and ginger.
2. Then add sea bass and cook the fish for 3 minutes per side.
3. Then close the lid and simmer the fish for 3 minutes over low heat.

**Nutrition: Calories:** 216 kcal; **Protein:** 24 g; **Carbohydrates:** 1.1 g; **Fat:** 12.3 g; **Fiber:** 0.2 g; **Cholesterol:** 54 mg; **Sodium:** 123 mg; **Potassium:** 354 mg

## 289. Yogurt Shrimps

**Preparation time:** 5 minutes
**Cooking time:** 10 minutes
**Servings:** 2
**Ingredients:**
- 2 lb. shrimp, peeled
- 1 tbsp. margarine
- ¼ cup low-fat yogurt
- 1 tsp. lemon zest, grated
- 1 chili pepper, chopped

**Directions:**
1. Melt the margarine in the skillet, add chili pepper, and roast it for 1 minute.
2. Then add shrimps and lemon zest.
3. Roast the shrimps for 2 minutes per side.
4. After this, add yogurt, stir the shrimps well and cook for 5 minutes.

**Nutrition: Calories:** 137 kcal; **Protein:** 21.4 g; **Carbohydrates:** 2.4 g; **Fat:** 4 g; **Fiber:** 0.1 g; **Cholesterol:** 192 mg; **Sodium:** 257 mg; **Potassium:** 187 mg

## 290. Aromatic Salmon with Fennel Seeds

**Preparation time:** 8 minutes
**Cooking time:** 10 minutes
**Servings:** 2
**Ingredients:**
- 4 medium salmon fillets, skinless and boneless
- 1 tbsp. fennel seeds
- 2 tbsp. olive oil
- 1 tbsp. lemon juice
- 1 tbsp. water

**Directions:**
1. Heat up olive oil in the skillet.
2. Add fennel seeds and roast them for 1 minute.
3. Add salmon fillets and sprinkle with lemon juice.
4. Add water and roast the fish for 4 minutes per side over medium heat.

**Nutrition: Calories:** 301 kcal; **Protein:** 4.8 g; **Carbohydrates:** 0.8 g; **Fat:** 18.2 g; **Fiber:** 0.6 g; **Cholesterol:** 78 mg; **Sodium:** 81 mg; **Potassium:** 713 mg

## 291. Shrimp Quesadillas

**Preparation time:** 16 minutes
**Cooking time:** 5 minutes
**Servings:** 2
**Ingredients:**
- 2 whole-wheat tortillas
- ½ tsp. cumin, ground
- 4 cilantro leaves
- 3 oz. shrimp, diced and cooked
- plump tomato, de-seeded
- ¾ cup non-fat mozzarella cheese, grated
- ¼ cup red onion, diced

**Directions:**
1. In a medium bowl, combine the grated mozzarella cheese and the warm, cooked shrimp. Add the ground cumin, red onion, and tomato. Mix together. Spread the mixture evenly on the tortillas.
2. Heat a non-stick frying pan. Place the tortillas in the pan then heat until they are crisp.
3. Add the cilantro leaves. Fold over the tortillas. Press down for 1–2 minutes. Slice the tortillas into wedges. Serve immediately.

**Nutrition: Calories:** 99 kcal; **Fat:** 9 g; **Carbs:** 7.2 g; **Protein:** 59 g; **Sugars:** 4 g; **Sodium:** 500 mg

## 292. The OG Tuna Sandwich

**Preparation time:** 15 minutes
**Cooking time:** 5 minutes
**Servings:** 2
**Ingredients:**
- 30 g olive oil
- Medium cucumber, peeled and diced
- ½ g pepper
- Whole-wheat bread slices
- 85 g onion, diced
- 2 ½ g salt
- 1 can flavored tuna
- 85 g spinach, shredded

**Directions:**
1. Grab your blender and add the spinach, tuna, onion, oil, salt, and pepper in, and pulse for about 10 to 20 seconds.
2. In the meantime, toast your bread and add your diced cucumber to a bowl, which you can pour your tuna mixture in. Carefully mix and add the mixture to the bread once toasted.
3. Slice in half and serve, while storing the remaining mixture in the fridge.

**Nutrition: Calories:** 302 kcal; **Fat:** 5.8 g; **Carbs:** 36.62 g; **Protein:** 28 g; **Sugars:** 3.22 g; **Sodium:** 445 mg

## 293. Easy to Understand Mussels

**Preparation time:** 10 minutes
**Cooking time:** 10 minutes
**Servings:** 2
**Ingredients:**
- 2 lb. mussels, cleaned
- 4 garlic cloves, minced
- 2 shallots, chopped
- Lemon and parsley
- 2 tbsp. Butter
- ½ cup broth
- ½ cup white wine

**Directions:**
1. Clean the mussels and remove the beard
2. Discard any mussels that do not close when tapped against a hard surface
3. Set your pot to Sauté mode and add chopped onion and butter
4. Stir and sauté onions
5. Add garlic and cook for 1 minute
6. Add broth and wine
7. Lock up the lid and cook for 5 minutes on HIGH pressure
8. Release the pressure naturally over 10 minutes
9. Serve with a sprinkle of parsley and enjoy!

**Nutrition: Calories:** 286 kcal; **Fat:** 14 g; **Carbs:** 12 g; **Protein:** 28 g; **Sugars:** 0 g; **Sodium:** 314 mg

## 294. Citrus-Glazed Salmon with Zucchini Noodles

**Preparation time:** 15 minutes
**Cooking time:** 20 minutes
**Servings:** 4
**Ingredients:**
- 4 (5- to 6-oz.) pieces salmon
- ½ tsp. Kosher salt
- ¼ tsp. black pepper, freshly ground
- 2 tbsp. extra-virgin olive oil
- 1 cup orange juice, freshly squeezed
- 1 tsp. low-sodium soy sauce
- Zucchinis (about 16 oz.), spiralized
- 1 tbsp. fresh chives, chopped
- 1 tbsp. fresh parsley, chopped

**Directions:**
1. Preheat the oven to 350°F. Flavor the salmon with salt plus black pepper. Heat up the olive oil in a large oven-safe skillet or sauté pan over medium-high heat. Add the salmon, skin-side down, and sear for 5 minutes, or until the skin is golden brown and crispy.

2. Flip the salmon over, then transfer to the oven until your desired doneness is reached—about 5 minutes. Place the salmon on a cutting board to rest.
3. Place the same pan on the stove over medium-high heat. Add the orange juice and soy sauce to deglaze the pan. Bring to a simmer, scraping up any brown bits, and simmering 5 to 7 minutes.
4. Split or divide the zucchini noodles into 4 plates and place 1 piece of salmon on each. Pour the orange glaze over the salmon and zucchini noodles. Garnish with chives and parsley.

**Nutrition: Calories:** 280 kcal; **Fat:** 13 g; **Sodium:** 255 mg; **Carbohydrates:** 11 g; **Protein:** 30 g

### 295. Salmon Cakes with Bell Pepper plus Lemon Yogurt

**Preparation time:** 15 minutes
**Cooking time:** 15 minutes
**Servings:** 4
**Ingredients:**

- ¼ cup whole-wheat bread crumbs
- ¼ cup mayonnaise
- 1 large egg, beaten
- 1 tbsp. chives, chopped
- 1 tbsp. fresh parsley, chopped
- Zest of 1 lemon
- ¾ tsp. Kosher salt, divided
- ¼ tsp. black pepper, freshly ground
- 5 to 6-oz. cans no-salt salmon, boneless, skinless, drained, and finely flaked
- ½ bell pepper, diced small
- 2 tbsp. extra-virgin olive oil, divided
- 1 cup plain Greek yogurt
- Juice of 1 lemon

**Directions:**
1. Mix the bread crumbs, mayonnaise, egg, chives, parsley, lemon zest, ½ tsp. of salt, and black pepper in a large bowl. Add the salmon and the bell pepper and stir gently until well combined. Shape the mixture into 8 patties.
2. Heat up 1 tbsp. of the olive oil in a large skillet over medium-high heat. Cook half the cakes until the bottoms are golden brown, 4 to 5 minutes. Adjust the heat to medium if the bottoms start to burn.
3. Flip the cakes and cook until golden brown, an additional 4 to 5 minutes. Repeat the process with the rest of the 1 tbsp. olive oil and the rest of the cakes.
4. Mix the yogurt, lemon juice, and the remaining ¼ tsp. salt in a small bowl. Serve with the salmon cakes.

**Nutrition: Calories:** 330 kcal; **Fat:** 23 g; **Sodium:** 385 mg; **Carbohydrates:** 9 g; **Protein:** 21 g

### 296. Halibut in Parchment with Zucchini, Shallots, and Herbs

**Preparation time:** 15 minutes
**Cooking time:** 15 minutes
**Servings:** 4
**Ingredients:**

- ½ cup zucchini, diced small
- 2 shallot, minced
- 4 (5-oz.) halibut fillets (about 1 inch thick)
- 4 tsp. extra-virgin olive oil
- ¼ tsp. Kosher salt
- ⅛ tsp. black pepper, freshly ground
- 1 lemon, sliced into ⅛-inch-thick rounds
- 8 sprigs of thyme

**Directions:**
1. Preheat the oven to 450°F. Combine the zucchini and shallots in a medium bowl. Cut 4 (15x24-inch) pieces of parchment paper. Fold each sheet in half horizontally.
2. Draw a large half heart on one side of each folded sheet, with the fold along the heart center. Cut out the heart, open the parchment, and lay it flat.
3. Place a fillet near the center of each parchment heart. Drizzle 1 teaspoon of olive oil on each fillet. Sprinkle with salt and pepper. Top each fillet with lemon slices and 2 sprigs of thyme. Sprinkle each fillet with ¼ of the zucchini and shallot mixture. Fold the parchment over.
4. Starting at the top, fold the parchment edges over, and continue all the way around to make a packet. Twist the end tightly to secure. Arrange the 4 packets on a baking sheet. Bake for about 15 minutes. Place on plates; cut open. Serve immediately.

**Nutrition: Calories:** 190 kcal; **Fat:** 7 g; **Sodium:** 170 mg; **Carbohydrates:** 5 g; **Protein:** 27 g

### 297. Flounder with Tomatoes and Basil

**Preparation time:** 15 minutes
**Cooking time:** 20 minutes
**Servings:** 4
**Ingredients:**

- 1-lb. cherry tomatoes
- 4 garlic cloves, sliced

- 2 tbsp. extra-virgin olive oil
- 2 tbsp. lemon juice
- 2 tbsp. basil, cut into ribbons
- ½ tsp. Kosher salt
- ¼ tsp. black pepper, freshly ground
- 4 (5- to 6-oz.) flounder fillets

**Directions:**
1. Preheat the oven to 425°F.
2. Mix the tomatoes, garlic, olive oil, lemon juice, basil, salt, and black pepper in a baking dish. Bake for 5 minutes.
3. Remove, then arrange the flounder on top of the tomato mixture. Bake until the fish is opaque and begins to flake, about 10 to 15 minutes, depending on thickness.

**Nutrition: Calories:** 215 kcal; **Fat:** 9 g; **Sodium:** 261 mg; **Carbohydrates:** 6 g; **Protein:** 28 g

## 298. Grilled Mahi-Mahi with Artichoke Caponata

**Preparation time:** 15 minutes
**Cooking time:** 30 minutes
**Servings:** 4
**Ingredients:**
- 2 tbsp. extra-virgin olive oil
- 2 celery stalks, diced
- 2 onion, diced
- 2 garlic cloves, minced
- ½ cup cherry tomatoes, chopped
- ¼ cup white wine
- 1 tbsp. white wine vinegar
- 1 can artichoke hearts, drained and chopped
- ¼ cup green olives, pitted and chopped
- 1 tbsp. capers, chopped
- ¼ tsp. red pepper flakes
- 2 tbsp. fresh basil, chopped
- (5- to 6-oz. each) skinless mahi-mahi fillets
- ½ tsp. Kosher salt
- ¼ tsp. black pepper, freshly ground
- Olive oil cooking spray

**Directions:**
1. Warm-up olive oil in a skillet over medium heat then put the celery and onion and sauté 4 to 5 minutes. Add the garlic and sauté 30 seconds. Add the tomatoes and cook within 2 to 3 minutes. Add the wine and vinegar to deglaze the pan, increasing the heat to medium-high.
2. Add the artichokes, olives, capers, and red pepper flakes and simmer, reducing the liquid by half, about 10 minutes. Mix in the basil.
3. Season the mahi-mahi with salt and pepper. Heat a grill skillet or grill pan over medium-high heat and coat with olive oil cooking spray. Add the fish and cook within 4 to 5 minutes per side. Serve topped with the artichoke caponata.

**Nutrition: Calories:** 245 kcal; **Fat:** 9 g; **Sodium:** 570 mg; **Carbohydrates:** 10 g; **Protein:** 28 g

## 299. Cod and Cauliflower Chowder

**Preparation time:** 15 minutes
**Cooking time:** 40 minutes
**Servings:** 4
**Ingredients:**
- 2 tbsp. extra-virgin olive oil
- 2 leek, sliced thinly
- 4 garlic cloves, sliced
- 1 medium head cauliflower, coarsely chopped
- 1 tsp. Kosher salt
- ¼ tsp. black pepper, freshly ground
- 4 pints cherry tomatoes
- 2 cups no-salt-added vegetable stock
- ¼ cup green olives, pitted and chopped
- 1 to 1½ lb. cod
- ¼ cup fresh parsley, minced

**Directions:**
1. Heat up the olive oil in a Dutch oven or large pot over medium heat. Add the leek and sauté until lightly golden brown, about 5 minutes.
2. Add the garlic and sauté within 30 seconds. Add the cauliflower, salt, and black pepper and sauté 2 to 3 minutes.
3. Add the tomatoes and vegetable stock; increase the heat to high and boil, then turn the heat to low and simmer within 10 minutes.
4. Add the olives and mix. Add the fish, cover, and simmer 20 minutes or until the fish is opaque and flakes easily. Gently mix in the parsley.

**Nutrition: Calories:** 270 kcal; **Fat:** 9 g; **Sodium:** 545 mg; **Potassium:** 1475 mg; **Carbohydrates:** 19 g; **Protein:** 3 0g

## 300. Sardine Bruschetta with Fennel and Lemon Cream

**Preparation time:** 15 minutes
**Cooking time:** 0 minutes
**Servings:** 4
**Ingredients:**
- ⅓ cup plain Greek yogurt
- 2 tbsp. mayonnaise
- 2 tbsp. lemon juice, divided

- 2 tsp. lemon zest
- ¾ tsp. Kosher salt, divided
- 2 fennel bulb, cored and thinly sliced
- ¼ cup parsley, chopped, plus more for garnish
- ¼ cup fresh mint, chopped
- 2 tsp. extra-virgin olive oil
- ⅛ tsp. black pepper, freshly ground
- 8 slices multigrain bread, toasted
- (4.4-oz.) cans sardines, smoked

**Directions**:
1. Mix the yogurt, mayonnaise, 1 tbsp. of the lemon juice, the lemon zest, and ¼ tsp. of the salt in a small bowl.
2. Mix the remaining ½ tsp. salt, the remaining 1 tbsp. lemon juice, the fennel, parsley, mint, olive oil, and black pepper in a separate small bowl.
3. Spoon 1 tbsp. of the yogurt mixture on each piece of toast.
4. Divide the fennel mixture evenly on top of the yogurt mixture. Divide the sardines among the toasts, placing them on top of the fennel mixture.
5. Garnish with more herbs, if desired.

**Nutrition: Calories:** 400 kcal; **Fat:** 16 g; **Sodium:** 565 mg; **Carbohydrates:** 51 g; **Protein:** 16 g

### 301. Chopped Tuna Salad

**Preparation time:** 15 minutes
**Cooking time:** 0 minutes
**Servings:** 4
**Ingredients:**
- 2 tbsp. extra-virgin olive oil
- 2 tbsp. lemon juice
- 2 tsp. Dijon mustard
- ½ tsp. Kosher salt
- ¼ tsp. black pepper, freshly ground
- 12 olives, pitted and chopped
- ½ cup celery, diced
- ½ cup red onion, diced
- ½ cup red bell pepper, diced
- ½ cup fresh parsley, chopped
- 2 (6-oz.) cans no-salt-added tuna packed in water, drained
- 6 cups baby spinach

**Directions**:
1. Mix the olive oil, lemon juice, mustard, salt, and black pepper in a medium bowl. Add in the olives, celery, onion, bell pepper, and parsley and mix well.
2. Add the tuna and gently incorporate. Divide the spinach evenly among 4 plates or bowls. Spoon the tuna salad evenly on top of the spinach.

**Nutrition: Calories:** 220 kcal; **Fat:** 11 g; **Sodium:** 396 mg; **Carbohydrates:** 7 g; **Protein:** 25 g

### 302. Monkfish with Sautéed Leeks, Fennel, and Tomatoes

**Preparation time:** 15 minutes
**Cooking time:** 35 minutes
**Servings:** 4
**Ingredients:**
- 1½ lb. monkfish
- 2 tbsp. lemon juice, divided
- 2 tsp. Kosher salt, divided
- ⅛ tsp. black pepper, freshly ground
- 2 tbsp. extra-virgin olive oil
- 1 leek, sliced in half lengthwise, and thinly sliced
- ½ onion, julienned
- 2 garlic cloves, minced
- bulbs fennel, cored and thinly sliced, plus ¼ cup fronds for garnish
- 1 (14.5-oz.) can no-salt-added diced tomatoes
- 1 tbsp. fresh parsley, chopped
- 2 tbsp. fresh oregano, chopped
- ¼ tsp. red pepper flakes

**Directions**:
1. Place the fish in a medium baking dish and add 2 tbsp. of the lemon juice, ¼ tsp. of the salt, plus the black pepper. Place in the refrigerator.
2. Warm-up olive oil in a large skillet over medium heat, then put the leek and onion and sauté until translucent, about 3 minutes. Add the garlic and sauté within 30 seconds. Add the fennel and sauté 4 to 5 minutes. Add the tomatoes and simmer for 2 to 3 minutes.
3. Stir in the parsley, oregano, red pepper flakes, the remaining ¾ tsp. salt, and the remaining 1 tbsp. lemon juice. Put the fish over the leek mixture, cover, and simmer for 20 to 25 minutes. Garnish with the fennel fronds.

**Nutrition: Calories:** 220 kcal; **Fat:** 9 g; **Sodium:** 345 mg; **Carbohydrates:** 11 g; **Protein:** 22 g

### 303. Caramelized Fennel and Sardines with Penne

**Preparation time:** 15 minutes
**Cooking time:** 30 minutes
**Servings:** 4
**Ingredients:**
- 8 oz. whole-wheat penne

- 2 tbsp. extra-virgin olive oil
- 2 bulb fennel, cored and thinly sliced, plus ¼ cup fronds
- 4 celery stalks, thinly sliced, plus ½ cup leaves
- 2 garlic cloves, sliced
- ¾ tsp. Kosher salt
- ¼ tsp. black pepper, freshly ground
- Zest of 1 lemon
- Juice of 1 lemon
- 2 (4.4-oz.) cans sardines packed in olive oil, boneless, skinless, undrained

**Directions**:
1. Cook the penne, as stated in the package directions. Drain, reserving 1 cup of pasta water. Warm-up olive oil in a large skillet over medium heat, then put the fennel and celery and cook within 10 to 12 minutes. Add the garlic and cook within 1 minute.
2. Add the penne, reserved pasta water, salt, and black pepper. Adjust the heat to medium-high and cook for 1 to 2 minutes.
3. Remoe, then stir in the lemon zest, lemon juice, fennel fronds, and celery leaves. Break the sardines into bite-size pieces and gently mix in, along with the oil they were packed in.

**Nutrition: Calories:** 400 kcal; **Fat:** 15 g; **Sodium:** 530 mg; **Carbohydrates:** 46 g; **Protein:** 22 g

## 304. Coppin

**Preparation time:** 15 minutes
**Cooking time:** 35 minutes
**Servings:** 4
**Ingredients:**
- 2 tbsp. extra-virgin olive oil
- 2 onion, diced
- 2 bulb fennel, chopped, plus ½ cup fronds for garnish
- 1-quart no-salt-added vegetable stock
- 4 garlic cloves, smashed
- 8 thyme sprigs
- 1 tsp. Kosher salt
- ¼ tsp. red pepper flakes
- 2 lb. bay leaf, dried
- 2 bunch kale, stemmed and chopped
- 12 littleneck clams tightly closed, scrubbed
- 1-lb. fish (cod, halibut, and bass are all good choices)
- ¼ cup fresh parsley, chopped

**Directions**:
1. Heat up the olive oil in a large stockpot over medium heat. Add the onion and fennel and sauté for about 5 minutes. Add the vegetable stock, garlic, thyme, salt, red pepper flakes, and bay leaf. Adjust the heat to medium-high, and simmer. Add the kale, cover, and simmer within 5 minutes.
2. Carefully add the clams, cover, and simmer for about 15 minutes until they open. Remove the clams and set aside. Discard any clams that do not open.
3. Add the fish, cover, and simmer within 5 to 10 minutes, depending on the fish's thickness, until opaque and easily separated. Gently mix in the parsley. Divide the cioppino among 4 bowls. Place 3 clams in each bowl and garnish with the fennel fronds.

**Nutrition: Calories:** 285 kcal; **Fat:** 9 g; **Sodium:** 570 mg; **Carbohydrates:** 19 g; **Protein:** 32 g

## 305. Green Goddess Crab Salad with Endive

**Preparation time:** 15 minutes
**Cooking time:** 10 minutes
**Servings:** 4
**Ingredients:**
- 1-lb. lump crabmeat
- ⅔ cup plain Greek yogurt
- 3 tbsp. mayonnaise
- 3 tbsp. fresh chives, chopped, plus additional for garnish
- 3 tbsp. fresh parsley, chopped, plus extra for garnish
- 3 tbsp. fresh basil, chopped, plus extra for garnish - Zest of 1 lemon
- Juice of 1 lemon
- ½ tsp. Kosher salt
- ¼ tsp. black pepper, freshly ground
- 4 endives, ends cut off, and leaves separated

**Directions**:
1. In a medium bowl, combine the crab, yogurt, mayonnaise, chives, parsley, basil, lemon zest, lemon juice, salt, plus black pepper, and mix until well combined.
2. Place the endive leaves on 4 salad plates. Divide the crab mixture evenly on top of the endive. Garnish with additional herbs, if desired.

**Nutrition: Calories:** 200 kcal; **Fat:** 9 g; **Sodium:** 570 mg; **Carbohydrates:** 44 g; **Protein:** 25 g

## 306. Seared Scallops with Blood Orange Glaze

**Preparation time:** 15 minutes
**Cooking time:** 20 minutes
**Servings:** 4
**Ingredients:**
- 3 tbsp. extra-virgin olive oil, divided
- 3 garlic cloves, minced
- ½ tsp. Kosher salt, divided
- 4 blood oranges, juiced
- 2 tsp. blood orange zest
- ½ tsp. red pepper flakes
- 1-lb. scallops, small side muscle removed
- ¼ tsp. black pepper, freshly ground
- ¼ cup fresh chives, chopped

**Directions:**
1. Heat up 1 tbsp. of the olive oil in a small saucepan over medium-high heat. Add the garlic and ¼ tsp. of the salt and sauté for 30 seconds.
2. Add the orange juice and zest, bring to a boil, reduce the heat to medium-low, and cook within 20 minutes, or until the liquid reduces by half and becomes a thicker syrup consistency. Remove and mix in the red pepper flakes.
3. Pat the scallops dry with a paper towel and season with the remaining ¼ tsp. salt and the black pepper. Heat up the remaining 2 tbsp. of olive oil in a large skillet on medium-high heat. Add the scallops gently and sear.
4. Cook on each side within 2 minutes. If cooking in 2 batches, use 1 tbsp. of oil per batch. Serve the scallops with the blood orange glaze and garnish with the chives.

**Nutrition: Calories:** 140 kcal; **Fat:** 4 g; **Sodium:** 570 mg; **Carbohydrates:** 12 g; **Protein:** 15 g

## 307. Lemon Garlic Shrimp

**Preparation time:** 15 minutes
**Cooking time:** 10 minutes
**Servings:** 4
**Ingredients:**
- 2 tbsp. extra-virgin olive oil
- 3 garlic cloves, sliced
- ½ tsp. Kosher salt
- ¼ tsp. red pepper flakes
- 1-lb. large shrimp, peeled and deveined
- ½ cup white wine
- 3 tbsp. fresh parsley, minced
- Zest of ½ lemon
- Juice of ½ lemon

**Directions:**
1. Heat up the olive oil in a wok or large skillet over medium-high heat. Add the garlic, salt, and red pepper flakes and sauté until the garlic starts to brown, 30 seconds to 1 minute.
2. Add the shrimp and cook within 2 to 3 minutes on each side. Pour in the wine and deglaze the wok, scraping up any flavorful brown bits, for 1 to 2 minutes. Turn off the heat; mix in the parsley, lemon zest, and lemon juice.

**Nutrition: Calories:** 200 kcal; **Fat:** 9 g; **Sodium:** 310 mg; **Carbohydrates:** 3 g; **Protein:** 23 g

## 308. Shrimp Fra Diavolo

**Preparation time:** 15 minutes
**Cooking time:** 10 minutes
**Servings:** 4
**Ingredients:**
- 2 tbsp. extra-virgin olive oil
- onion, diced small
- 1 fennel bulb, cored and diced small, plus ¼ cup fronds for garnish
- 1 bell pepper, diced small
- ½ tsp. oregano, dried
- ½ tsp. thyme, dried
- ½ tsp. Kosher salt
- ¼ tsp. red pepper flakes
- 1 (14.5-oz.) can no-salt-added diced tomatoes
- 1-lb. shrimp, peeled and deveined
- Juice of 1 lemon
- Zest of 1 lemon
- tbsp. fresh parsley, chopped, for garnish

**Directions:**
1. Heat up the olive oil in a large skillet or sauté pan over medium heat. Add the onion, fennel, bell pepper, oregano, thyme, salt, and red pepper flakes and sauté until translucent, about 5 minutes.
2. Drizzle the pan using the canned tomatoes' juice, scraping up any brown bits, and bringing to a boil. Add the diced tomatoes and the shrimp. Lower heat to a simmer within 3 minutes.
3. Turn off the heat. Add the lemon juice and lemon zest, and toss well to combine. Garnish with the parsley and the fennel fronds.

**Nutrition: Calories:** 240 kcal; **Fat:** 9 g; **Sodium:** 335 mg; **Carbohydrates:** 13 g; **Protein:** 2 5g

## 309. Fish Amandine

**Preparation time:** 15 minutes
**Cooking time:** 15 minutes
**Servings:** 4
**Ingredients:**
- 4-oz. tilapia or halibut fillets, skinless, trout, (½- to 1-inch thick)
- ¼ cup buttermilk - ½ tsp. dry mustard
- ⅛ tsp. red pepper, crushed
- 1 tbsp. butter, melted - ¼ tsp. salt
- ½ cup panko bread crumbs
- 2 tbsp. fresh parsley, chopped
- ¼ cup almonds, sliced, coarsely chopped
- 2 tbsp. Parmesan cheese, grated

**Directions:**
1. Defrost fish, if frozen. Preheat oven to 450°F. Grease a shallow baking pan; set aside. Rinse fish; pat dry with paper towels.
2. Pour buttermilk into a shallow dish. In an extra shallow dish, mix bread crumbs, dry mustard, parsley, and salt. Soak fish into buttermilk, then into crumb mixture, turning to coat. Put coated fish in the ready baking pan.
3. Flavor the fish with almonds plus Parmesan cheese; drizzle with melted butter. Sprinkle with crinkled red pepper. Bake for 5 minutes per ½-inch thickness of fish or until fish flakes easily when checked with a fork.

**Nutrition: Calories:** 209 kcal; **Fat:** 8.7 g; **Sodium:** 302 mg; **Carbohydrates:** 6.7 g; **Protein:** 26.2 g

## 310. Air-Fryer Fish Cakes

**Preparation time:** 15 minutes
**Cooking time:** 10 minutes
**Servings:** 2
**Ingredients:**
- Cooking spray
- 10 oz. white fish, finely chopped
- ⅔ cup whole-wheat panko breadcrumbs
- 3 tbsp. fresh Cilantro, finely chopped
- 2 tbsp. Thai sweet chili sauce
- 2 tbsp. canola mayonnaise
- large egg
- ⅛ tsp. salt
- ¼ tsp. pepper, ground
- lime wedges

**Directions:**
1. Oil the basket of an air fryer with cooking spray.
2. Put fish, cilantro, panko, chili sauce, egg, mayonnaise, pepper, and salt in a medium bowl; stir until well mixed. Shape the mixture into four 3-inch-diameter cakes.
3. Oil the cakes with cooking spray; place in the basket. Cook at 400°F until the cakes are browned for 9 to 10 minutes. Serve with lime wedges.

**Nutrition: Calories:** 399 kcal; **Fat:** 15.5 g; **Sodium:** 537 mg; **Carbohydrates:** 27.9 g; **Protein:** 34.6 g

## 311. Pesto Shrimp Pasta

**Preparation time:** 15 minutes
**Cooking time:** 12 minutes
**Servings:** 4
**Ingredients:**
- ⅛ tsp. pepper, freshly cracked
- 1 cup orzo, dried
- 4 tsp. packaged pesto sauce mix
- 1 lemon, halved
- ⅛ tsp. coarse salt
- 1-lb. medium shrimp, thawed
- 1 medium zucchini, halved lengthwise and sliced
- 1 tbsp. olive oil, divided
- 1-oz. Parmesan cheese, shaved

**Directions:**
1. Prepare orzo pasta concerning package directions. Drain; reserving ¼ cup of the pasta cooking water. Mix 1 tsp. of the pesto mix into the kept cooking water and set aside.
2. Mix 3 tsp. of the pesto mix plus 1 tbsp. of the olive oil in a large plastic bag. Seal and shake to mix. Put the shrimp in the bag; seal, and turn to coat. Set aside.
3. Sauté zucchini in a big skillet over moderate heat for 1 to 2 minutes, stirring repeatedly. Put the pesto-marinated shrimp in the skillet and cook for 5 minutes or until the shrimp is dense.
4. Put the cooked pasta in the skillet with the zucchini and shrimp combination. Stir in the kept pasta water until absorbed, grating up any seasoning in the bottom of the pan. Season with pepper and salt. Squeeze the lemon over the pasta. Top with Parmesan then serve.

**Nutrition: Calories:** 361 kcal; **Fat:** 10.1 g; **Sodium:** 502 mg; **Carbohydrates:** 35.8 g; **Protein:** 31.6 g

## 312. Easy Shrimp and Mango

**Preparation time:** 10 minutes
**Cooking time:** 0 minutes
**Servings:** 4
**Ingredients:**
- 3 tbsp. balsamic vinegar
- 3 tbsp. coconut sugar
- 6 tbsp. avocado mayonnaise
- 3 mangos, peeled and cubed
- 3 tbsp. parsley, finely chopped
- 2 lb. shrimp, peeled, deveined, and cooked

**Directions:**
1. In a bowl, mix vinegar with sugar and mayo and whisk.
2. In another bowl, combine the mango with the parsley and shrimp, and add the mayo mix, toss and serve. Enjoy!

**Nutrition: Calories:** 204 kcal; **Fat:** 3 g; **Fiber:** 2 g; **Carbs:** 8 g; **Protein:** 8 g

## 313. Spring Salmon Mix

**Preparation time:** 10 minutes
**Cooking time:** 0 minutes
**Servings:** 4
**Ingredients:**
- 2 tbsp. scallions, chopped
- 2 tbsp. sweet onion, chopped
- ½ tsp. lime juice - 2 tbsp. chives, minced
- 2 tbsp. olive oil
- 1 lb. salmon, smoked flaked
- 1 cup cherry tomatoes, halved
- Black pepper to the taste
- 1 tbsp. parsley, chopped

**Directions:**
1. In a bowl, mix the scallions with sweet onion, lime juice, chives, oil, salmon, tomatoes, black pepper, and parsley, toss and serve.
2. Enjoy!

**Nutrition: Calories:** 200 kcal; **Fat:** 8 g; **Fiber:** 3 g; **Carbs:** 8 g; **Protein:** 6 g

## 314. Smoked Salmon and Green Beans

**Preparation time:** 10 minutes
**Cooking time:** 0 minutes
**Servings:** 4
**Ingredients:**
- 3 tbsp. balsamic vinegar
- 2 tbsp. olive oil
- ⅓ cup Kalamata olives, pitted and minced
- 2 Garlic clove, minced
- Black pepper to the taste
- ½ tsp. lemon zest, grated
- lb. green beans, blanched and halved
- ½ lb. cherry tomatoes, halved
- ½ fennel bulb, sliced
- ½ red onion, sliced
- 2 cups baby arugula
- ¾ lb. smoked salmon, flaked

**Directions:**
1. In a bowl, combine the green beans with cherry tomatoes, fennel, onion, arugula, and salmon and toss.
2. Add vinegar, oil, olives, garlic, black pepper, and lemon zest, toss and serve.
3. Enjoy!

**Nutrition: Calories** 212 kcal; **Fat:** 3 g; **Fiber:** 3 g; **Carbs:** 6 g; **Protein:** 4 g

## 315. Saffron Shrimp

**Preparation time:** 10 minutes
**Cooking time:** 30 minutes
**Servings:** 4
**Ingredients:**
- 1 tsp. lemon juice
- Black pepper to the taste
- ½ cup avocado mayo
- ½ tsp. sweet paprika
- 2 tbsp. olive oil
- 2 Fennel bulb, chopped
- 1 yellow onion, chopped
- 2 Garlic cloves, minced
- 1 cup canned tomatoes, no-salt-added and chopped
- 1 and ½ lb. big shrimp, peeled and deveined
- ¼ tsp. saffron powder

**Directions:**
1. In a bowl, combine the garlic with lemon juice, black pepper, mayo, and paprika, and whisk.
2. Add the shrimp and toss.
3. Heat up a pan with the oil over medium-high heat, add the shrimp, fennel, onion, and garlic mix, toss and cook for 4 minutes.
4. Add tomatoes and saffron, toss, divide into bowls and serve. Enjoy!

**Nutrition: Calories:** 210 kcal; **Fat:** 2 g; **Fiber:** 5 g; **Carbs:** 8 g; **Protein:** 4 g

## 316. Crab, Zucchini and Watermelon Soup

**Preparation time:** 4 hours
**Cooking time:** 0 minutes
**Servings:** 4
**Ingredients:**
- ¼ cup basil, chopped
- 2 lb. tomatoes
- 5 cups watermelon, cubed
- ¼ cup red wine vinegar
- ⅓ cup olive oil
- 2 garlic cloves, minced
- Zucchini, chopped
- Black pepper to the taste
- 1 cup crabmeat

**Directions:**
1. In your food processor, mix tomatoes with basil, vinegar, 4 cups watermelon, garlic, ⅓ cup oil, and black pepper to the taste, pulse, pour into a bowl, and keep in the fridge for 1 hour.
2. Divide this into bowls, add zucchini, crab, and the rest of the watermelon and serve.
3. Enjoy!

**Nutrition: Calories:** 231 kcal; **Fat:** 3 g; **Fiber:** 3 g; **Carbs:** 6 g; **Protein:** 8 g

## 317. Shrimp and Orzo

**Preparation time:** 10 minutes
**Cooking time:** 30 minutes
**Servings:** 4
**Ingredients:**
- 2 lb. shrimp, peeled and deveined
- Black pepper to the taste
- 2 garlic cloves, minced
- 2 tbsp. olive oil
- ½ tsp. oregano, dried
- 1 yellow onion, chopped
- 2 cups low-sodium chicken stock
- 4 oz. orzo
- ½ cup water
- 4 oz. canned tomatoes, no-salt-added and chopped
- Juice of 1 lemon

**Directions:**
1. Heat up a pan with the oil over medium-high heat, add onion, garlic, and oregano, stir, and cook for 4 minutes.
2. Add orzo, stir and cook for 2 more minutes.
3. Add stock and the water, bring to a boil, cover, reduce heat to low, and cook for 12 minutes.
4. Add lemon juice, tomatoes, black pepper, and shrimp, introduce in the oven, and bake at 400°F for 15 minutes.
5. Divide between plates and serve.
6. Enjoy!

**Nutrition: Calories:** 228 kcal; **Fat:** 4 g; **Fiber:** 3 g; **Carbs:** 7 g; **Protein:** 8 g

## 318. Lemon and Garlic Scallops

**Preparation time:** 10 minutes
**Cooking time:** 5 minutes
**Servings:** 4
**Ingredients:**
- 2 tbsp. olive oil - ¼ lb. scallops, dried
- 2 tbsp. all-purpose flour
- ¼ tsp. sunflower seeds
- 4–5 garlic cloves, minced
- 1 scallion, chopped
- 1 pinch sage, ground - 1 lemon juice
- 2 tbsp. parsley, chopped

**Directions:**
1. Take a nonstick skillet and place over medium-high heat.
2. Add oil and allow the oil to heat up.
3. Take a medium-sized bowl and add scallops alongside sunflower seeds and flour.
4. Place the scallops in the skillet and add scallions, garlic, and sage.
5. Sauté for 3-4 minutes until they show an opaque texture.
6. Stir in lemon juice and parsley.
7. Remove heat and serve hot!

**Nutrition: Calories:** 151 kcal; **Fat:** 4 g; **Carbohydrates:** 10 g; **Protein:** 18 g

## 319. Walnut Encrusted Salmon

**Preparation time:** 10 minutes
**Cooking time:** 14 minutes
**Servings:** 34
**Ingredients:**
- ½ cup walnuts
- 2 tbsp. stevia
- ½ tbsp. Dijon mustard
- ¼ tsp. dill
- 2 salmon fillets (3 oz. each)
- 2 tbsp. olive oil
- Sunflower seeds and pepper to taste

**Directions:**
1. Preheat your oven to 350°F.
2. Add walnuts, mustard, stevia to a food processor and process until your desired consistency is achieved.

3. Take a frying pan and place it over medium heat.
4. Add oil and let it heat up.
5. Add salmon and sear for 3 minutes.
6. Add walnut mix and coat well.
7. Transfer coated salmon to baking sheet, bake in the oven for 8 minutes.
8. Serve and enjoy!

**Nutrition: Calories:** 373 kcal; **Fat:** 43 g; **Carbohydrates:** 4 g; **Protein:** 20 g

## 320. Roasted Lemon Swordfish

**Preparation time:** 10 minutes
**Cooking time:** 70-80 minutes
**Servings:** 4
**Ingredients:**
- ¼ cup parsley, chopped
- ½ tsp. garlic, chopped
- ½ tsp. canola oil
- 4 swordfish fillets (6 oz. each)
- ¼ tsp. sunflower seeds
- 1 tbsp. sugar
- 2 Lemons, quartered and seeds removed

**Directions:**
1. Preheat your oven to 375°F.
2. Take a small-sized bowl and add sugar, sunflower seeds, lemon wedges.
3. Toss well to coat them.
4. Take a shallow baking dish and add lemons; cover with aluminum foil.
5. Roast for about 60 minutes until lemons are tender and browned (Slightly).
6. Heat your grill and place the rack about 4 inches away from the source of heat.
7. Take a baking pan and coat it with cooking spray. Transfer fish fillets to the pan and brush with oil on top spread garlic on top.
8. Grill for about 5 minutes on each side until the fillet turns opaque.
9. Transfer fish to a serving platter, squeeze roasted lemon on top. Sprinkle parsley, serve with a lemon wedge on the side.
10. Enjoy!

**Nutrition: Calories:** 280 kcal; **Fat:** 12 g; **Net Carbohydrates:** 4 g; **Protein:** 34 g

## 321. Especial Glazed Salmon

**Preparation time:** 45 minutes
**Cooking time:** 10 minutes
**Servings:** 4
**Ingredients:**
- 4 pieces salmon fillets (5 oz. each)
- 4 tbsp. coconut aminos
- 4 tsp. olive oil - 2 tsp. ginger, minced
- 4 tsp. garlic, minced
- 2 tbsp. sugar-free ketchup
- 4 tbsp. dry white wine
- 2 tbsp. red boat fish sauce, low-sodium

**Directions:**
1. Take a bowl and mix in coconut aminos, garlic, ginger, fish, sauce, and mix.
2. Add salmon and let it marinate for 15-20 minutes.
3. Take a skillet/pan and place it over medium heat.
4. Add oil and let it heat up.
5. Add salmon fillets and cook on high heat for 3-4 minutes per side.
6. Remove dish once crispy.
7. Add sauce and wine.
8. Simmer for 5 minutes on low heat.
9. Return salmon to the glaze and flip until both sides are glazed. Serve and enjoy!

**Nutrition: Calories:** 372 kcal; **Fat:** 24 g; **Carbohydrates:** 3 g; **Protein:** 35 g

## 322. Generous Stuffed Salmon Avocado

**Preparation time:** 10 minutes
**Cooking time:** 30 minutes
**Servings:** 2
**Ingredients:**
- 2 ripe organic avocado
- 4 oz. wild-caught smoked salmon
- 4 oz. cashew cheese
- 2 tbsp. extra virgin olive oil
- 2 Sunflower seeds as needed

**Directions:**
1. Cut avocado in half and deseed.
2. Add the rest of the ingredients to a food processor and process until coarsely chopped.
3. Place mixture into the avocado.
4. Serve and enjoy!

**Nutrition: Calories:** 525 kcal; **Fat:** 48 g; **Carbohydrates:** 4 g; **Protein:** 19 g

## 323. Spanish Mussels

**Preparation time:** 10 minutes
**Cooking time:** 23 minutes
**Servings:** 4
**Ingredients:**
- 3 tbsp. olive oil - Pepper to taste
- 2 lb. mussels, scrubbed
- 3 cups tomatoes, canned and crushed

- 2 shallot, chopped
- 2 garlic cloves, minced
- 2 cups low-sodium vegetable stock
- ⅓ cup cilantro, chopped

**Directions**:
1. Take a pan and place it over medium-high heat, add shallot and stir-cook for 3 minutes.
2. Add garlic, stock, tomatoes, pepper, stir and reduce heat, simmer for 10 minutes.
3. Add mussels, cilantro, and toss.
4. Cover and cook for 10 minutes more.
5. Serve and enjoy!

**Nutrition: Calories:** 210 kcal; **Fat:** 2 g; **Carbohydrates:** 5 g; **Protein:** 8 g

### 324. Tilapia Broccoli Platter

**Preparation time:** 4 minutes
**Cooking time:** 14 minutes
**Servings:** 2
**Ingredients:**
- 6 oz. tilapia, frozen
- 1 tbsp. almond butter
- 2 tbsp. garlic, minced
- 1 tsp. lemon pepper seasoning
- 1 cup broccoli florets, fresh

**Directions**:
1. Preheat your oven to 350°F.
2. Add fish in aluminum foil packets.
3. Arrange broccoli around fish.
4. Sprinkle lemon pepper on top.
5. Close the packets and seal.
6. Bake for 14 minutes.
7. Take a bowl and add garlic and almond butter, mix well and keep the mixture on the side.
8. Remove the packet from the oven and transfer to a platter.
9. Place almond butter on top of the fish and broccoli, serve and enjoy!

**Nutrition: Calories:** 362 kcal; **Fat:** 25 g; **Carbohydrates:** 2 g; **Protein:** 29 g

### 325. Salmon with Peas and Parsley Dressing

**Preparation time:** 15 minutes
**Cooking time:** 15 minutes
**Servings:** 4
**Ingredients:**
- 16 oz. salmon fillets, boneless and skin-on
- 1 tbsp. parsley, chopped
- 10 oz. peas
- 9 oz. vegetable stock, low-sodium
- 2 cups water
- ½ tsp. oregano, dried
- ½ tsp. sweet paprika
- 2 Garlic cloves, minced
- A pinch black pepper

**Directions**:
1. Add garlic, parsley, paprika, oregano, and stock to a food processor and blend.
2. Add water to your Instant Pot.
3. Add steam basket.
4. Add fish fillets inside the steamer basket.
5. Season with pepper.
6. Lock the lid and cook on HIGH pressure for 10 minutes.
7. Release the pressure naturally over 10 minutes.
8. Divide the fish amongst plates.
9. Add peas to the steamer basket and lock the lid again, cook on HIGH pressure for 5 minutes.
10. Quick-release the pressure.
11. Divide the peas next to your fillets and serve with the parsley dressing drizzled on top
12. Enjoy!

**Nutrition: Calories:** 315 kcal; **Fat:** 5 g; **Carbohydrates:** 14 g; **Protein:** 16 g

### 326. Mackerel and Orange Medley

**Preparation time:** 10 minutes
**Cooking time:** 10 minutes
**Servings:** 4
**Ingredients:**
- 4 mackerel fillets, skinless and boneless
- 4 spring onion, chopped
- tsp. olive oil
- 1-inch ginger piece, grated
- Black pepper as needed
- Juice and zest of 1 whole orange
- 1 cup low-sodium fish stock

**Directions**:
1. Season the fillets with black pepper and rub olive oil. Add stock, orange juice, ginger, orange zest, and onion to Instant Pot.
2. Place a steamer basket and add the fillets.
3. Lock the lid and cook on HIGH pressure for 10 minutes.
4. Release the pressure naturally over 10 minutes.
5. Divide the fillets amongst plates and drizzle the orange sauce from the pot over the fish.
6. Enjoy!

**Nutrition: Calories:** 200 kcal; **Fat:** 4 g; **Carbohydrates:** 19 g; **Protein:** 14 g

### 327. Spicy Chili Salmon

**Preparation time:** 10 minutes
**Cooking time:** 7 minutes
**Servings:** 4
**Ingredients:**

- 4 salmon fillets, boneless and skin-on
- 2 tbsp. assorted chili peppers, chopped
- 1 lemon juice
- lemon, sliced
- 1 cup water
- Black pepper

**Directions:**

1. Add water to the Instant Pot.
2. Add steamer basket and add salmon fillets, season the fillets with salt and pepper.
3. Drizzle lemon juice on top.
4. Top with lemon slices.
5. Lock the lid and cook on HIGH pressure for 7 minutes.
6. Release the pressure naturally over 10 minutes.
7. Divide the salmon and lemon slices between serving plates.
8. Enjoy!

**Nutrition: Calories:** 281 kcal; **Fat:** 8 g; **Carbs:** 19 g; **Protein:** 7 g

### 328. Simple One-Pot Mussels

**Preparation time:** 10 minutes
**Cooking time:** 5 minutes
**Servings:** 4
**Ingredients:**

- 2 tbsp. butter
- 2 shallots, chopped
- 4 minced garlic cloves
- ½ cup broth
- ½ cup white wine
- 2 lb. mussels, cleaned
- Lemon and parsley, for serving

**Directions:**

1. Clean the mussels and remove the beard.
2. Discard any mussels that do not close when tapped against a hard surface.
3. Set your pot to Sauté mode and add chopped onion and butter. Stir and sauté onions.
4. Add garlic and cook for 1 minute. Add broth and wine. Lock the lid and cook for 5 minutes on HIGH pressure. Release the pressure naturally over 10 minutes.
5. Serve with a sprinkle of parsley and enjoy!

**Nutrition: Calories:** 286 kcal; **Fat:** 14 g; **Carbs:** 12 g; **Protein:** 28 g

### 329. Lemon Pepper and Salmon

**Preparation time:** 5 minutes
**Cooking time:** 6 minutes
**Servings:** 3
**Ingredients:**

- ¾ cup water
- 2 Few sprigs of parsley, basil, tarragon, basil
- 2 lb. salmon, skin on
- 1 tsp. ghee
- ¼ tsp. salt
- ½ tsp. pepper
- ½ lemon, thinly sliced
- 1 whole carrot, julienned

**Directions:**

1. Set your pot to Sauté mode and water and herbs.
2. Place a steamer rack inside your pot and place salmon.
3. Drizzle the ghee on top of the salmon and season with salt and pepper.
4. Cover lemon slices.
5. Lock the lid and cook on HIGH pressure for 3 minutes.
6. Release the pressure naturally over 10 minutes.
7. Transfer the salmon to a serving platter.
8. Set your pot to Sauté mode and add vegetables.
9. Cook for 1-2 minutes.
10. Serve with vegetables and salmon.
11. Enjoy!

**Nutrition: Calories:** 464 kcal; **Fat:** 34 g; **Carbohydrates:** 3 g; **Protein:** 34 g

### 330. Simple Sautéed Garlic and Parsley Scallops

**Preparation time:** 5 minutes
**Cooking time:** 25 minutes
**Servings:** 4
**Ingredients:**

- 8 tbsp. almond butter
- 2 garlic cloves, minced
- 16 large sea scallops
- Sunflower seeds and pepper to taste
- ½ tbsp. olive oil

**Directions:**

1. Seasons scallops with sunflower seeds and pepper.
2. Take a skillet, place it over medium heat, add oil and let it heat up.
3. Sauté scallops for 2 minutes per side, repeat until all scallops are cooked.
4. Add almond butter to the skillet and let it melt.

5. Stir in garlic and cook for 15 minutes.
6. Return scallops to skillet and stir to coat.
7. Serve and enjoy!

**Nutrition: Calories:** 417 kcal; **Fat:** 31 g; **Net Carbohydrates:** 5 g; **Protein:** 29 g

---

### 331. Salmon and Cucumber Platter

**Preparation time:** 10 minutes
**Cooking time:** 0 minutes
**Servings:** 4
**Ingredients:**

- 2 cucumbers, cubed
- 2 tsp. fresh squeezed lemon juice
- 4 oz. non-fat yogurt
- 1 tsp. lemon zest, grated
- Pepper to taste
- 1 tsp. dill, chopped
- 8 oz. smoked salmon, flaked

**Directions:**

1. Take a bowl and add cucumbers, lemon juice, lemon zest, pepper, dill, salmon, and yogurt, and toss well.
2. Serve cold.
3. Enjoy!

**Nutrition: Calories:** 242 kcal; **Fat:** 3 g; **Carbohydrates:** 3 g; **Protein:** 3 g

# CHAPTER 11:
# Meat Dishes

## 332. Tarragon Pork Steak with Tomatoes

**Preparation time:** 10 minutes
**Cooking time:** 22 minutes
**Servings:** 4
**Ingredients:**
- 4 medium pork steaks
- Black pepper to the taste
- 1 tbsp. olive oil
- 8 cherry tomatoes, halved
- A handful tarragon, chopped

**Directions:**
1. Heat up a pan with the oil over medium-high heat, add steaks, season with black pepper, cook them for 6 minutes on each side, and divide between plates.
2. Heat up the same pan over medium heat, add the tomatoes and the tarragon, cook for 10 minutes, divide next to the pork and serve. Enjoy!

**Nutrition: Calories:** 263 kcal; **Fat:** 4 g; **Fiber:** 6 g; **Carbs:** 12 g; **Protein:** 16 g

## 333. Pork Meatballs

**Preparation time:** 10 minutes
**Cooking time:** 10 minutes
**Servings:** 4
**Ingredients:**
- 1 lb. pork, ground

- ⅓ cup cilantro, chopped
- 1 cup red onion, chopped
- 4 garlic cloves, minced
- 1 tbsp. ginger, grated
- 1 Thai chili, chopped
- 2 tbsp. olive oil

**Directions:**
1. In a bowl, combine the meat with cilantro, onion, garlic, ginger, and chili, stir well and shape medium meatballs out of this mix.
2. Heat up a pan with the oil over medium-high heat, add the meatballs, cook them for 5 minutes on each side, divide them between plates and serve with a side salad.
3. Enjoy!

**Nutrition: Calories:** 220 kcal; **Fat:** 4 g; **Fiber:** 2 g; **Carbs:** 8 g; **Protein:** 14 g

---

## 334. Lamb Chops with Rosemary

**Preparation time:** 5 minutes
**Cooking time:** 15 minutes
**Servings:** 4
**Ingredients:**
- 1 lb. lamb chops
- ½ tsp. black pepper, freshly ground
- 1 tbsp. olive oil
- 5 garlic cloves
- 1 tbsp. fresh rosemary, chopped

**Directions:**
1. Adjust the oven rack to the top third of the oven. Preheat broiler. Line a baking sheet with foil.
2. Place the garlic, rosemary, pepper, and olive oil into a small bowl and stir well to combine.
3. Place the lamb chops on a baking sheet and brush half of the garlic-rosemary mixture equally between the chops, coating well. Place the sheet beneath the broiler and broil for 4–5 minutes. Remove from oven and carefully flip over the chops. Divide the remaining garlic-rosemary mixture evenly between the chops and spread to coat. Return pan to oven and broil for another 3 minutes.
4. Remove from oven and serve immediately.

**Nutrition: Calories:** 185 kcal; **Fat:** 9 g; **Carbs:** 1 g; **Protein:** 23 g; **Sugars:** 0 g; **Sodium:** 72.8 mg

---

## 335. Cane Wrapped Around In Prosciutto

**Preparation time:** 3 minutes
**Cooking time:** 5 minutes
**Servings:** 4
**Ingredients:**
- 80 oz. prosciutto, sliced
- 1 lb. thick asparagus

**Directions:**
1. The first step here is to prepare your instant pot by pouring in about 2 cups of water
2. Take the asparagus and wrap them up in prosciutto spears. Once all of the asparagus are wrapped, gently place the processed asparaguses in the cooking basket inside your pot in layers. Turn up the heat to a high temperature, and when there is a pressure build-up, take down the heat and let it cook for about 2-3 minutes at the high pressure. Once the timer runs out, gently open the cover of the pressure cooker
3. Take out the steamer basket from the pot instantly and toss the asparaguses on a plate to serve
4. Eat warm or let them come down to room temperature

**Nutrition: Calories:** 212 kcal; **Fat:** 14 g; **Carbs:** 11 g; **Protein:** 12 g; **Sugars:** 367.6 g; **Sodium:** 0 mg

---

## 336. Beef Veggie Pot Meal

**Preparation time:** 45-50 minutes
**Cooking time:** 40 minutes
**Servings:** 2-3
**Ingredients:**
- 1 tsp. butter
- ¼ cabbage head, shredded
- 2 carrots, peeled and sliced
- 1 tbsp. flour
- 4 tbsp. sour cream
- 1 onion, chopped
- 10 oz. beef tenderloin, sliced and boiled

**Directions:**
1. In a saucepan, add the butter, cabbage, carrots, and onions.
2. Cook on medium-high heat until the veggies get softened.
3. Add the beef meat and stir the mix.
4. In a mixing bowl, beat the cream with flour until smooth.
5. Add the sauce over the beef.
6. Cover and cook for 40 minutes.

7. Serve warm.

**Nutrition: Calories:** 245.5 kcal; **Fat:** 10.2 g; **Carbs:** 18.4 g; **Protein:** 19.0 g; **Sugars:** 5.5 g; **Sodium:** 188.2 mg

### 337. Braised Beef Shanks

**Preparation time:** 10 minutes
**Cooking time:** 4-6 hours
**Servings:** 2
**Ingredients:**

- Black pepper, freshly ground
- 5 garlic cloves, minced
- 1½ lb. lean beef shanks
- 2 sprigs fresh rosemary
- 1 cup low-fat, low-sodium beef broth
- 1 tbsp. fresh lime juice

**Directions:**

1. In a slow cooker, add all ingredients and mix. Set the slow cooker on low.
2. Cover and cook for 4-6 hours.

**Nutrition: Calories:** 50 kcal; **Fat:** 1 g; **Carbs:** 0.8 g; **Protein:** 8 g; **Sugars:** 0 g; **Sodium:** 108 mg

### 338. Beef with Mushrooms

**Preparation time:** 15 minutes
**Cooking time:** 8 hours
**Servings:** 8
**Ingredients:**

- 2 cup salt-free tomato paste
- 2 cup fresh mushrooms, sliced
- 2 cup low-fat, low-sodium beef broth
- 2 lb. lean beef stew meat, cubed
- 1 cup fresh parsley leaves, chopped
- black pepper, freshly ground
- 4 garlic cloves, minced

**Directions:**

1. In a slow cooker, add all ingredients except lemon juice, and stir to combine.
2. Set the slow cooker on low.
3. Cover and cook for about 8 hours.
4. Serve hot with the drizzling of lemon juice.

**Nutrition: Calories:** 260 kcal; **Fat:** 12 g; **Carbs:** 18 g; **Protein:** 44 g; **Sugars:** 4 g; **Sodium:** 480 mg

### 339. Lemony Braised Beef Roast

**Preparation time:** 15 minutes
**Cooking time:** 6-8 hours
**Servings:** 6
**Ingredients:**

- 1 tbsp. fresh rosemary, minced
- ½ cup low-fat, low-sodium beef broth
- Black pepper, freshly ground
- 2 lb. lean beef pot roast
- 1 onion, sliced
- 2 garlic cloves, minced
- ¼ cup fresh lemon juice
- 1 tsp. cumin, ground

**Directions:**

1. In a large slow cooker, add all ingredients and mix well. Set the slow cooker on low.
2. Cover and cook for about 6-8 hours.

**Nutrition: Calories:** 344 kcal; **Fat:** 2.8 g; **Carbs:** 18 g; **Protein:** 32 g; **Sugars:** 2.4 g; **Sodium:** 278 mg

### 340. Grilled Fennel-Cumin Lamb Chops

**Preparation time:** 10 minutes
**Cooking time:** 30 minutes
**Servings:** 2
**Ingredients:**

- ¼ tsp. salt
- 1 large garlic clove, minced
- ⅛ tsp. black pepper, cracked
- ¾ tsp. fennel seeds, crushed
- ¼ tsp. coriander, ground
- 4–6 lamb rib chops, sliced
- ¾ tsp. cumin, ground

**Directions:**

1. Trim fat from chops. Place the chops on a plate.
2. In a small bowl, combine the garlic, fennel seeds, cumin, salt, coriander, and black pepper. Sprinkle the mixture evenly over chops; rub in with your fingers. Cover the chops with plastic wrap and marinate in the refrigerator for at least 30 minutes or up to 24 hours.
3. Grill chops on the rack of an uncovered grill directly over medium coals until chops are desired doneness.

**Nutrition: Calories:** 239 kcal; **Fat:** 12 g; **Carbs:** 2 g; **Protein:** 29 g; **Sugars:** 0 g; **Sodium:** 409 mg

### 341. Beef Heart

**Preparation time:** 40 minutes
**Cooking time:** 30 minutes
**Servings:** 4
**Ingredients:**

- 1 large onion, chopped
- 1 cup water
- 2 tomatoes, peeled and chopped
- 1 beef heart, boiled
- 2 tbsp. tomato paste

**Directions**:
1. Boil the beef heart until half-done.
2. Sauté the onions with tomatoes until soft.
3. Cut the beef heart into cubes and add to tomato and onion mixture.
4. Add water and tomato paste. Stew on low heat for 30 minutes.

**Nutrition: Calories:** 138 kcal; **Fat:** 3 g; **Carbs:** 0.1 g; **Protein:** 24.2 g; **Sugars:** 0 g; **Sodium:** 50.2 mg

---

### 342. Jerk Beef and Plantain Kabobs

**Preparation time:** 10 minutes
**Cooking time:** 15 minutes
**Servings:** 4
**Ingredients:**
- 2 ripe plantains, peeled and sliced
- 2 tbsp. Red wine vinegar
- Lime wedges
- 1 tbsp. cooking oil
- 1 medium red onion, sliced
- 12 oz. beef sirloin steak, sliced and boneless
- 1 tbsp. Jamaican jerk seasoning

**Directions**:
1. Trim fat from meat. Cut into 1-inch pieces. In a small bowl, stir together red wine vinegar, oil, and jerk seasoning. Toss meat cubes with half of the vinegar mixture. On long skewers, alternately thread meat, plantain chunks, and onion wedges, leaving a ¼-inch space between pieces.
2. Brush plantains and onion wedges with remaining vinegar mixture.
3. Place skewers on the rack of an uncovered grill directly over medium coals. Grill for 12 to 15 minutes or until meat is desired doneness, turning occasionally.
4. Serve with lime wedges.

**Nutrition: Calories:** 260 kcal; **Fat:** 7 g; **Carbs:** 21 g; **Protein:** 26 g; **Sugars:** 2.5 g; **Sodium:** 358 mg

---

### 343. Beef Pot

**Preparation time:** 10 minutes
**Cooking time:** 40 minutes
**Servings:** 2
**Ingredients:**
- 4 tbsp. Sour cream
- ¼ cabbage head, shredded
- 1 tsp. butter
- 2 carrots, peeled and sliced
- 1 onion, chopped
- 10 oz. beef tenderloin, boiled and sliced
- 1 tbsp. flour

**Directions**:
1. Sauté the cabbage, carrots, and onions in butter.
2. Spray a pot with cooking spray.
3. In layers, place the sautéed vegetables, then beef, then another layer of vegetables.
4. Beat the sour cream with flour until smooth and pour over the beef.
5. Cover and bake at 400°F for 40 minutes.

**Nutrition: Calories:** 210 kcal; **Fat:** 30 g; **Carbs:** 4 g; **Protein:** 14 g; **Sugars:** 1 g; **Sodium:** 600 mg

---

### 344. Beef with Cucumber Raito

**Preparation time:** 10 minutes
**Cooking time:** 30 minutes
**Servings:** 2
**Ingredients:**
- ½ tsp. lemon-pepper seasoning
- ¼ cup cucumber, coarsely shredded and unpeeled
- Black pepper and salt
- 1 tbsp. red onion, finely chopped
- ¼ tsp. sugar
- 1 lb. beef sirloin steak, sliced, de-boned
- 8 oz. plain Fat-free yogurt
- 1 tbsp. fresh mint, snipped

**Directions**:
1. Preheat broiler.
2. In a small bowl, combine yogurt, cucumber, onion, snipped mint, and sugar. Season to taste with salt and pepper; set aside
3. Trim fat from meat. Sprinkle meat with lemon-pepper seasoning.
4. Place meat on the unheated rack of a broiler pan. Broil 3 to 4 inches from heat, turning meat over after half of the broiling time.
5. Allow 15 to 17 minutes for medium-rare (145°F) and 20 to 22 minutes for medium (160°F).
6. Cut steak across the grain into thin slices.
7. Serve and enjoy.

**Nutrition: Calories:** 176 kcal; **Fat:** 3 g; **Carbs:** 5 g; **Protein:** 28 g; **Sugars:** 8.9 g; **Sodium:** 88.3 mg

---

### 345. Bistro Beef tenderloin

**Preparation time:** 10 minutes
**Cooking time:** 45 minutes
**Servings:** 12
**Ingredients:**
- 2 tbsp. Extra-virgin olive oil

- 2 tbsp. Dijon mustard
- 1 tsp. Kosher salt
- ⅔ cup mixed fresh herbs, chopped
- 3 lb. beef tenderloin, trimmed
- ½ tsp. pepper, freshly ground

**Directions:**
1. Preheat oven to 400°F.
2. Tie kitchen string around tenderloin in 3 places, so it doesn't flatten while roasting.
3. Rub the tenderloin with oil; pat on salt and pepper. Place in a large roasting pan.
4. Roast until a thermometer inserted into the thickest part of the tenderloin registers 140°F for medium-rare, about 45 minutes, turning 2 or 3 times during roasting to ensure even cooking.
5. Transfer to a cutting board; let rest for 10 minutes. Remove the string.
6. Place herbs on a large plate. Coat the tenderloin evenly with mustard; then roll in the herbs, pressing gently to adhere. Slice and serve.

**Nutrition: Calories:** 280 kcal; **Fat:** 20.6 g; **Carbs:** 0.9 g; **Protein:** 22.2 g; **Sugars:** 0 g; **Sodium:** 160 mg

---

### 346. The Surprising No "Noodle" Lasagna

**Preparation time:** 10 minutes
**Cooking time:** 10 minutes
**Servings:** 8
**Ingredients:**
- ½ cup Parmesan cheese
- 2 garlic cloves, minced
- 8 oz. Mozzarella, sliced
- 1 lb. beef, ground
- 25 oz. marinara sauce
- 1 small-sized onion
- 1 ½ cup ricotta cheese
- 1 large-sized egg

**Directions:**
1. Set your pot to Sauté mode and add garlic, onion, and ground beef.
2. Take a small bowl and add ricotta and parmesan with egg, and mix.
3. Drain the grease and transfer the beef to a 1 and a ½ quart soufflé dish.
4. Add marinara sauce to the browned meat and reserve half.
5. Top the remaining meat sauce with half of your mozzarella cheese.
6. Spread half of the ricotta cheese over the mozzarella layer.
7. Top with the remaining meat sauce.
8. Add a final layer of mozzarella cheese on top.
9. Spread any remaining ricotta cheese mixture over the mozzarella.
10. Carefully add this mixture to your Soufflé Dish.
11. Pour 1 cup of water to your pot.
12. Place it over a trivet.
13. Lock up the lid and cook on HIGH pressure for 10 minutes.
14. Release the pressure naturally over 10 minutes.
15. Serve and enjoy!

**Nutrition: Calories:** 607 kcal; **Fat:** 23 g; **Carbs:** 65 g; **Protein:** 33 g; **Sugars:** 0.31 g; **Sodium:** 128 mg

---

### 347. Lamb Chops with Kale

**Preparation time:** 10 minutes
**Cooking time:** 35 minutes
**Servings:** 4
**Ingredients:**
- 1 tbsp. olive oil
- 1 sliced yellow onion
- 1 cup torn kale
- 2 tbsp. low-sodium tomato paste
- ¼ tsp. black pepper
- ½ cup low-sodium veggie stock
- 1 lb. lamb chops

**Directions:**
1. Grease a roasting pan with the oil, arrange the lamb chops inside, also add the kale and the other ingredients, and toss gently.
2. Bake everything at 390°F for 35 minutes, divide between plates and serve.

**Nutrition: Calories:** 275 kcal; **Fat:** 11.8 g; **Carbs:** 7.3 g; **Protein:** 33.6 g; **Sugars:** 0.1 g; **Sodium:** 280 mg

---

### 348. Beef and Vegetable Stir-Fry

**Preparation time:** 20 minutes
**Cooking time:** 30 minutes
**Servings:** 4

**Ingredients:**
- 1 lb. skirt steak, thinly sliced
- 2 tbsp. sesame seeds
- ¾ cup stir-fry sauce
- 1 red bell pepper, thinly sliced
- 2 scallions, thinly sliced
- 2 tbsp. canola oil
- ¼ tsp. black pepper, ground
- 1 broccoli head, sliced
- 1½ cup fluffy brown rice

**Directions:**
1. Prepare the Stir-Fry Sauce.

2. Heat the canola oil in a large wok or skillet over medium-high heat. Season the steak with black pepper and cook for 4 minutes, until crispy on the outside and pink on the inside. Remove the steak from the skillet and place the broccoli and peppers in the hot oil. Stir-fry for 4 minutes, stirring or tossing occasionally, until crisp and slightly tender.
3. Place the steak back in the skillet with the vegetables. Pour the stir-fry sauce over the steak and vegetables and let simmer for 3 minutes. Remove from the heat. Serve the stir-fry over rice and top with the scallions and sesame seeds.
4. For leftovers, divide the stir-fry evenly into microwaveable airtight containers and store in the refrigerator for up to 5 days. Reheat in the microwave on high for 2 to 3 minutes, until heated through.

**Nutrition:** **Calories:** 408 kcal; **Fat:** 18 g; **Carbs:** 36 g; **Protein:** 31 g; **Sugars:** 5.5 g; **Sodium:** 197 mg

### 349. Simple Veal Chops

**Preparation time:** 10 minutes
**Cooking time:** 10 minutes
**Servings:** 4
**Ingredients:**
- 3 tbsp. essential olive oil
- 1 lemon zest, grated
- 3 tbsp. whole-wheat flour
- 1 ½ cup whole-wheat breadcrumbs
- Black pepper
- 1 tbsp. milk
- 4 veal rib chops
- 2 eggs

**Directions:**
1. Put whole-wheat flour within a bowl.
2. In another bowl, mix eggs with milk and whisk
3. In ⅓ bowl, mix the breadcrumbs with lemon zest.
4. Season veal chops with black pepper, dredge them in flour, and dip inside egg mix then in breadcrumbs.
5. Heat up a pan because of the oil over medium-high heat, add veal chops, cook for 2 main minutes on both sides and transfer to some baking sheet, introduce them inside the oven at 350°F, bake for quarter-hour, divide between plates and serve utilizing a side salad.
6. Enjoy!

**Nutrition:** **Calories:** 270 kcal; **Fat:** 6 g; **Carbs:** 10 g; **Protein:** 16 g; **Sugars:** 0 g; **Sodium:** 320 mg

### 350. Beef and Barley Farmers Soup

**Preparation time:** 10 minutes
**Cooking time:** 20 minutes
**Servings:** 4
**Ingredients:**
- 1 diced onion
- 15 g sunflower oil
- 15 g balsamic vinegar
- 900 g Campbell's red and white vegetable beef soup bowl
- 2 green onion stalks, thinly sliced
- 1 carrot, diced
- 340 g cubed lean beef
- 1 celery stalk, julienned
- 1 garlic clove, minced
- 85 g pot barley

**Directions:**
1. Throw a cast iron pan or a deep saucepan on medium heat with the oil and cubed beef to allow the 2 to cook. Wait till beef is properly browned on all sides, and then add in the diced vegetables. Cover and cook for an additional 3-5 minutes, stirring occasionally.
2. Add in a combination of the broth, vinegar, and barley; reduce the flame and bring to a boil. Continue to cook for about 20 minutes, or until thickened to preferred consistency.
3. Top with chopped green onions and serve!

**Nutrition:** **Calories:** 279 kcal; **Fat:** 7.6 g; **Carbs:** 28.91 g; **Protein:** 24.82 g; **Sugars:** 3 g; **Sodium:** 590 mg

### 351. Simple Pork and Capers

**Preparation time:** 10 minutes
**Cooking time:** 10 minutes
**Servings:** 2
**Ingredients:**
- 8 oz. pork, cubed
- 1 cup low-sodium chicken stock
- Black pepper
- 2 tbsp. organic extra virgin olive oil
- 1 garlic oil, minced
- 2 tbsp. Capers

**Directions:**
1. Heat up a pan with the oil over medium-high heat, add the pork season with black pepper and cook for 4 minutes on both sides.
2. Add garlic, capers, and stock, stir and cook for 7 minutes more. Divide everything between plates and serve.

3. Enjoy!

**Nutrition:** **Calories:** 224, **Fat:** 12 g, **Carbs:** 12 g, **Protein:** 10 g, **Sugars:** 5 g, **Sodium:** 5 mg

### 352. A "Boney" Pork Chop

**Preparation time:** 20 minutes
**Cooking time:** 30 minutes
**Servings:** 4
**Ingredients:**
- 1 cup baby carrots
- Flavored vinegar
- 3 tbsp. Worcestershire sauce
- Ground pepper
- 1 chopped onion
- 4 ¾ bone-in thick pork chops
- ¼ cup divided butter
- 1 cup vegetables

**Directions:**
1. Take a bowl and add pork chops, season with pepper and flavored vinegar
2. Take a skillet and place it over medium heat, add 2 tsp. of butter and melt it
3. Toss the pork chops and brown them
4. Each side should take about 3-5 minutes
5. Set your pot to sauté mode and add 2 tbsp. of butter, add carrots and sauté them
6. Pour broth and Worcestershire
7. Add pork chops and lock up the lid
8. Cook on HIGH pressure for 13 minutes
9. Release the pressure naturally
10. Enjoy!

**Nutrition:** **Calories:** 715, **Fat:** 37.4 g, **Carbs:** 2 g, **Protein:** 20.7 g, **Sugars:** 0 g, **Sodium:** 276 mg

### 353. Roast and Mushrooms

**Preparation time:** 10 minutes
**Cooking time:** 20 minutes
**Servings:** 4
**Ingredients:**
- 1 tsp. Italian seasoning
- 12 oz. low-sodium beef stock
- 3 ½ lb. pork roast
- 4 oz. mushrooms, sliced

**Directions:**
1. In a roasting pan, combine the roast with mushrooms, stock, and Italian seasoning, and toss
2. Introduce inside the oven and bake at 350°F for starters hour and 20 minutes.
3. Slice the roast, and divide it along while using a mushroom mix between plates and serve.

4. Enjoy!

**Nutrition:** **Calories:** 310 kcal; **Fat:** 16 g; **Carbs:** 10 g; **Protein:** 22 g, **Sugars:** 4 g; **Sodium:** 600 mg

### 354. Pork and Celery Mix

**Preparation time:** 10 minutes
**Cooking time:** 30 minutes
**Servings:** 8
**Ingredients:**
- 3 tsp. Fenugreek powder
- Black pepper
- 1 tbsp. organic olive oil
- 1 ½ cup coconut cream
- 26 oz. celery leaves and stalks, chopped
- 1 lb. pork meat, cubed
- 1 tbsp. onion, chopped

**Directions:**
1. Heat up a pan while using oil over medium-high heat, add the pork as well as the onion, black pepper, and fenugreek, toss, and brown for 5 minutes.
2. Add the celery too because coconut cream, toss, cook over medium heat for 20 minutes, divide everything into bowls and serve.
3. Enjoy!

**Nutrition:** **Calories:** 340 kcal; **Fat:** 5 g; **Carbs:** 8 g; **Protein:** 14 g; **Sugars:** 2.1 g; **Sodium:** 200 mg

### 355. Pork and Dates Sauce

**Preparation time:** 10 minutes
**Cooking time:** 40 minutes
**Servings:** 6
**Ingredients:**
- 2 tbsp. water
- 2 tbsp. mustard
- ⅓ cup dates, pitted
- Black pepper
- ¼ tsp. onion powder
- ¼ cup coconut amino
- 1 ½ lb. pork tenderloin
- ¼ tsp. paprika, smoked

**Directions:**
1. In your blender, mix dates with water, coconut amino, mustard, paprika, pepper, and onion powder and blend well.
2. Put pork tenderloin within the roasting pan, add the dates sauce, toss to coat perfectly, introduce everything inside the oven at 400°F, bake for 40 minutes, slice the meat, divide it as well since the sauce is between plates and serve.

3. Enjoy!

**Nutrition: Calories:** 240 kcal; **Fat:** 8 g; **Carbs:** 13 g; **Protein:** 24 g; **Sugars:** 0 g; **Sodium:** 433 mg

### 356. Pork Roast and Cranberry Roast

**Preparation time:** 10 minutes
**Cooking time:** 30 minutes
**Servings:** 4
**Ingredients:**
- 2 garlic cloves, minced
- ½ tsp. ginger, grated
- Black pepper
- ½ cup low-sodium veggie stock
- 1 ½ lb. pork loin roast
- 1 tbsp. coconut flour
- ½ cup cranberries
- Juice of ½ lemon

**Directions:**
1. Put the stock in the little pan, get hot over medium-high heat, add black pepper, ginger, garlic, cranberries, fresh freshly squeezed lemon juice along using the flour, whisk well and cook for 10 minutes. Put the roast in the pan, add the cranberry sauce at the very top, introduce inside the oven, and bake at 375°F for an hour and 20 minutes.
2. Slice the roast, and divide it along using the sauce between plates and serve.
3. Enjoy!

**Nutrition: Calories:** 330 kcal; **Fat:** 13 g; **Carbs:** 13 g; **Protein:** 25 g; **Sugars:** 7 g; **Sodium:** 150 mg

### 357. Easy Pork Chops

**Preparation time:** 10 minutes
**Cooking time:** 10 minutes
**Servings:** 4
**Ingredients:**
- 1 cup low-sodium chicken stock
- 1 tsp. sweet paprika
- 4 pork chops, boneless
- ¼ tsp. black pepper
- 1 tbsp. extra-virgin olive oil

**Directions:**
1. Heat up a pan while using the oil over medium-high heat, add pork chops, brown them for 5 minutes on either sides, add paprika, black pepper, and stock, toss, cook for 15 minutes more, divide between plates, and serve by using a side salad.

2. Enjoy!

**Nutrition: Calories:** 272 kcal; **Fat:** 4 g; **Carbs:** 14 g; **Protein:** 17 g; **Sugars:** 0.2 g; **Sodium:** 68 mg

### 358. Pork and Roasted Tomatoes Mix

**Preparation time:** 10 minutes
**Cooking time:** 15 minutes
**Servings:** 6
**Ingredients:**
- ½ cup yellow onion, chopped
- 2 cup zucchinis, chopped
- 1 lb. pork meat, ground
- ¾ cup low-fat cheddar cheese, shredded
- Black pepper
- 15 oz. no-salt-added, chopped and canned roasted tomatoes

**Directions:**
1. Heat up a pan over medium-high heat, add pork, onion, black pepper, and zucchini, stir and cook for 7 minutes.
2. Add roasted tomatoes, stir, bring to a boil, cook over medium heat for 8 minutes, divide into bowls, sprinkle cheddar on the top, and serve.
3. Enjoy!

**Nutrition: Calories:** 270 kcal; **Fat:** 5 g; **Carbs:** 10 g; **Protein:** 12 g; **Sugars:** 8 g; **Sodium:** 390 mg

### 359. Provence Pork Medallions

**Preparation time:** 10 minutes
**Cooking time:** 20 minutes
**Servings:** 4
**Ingredients:**
- 1 tsp. Herb de Provence
- Pepper.
- ½ cup dry white wine
- 16 oz. pork tenderloins
- Salt

**Directions:**
1. Season pork lightly with salt and pepper.
2. Place the pork between 2 pieces of parchment paper and lb. with a mallet.
3. You need to have ¼-inch thick meat.
4. In a large non-stick frying pan, cook the pork over medium-high heat for 2–3 minutes per side.
5. Remove from the heat and sprinkle with herb de Provence. Remove the pork from the skillet and place aside. Keep warm.
6. Place the skillet over heat again. Add the wine and cook, stirring to scrape down the bits.

7. Cook until reduced slightly and pour over pork. Serve.

**Nutrition: Calories:** 105.7 kcal; **Fat:** 1.7 g; **Carbs:** 0.8 g; **Protein:** 22.6 g; **Sugars:** 0 g; **Sodium:** 67 mg

## 360. Garlic Pork Shoulder

**Preparation time:** 10 minutes
**Cooking time:** 4 hours
**Servings:** 6
**Ingredients:**
- 2 tsps. Sweet paprika
- 4 lb. pork shoulder
- 3 tbsp. Extra virgin essential olive oil
- Black pepper
- 3 tbsp. garlic, minced

**Directions:**
1. In a bowl, mix extra virgin extra virgin olive oil with paprika, black pepper, and whisk well.
2. Brush pork shoulder with this mix, arrange inside a baking dish, and introduce inside the oven at 425°F for 20 or so minutes.
3. Reduce heat to 325°F and bake for 4 hours.
4. Slice the meat, and divide it between plates and serve, having a side salad.
5. Enjoy!

**Nutrition: Calories:** 321 kcal; **Fat:** 6 g; **Carbs:** 12 g; **Protein:** 18 g; **Sugars:** 0 g; **Sodium:** 470 mg

## 361. Grilled Flank Steak with Lime Vinaigrette

**Preparation time:** 10 minutes
**Cooking time:** 10 minutes
**Servings:** 6
**Ingredients:**
- 2 tbsp. lime juice, freshly squeezed
- 2 tbsp. extra virgin olive oil
- ½ tsp. black pepper, ground
- ¼ cup fresh cilantro, chopped
- 1 tbsp. cumin, ground
- ¼ tsp. red pepper flakes
- ¾ lb. flank steak

**Directions:**
1. Heat the grill to low, medium heat
2. In a food processor, place all ingredients except for the cumin, red pepper flakes, and flank steak. Pulse until smooth. This will be the vinaigrette sauce. Set aside.
3. Season the flank steak with ground cumin and red pepper flakes and allowing marinate for at least 10 minutes.
4. Place the steak on the grill rack and cook for 5 minutes on each side. Cut into the center to check the doneness of the meat. You can also insert a meat thermometer to check the internal temperature.
5. Remove from the grill and allowing stand for 5 minutes.
6. Slice the steak to 2 inches long and toss the vinaigrette to flavor the meat.
7. Serve with salad if desired.

**Nutrition: Calories: per Servings:** 103 kcal; **Protein:** 13 g; **Carbs:** 1 g; **Fat:** 5 g; **Saturated Fat:** 1 g; **Sodium:** 73 mg

## 362. Asian Pork tenderloin

**Preparation time:** 10 minutes
**Cooking time:** 15 minutes
**Servings:** 4
**Ingredients:**
- 2 tbsp. sesame seeds
- 1 tsp. coriander, ground
- ⅛ tsp. cayenne pepper
- ⅛ tsp. celery seed
- ½ tsp. onion, minced
- ¼ tsp. cumin, ground
- ⅛ tsp. cinnamon, ground
- 1 tbsp. sesame oil
- 1-lb. pork tenderloin sliced into 4 equal portions

**Directions:**
1. Preheat the oven to 400°F.
2. In a skillet, toast the sesame seeds over low heat and set aside. Allow the sesame seeds to cool.
3. In a bowl, combine the rest of the ingredients except for the pork tenderloin. Stir in the toasted sesame seeds.
4. Place the pork tenderloin in a baking dish and rub the spices on both sides.
5. Place the baking dish with the pork in the oven and bake for 15 minutes or until the internal temperature of the meat reaches to 170°F.
6. Serve warm.

**Nutrition: Calories:** 248 kcal; **Protein:** 26 g; **Carbs:** 0 g; **Fat:** 16 g; **Saturated Fat:** 5 g; **Sodium:** 57 mg

## 363. Simple Beef Brisket and Tomato Soup

**Preparation time:** 10 minutes
**Cooking time:** 3 hours
**Servings:** 8
**Ingredients:**
- 1 tbsp. olive oil

- 2 ½ lb. beef brisket, trimmed of fat and cut into 8 equal parts
- A dash black pepper, ground
- 1 ½ cups onions, chopped
- 4 garlic cloves, smashed
- 1 tsp. thyme, dried
- 1 cup ripe Roma tomatoes, chopped
- ¼ cup red wine vinegar
- 1 cup beef stock, low-sodium or homemade

**Directions:**
1. In a heavy pot, heat the oil over medium-high heat.
2. Season the brisket with ground black pepper and place in the pot.
3. Cook while stirring constantly until the beef turns brown on all sides.
4. Stir in the onions and cook until fragrant. Add in the garlic and thyme and cook for another minute until fragrant.
5. Pour in the rest of the ingredients and bring to a boil.
6. Cook until the beef is tender. This may take about 3 hours or more.

**Nutrition:** Calories: 229 kcal; **Protein:** 31 g; **Carbs:** 6 g; **Fat:** 9 g; **Saturated Fat:** 3 g; **Sodium:** 184 mg

### 364. Beef Stew with Fennel and Shallots

**Preparation time:** 10 minutes
**Cooking time:** 40 minutes
**Servings:** 6
**Ingredients:**
- 1 tbsp. olive oil
- 1-lb. lean beef stew meat, boneless, trimmed from fat and cut into cubes
- ½ fennel bulb, trimmed and sliced thinly
- 3 large shallots, chopped
- ¾ tsp. black pepper, ground
- 2 fresh thyme sprigs
- 1 bay leaf
- 3 cups low-sodium beef broth
- ½ cup red wine
- 4 large carrots, peeled and cut into chunks
- 4 large white potatoes, peeled and cut into chunks
- 3 Portobello mushrooms, cleaned and cut into chunks
- ⅓ cup Italian parsley, chopped

**Directions:**
1. Heat oil in a pot over medium heat and stir in the beef cubes for 5 minutes or until all sides turn brown.
2. Stir in the fennel, shallots, black pepper, and thyme for one minute or until the ingredients become fragrant.
3. Stir in the bay leaf, broth, red wine, carrots, white potatoes, and mushrooms.
4. Bring to a boil and cook for 30 minutes or until everything is tender.
5. Stir in the parsley last.

**Nutrition:** Calories: 244 kcal; **Protein:** 21 g; **Carbs:** 22 g; **Fat:** 8 g; **Saturated Fat:** 2 g; **Sodium:** 184 mg

### 365. Rustic Beef and Barley Soup

**Preparation time:** 10 minutes
**Cooking time:** 40 minutes
**Servings:** 6
**Ingredients:**
- 1 tsp. olive oil
- 1-lb. beef round steak, sliced into strips
- 2 cups yellow onion, chopped
- 1 cup diced celery
- 4 cloves of garlic, chopped
- 1 cup Roma tomatoes, diced
- ½ cup sweet potato, diced
- ½ cup mushrooms, diced
- 1 cup carrots, diced
- ¼ cup barley, uncooked
- 3 cups low-sodium vegetable stock
- 1 tsp. sage, dried
- 1 paprika
- A dash black pepper to taste
- 1 cup kale, chopped

**Directions:**
1. In a large pot, heat the oil over medium flame and stir in the beef. Cook for 5 minutes while stirring constantly until all sides turn brown.
2. Stir in the onion, celery, and garlic until fragrant.
3. Add in the rest of the ingredients except for the kale.
4. Bring to a boil and cook for 30 minutes until everything is tender.
5. Stir in the kale last and cook for another 5 minutes.

**Nutrition:** Calories: per Servings: 246 kcal; **Protein:** 21 g; **Carbs:** 24 g; **Fat:** 4 g; **Saturated Fat:** 1 g; **Sodium:** 13 mg

## 366. Beef Stroganoff

**Preparation time:** 10 minutes
**Cooking time:** 25 minutes
**Servings:** 4
**Ingredients:**

- ½ cup onion, chopped
- ½ lb. beef round steak, boneless, cut into ¾ inch thick
- 4 cups pasta noodles
- ½ cup Fat-free cream of mushroom soup
- ½ cup water
- ½ tsp. paprika
- ½ cup Fat-free sour cream

**Directions:**
1. In a non-stick frying pan, sauté the onions over low to medium heat without oil while constantly stirring for about 5 minutes.
2. Stir in the beef and cook for another 5 minutes until the beef is tender and turns brown on all sides. Set aside.
3. In a large pot, fill it with water until ¾ full and bring to a boil. Cook the noodles until done according to package instructions. Drain the noodles and set aside.
4. In a saucepan, whisk the mushroom soup and water. Bring to a boil over medium heat and stir constantly until the sauce has reduced. Add in paprika and sour cream.
5. Assemble the stroganoff by placing the pasta in a bowl and pouring over the sauce. Top with the meat.
6. Serve warm.

**Nutrition: Calories:** 273 kcal; **Protein:** 20 g; **Carbs:** 37 g; **Fat:** 5 g; **Saturated Fat:** 2 g; **Sodium:** 193 mg

## 367. Curried Pork tenderloin in Apple Cider

**Preparation time:** 10 minutes
**Cooking time:** 26 minutes
**Servings:** 6
**Ingredients:**

- 16 oz. pork tenderloin, cut into 6 pieces
- 1 ½ tbsp. curry powder
- 1 tbsp. extra-virgin olive oil
- 2 medium onions, chopped
- 2 cups apple cider, organic and unsweetened
- 1 tart apple, peeled and chopped into chunks

**Directions:**
1. In a bowl, season the pork with the curry powder and set aside.
2. Heat oil in a pot over medium flame.
3. Sauté the onions for one minute until fragrant.
4. Stir in the seasoned pork tenderloin and cook for 5 minutes or until lightly golden.
5. Add in the apple cider and apple chunks.
6. Close the lid and bring to a boil.
7. Allow to simmer for 20 minutes.

**Nutrition: Calories:** 244 kcal; **Protein:** 24 g; **Carbs:** 18 g; **Fat:** 8 g; **Saturated Fat:** 2 g; **Sodium:** 70 mg

## 368. Pork Medallions with 5 Spice Powder

**Preparation time:** 10 minutes
**Cooking time:** 25 minutes
**Servings:** 4
**Ingredients:**

- 1 tbsp. olive oil
- 3 garlic cloves, minced
- 1-lb. pork tenderloin, fat trimmed
- 2 tbsp. low-sodium soy sauce
- 1 tbsp. green onion, minced
- ¾ tsp. five spice powder
- ½ cup water
- ¼ cup dry white wine
- ⅓ cup onion, chopped
- ½ head green cabbage, thinly sliced and wilted
- 1 tbsp. fresh parsley, chopped

**Directions:**
1. In a bowl, combine the olive oil, garlic, pork tenderloin, soy sauce, green onion, and five-spice powder. Mix until well combined and allowing marinate in the fridge for at least 2 hours.
2. Heat the oven to 400°F.
3. Remove the pork from the marinade and pat dry.
4. On a skillet, sear the meat on all sides until slightly brown before transferring into a heat-proof baking dish.
5. Place inside the oven and roast the pork for 20 minutes.
6. Meanwhile, pour the water, dry white wine, and onions in the skillet where you seared the pork and deglaze. Allow to simmer until the sauce has reduced.
7. Serve the pork medallions with wilted cabbages and drizzle the sauce on top.

**Nutrition: Calories:** 219 kcal; **Protein:** 25 g; **Carbs:** 5 g; **Fat:** 11 g; **Saturated Fat:** 2 g; **Sodium:** 296 mg

## 369. Grilled Pork Fajitas

**Preparation time:** 10 minutes
**Cooking time:** 15 minutes
**Servings:** 8

**Ingredients:**
- ½ tsp. paprika
- ½ tsp. oregano
- ¼ tsp. coriander, ground
- ¼ tsp. garlic powder
- 1 tbsp. chili powder
- 1-lb. pork tenderloin, fat trimmed and cut into large strips
- 1 onion, sliced
- 8 whole-wheat flour tortillas, warmed
- 4 medium tomatoes, chopped
- 4 cups lettuce, shredded

**Directions:**
1. In a bowl, mix the paprika, oregano, coriander, garlic powder, and chili powder.
2. Sprinkle the spice mixture on the pork tenderloin strips and toss to coat the meat with the spices.
3. Prepare the grill and heat to 400°F.
4. Place the meat and onion in a grill basket and broil for 20 minutes or until all sides have browned.
5. Assemble the fajitas by placing in the center of the tortillas the grilled pork and onions. Add in the tomatoes and lettuce before rolling the fajitas.

**Nutrition: Calories:** 250 kcal; **Protein:** 20 g; **Carbs:** 29 g; **Fat:** 6 g; **Saturated Fat:** 2 g; **Sodium:** 234 mg

## 370. New York Strip Steak with Mushroom Sauce

**Preparation time:** 10 minutes
**Cooking time:** 20 minutes
**Servings:** 2

**Ingredients:**
- 2 New York Strip steaks (4 oz. each), trimmed from fat
- 3 garlic cloves, minced
- 2 oz. shiitake mushrooms, sliced
- 2 oz. button mushrooms, sliced
- ¼ tsp. thyme
- ¼ tsp. rosemary
- ¼ cup low-sodium beef broth

**Directions:**
1. Heat the grill to 350°F.
2. Position the grill rack 6 inches from the heat source.
3. Grill the steaks for 10 minutes on each side or until slightly pink on the inside.
4. Meanwhile, prepare the sauce. In a small nonstick pan, water-sauté the garlic, mushrooms, thyme, and rosemary for a minute. Pour in the broth and bring to a boil. Allow the sauce to simmer until the liquid is reduced.
5. Top the steaks with the mushroom sauce.
6. Serve warm.

**Nutrition: Calories:** 270 kcal; **Protein:** 23 g; **Carbs:** 4 g; **Fat:** 6 g; **Saturated Fat:** 2 g; **Sodium:** 96 mg

## 371. Pork Chops with Black Currant Jam

**Preparation time:** 10 minutes
**Cooking time:** 20 minutes
**Servings:** 6

**Ingredients:**
- ¼ cup black currant jam
- 2 tbsp. Dijon mustard
- 1 tsp. olive oil
- 6 center cut pork loin chops, trimmed from fat
- ⅓ cup wine vinegar
- ⅛ tsp. black pepper, ground
- 6 orange slices

**Directions:**
1. In a small bowl, mix together the jam and mustard. Set aside.
2. In a nonstick pan, heat the oil over medium flames and sear the pork chops for 5 minutes on each side or until all sides turn brown.
3. Brush the pork chops with the mustard mixture and turn the flame to low. Cook for 2 more minutes on each side. Set aside.
4. Using the same frying pan, pour in the wine vinegar to deglaze the pan. Season with ground black pepper and allow to simmer for at least 5 minutes or until the vinegar has reduced.
5. Pour over the pork chops and garnish with orange slices on top.

**Nutrition: Calories:** 198 kcal; **Protein:** 25 g; **Carbs:** 11 g; **Fat:** 6 g; **Saturated Fat:** 2 g; **Sodium:** 188 mg

## 372. Pork Medallion with Herbes de Provence

**Preparation time:** 10 minutes
**Cooking time:** 15 minutes
**Servings:** 2

**Ingredients:**
- 8 oz. pork medallion, trimmed from fat

- black pepper, freshly ground, to taste
- ½ tsp. Herbs de Provence
- ¼ cup dry white wine

**Directions:**
1. Season the meat with black pepper.
2. Place the meat in between sheets of wax paper and pound on a mallet until about ¼ inch thick.
3. In a nonstick skillet, sear the pork over medium heat for 5 minutes on each side or until the meat is slightly brown.
4. Remove meat from the skillet and sprinkle with Herbs de Provence.
5. Using the same skillet, pour the wine and scrape the sides to deglaze. Allow to simmer until the wine is reduced.
6. Pour the wine sauce over the pork.
7. Serve immediately.

**Nutrition:** **Calories:** 120 kcal; **Protein:** 24 g; **Carbs:** 1 g; **Fat:** 2 g; **Saturated Fat:** 0.5 g; **Sodium:** 62 mg

### 373. Pork tenderloin with Apples and Balsamic Vinegar

**Preparation time:** 10 minutes
**Cooking time:** 25 minutes
**Servings:** 4
**Ingredients:**
- 1 tbsp. olive oil
- 1-lb. pork tenderloin, trimmed from fat
- black pepper, freshly ground
- 2 cups onion, chopped
- 2 cups apple, chopped
- 1 ½ tbsp. fresh rosemary, chopped
- 1 cup low-sodium chicken broth
- 1 ½ tbsp. balsamic vinegar

**Directions:**
1. Heat the oven to 450°F.
2. Heat the oil in a large skillet over medium flame.
3. Sear the pork and season with black pepper. Cook the pork for 3 minutes until all sides turn light brown. Remove from the heat and place in a baking pan.
4. Roast the pork for 15 minutes.
5. Meanwhile, place the onion, apples, and rosemary on the skillet where the pork is seared. Continue stirring for 5 minutes. Pour in broth and balsamic vinegar and allowing simmer until the sauce thickens.
6. Serve the roasted pork with the onion and apple sauce.

**Nutrition:** **Calories:** 240 kcal; **Protein:** 26 g; **Carbs:** 17 g; **Fat:** 6 g; **Saturated Fat:** 1 g; **Sodium:** 83 mg

### 374. Pork with Apples and Blue Cheese

**Preparation time:** 10 minutes
**Cooking time:** 25 minutes
**Servings:** 4
**Ingredients:**
- 1-lb. pork tenderloin, trimmed from fat
- ½ tsp. white pepper
- 2 tsp. black pepper
- ¼ tsp. cayenne pepper
- 1 tsp. paprika
- 2 apples, sliced
- ½ cup apple juice, unsweetened
- ¼ cup blue cheese, crumbled

**Directions:**
1. Heat the oven to 350°F.
2. Season the tenderloin with white pepper, black pepper, cayenne pepper, and paprika.
3. Heat a non-stick pan over medium flame and sear the meat for 3 minutes on each side. Transfer to a baking dish and roast in the oven for 20 minutes or until the internal temperature is at 155°F. Remove from the oven to cool.
4. While the pork is roasting, prepare the sauce. Using the same skillet used to sear the meat, sauté the apples for 3 minutes. Add the apple juice and allow the sauce to thicken for at least 10 minutes.
5. Serve the pork with the apple sauce and sprinkle with blue cheese on top.

**Nutrition:** **Calories:** 235 kcal; **Protein:** 26 g; **Carbs:** 17 g; **Fat:** 3 g; **Saturated Fat:** 1 g; **Sodium:** 145 mg

### 375. Pork tenderloin with Fennel Sauce

**Preparation time:** 10 minutes
**Cooking time:** 30 minutes
**Servings:** 4
**Ingredients:**
- 4 pork tenderloin fillets, trimmed from fat and cut into 4 portions
- 1 tbsp. olive oil
- 1 tsp. fennel seeds
- 1 fennel bulb, cored and sliced thinly
- 1 sweet onion, sliced thinly
- ½ cup dry white wine
- 12 oz. low-sodium chicken broth
- 1 orange, sliced for garnish

**Directions:**
1. Place the pork slices in between wax paper and lb. with a mallet to about ¼-inch thick.

2. Heat oil in a skillet and fry the fennel seeds for 3 minutes or until fragrant.
3. Stir in the pork and cook on all sides for 3 minutes or until golden brown. Remove the pork from the skillet and set aside.
4. Using the same skillet, add the fennel bulb slices and onion. Sauté for 5 minutes, and then set aside.
5. Add the wine and chicken broth in the skillet and bring to a boil until the sauce reduces in half.
6. Return the pork to the skillet and cook for another 5 minutes.
7. Serve the pork with sauce and vegetables.

**Nutrition:** **Calories:** 276 kcal; **Protein:** 29 g; **Carbs:** 13 g; **Fat:** 12 g; **Saturated Fat:** 3 g; **Sodium:** 122 mg

### 376. Spicy Beef Kebabs

**Preparation time:** 10 minutes
**Cooking time:** 10 minutes
**Servings:** 8
**Ingredients:**
- 2 yellow onions, minced
- 2 tbsp. fresh lemon juice
- 1 ½ lb. lean beef, ground and minced
- ¼ cup bulgur, soaked in water for 30 minutes, then rinse
- ¼ cup pine nuts, chopped
- 2 garlic cloves, minced
- 1 tsp. cumin, ground
- ½ tsp. cinnamon, ground
- ½ tsp. cardamom, ground
- ½ tsp. black pepper, freshly ground
- 16 wooden skewers, soaked in water for 30 minutes

**Directions:**
1. In a mixing bowl, combine all ingredients except for the skewers. Mix well unto
2. Form a sausage from the meat mixture and thread it into the skewers. If the sausage is crumbly, add a tbsp. of water at a time until it holds well together. Refrigerate the skewered meat sausages until ready to cook.
3. Heat the grill to 350°F and place the grill rack 6 inches from the heat source.
4. Place the skewered kebabs on the grill and broil for 5 minutes on each side.
5. Serve with yogurt if desired.

**Nutrition:**
**Calories:** 219 kcal; **Protein:** 23 g; **Carbs:** 3 g; **Fat:** 12 g; **Saturated Fat:** 3 g; **Sodium:** 53 mg

### 377. Spicy Beef Curry

**Preparation time:** 10 minutes
**Cooking time:** 40 minutes
**Servings:** 6
**Ingredients:**
- 1 medium Serrano pepper, cut into thirds
- 4 garlic cloves, minced
- 1 2-inch piece ginger, peeled and chopped
- 1 yellow onion, chopped
- 2 tbsp. coriander, ground
- 2 tsp. cumin, ground
- ½ tsp. turmeric, ground
- 2 tsp. garam masala
- 1 tbsp. olive oil
- 2 lb. beef, cut into chunks
- 1 cup ripe tomatoes, diced
- 2 cups water
- 1 cup fresh cilantro for garnish

**Directions:**
1. In a food processor, pulse the serrano peppers, garlic, ginger, onion, coriander, cumin, turmeric, and garam masala until well-combined.
2. Heat oil over medium heat in a skillet and sauté the spice mixture for 2 minutes or until fragrant.
3. Stir in the beef and allowing cook while stirring constantly for 3 minutes or until the beef turns brown.
4. Stir in the tomatoes and sauté for another 3 minutes.
5. Add in the water and bring to a boil.
6. Once boiling, turn the heat to low and allowing simmer for 30 minutes or until the meat is tender.
7. Add cilantro last before serving.

**Nutrition:** **Calories:** 181 kcal; **Protein:** 16 g; **Carbs:** 5 g; **Fat:** 8 g; **Saturated Fat:** 2 g; **Sodium:** 74 mg

# CHAPTER 12: STEWS AND SOUPS

## 378. Chicken Wild Rice Soup

**Preparation time:** 10 minutes
**Cooking time:** 15 minutes
**Servings:** 6
**Ingredients:**

- ⅔ cup wild rice, uncooked
- 1 tbsp. onion, chopped finely
- 1 tbsp. fresh parsley, chopped
- 1 cup carrots, chopped
- 8-oz. chicken breast, cooked
- 2 tbsp. butter
- ¼ cup all-purpose white flour
- 5 cups low-sodium chicken broth
- 1 tbsp. almonds, slivered

**Directions:**

1. Start by adding rice and 2 cups broth along with ½ cup water to a cooking pot. Cook the chicken until the rice is al dente and set it aside. Add butter to a saucepan and melt it.
2. Stir in onion and sauté until soft, then add the flour and the remaining broth.
3. Stir it and then cook for it 1 minute, then add the chicken, cooked rice, and carrots. Cook for 5 minutes on simmer. Garnish with almonds. Serve fresh.

**Nutrition: Calories:** 287 kcal; **Protein:** 21 g; **Fat:** 35 g

## 379. Classic Chicken Soup

**Preparation time:** 10 minutes
**Cooking time:** 25 minutes
**Servings:** 2
**Ingredients:**
- 1 ½ cups low-sodium vegetable broth
- 1 cup water
- ¼ tsp. poultry seasoning
- ¼ tsp. black pepper
- 1 cup chicken strips
- ¼ cup carrot
- 2-oz. egg noodles, uncooked

**Directions:**
1. Gather all the ingredients into a slow cooker and toss it. Cook soup on high heat for 25 minutes. Serve warm.

**Nutrition: Calories:** 103 kcal; **Protein:** 8 g; **Fat:** 11 g

## 380. Cucumber Soup

**Preparation time:** 10 minutes
**Cooking time:** 0 minute
**Servings:** 4
**Ingredients:**
- 2 medium cucumbers
- ⅓ cup sweet white onion
- 1 green onion
- ¼ cup fresh mint
- 2 tbsp. fresh dill
- 2 tbsp. lemon juice
- ⅔ cup water
- ½ cup half and half cream
- ⅓ cup sour cream
- ½ tsp. pepper
- Fresh dill sprigs for garnish

**Directions:**
1. Situate all of the ingredients into a food processor and toss. Puree the mixture and refrigerate for 2 hours. Garnish with dill sprigs. Enjoy fresh.

**Nutrition: Calories:** 77 kcal; **Protein:** 2 g; **Fat:** 6 g

## 381. Squash and Turmeric Soup

**Preparation time:** 10 minutes
**Cooking time:** 30 minutes
**Servings:** 4
**Ingredients:**
- 4 cups low-sodium vegetable broth
- 2 medium zucchini squash
- 2 medium yellow crookneck squash
- 1 small onion
- ½ cup green peas, frozen
- 2 tbsp. olive oil
- ½ cup plain nonfat Greek yogurt
- 2 tsp. turmeric

**Directions:**
1. Warm the broth in a saucepan on medium heat. Toss in onion, squash, and zucchini. Let it simmer for approximately 25 minutes; then add oil and green peas.
2. Cook for another 5 minutes, then allowing it to cool.
3. Puree the soup using a handheld blender; then add Greek yogurt and turmeric. Refrigerate it overnight and serve fresh.

**Nutrition: Calories:** 100 kcal; **Protein:** 4 g; **Fat:** 10 g

## 382. Leek, Potato, and Carrot Soup

**Preparation time:** 15 minutes
**Cooking time:** 25 minutes
**Servings:** 4
**Ingredients:**
- 1 leek
- ¾ cup potatoes, diced and boiled
- ¾ cup carrots, diced and boiled
- 1 garlic clove
- 1 tbsp. oil
- Pepper, crushed, to taste
- 3 cups low-sodium chicken stock
- Parsley, chopped, for garnish
- 1 bay leaf
- ¼ tsp. cumin, ground

**Directions:**
1. Trim off and take away a portion of the coarse inexperienced portions of the leek, at that factor reduce daintily and flush altogether in virus water. Channel properly. Warmth the oil in an extensively based pot. Include the leek and garlic, and sear over low warmth for 2-3 minutes, till sensitive. Include the inventory, inlet leaf, cumin, and pepper. Heat the mixture, mix constantly. Include the bubbled potatoes and carrots and stew for 10-15 minutes. Modify the flavoring, eliminate the inlet leaf, and serve sprinkled generously with slashed parsley.
2. To make a pureed soup, manner the soup in a blender or nourishment processor till smooth Come again to the pan. Include ½ field milk. Bring to bubble and stew for 2-3minutes

**Nutrition: Calories:** 315 kcal; **Fat:** 8 g; **Protein:** 15 g

## 383. Bell Pepper Soup

**Preparation time:** 30 minutes
**Cooking time:** 35 minutes
**Servings:** 4
**Ingredients:**
- 4 cups low-sodium chicken broth
- 3 red peppers
- 2 medium onions
- 3 tbsp. lemon juice
- 1 tbsp. lemon zest, finely minced
- A pinch cayenne peppers
- ¼ tsp. cinnamon
- ½ cup finely minced fresh cilantro

**Directions:**
1. In a medium stockpot, consolidate each one of the fixings except for the cilantro and warmth to the point of boiling over excessive warm temperature.
2. Diminish the warmth and stew, ordinarily secured, for around 30 minutes, till thickened.
3. Cool marginally. Utilizing a hand blender or nourishment processor, puree the soup. Include the cilantro and tenderly heat.

**Nutrition: Calories:** 265 kcal; **Fat:** 8 g; **Protein:** 5 g

## 384. Yucatan Soup

**Preparation time:** 10 minutes
**Cooking time:** 20 minutes
**Servings:** 4
**Ingredients:**
- ½ cup onion, chopped
- 8 cloves garlic, chopped
- 2 Serrano chili peppers, chopped
- 1 medium tomato, chopped
- 1 ½ cups chicken breast, cooked, shredded
- 2 6-inch corn tortillas, sliced
- 1 tbsp. olive oil
- 4 cups chicken broth

- 1 bay leaf
- ¼ cup lime juice
- ¼ cup cilantro, chopped
- 1 tsp. black pepper

**Directions**:
1. Spread the corn tortillas in a baking sheet and bake them for 3 minutes at 400°F. Place a suitably-sized saucepan over medium heat and add oil to heat.
2. Toss in chili peppers, garlic, and onion, then sauté until soft. Stir in broth, tomatoes, bay leaf, and chicken.
3. Let this chicken soup cook for 10 minutes on a simmer. Stir in cilantro, lime juice, and black pepper. Garnish with baked corn tortillas. Serve.

**Nutrition: Calories:** 215 kcal; **Protein:** 21 g; **Fat:** 32 g

## 385. Zesty Taco Soup

**Preparation time:** 10 minutes
**Cooking time:** 7 hours
**Servings:** 2
**Ingredients:**
- 1 ½ lb. chicken breast
- 15 ½ oz. dark red kidney beans, canned
- 15 ½ oz. white corn, canned
- 1 cup tomatoes, canned
- ½ cup onion
- 15 ½ oz. yellow hominy, canned
- ½ cup green bell peppers
- 1 garlic clove
- 1 medium Jalapeño
- 1 tbsp. package McCormick
- 2 cups chicken broth

**Directions**:
1. Add drained beans, hominy, corn, onion, garlic, jalapeno pepper, chicken, and green peppers to a Crockpot.
2. Cover the beans-corn mixture and cook for 1 hour on "high" temperature. Set heat to "low" and continue cooking for 6 hours. Shred the slow-cooked chicken and return to the taco soup. Serve warm.

**Nutrition: Calories:** 191 kcal; **Protein:** 21 g; **Fat:** 20 g

## 386. Southwestern Posole

**Preparation time:** 10 minutes
**Cooking time:** 53 minutes
**Servings:** 4
**Ingredients:**
- 1 tbsp. olive oil
- 1-lb. pork loin, diced
- ½ cup onion, chopped
- 1 garlic clove, chopped
- 28 oz. white hominy, canned
- 4 oz. green chili, canned and diced
- 4 cups chicken broth
- ¼ tsp. black pepper

**Directions**:
1. Place a suitably-sized cooking pot over medium heat and add oil to heat. Toss in pork pieces and sauté for 4 minutes.
2. Stir in garlic and onion, then stir for 4 minutes, or until onion is soft.
3. Add the remaining ingredients; then cover the pork soup. Cook this for 45 minutes, or until the pork is tender. Serve warm.

**Nutrition: Calories:** 286 kcal; **Protein:** 25 g; **Fat:** 15 g

## 387. Spring Vegetable Soup

**Preparation time:** 10 minutes
**Cooking time:** 45 minutes
**Servings:** 4
**Ingredients:**
- 1 cup fresh green beans
- ¾ cup celery
- ½ cup onion
- ½ cup carrots
- ½ cup mushrooms
- ½ cup corn, frozen
- 1 medium Roma tomato
- 2 tbsp. olive oil
- 4 cups vegetable broth
- 1 tsp. oregano leaves, dried
- 1 tsp. garlic powder

**Directions**:
1. Place a suitably-sized cooking pot over medium heat and add olive oil to heat. Toss in onion and celery, then sauté until soft. Stir in the corn and rest of the ingredients and cook the soup to boil.

2. Now reduce its heat to a simmer and cook for 45 minutes. Serve warm.

**Nutrition:** **Calories:** 115 kcal; **Protein:** 3 g; **Fat:** 13 g

### 388. Seafood Corn Chowder

**Preparation time:** 10 minutes
**Cooking time:** 12 minutes
**Servings:** 4
**Ingredients:**

- 1 tbsp. butter
- 1 cup onion
- ⅓ cup celery
- ½ cup green bell pepper
- ½ cup red bell pepper
- 1 tbsp. white flour
- 14 oz. chicken broth
- 2 cups cream
- 6 oz. evaporated milk
- 10 oz. surimi imitation crab chunks
- 2 cups corn kernels, frozen
- ½ tsp. black pepper
- ½ tsp. paprika

**Directions:**

1. Place a suitably-sized saucepan over medium heat and add butter to melt. Toss in onion, green and red peppers, and celery, then sauté for 5 minutes. Stir in flour and whisk well for 2 minutes.
2. Pour in chicken broth and stir until it boils. Add evaporated milk, corn, surimi crab, paprika, black pepper, and creamer. Cook for 5 minutes, then serves warm.

**Nutrition:** **Calories:** 175 kcal; **Protein:** 8 g; **Fat:** 7 g

### 389. Beef Sage Soup

**Preparation time:** 10 minutes
**Cooking time:** 20 minutes
**Servings:** 4
**Ingredients:**

- ½ lb. beef, ground
- ½ tsp. sage, ground
- ½ tsp. black pepper
- ½ tsp. basil dried
- ½ tsp. garlic powder
- 4 slices bread, cubed
- 2 tbsp. olive oil
- 1 tbsp. herb seasoning blend
- 2 garlic cloves, minced
- 3 cups chicken broth
- 1 ½ cups water
- 4 tbsp. fresh parsley
- 2 tbsp. parmesan cheese

**Directions:**

1. Preheat your oven to 375ºF. Mix beef with sage, basil, black pepper, and garlic powder in a bowl, then set it aside. Throw in the bread cubes with olive oil on a baking sheet and bake them for 8 minutes.
2. Meanwhile, sauté the beef mixture in a greased cooking pot until it is browned. Stir in garlic and sauté for 2 minutes; then add parsley, water, and broth. Cover the beef soup and cook for 10 minutes on a simmer. Garnish the soup with parmesan cheese and baked bread. Serve warm.

**Nutrition:** **Calories:** 336 kcal; **Protein:** 26 g; **Fat:** 16 g

### 390. Cabbage Borscht

**Preparation time:** 10 minutes
**Cooking time:** 90 minutes
**Servings:** 6
**Ingredients:**

- 2 lb. beef steaks
- 6 cups cold water
- 2 tbsp. olive oil
- ½ cup tomato sauce
- 1 medium cabbage, chopped
- 1 cup onion, diced
- 1 cup carrots, diced
- 1 cup turnips, peeled and diced
- 1 tsp. pepper - 6 tbsp. lemon juice
- 4 tbsp. sugar

**Directions:**

1. Start by placing steak in a large cooking pot and pour enough water to cover it. Cover the beef pot and cook it on a simmer until it is tender, then shred it using a fork. Add olive oil, onion, tomato sauce, carrots, turnips, and shredded steak to the cooking liquid in the pot.
2. Stir in black pepper, sugar, and lemon juice to season the soup. Cover the cabbage soup and cook on low heat for 1 ½ hour. Serve warm.

**Nutrition:** **Calories:** 212 kcal; **Protein:** 19 g; **Fat:** 10 g

### 391. Ground Beef Soup

**Preparation time:** 10 minutes
**Cooking time:** 30 minutes
**Servings:** 4
**Ingredients:**

- 1-lb. lean beef, ground
- ½ cup onion, chopped

- 2 tsp. lemon-pepper seasoning blend
- 1 cup beef broth - 2 cups water
- ⅓ cup white rice, uncooked
- 3 cups mixed vegetables, frozen
- 1 tbsp. sour cream

**Directions**:
1. Spray a saucepan with cooking oil and place it over medium heat. Toss in onion and ground beef, then sauté until brown. Stir in broth and the rest of the ingredients; then boil it.
2. Reduce heat to a simmer; then cover the soup to cook for 30 minutes. Garnish with sour cream. Enjoy.

**Nutrition: Calories:** 223 kcal; **Protein:** 20 g; **Fat:** 20 g

## 392. Mexican Tortilla Soup

**Preparation time:** 7 minutes
**Cooking time:** 40 minutes
**Servings:** 4
**Ingredients:**
- 1-lb. chicken breasts
- 1 can (15 oz.) whole tomatoes, peeled
- 1 can (10 oz.) red enchilada sauce
- 1 and ½ tsp. garlic, minced
- 1 yellow onion, diced
- 1 can (4 oz.) fire-roasted green chili, diced
- 1 can (15 oz.) black beans
- 1 can (15 oz.) fire-roasted corn
- 1 container (32 oz.) chicken stock
- 1 tsp. cumin, ground
- 2 tsp. chili powder
- ¾ tsp. paprika
- 1 bay leaf
- 1 tbsp. cilantro, chopped

**Directions**:
1. Set your Instant Pot on Sauté mode.
2. Toss olive oil, onion, and garlic into the insert of the Instant Pot.
3. Sauté for 4 minutes, then add chicken and remaining ingredients.
4. Mix well gently, then seal and lock the lid.
5. Select Manual mode for 7 minutes at high pressure.
6. Once done, release the pressure completely; then remove the lid.
7. Adjust seasoning as needed.
8. Garnish with desired toppings.

**Nutrition: Calories:** 390 kcal; **Protein:** 29.5 g; **Fat:** 26.5 g

## 393. Chicken Noodle Soup

**Preparation time:** 9 minutes
**Cooking time:** 35 minutes
**Servings:** 6
**Ingredients:**
- 1 tbsp. olive oil
- 1 ½ cups carrots
- 1 ½ cup celery, diced
- 1 cup yellow onion, chopped
- 3 tbsp. garlic, minced
- 8 cups low-sodium chicken broth
- 2 tsp. fresh thyme, minced
- 2 tsp. fresh rosemary, minced
- 1 bay leaf
- 2 ½ lb. chicken thighs
- 3 cups wide egg noodles
- 1 tbsp. fresh lemon juice
- ¼ cup fresh parsley, chopped

**Directions**:
1. Preheat olive oil in the insert of the Instant Pot on Sauté mode.
2. Add onion, celery, and carrots and sauté them for minutes.
3. Stir in garlic and sauté for 1 minute.
4. Add bay leaf, thyme, broth, rosemary, salt, and pepper.
5. Seal and secure the Instant Pot lid and select Manual mode for 10 minutes at high pressure.
6. Once done, release the pressure completely; then remove the lid.
7. Add noodles to the insert and switch the Instant Pot to sauté mode.
8. Cook the soup for 6 minutes until noodles are all done.
9. Pull out chicken and shred it using a fork.
10. Return the chicken to the soup; then add lemon juice and parsley.

**Nutrition: Calories:** 333 kcal; **Protein:** 44.7 g; **Fat:** 13.7 g

## 394. Cheesy Broccoli Soup

**Preparation time:** 11 minutes
**Cooking time:** 30 minutes
**Servings:** 4
**Ingredients:**
- ½ cup heavy whipping cream
- 1 cup broccoli
- 1 cup cheddar cheese
- Salt, to taste
- 1½ cups chicken broth

**Directions**:
1. Cook chicken broth in a large pot and add broccoli.
2. Boil and stir in the rest of the ingredients.
3. Simmer on low heat for 21 minutes.
4. Ladle out into a bowl and serve hot.

**Nutrition**: **Calories**: 188 kcal; **Fat**: 15 g; **Protein**: 9.8 g

## 395. Rich Potato Soup

**Preparation time**: 6 minutes
**Cooking time**: 30 minutes
**Servings**: 4
**Ingredients**:
- 1 tbsp. butter
- 1 medium onion, diced
- 3 cloves garlic, minced
- 3 cups chicken broth
- 1 can/box cream of chicken soup
- 7–8 medium-sized russet potatoes
- 1 ½ tsp. salt
- 1 cup milk
- 1 tbsp. flour
- 2 cups cheddar cheese, shredded

**Garnish**:
- 5–6 slices bacon, chopped
- Green onions, sliced
- Cheddar cheese, shredded

**Directions**:
1. Heat butter in the insert of the Instant Pot on sauté mode.
2. Add onions and sauté for 4 minutes until soft.
3. Stir in garlic and sauté it for 1 minute.
4. Add potatoes, cream of chicken, broth, salt, and pepper to the insert.
5. Mix well, then seal and lock the lid.
6. Cook this mixture for 10 minutes at Manual Mode with high pressure.
7. Meanwhile, mix flour with milk in a bowl and set it aside.
8. Once the instant pot beeps, release the pressure completely.
9. Remove the Instant Pot lid and switch the instant pot to Sauté mode.
10. Pour in flour slurry and stir; cook the mixture for 5 minutes until it thickens.
11. Add 2 cups of cheddar cheese and let it melt.
12. Garnish it as desired.

**Nutrition**: **Calories**: 784 kcal; **Protein**: 34 g; **Fat**: 46.5 g

## 396. Mediterranean Lentil Soup

**Preparation time**: 9 minutes
**Cooking time**: 20 minutes
**Servings**: 4
**Ingredients**:
- 1 tbsp. olive oil
- ½ cup red lentils
- 1 medium yellow or red onion
- 2 garlic cloves
- ½ tsp. cumin, ground
- ½ tsp. coriander, ground
- ½ tsp. sumac, ground
- ½ tsp. red chili flakes
- ½ tsp. parsley, dried
- ¾ tsp. mint flakes, dried
- 2 cups water
- juice of ½ lime

**Directions**:
1. Preheat oil in the insert of your Instant Pot on Sauté mode.
2. Add onion and sauté until it turns golden brown.
3. Toss in the garlic, parsley sugar, mint flakes, red chili flakes, sumac, coriander, and cumin.
4. Stir cook this mixture for 2 minutes.
5. Add water, lentils, salt, and pepper. Stir gently.
6. Seal and lock the Instant Pot lid and select Manual mode for 8 minutes at high pressure.
7. Once done, release the pressure completely; then remove the lid.
8. Stir well; then add lime juice.

**Nutrition**: **Calories**: 525 kcal; **Protein**: 30 g; **Fat**: 19.3 g

## 397. Sausage Kale Soup with Mushrooms

**Preparation time**: 8 minutes
**Cooking time**: 70 minutes
**Servings**: 6
**Ingredients**:
- 2 cups fresh kale
- 4 oz. mushrooms, sliced
- 6 cups chicken bone broth
- 1-lb. sausage, cooked and sliced

**Directions**:
1. Heat chicken broth with 2 cans of water in a large pot and bring to a boil.
2. Stir in the remaining ingredients and allow the soup to simmer on low heat for about 1 hour.
3. Dish out and serve hot.

**Nutrition**: **Calories**: 259 kcal; **Fat**: 20 g; **Protein**: 14 g

## 398. Classic Minestrone

**Preparation time:** 12 minutes
**Cooking time:** 25 minutes
**Servings:** 6
**Ingredients:**
- 2 tbsp. olive oil
- 3 garlic cloves
- 1 onion, diced
- 2 carrots
- 2 stalks celery
- 1 ½ tsp. basil, dried
- 1 tsp. oregano, dried
- ½ tsp. fennel seed
- 6 cups low-sodium chicken broth
- 1 (28-oz.) can tomatoes
- 1 (16-oz.) can kidney beans
- 1 zucchini
- 1 Parmesan rind
- 1 bay leaf
- 1 bunch kale leaves, chopped
- 2 tsp. red wine vinegar
- ⅓ cup Parmesan, freshly grated
- 2 tbsp. fresh parsley leaves, chopped

**Directions:**
1. Preheat olive oil in the insert of the Instant Pot on Sauté mode. Add carrots, celery, and onion, sauté for 3 minutes. Stir in fennel seeds, oregano, and basil. Stir cook for 1 minute.
2. Add stock, beans, tomatoes, parmesan, bay leaf, and zucchini.
3. Secure and seal the Instant Pot lid, then select Manual mode to cook for minutes at high pressure. Once done, release the pressure completely; then remove the lid. Add kale and let it sit for 2 minutes in the hot soup. Stir in red wine, vinegar, pepper, and salt. Garnish with parsley and parmesan.

**Nutrition: Calories:** 805 kcal; **Protein:** 124 kcal; **Fat:** 34 g

## 399. Turkey Meatball and Ditalini Soup

**Preparation time:** 15 minutes
**Cooking time:** 40 minutes
**Servings:** 4
**Ingredients:**
Meatballs:
- 1 lb. 93% lean turkey, ground
- ⅓ cup seasoned breadcrumbs
- 3 tbsp. Pecorino Romano cheese, grated
- 1 large egg, beaten
- 1 clove garlic, crushed
- 1 tbsp. fresh parsley, minced
- ½ tsp. Kosher salt

Soup:
- 1 tsp. olive oil - ½ cup onion
- ½ cup celery - ½ cup carrot
- 3 cloves garlic
- 1 can San Marzano tomatoes
- 4 cups reduced-sodium chicken broth
- 4 torn basil leaves
- 2 bay leaves - 1 cup ditalini pasta
- 1 cup zucchini, diced small
- Parmesan rind, optional
- parmesan cheese, grated, optional for serving

**Directions:**
1. Thoroughly combine turkey with egg, garlic, parsley, salt, pecorino, and breadcrumbs in a bowl. Make 30 equal-sized meatballs out of this mixture. Preheat olive oil in the insert of the Instant Pot on Sauté mode.
2. Sear the meatballs in the heated oil in batches until brown. Set the meatballs aside in a plate.
3. Add more oil to the insert of the Instant Pot. Stir in carrots, garlic, celery, and onion. Sauté for 4 minutes. Add basil, bay leaves, tomatoes, and Parmesan rind. Return the seared meatballs to the pot along with the broth. Secure and sear the Instant Pot lid and select Manual mode for 15 minutes at high pressure. Once done, release the pressure completely; then remove the lid. Add zucchini and pasta, and cook it for 4 minutes on Sauté mode.
4. Garnish with cheese and basil.

**Nutrition: Calories:** 261 kcal; **Protein:** 37 g; **Fat:** 7 g

## 400. Mint Avocado Chilled Soup

**Preparation time:** 6 minutes
**Cooking time:** 0 minutes
**Servings:** 2
**Ingredients:**
- 1 cup coconut milk, chilled
- 1 medium ripe avocado
- 1 tbsp. lime juice Salt, to taste
- 20 fresh mint leaves

**Directions:**
1. Put all the ingredients into an immersion blender and blend until a thick mixture is formed. Allow to cool for 10 minutes and serve chilled.

**Nutrition: Calories:** 286 kcal; **Fat:** 27 g; **Protein:** 4.2 g

# CHAPTER 13:
# Vegetarian

## 401. Lentil-Stuffed Zucchini Boats

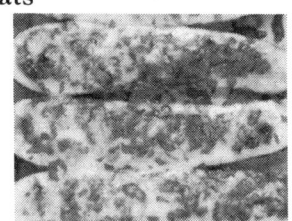

**Preparation time:** 15 minutes
**Cooking time:** 45 minutes
**Servings:** 2
**Ingredients:**

- 2 medium zucchinis, halved lengthwise and seeded
- 2 ¼ cups water, divided
- 1 cup green or red lentils, dried and rinsed
- 2 tsp. olive oil
- ⅓ cup onion, diced
- 2 tbsp. tomato paste
- ½ tsp. oregano
- ¼ tsp. garlic powder
- Pinch salt
- ¼ cup part-skim mozzarella cheese, grated

**Directions:**

1. Preheat the oven to 375°F. Line a baking sheet with parchment paper. Place the zucchini, hollow sides up, on the baking sheet, and set aside.
2. Boil 2 cups of water to a boil over high heat in a medium saucepan and add the lentils. Lower the heat, and then simmer within 20 to 25 minutes. Drain and set aside. Heat up the olive oil in a medium skillet over medium-low heat. Sauté the onions until they are translucent, about 4 minutes. Lower the heat and add the cooked lentils, tomato paste, oregano, garlic powder, and salt.
3. Add the last quarter cup of water and simmer for 3 minutes, until the liquid reduces and forms a sauce. Remove from heat.

4. Stuff each zucchini half with the lentil mixture, dividing it evenly, and top with cheese, bake for 25 minutes, and serve. The zucchini should be fork-tender, and the cheese should be melted.

**Nutrition: Calories:** 479 kcal; **Fat:** 9 g; **Carbohydrates:** 74 g; **Fiber:** 14 g; **Protein:** 31 g; **Sodium:** 206 mg; **Potassium:** 1389 mg

## 402. Baked Eggplant Parmesan

**Preparation time:** 15 minutes
**Cooking time:** 35 minutes
**Servings:** 4
**Ingredients:**
- 1 small to medium eggplant, cut into ¼-inch slices
- ½ tsp. salt-free Italian seasoning blend
- 1 tbsp. olive oil
- ¼ cup onion, diced
- ½ cup yellow or red bell pepper, diced
- 2 garlic cloves, pressed or minced
- 1 (8-oz.) can tomato sauce
- 3 oz. fresh mozzarella, cut into 6 pieces
- 1 tbsp. Parmesan cheese, grated and divided
- 5 to 6 fresh basil leaves, chopped

**Directions:**
1. Preheat an oven-style air fryer to 400°F.
2. Working in 2 batches, place the eggplant slices onto the air-fryer tray and sprinkle them with Italian seasoning. Bake for 7 minutes. Repeat with the remaining slices, andthen set them aside on a plate.
3. In a medium skillet, heat the oil over medium heat and sauté the onion and peppers until softened for about 5 minutes. Add the garlic and sauté for 1 to 2 more minutes. Add the tomato sauce and stir to combine. Remove the sauce from the heat.
4. Spray a 9x6-inch casserole dish with cooking spray. Spread one-third of the sauce into the bottom of the dish. Layer eggplant slices onto the sauce. Sprinkle with half of the Parmesan cheese.
5. Continue layering the sauce and eggplant, ending with the sauce. Place the mozzarella pieces on the top.
6. Sprinkle the remaining Parmesan evenly over the entire dish. Bake in the oven for 20 minutes. Garnish with fresh basil, cut into four servings, and serve.

**Nutrition: Calories:** 213 kcal; **Fat:** 12 g; **Carbohydrates:** 20 g; **Fiber:** 7 g; **Protein:** 10 g; **Sodium:** 222 mg; **Potassium:** 763 mg

## 403. Sweet Potato Rice with Spicy Peanut Sauce

**Preparation time:** 15 minutes
**Cooking time:** 25 minutes
**Servings:** 2
**Ingredients:**
- ½ cup basmati rice
- 2 tsp. olive oil, divided
- 1 (8-oz.) can chickpeas, drained and rinsed
- 2 medium sweet potatoes, small cubes
- ¼ tsp. cumin, ground
- 1 cup water
- ⅛ tsp. salt
- 2 tbsp. cilantro, chopped
- 3 tbsp. peanut butter
- 1 tbsp. sriracha
- 2 tsp. reduced-sodium soy sauce
- ½ tsp. garlic powder
- ¼ tsp. ground ginger

**Directions:**
1. Heat up 1 tsp. of oil in a large nonstick skillet over medium-high heat. Add the chickpeas and heat for 3 minutes. Stir and cook until lightly browned. Transfer the chickpeas to a small bowl.
2. Put the rest of the1 tsp. of oil into the skillet; then add the potatoes and cumin, distributing them evenly. Cook the potatoes until they become lightly browned before turning them.
3. While the potatoes are cooking, boil the water with the salt in a large saucepan over medium-high heat. Put the rice in the boiling water, adjust the heat to low, cover, and simmer for 20 minutes.
4. When the potatoes have fully cooked, about 10 minutes in total, remove the skillet from the heat. Transfer the potatoes and chickpeas to the rice, folding all gently. Add the chopped cilantro.
5. In a small bowl, whisk the peanut butter, sriracha, soy sauce, garlic powder, and ginger until well blended.

6. Divide the rice mixture between 2 serving bowls. Drizzle with the sauce and serve.

**Nutrition: Calories:** 667 kcal; **Fat:** 22 g; **Carbohydrates:** 100 g; **Fiber:** 14 g; **Protein:** 20 g; **Sodium:** 563 mg; **Potassium:** 963 mg

## 404. Vegetable Red Curry

**Preparation time:** 15 minutes
**Cooking time:** 25 minutes
**Servings:** 2
**Ingredients:**

- 2 tsp. olive oil
- 1 cup sliced carrots
- ½ cup onion, chopped
- 1 garlic clove, pressed or minced
- 2 bell peppers, seeded and thinly sliced
- 1 cup cauliflower, chopped
- ⅔ cup light coconut milk
- ½ cup low-sodium vegetable broth
- 1 tbsp. tomato paste
- 1 tsp. curry powder
- ½ tsp. cumin, ground
- ½ tsp. coriander, ground
- ¼ tsp. turmeric
- 2 cups fresh baby spinach
- 1 cup quick-cooking brown rice

**Directions:**

1. Heat-up oil in a large nonstick skillet over medium heat.
2. Add the carrots, onion, and garlic and cook for 2 to 3 minutes.
3. Reduce the heat to medium-low, add the peppers and cauliflower to the skillet, cover, and cook within 5 minutes.
4. Add the coconut milk, broth, tomato paste, curry powder, cumin, coriander, and turmeric, stirring to combine. Simmer, covered (vent the lid slightly), for 10 to 15 minutes until the curry is slightly reduced and thickened.
5. Uncover, add the spinach, and stir for 2 minutes until it is wilted and mixed into the vegetables. Remove from the heat.
6. Cook the rice as stated in the package instructions. Serve the curry over the rice.

**Nutrition: Calories:** 584 kcal; **Fat:** 16 g; **Carbohydrates:** 101 g; **Fiber:** 10 g; **Protein:** 13 g; **Sodium:** 102 mg; **Potassium:** 1430 mg

## 405. Black Bean Burgers

**Preparation time:** 15 minutes
**Cooking time:** 20 minutes
**Servings:** 4
**Ingredients:**

- ½ cup quick-cooking brown rice
- 2 tsp. canola oil, divided
- ½ cup carrots, finely chopped
- ¼ cup onion, finely chopped
- 1 can black beans, drained
- 1 tbsp. salt-free mesquite seasoning blend - 4 small, hard rolls

**Directions:**

1. Cook the rice as stated in the package directions and set aside. Heat up 1 tsp. of oil in a large nonstick skillet over medium heat. Add the carrots and onions and cook until the onions are translucent about 4 minutes. Adjust the heat to low, and cook again for 5 to 6 minutes, until the carrots are tender.
2. Add the beans and seasoning to the skillet and continue cooking for 2 to 3 more minutes. Pulse bean mixture in a food processor within 3 to 4 times or until the mixture is coarsely blended. Put the butter in a medium bowl and fold in the brown rice until well combined.
3. Divide the mixture evenly and form it into 4 patties with your hands. Heat the remaining oil in the skillet. Cook the patties within 4 to 5 minutes per side, turning once. Serve the burgers on the rolls with your choice of toppings.

**Nutrition: Calories:** 368 kcal; **Fat:** 6 g; **Carbohydrates:** 66 g; **Fiber:** 8 g; **Protein:** 13 g; **Sodium:** 322 mg; **Potassium:** 413 mg

## 406. Summer Barley Pilaf with Yogurt Dill Sauce

**Preparation time:** 15 minutes
**Cooking time:** 30 minutes
**Servings:** 3
**Ingredients:**

- 2 ⅔ cups low-sodium vegetable broth
- 2 tsp. avocado oil
- 1 small zucchini, diced
- ⅓ cup almonds, slivered
- 2 scallions, sliced
- 1 cup barley
- ½ cup plain nonfat Greek yogurt
- 2 tsp. lemon zest, grated
- ¼ tsp. dill, dried

**Directions**:
1. Boil the broth in a large saucepan. Heat up the oil in a skillet. Add the zucchini and sauté 3 to 4 minutes. Add the almonds and the white parts of the scallions and sauté for 2 minutes. Remove, and transfer it to a small bowl.
2. Add the barley to the skillet and sauté for 2 to 3 minutes to toast. Transfer the barley to the boiling broth and reduce the heat to low, cover, and simmer for 25 minutes or until tender.
3. Remove, and let stand within 10 minutes or until the liquid is absorbed.
4. Simultaneously, mix the yogurt, lemon zest, and dill in a small bowl and set aside. Fluff the barley with a fork. Add the zucchini, almond, and onion mixture and mix gently. To serve, divide the pilaf between 2 bowls and drizzle the yogurt over each bowl.

**Nutrition: Calories:** 545 kcal; **Fat:** 15 g; **Carbohydrates:** 87 g; **Fiber:** 19 g; **Protein:** 21 g; **Sodium:** 37 mg; **Potassium:** 694 mg

## 407. Lentil Quinoa Gratin with Butternut Squash

**Preparation time:** 15 minutes
**Cooking time:** 1 hour and 15 minutes
**Servings:** 3
**Ingredients:**
**For the Lentils and Squash:**
- Nonstick cooking spray
- 2 cups water
- ½ cup green or red lentils, dried and rinsed
- Pinch salt
- 1 tsp. olive oil, divided
- ½ cup quinoa
- ¼ cup shallot, diced
- 2 cups butternut squash, frozen and cubed
- ¼ cup low-fat milk
- 1 tsp. fresh rosemary, chopped
- black pepper, freshly ground

**For the Gratin Topping:**
- ¼ cup panko bread crumbs
- 1 tsp. olive oil
- ⅓ cup Gruyere cheese, shredded

**Directions**:
1. Preheat the oven to 400°F. Spray a 1½-quart casserole dish or an 8-by-8-inch baking dish with cooking spray.
2. In a medium saucepan, stir the water, lentils, and salt and boil over medium-high heat. Lower the heat once the water is boiling, cover, and simmer for 20 to 25 minutes. Then drain and transfer the lentils to a large bowl and set aside.
3. In the same saucepan, heat-up ½ tsp. of oil over medium heat. Add the quinoa and quickly stir for 1 minute to toast it lightly. Cook according to the package directions, about 20 minutes.
4. While the quinoa cooks, heat the remaining olive oil in a medium skillet over medium-low heat, add the shallots, and sauté them until they are translucent, about 3 minutes.
5. Add the squash, milk, and rosemary and cook for 1 to 2 minutes. Remove, then transfer to the lentil bowl. Add in the quinoa and gently toss all. Season with pepper to taste. Transfer the mixture to the casserole dish.
6. For the gratin topping, mix the panko bread crumbs with the olive oil in a small bowl. Put the bread crumbs over the casserole and top them with the cheese. Bake the casserole for 25 minutes and serve.

**Nutrition: Calories:** 576 kcal; **Fat:** 15 g; **Carbohydrates:** 87 g; **Fiber:** 12 g; **Protein:** 28 g; **Sodium:** 329 mg; **Potassium:** 1176 mg

## 408. Brown Rice Casserole with Cottage Cheese

**Preparation time:** 15 minutes
**Cooking time:** 45 minutes
**Servings:** 3
**Ingredients:**
- Nonstick cooking spray
- 1 cup quick-cooking brown rice
- 1 tsp. olive oil
- ½ cup sweet onion, diced
- 1 (10-oz.) bag fresh spinach
- 1½ cups low-fat cottage cheese
- 1 tbsp. Parmesan cheese, grated
- ¼ cup sunflower seed kernels

**Directions**:
1. Preheat the oven to 375°F. Spray a small 1½-quart casserole dish with cooking spray. Cook the rice, as stated in the package directions. Set aside. Warm-up the oil in a large nonstick skillet over medium-low heat.
2. Add the onion and sauté for 3 to 4 minutes. Add the spinach and cover the skillet, cooking for 1 to 2 minutes until the spinach wilts. Remove the skillet from the heat.
3. In a medium bowl, mix the rice, spinach mixture, and cottage cheese. Transfer the mixture to the prepared casserole dish.

4. Top with the Parmesan cheese and sunflower seeds, bake for 25 minutes until lightly browned, and serve.

**Nutrition: Calories:** 334 kcal; **Fat:** 9 g; **Carbohydrates:** 47 g; **Fiber:** 5 g; **Protein:** 19 g; **Sodium:** 425 mg; **Potassium:** 553 mg

## 409. Quinoa-Stuffed Peppers

**Preparation time:** 15 minutes
**Cooking time:** 35 minutes
**Servings:** 2
**Ingredients:**

- 2 large green bell peppers, halved
- 1½ tsp. olive oil, divided
- ½ cup quinoa
- ½ cup onion, minced
- 1 garlic clove, pressed or minced
- 1 cup Portobello mushrooms, chopped
- 3 tbsp. Parmesan cheese, grated and divided
- 4 oz. tomato sauce

**Directions:**

1. Preheat the oven to 400°F. Put the pepper halves on your prepared baking sheet. Brush the insides of peppers with ½ tsp. olive oil and bake for 10 minutes.
2. Remove the baking sheet, then set aside. While the peppers bake, cook the quinoa in a large saucepan over medium heat according to the package directions and set aside.
3. Warm-up the rest of the oil in a medium-size skillet over medium heat. Add the onion and sauté until it's translucent, about 3 minutes. Put the garlic and cook within 1 minute.
4. Put the mushrooms in the skillet, adjust the heat to medium-low, cover, and cook within 5 to 6 minutes. Uncover, and if there's still liquid in the pan, reduce the heat and cook until the liquid evaporates.
5. Add the mushroom mixture, 1 tbsp. of Parmesan, and the tomato sauce to the quinoa and gently stir to combine. Carefully spoon the quinoa mixture into each pepper half and sprinkle with the remaining Parmesan. Return the peppers to the oven, bake for 10 to 15 more minutes until tender, and serve.

**Nutrition: Calories:** 292 kcal; **Fat:** 9 g; **Carbohydrates:** 45 g; **Fiber:** 8 g; **Protein:** 12 g; **Sodium:** 154 mg; **Potassium:** 929 mg

## 410. Greek Flatbread with Spinach, Tomatoes, and Feta

**Preparation time:** 15 minutes
**Cooking time:** 9 minutes
**Servings:** 2
**Ingredients:**

- 2 cups fresh baby spinach, coarsely chopped
- 2 tsp. olive oil
- 2 slices Naan, or another flatbread
- ¼ cup black olives, sliced
- 2 plum tomatoes, thinly sliced
- 1 tsp. salt-free Italian seasoning blend
- ¼ cup feta cheese, crumbled

**Directions:**

1. Preheat the oven to 400°F. Heat 3 tbsp. of water in a small skillet over medium heat. Add the spinach, cover, and steam until wilted, about 2 minutes. Drain off any excess water, then put aside.
2. Drizzle the oil evenly onto both flatbreads. Top each evenly with spinach, olives, tomatoes, seasoning, and feta. Bake the flatbreads within 5 to 7 minutes, or until lightly browned. Cut each into four pieces and serve hot.

**Nutrition: Calories:** 411 kcal; **Fat:** 15 g; **Carbohydrates:** 53 g; **Fiber:** 7 g; **Protein:** 15 g; **Sodium:** 621 mg; **Potassium:** 522 mg

## 411. Mushroom Risotto with Peas

**Preparation time:** 15 minutes
**Cooking time:** 20 minutes
**Servings:** 2
**Ingredients:**

- 2 cups low-sodium vegetable or chicken broth
- 1 tsp. olive oil
- 8 oz. baby Portobello mushrooms, thinly sliced
- ½ cup peas, frozen
- 1 tsp. butter
- 1 cup Arborio rice
- 1 tbsp. Parmesan cheese, grated

**Directions:**

1. Pour the broth into a microwave-proof glass measuring cup. Microwave on high for 1½ minutes or until hot. Warm-up oil over medium heat in a large saucepan. Add the mushrooms and stir for 1 minute. Cover and cook until soft, about 3 more minutes. Stir in the peas and reduce the heat to low.

2. Put the mushroom batter to the saucepan's sides and add the butter to the middle, heating until melted. Put the rice in the saucepan and stir for 1 to 2 minutes to lightly toast. Add the hot broth, ½ cup at a time, and stir gently.
3. As the broth is cooked into the rice, continue adding more broth, ½ cup at a time, stirring after each addition, until all broth is added. Once all of the liquid is absorbed (this should take 15 minutes), remove from the heat. Serve immediately, topped with Parmesan cheese.

**Nutrition: Calories:** 430 kcal; **Fat:** 6 g; **Carbohydrates:** 83 g; **Fiber:** 5 g; **Protein:** 10 g; **Sodium:** 78 mg; **Potassium:** 558 mg

## 412. Loaded Tofu Burrito with Black Beans

**Preparation time:** 15 minutes
**Cooking time:** 20 minutes
**Servings:** 2
**Ingredients:**
- 4 oz. extra-firm tofu, pressed and cut into 2-inch cubes
- 2 tsp. mesquite salt-free seasoning, divided
- 2 tsp. canola oil
- 1 cup bell peppers, thinly sliced
- ½ cup onions, diced
- ⅔ cup black beans, drained
- 2 (10-inch) whole-wheat tortillas
- 1 tbsp. sriracha
- Nonfat Greek yogurt, for serving

**Directions:**
1. Put the tofu and 1 tsp. of seasoning in a medium zip-top plastic freezer bag and toss until the tofu is well coated.
2. Heat up the oil in a medium skillet over medium-high heat. Put the tofu in the skillet. Don't stir; allow the tofu to brown before turning. When lightly browned, about 6 minutes, transfer the tofu from the skillet to a small bowl and set aside.
3. Put the peppers plus onions in the skillet and sauté until tender, about 5 minutes. Lower the heat to medium-low, then put the beans and the remaining seasoning. Cook within 5 minutes.
4. For the burritos, lay each tortilla flat on a work surface. Place half of the tofu in the center of each tortilla, top with half of the pepper-bean mixture, and drizzle with the sriracha.
5. Fold the bottom portion of each tortilla up and over the tofu mixture.
6. Then fold each side into the middle, tuck in, and tightly roll it up toward the open end. Serve with a dollop of yogurt.

**Nutrition: Calories:** 327 kcal; **Fat:** 12 g; **Carbohydrates:** 41 g; **Fiber:** 11 g; **Protein:** 16 g; **Sodium:** 282 mg

## 413. Southwest Tofu Scramble

**Preparation time:** 15 minutes
**Cooking time:** 15 minutes
**Servings:** 1
**Ingredients:**
- ½ tbsp. olive oil - ½ red onion, chopped
- 2 cups spinach, chopped
- 8 oz. firm tofu, drained well
- 1 tsp. cumin, ground
- ½ tsp. garlic powder

**Optional for Servings:** sliced avocado or sliced tomatoes

**Directions:**
1. Heat up the olive oil in a medium skillet over medium heat. Put the onion and cook within 5 minutes. Add the spinach and cover to steam for 2 minutes.
2. Using a spatula, move the veggies to one side of the pan. Crumble the tofu into the open area in the pan, breaking it up with a fork. Add the cumin and garlic to the crumbled tofu and mix well. Sauté for 5 to 7 minutes until the tofu is slightly browned.
3. Serve immediately with whole-grain bread, fruit, or beans. Top with optional sliced avocado and tomato, if using.

**Nutrition: Calories:** 267 kcal; **Fat:** 17 g; **Sodium:** 75 mg; **Carbohydrate:** 13 g; **Protein:** 23 g

## 414. Black-Bean and Vegetable Burrito

**Preparation time:** 15 minutes
**Cooking time:** 15 minutes
**Servings:** 4
**Ingredients:**
- ½ tbsp. olive oil
- 2 red or green bell peppers, chopped
- 1 zucchini or summer squash, diced
- ½ tsp. chili powder
- 1 tsp. cumin
- Black pepper, freshly ground
- 2 cans black beans, drained and rinsed
- 1 cup cherry tomatoes, halved
- 4 (8-inch) whole-wheat tortillas

- **Optional for Servings:** spinach; avocado, sliced; scallions, chopped, or hot sauce

**Directions:**
1. Heat up the oil in a large sauté pan over medium heat. Add the bell peppers and sauté until crisp-tender, about 4 minutes. Add the zucchini, chili powder, cumin, and black pepper to taste, and continue to sauté until the vegetables are tender, about 5 minutes.
2. Add the black beans and cherry tomatoes and cook within 5 minutes. Divide between 4 burritos and serve topped with optional ingredients as desired. Enjoy immediately.

**Nutrition: Calories:** 311 kcal; **Fat:** 6 g; **Sodium:** 499 mg; **Carbohydrate:** 52 g; **Protein:** 19 g

## 415. Baked Eggs in Avocado

**Preparation time:** 15 minutes
**Cooking time:** 15 minutes
**Servings:** 2
**Ingredients:**

- 2 avocados - 2 limes juice
- Black pepper, freshly ground - 4 eggs
- 2 (8-inch) whole-wheat or corn tortillas, warmed
- **Optional for Servings:** cherry tomatoes, halved, and cilantro, chopped

**Directions:**
1. Adjust the oven rack to the middle position and preheat the oven to 450°F. Scrape out the center of halved avocado using a spoon about 1½ tbsp. Press lime juice over the avocados and season with black pepper to taste, and then place it on a baking sheet. Crack an egg into the avocado.
2. Bake within 10 to 15 minutes. Remove from oven and garnish with optional cilantro and cherry tomatoes and serve with warm tortillas.

**Nutrition: Calories:** 534 kcal; **Fat:** 39 g; **Sodium:** 462 mg; **Potassium:** 1,095 mg; **Carbohydrate:** 30 g; **Fiber:** 20 g; **Sugars:** 3 g; **Protein:** 23 g

## 416. Red Beans and Rice

**Preparation time:** 15 minutes
**Cooking time:** 45 minutes
**Servings:** 2
**Ingredients:**

- ½ cup dry brown rice
- 1 cup water, plus ¼ cup
- 1 can red beans, drained
- 1 tbsp. cumin, ground
- 1 lime juice

- 4 handfuls fresh spinach
- **Optional toppings:** avocado, tomatoes, chopped; Greek yogurt, onions

**Directions:**
1. Mix rice plus water in a pot and bring to a boil. Cover and reduce heat to a low simmer. Cook within 30 to 40 minutes or according to package directions. Meanwhile, add the beans, ¼ cup of water, cumin, and lime juice to a medium skillet. Simmer within 5 to 7 minutes. Once the liquid is mostly gone, remove from the heat and add the spinach. Cover and let spinach wilt slightly, 2 to 3 minutes. Mix in with the beans. Serve beans with rice. Add toppings, if using.

**Nutrition: Calories:** 232 kcal; **Fat:** 2 g; **Sodium:** 210 mg; **Carbohydrate:** 41 g; **Protein:** 13 g

## 417. Hearty Lentil Soup

**Preparation time:** 15 minutes
**Cooking time:** 30 minutes
**Servings:** 4
**Ingredients:**

- 1 tbsp. olive oil
- 2 carrots, peeled and chopped
- 2 celery stalks, diced
- 1 onion, chopped
- 1 tsp. thyme, dried
- ½ tsp. garlic powder
- Black pepper, freshly ground
- 1 (28-oz.) can no-salt diced tomatoes, drained
- 1 cup dry lentils - 5 cups water
- Salt

**Directions:**
1. Heat up the oil in a large Dutch oven or pot over medium heat. Once the oil is simmering, add the carrot, celery, and onion. Cook, often stirring within 5 minutes.
2. Add the thyme, garlic powder, and black pepper. Cook within 30 seconds. Pour in the drained diced tomatoes and cook for a few more minutes, often stirring to enhance their flavor. Put the lentils, water, plus a pinch of salt. Raise the heat and bring to a boil, then partially cover the pot and reduce heat to maintain a gentle simmer. Cook within 30 minutes, or until lentils are tender but still hold their shape. Ladle into serving bowls and serve with a fresh green salad and whole-grain bread.

**Nutrition: Calories:** 168 kcal; **Fat:** 4 g; **Sodium:** 130 mg; **Carbohydrate:** 35 g; **Protein:** 10 g

## 418. Black-Bean Soup

**Preparation time:** 15 minutes
**Cooking time:** 20 minutes
**Servings:** 4
**Ingredients:**
- 1 yellow onion
- 1 tbsp. olive oil
- 2 cans black beans, drained
- 1 cup fresh tomatoes, diced
- 5 cups low-sodium vegetable broth
- ¼ tsp. black pepper, freshly ground
- ¼ cup fresh cilantro, chopped

**Directions:**
1. Cook or sauté the onion in the olive oil within 4 to 5 minutes in a large saucepan over medium heat.
2. Put the black beans, tomatoes, vegetable broth, and black pepper. Boil, and then adjust heat to simmer within 15 minutes.
3. Remove, then work in batches, ladle the soup into a blender, and process until somewhat smooth. Put it back in the pot, add the cilantro, and heat until warmed through. Serve immediately.

**Nutrition: Calories:** 234 kcal; **Fat:** 5 g; **Sodium:** 363 mg; **Carbohydrate:** 37 g; **Protein:** 11 g

## 419. Loaded Baked Sweet Potatoes

**Preparation time:** 15 minutes
**Cooking time:** 20 minutes
**Servings:** 4
**Ingredients:**
- 4 sweet potatoes
- ½ cup non-fat or low-fat plain Greek yogurt
- Black pepper, freshly ground
- 1 tsp. olive oil
- 1 red bell pepper, cored and diced
- ½ red onion, diced
- 1 tsp. cumin, ground
- 1 (15-oz.) can chickpeas, drained and rinsed

**Directions:**
1. Prick the potatoes using a fork and cook on your microwave's potato setting until potatoes are soft and cooked through, about 8 to 10 minutes for 4 potatoes. If you don't have a microwave, bake at 400°F for about 45 minutes.
2. Combine the yogurt and black pepper in a small bowl and mix well. Heat the oil in a medium pot over medium heat. Add bell pepper, onion, cumin, and additional black pepper to taste.
3. Add the chickpeas, stir to combine, and heat through about 5 minutes. Slice the potatoes lengthwise down the middle and top each half with a portion of the bean mixture followed by 1 to 2 tbsp. of the yogurt. Serve immediately.

**Nutrition: Calories:** 264 kcal; **Fat:** 2 g; **Sodium:** 124 mg; **Carbohydrate:** 51 g; **Protein:** 11 g

## 420. White Beans with Spinach and Pan-Roasted Tomatoes

**Preparation time:** 15 minutes
**Cooking time:** 10 minutes
**Servings:** 2
**Ingredients:**
- 1 tbsp. olive oil
- 4 small plum tomatoes, halved lengthwise
- 10 oz. spinach, frozen, defrosted and squeezed of excess water
- 2 garlic cloves, thinly sliced
- 2 tbsp. water
- ¼ tsp. black pepper, freshly ground
- 1 can white beans, drained
- Juice of 1 lemon

**Directions:**
1. Heat up the oil in a large skillet over medium-high heat. Put the tomatoes, cut-side down, and cook within 3 to 5 minutes; turn and cook within 1 minute more. Transfer to a plate.
2. Reduce heat to medium and add the spinach, garlic, water, and pepper to the skillet. Cook, tossing until the spinach is heated through, 2 to 3 minutes.
3. Return the tomatoes to the skillet, put the white beans and lemon juice, and toss until heated through 1 to 2 minutes.

**Nutrition: Calories:** 293 kcal; **Fat:** 9 g; **Sodium:** 267 mg; **Carbohydrate:** 43 g; **Protein:** 15 g

## 421. Black-Eyed Peas and Greens Power Salad

**Preparation time:** 15 minutes
**Cooking time:** 6 minutes
**Servings:** 2
**Ingredients:**
- 1 tbsp. olive oil
- 3 cups purple cabbage, chopped
- 5 cups baby spinach
- 1 cup carrots, shredded
- 1 can black-eyed peas, drained
- Juice of ½ lemon
- Salt

- Black pepper, freshly ground

**Directions:**
1. In a medium pan, add the oil and cabbage and sauté for 1 to 2 minutes on medium heat. Add in your spinach, cover for 3 to 4 minutes on medium heat, until greens are wilted. Remove from the heat and add to a large bowl.
2. Add in the carrots, black-eyed peas, and a splash of lemon juice. Season with salt and pepper, if desired. Toss and serve.

**Nutrition: Calories:** 320 kcal; **Fat:** 9 g; **Sodium:** 351 mg; **Potassium:** 544 mg; **Carbohydrate:** 49 g; **Protein:** 16 g

## 422. Butternut-Squash Macaroni and Cheese

**Preparation time:** 15 minutes
**Cooking time:** 20 minutes
**Servings:** 2
**Ingredients:**
- 1 cup whole-wheat ziti macaroni
- 2 cups butternut squash, peeled and cubed
- 1 cup non-fat or low-fat milk, divided
- Black pepper, freshly ground
- 1 tsp. Dijon mustard
- 1 tbsp. olive oil
- ¼ cup low-fat cheddar cheese, shredded

**Directions:**
1. Cook the pasta al dente. Put the butternut squash plus ½ cup milk in a medium saucepan and place over medium-high heat. Season with black pepper. Bring it to a simmer. Lower the heat, then cook until fork-tender, 8 to 10 minutes.
2. To a blender, add squash and Dijon mustard. Purée until smooth. Meanwhile, place a large sauté pan over medium heat and add olive oil.
3. Add the squash purée and the remaining ½ cup of milk. Simmer within 5 minutes. Add the cheese and stir to combine.
4. Add the pasta to the sauté pan and stir to combine. Serve immediately.

**Nutrition: Calories:** 373 kcal; **Fat:** 10 g; **Sodium:** 193 mg; **Carbohydrate:** 59 g; **Protein:** 14 g

## 423. Pasta with Tomatoes and Peas

**Preparation time:** 15 minutes
**Cooking time:** 15 minutes
**Servings:** 2
**Ingredients:**
- ½ cup whole-grain pasta of choice
- 8 cups water, plus ¼ for finishing
- 1 cup peas, frozen
- 1 tbsp. olive oil
- 1 cup cherry tomatoes, halved
- ¼ tsp. black pepper, freshly ground
- 1 tsp. basil, dried
- ¼ cup Parmesan cheese, grated (low-sodium)

**Directions:**
1. Cook the pasta al dente. Add the water to the same pot you used to cook the pasta, and when it's boiling, add the peas. Cook within 5 minutes. Drain and set aside.
2. Heat up the oil in a large skillet over medium heat. Add the cherry tomatoes, put a lid on the skillet and let the tomatoes soften for about 5 minutes, stirring a few times.
3. Season with black pepper and basil. Toss in the pasta, peas, and ¼ cup of water, stir and remove from the heat. Serve topped with Parmesan.

**Nutrition: Calories:** 266 kcal; **Fat:** 12 g; **Sodium:** 320 mg; **Carbohydrate:** 30 g; **Protein:** 13 g

## 424. Healthy Vegetable Fried Rice

**Preparation time:** 15 minutes
**Cooking time:** 10 minutes
**Servings:** 4
**Ingredients:**
**For the sauce:**
- ⅓ cup garlic vinegar
- 1½ tbsp. dark molasses
- 1 tsp. onion powder

**For the fried rice:**
- 1 tsp. olive oil
- 2 whole eggs, lightly beaten + 4 egg whites
- 1 cup mixed vegetables, frozen
- 1 cup Edamame, frozen
- 2 cups brown rice, cooked

**Directions:**
1. Prepare the sauce by combining the garlic vinegar, molasses, and onion powder in a glass jar. Shake well.
2. Heat up the oil in a large wok or skillet over medium-high heat. Add eggs and egg whites, let cook until the eggs set, for about 1 minute.
3. Break up eggs with a spatula or spoon into small pieces. Add frozen mixed vegetables and frozen edamame. Cook for 4 minutes, stirring frequently.

4. Add the brown rice and sauce to the vegetable-and-egg mixture. Cook for 5 minutes or until heated through. Serve immediately.

**Nutrition:** **Calories:** 210 kcal; **Fat:** 6 g; **Sodium:** 113 mg; **Carbohydrate:** 28 g; **Protein:** 13 g

### 425. Portobello-Mushroom Cheeseburgers

**Preparation time:** 15 minutes
**Cooking time:** 10 minutes
**Servings:** 4
**Ingredients:**
- 4 Portobello mushrooms, caps removed and brushed clean
- 1 tbsp. olive oil
- ½ tsp. black pepper, freshly ground
- 1 tbsp. red wine vinegar
- 4 slices reduced-fat Swiss cheese, sliced thin
- 4 whole-wheat 100-calorie sandwich thins
- ½ avocado, sliced thin

**Directions:**
1. Heat up a skillet or grill pan over medium-high heat. Clean the mushrooms and remove the stems. Brush each cap with olive oil and sprinkle with black pepper. Place in skillet cap-side up and cook for about 4 minutes. Flip and cook for another 4 minutes.
2. Sprinkle with the red wine vinegar and flip. Add the cheese and cook for 2 more minutes. For optimal melting, place a lid loosely over the pan. Meanwhile, toast the sandwich thins. Create your burgers by topping each with sliced avocado. Enjoy immediately.

**Nutrition:** **Calories:** 245 kcal; **Fat:** 12 g; **Sodium:** 266 mg; **Carbohydrate:** 28 g; **Protein:** 14 g

### 426. And-Rosemary Omelet

**Preparation time:** 15 minutes
**Cooking time:** 15 minutes
**Servings:** 2
**Ingredients:**
- ½ tbsp. olive oil
- 4 eggs
- ¼ cup Parmesan cheese, grated
- 1 (15-oz.) can chickpeas, drained and rinsed
- 2 cups baby spinach, packed
- 1 cup button mushrooms, chopped
- 2 sprigs rosemary, leaves picked (or 2 tsp. rosemary, dried)
- Salt
- Black pepper, freshly ground

**Directions:**
1. Warm oven to 400°F and puts a baking tray on the middle shelf. Line an 8-inch spring-form pan with baking paper and grease generously with olive oil. If you don't have a spring-form pan, grease an oven-safe skillet (or cast-iron skillet) with olive oil.
2. Lightly whisk the eggs and Parmesan. Place chickpeas in the prepared pan. Layer the spinach and mushrooms on top of the beans. Pour the egg mixture on top and scatter the rosemary. Season to taste with salt and pepper.
3. Place the pan on the preheated tray and bake until golden and puffy and the center feels firm and springy for about 15 minutes.
4. Remove from the oven, slice, and serve immediately.

**Nutrition: Calories:** 418 kcal; **Fat:** 19 g; **Sodium:** 595 mg; **Carbohydrate:** 33 g; **Protein:** 30 g

### 427. Chilled Cucumber-And-Avocado Soup with Dill

**Preparation time:** 15 minutes
**Cooking time:** 30 minutes
**Servings:** 4
**Ingredients:**
- 2 English cucumbers, peeled and diced, plus ¼ cup reserved for garnish
- 1 avocado, peeled, pitted, and chopped, plus ¼ cup reserved for garnish
- 1½ cups non-fat or low-fat plain Greek yogurt
- ½ cup cold water
- ⅓ cup dill, loosely packed, plus sprigs for garnish
- 1 tbsp. lemon juice, freshly squeezed
- ¼ tsp. black pepper, freshly ground
- ¼ tsp. salt
- 1 garlic clove

**Directions:**
1. Purée ingredients in a blender until smooth. If you prefer a thinner soup, add more water until you reach the desired consistency. Divide soup among 4 bowls.
2. Cover with plastic wrap and refrigerate within 30 minutes. Garnish with cucumber, avocado, and dill sprigs, if desired.

**Nutrition: Calories:** 142 kcal; **Fat:** 7 g; **Sodium:** 193 mg; **Carbohydrate:** 12 g; **Protein:** 11 g

## 428. Southwestern Bean-And-Pepper Salad

**Preparation time:** 6 minutes
**Cooking time:** 0 minutes
**Servings:** 4
**Ingredients:**
- 1 can pinto beans, drained
- 2 bell peppers, cored and chopped
- 1 cup corn kernels - Salt
- Black pepper, freshly ground
- 2 limes juice
- 1 tbsp. olive oil
- 1 avocado, chopped

**Directions:**
1. Mix beans, peppers, corn, salt, plus pepper in a large bowl. Press fresh lime juice, then mix in olive oil. Let the salad stand in the fridge within 30 minutes. Add avocado just before serving.

**Nutrition: Calories:** 245 kcal; **Fat:** 11 g; **Sodium:** 97 mg; **Carbohydrate:** 32 g; **Protein:** 8 g

## 429. Cauliflower Mashed Potatoes

**Preparation time:** 10 minutes
**Cooking time:** 10 minutes
**Servings:** 4
**Ingredients:**
- 16 cups water (enough to cover cauliflower)
- 1 head cauliflower (about 3 lb.), trimmed and cut into florets
- 4 garlic cloves
- 1 tbsp. olive oil
- ¼ tsp. salt
- ⅛ tsp. black pepper, freshly ground
- 2 tsp. parsley, dried

**Directions:**
1. Boil a large pot of water, then the cauliflower and garlic. Cook within 10 minutes, then strain. Move it back to the hot pan, and let it stand within 2 to 3 minutes with the lid on.
2. Put the cauliflower plus garlic in a food processor or blender. Add the olive oil, salt, pepper, and purée until smooth. Taste and adjust the salt and pepper.
3. Remove, then put the parsley, and mix until combined. Garnish with additional olive oil, if desired. Serve immediately.

**Nutrition: Calories:** 87 kcal; **Fat:** 4 g; **Sodium:** 210 mg; **Carbohydrate:** 12 g; **Protein:** 4 g

# CHAPTER 14:
# Side Dishes And Appetizer

## 430. Turmeric Endives

**Preparation time:** 10 minutes
**Cooking time:** 20 minutes
**Servings:** 4
**Ingredients:**
- 2 endives, halved lengthwise
- 2 tbsp. olive oil
- 1 tsp. rosemary, dried
- ½ tsp. turmeric powder
- A pinch black pepper

**Directions:**
1. Mix the endives with the oil and the other ingredients in a baking pan, toss gently, and bake at 400°F within 20 minutes.
2. Serve as a side dish.

**Nutrition:** **Calories:** 64 kcal; **Protein:** 0.2 g; **Carbohydrates:** 0.8 g; **Fat:** 7.1 g; **Fiber:** 0.6 g; **Sodium:** 3 mg; **Potassium:** 50 mg

## 431. Parmesan Endives

**Preparation time:** 10 minutes
**Cooking time:** 20 minutes
**Servings:** 4
**Ingredients:**
- 4 endives, halved lengthwise
- 1 tbsp. lemon juice
- 1 tbsp. lemon zest, grated
- 2 tbsp. fat-free parmesan, grated
- 2 tbsp. olive oil
- A pinch black pepper

**Directions**:
1. In a baking dish, combine the endives with the lemon juice and the other ingredients except for the parmesan and toss.
2. Sprinkle the parmesan on top, bake the endives at 400°F for 20 minutes, and serve.

**Nutrition**: **Calories**: 71 kcal; **Protein**: 0.9 g; **Carbohydrates**: 2.2 g; **Fat**: 7.1 g; **Fiber**: 0.9 g; **Sodium**: 71 mg; **Potassium**: 88 mg

### 432. Lemon Asparagus

**Preparation time**: 10 minutes
**Cooking time**: 20 minutes
**Servings**: 4
**Ingredients**:
- 1-lb. asparagus, trimmed
- 2 tbsp. basil pesto
- 1 tbsp. lemon juice
- A pinch black pepper
- 3 tbsp. olive oil
- 2 tbsp. cilantro, chopped

**Directions**:
1. Arrange the asparagus n a lined baking sheet, add the pesto and the other ingredients, toss, and bake at 400°F within 20 minutes. Serve as a side dish.

**Nutrition**: **Calories**: 114 kcal; **Protein**: 2.6 g; **Carbohydrates**: 4.5 g; **Fat**: 10.7 g; **Fiber**: 2.4 g; **Sodium**: 3 mg; **Potassium**: 240 mg

### 433. Lime Carrots

**Preparation time**: 10 minutes
**Cooking time**: 30 minutes
**Servings**: 4
**Ingredients**:
- 1-lb. baby carrots, trimmed
- 1 tbsp. sweet paprika
- 1 tsp. lime juice
- 3 tbsp. olive oil
- A pinch black pepper
- 1 tsp. sesame seeds

**Directions**:
1. Arrange the carrots on a lined baking sheet, add the paprika and the other ingredients except for the sesame seeds, toss, and bake at 400°F within 30 minutes. Divide the carrots between plates, sprinkle sesame seeds on top and serve as a side dish.

**Nutrition**: **Calories**: 139 kcal; **Protein**: 1.1 g; **Carbohydrates**: 10.5 g; **Fat**: 11.2 g; **Fiber**: 4 g; **Sodium**: 89 mg; **Potassium**: 313 mg

### 434. Garlic Potato Pan

**Preparation time**: 10 minutes
**Cooking time**: 1 hour
**Servings**: 8
**Ingredients**:
- 1-lb. gold potatoes, peeled and cut into wedges
- 2 tbsp. olive oil
- 1 red onion, chopped
- 2 garlic cloves, minced
- 2 cups coconut cream
- 1 tbsp. thyme, chopped
- ¼ tsp. nutmeg, ground
- ½ cup low-fat parmesan, grated

**Directions**:
1. Warm-up a pan with the oil over medium heat, put the onion plus the garlic, and sauté for 5 minutes. Add the potatoes and brown them for 5 minutes more.
2. Add the cream and the rest of the ingredients, toss gently, bring to a simmer and cook over medium heat within 40 minutes more. Divide the mix between plates and serve as a side dish.

**Nutrition**: **Calories**: 230 kcal; **Protein**: 3.6 g; **Carbohydrates**: 14.3 g; **Fat**: 19.1 g; **Fiber**: 3.3 g; **Cholesterol**: 6 mg; **Sodium**: 105 mg; **Potassium**: 426 mg

### 435. Balsamic Cabbage

**Preparation time:** 10 minutes
**Cooking time:** 20 minutes
**Servings:** 4
**Ingredients:**
- 1-lb. green cabbage, roughly shredded
- 2 tbsp. olive oil
- A pinch black pepper
- 1 shallot, chopped
- 2 garlic cloves, minced
- 2 tbsp. balsamic vinegar
- 2 tsp. hot paprika
- 1 tsp. sesame seeds

**Directions:**
1. Heat-up a pan with the oil over medium heat, add the shallot and the garlic, and sauté for 5 minutes. Add the cabbage and the other ingredients, toss, cook over medium heat for 15 minutes, divide between plates and serve.

**Nutrition:** **Calories:** 100 kcal; **Protein:** 1.8 g; **Carbohydrates:** 8.2 g; **Fat:** 7.5 g; **Fiber:** 3 g; **Sodium:** 22 mg; **Potassium:** 225 mg

### 436. Chili Broccoli

**Preparation time:** 10 minutes
**Cooking time:** 30 minutes
**Servings:** 4
**Ingredients:**
- 2 tbsp. olive oil - 1-lb. broccoli florets
- 2 garlic cloves, minced
- 2 tbsp. chili sauce
- 1 tbsp. lemon juice
- A pinch black pepper
- 2 tbsp. cilantro, chopped

**Directions:**
1. In a baking pan, combine the broccoli with the oil, garlic, and the other, toss a bit, and bake at 400°F for 30 minutes. Divide the mix between plates and serve as a side dish.

**Nutrition:** **Calories:** 103 kcal; **Protein:** 3.4 g; **Carbohydrates:** 8.3 g; **Fat:** 7.4 g; **Fiber:** 3 g; **Sodium:** 229 mg; **Potassium:** 383 mg

### 437. Hot Brussels sprouts

**Preparation time:** 10 minutes
**Cooking time:** 25 minutes
**Servings:** 4
**Ingredients:**
- 1 tbsp. olive oil
- 1-lb. Brussels sprouts, trimmed and halved
- 2 garlic cloves, minced
- ½ cup low-fat mozzarella, shredded
- A pinch pepper flakes, crushed

**Directions:**
1. In a baking dish, combine the sprouts with the oil and the other ingredients except for the cheese and toss.
2. Sprinkle the cheese on top, introduce in the oven and bake at 400°F for 25 minutes. Divide between plates and serve as a side dish.

**Nutrition:** **Calories:** 111 kcal; **Protein:** 10 g; **Carbohydrates:** 11.6 g; **Fat:** 3.9 g; **Fiber:** 5 g; **Cholesterol:** 4 mg; **Sodium:** 209 mg; **Potassium:** 447 mg

### 438. Paprika Brussels sprouts

**Preparation time:** 10 minutes
**Cooking time:** 25 minutes
**Servings:** 4
**Ingredients:**
- 2 tbsp. olive oil
- 1-lb. Brussels sprouts, trimmed and halved - 3 green onions, chopped
- 2 garlic cloves, minced
- 1 tbsp. balsamic vinegar
- 1 tbsp. sweet paprika
- A pinch black pepper

**Directions:**
1. In a baking pan, combine the Brussels sprouts with the oil and the other ingredients, toss and bake at 400°F within 25 minutes.
2. Divide the mix between plates and serve.

**Nutrition:** **Calories:** 121 kcal; **Protein:** 4.4 g; **Carbohydrates:** 12.6 g; **Fat:** 7.6 g; **Fiber:** 5.2 g; **Sodium:** 31 mg; **Potassium:** 521 mg

### 439. Creamy Cauliflower Mash

**Preparation time:** 10 minutes
**Cooking time:** 25 minutes
**Servings:** 4
**Ingredients:**
- 2 lb. cauliflower florets
- ½ cup coconut milk
- A pinch black pepper
- ½ cup low-fat sour cream
- 1 tbsp. cilantro, chopped
- 1 tbsp. chives, chopped

**Directions:**
1. Put the cauliflower in a pot, add water to cover, bring to a boil over medium heat, and cook for 25 minutes and drain.

2. Mash the cauliflower, add the milk, black pepper, and the cream, whisk well, divide between plates, sprinkle the rest of the ingredients on top, and serve.

**Nutrition:** **Calories:** 188 kcal; **Protein:** 6.1 g; **Carbohydrates:** 15 g; **Fat:** 13.4 g; **Fiber:** 6.4 g; **Cholesterol:** 13 mg; **Sodium:** 88 mg; **Potassium:** 811 mg

### 440. Avocado, Tomato, and Olives Salad

**Preparation time:** 5 minutes
**Cooking time:** 0 minutes
**Servings:** 4
**Ingredients:**
- 2 tbsp. olive oil
- 2 avocados, cut into wedges
- 1 cup Kalamata olives, pitted and halved
- 1 cup tomatoes, cubed
- 1 tbsp. ginger, grated
- A pinch black pepper
- 2 cups baby arugula
- 1 tbsp. balsamic vinegar

**Directions:**
1. In a bowl, combine the avocados with the Kalamata and the other ingredients, toss and serve as a side dish.

**Nutrition:** **Calories:** 320 kcal; **Protein:** 3 g; **Carbohydrates:** 13.9 g; **Fat:** 30.4 g; **Fiber:** 8.7 g; **Sodium:** 305 mg; **Potassium:** 655 mg

### 441. Radish and Olives Salad

**Preparation time:** 5 minutes
**Cooking time:** 0 minutes
**Servings:** 4
**Ingredients:**
- 2 green onions, sliced
- 1-lb. radishes, cubed
- 2 tbsp. balsamic vinegar
- 2 tbsp. olive oil
- 1 tsp. chili powder
- 1 cup black olives, pitted and halved
- A pinch black pepper

**Directions:**
1. Mix radishes with the onions and the other ingredients in a large salad bowl, toss, and serve as a side dish.

**Nutrition:** **Calories:** 123 kcal; **Protein:** 1.3 g; **Carbohydrates:** 6.9 g; **Fat:** 10.8 g; **Fiber:** 3.3 g; **Sodium:** 345 mg; **Potassium:** 306 mg

### 442. Spinach and Endives Salad

**Preparation time:** 5 minutes
**Cooking time:** 0 minutes
**Servings:** 4
**Ingredients:**
- 2 endives, roughly shredded
- 1 tbsp. dill, chopped
- ¼ cup lemon juice
- ¼ cup olive oil
- 2 cups baby spinach
- 2 tomatoes, cubed
- 1 cucumber, sliced
- ½ cups walnuts, chopped

**Directions:**
1. In a large bowl, combine the endives with the spinach and the other ingredients, toss and serve as a side dish.

**Nutrition:** **Calories:** 238 kcal; **Protein:** 5.7 g; **Carbohydrates:** 8.4 g; **Fat:** 22.3 g; **Fiber:** 3.1 g; **Sodium:** 24 mg; **Potassium:** 50 6mg

### 443. Basil Olives Mix

**Preparation time:** 5 minutes
**Cooking time:** 0 minutes
**Servings:** 4
**Ingredients:**
- 2 tbsp. olive oil
- 1 tbsp. balsamic vinegar
- A pinch of black pepper
- 4 cups corn
- 2 cups black olives, pitted and halved
- 1 red onion, chopped
- ½ cup cherry tomatoes halved
- 1 tbsp. basil, chopped
- 1 tbsp. jalapeno, chopped
- 2 cups romaine lettuce, shredded

**Directions:**
1. Mix the corn with the olives, lettuce, and the other ingredients in a large bowl, toss well, divide between plates and serve as a side dish.

**Nutrition:** **Calories:** 290 kcal; **Protein:** 6.2 g; **Carbohydrates:** 37.6 g; **Fat:** 16.1 g; **Fiber:** 7.4 g; **Sodium:** 613 mg; **Potassium:** 562 mg

### 444. Arugula Salad

**Preparation time:** 5 minutes
**Cooking time:** 0 minutes
**Servings:** 4
**Ingredients:**
- ¼ cup pomegranate seeds
- 5 cups baby arugula

- 6 tbsp. green onions, chopped
- 1 tbsp. balsamic vinegar
- 2 tbsp. olive oil
- 3 tbsp. pine nuts
- ½ shallot, chopped

**Directions**:
1. In a salad bowl, combine the arugula with the pomegranate and the other ingredients, toss and serve.

**Nutrition:** **Calories:** 120 kcal; **Protein:** 1.8 g; **Carbohydrates:** 4.2 g; **Fat:** 11.6 g; **Fiber:** 0.9 g; **Sodium:** 9 mg; **Potassium:** 163 mg

### 445. Spanish rice

**Preparation time:** 15 minutes
**Cooking time:** 1 hour and 35 minutes
**Servings:** 8
**Ingredients:**
- 2 cups brown rice
- .25 cup extra virgin olive oil
- 2 garlic cloves, minced
- 1 onion, diced
- 2 tomatoes, diced
- 1 jalapeno, seeded and diced
- 1 tbsp. tomato paste
- .5 cup cilantro, chopped
- 2.5 cups chicken broth, low-sodium

**Directions**:
1. Warm the oven to 375°F. Puree the tomatoes, onion, plus garlic using a blender or food processor. Measure out 2 cups of this vegetable puree to use and discard the excess.
2. Into a large oven-safe Dutch pan, heat the extra virgin olive oil over medium heat until hot and shimmering. Add in the jalapeno and rice to toast, cooking while occasionally stirring for 2 to 3 minutes.
3. Slowly stir the chicken broth into the rice, followed by the vegetable puree and tomato paste. Stir until combine and increase the heat to medium-high until the broth reaches a boil.
4. Cover the Dutch pan with an oven-safe lid, transfer the pot to the preheated oven, and bake within 1 hour and 15 minutes. Remove and stir the cilantro into the rice. Serve.

**Nutrition:** **Calories:** 265 kcal; **Sodium:** 32 mg; **Potassium:** 322 mg; **Carbs:** 40 g; **Fat:** 3 g; **Protein:** 5 g

### 446. Sweet Potatoes and Apples

**Preparation time:** 15 minutes
**Cooking time:** 40 minutes
**Servings:** 4
**Ingredients:**
- 2 sweet potatoes, sliced into 1" cubes
- 2 apples, cut into 1" cubes
- 3 tbsp. extra virgin olive oil, divided
- .25 tsp. black pepper, ground
- 1 tsp. cinnamon, ground
- 2 tbsp. maple syrup

**Directions**:
1. Warm the oven to 425°F and grease a large baking sheet with non-stick cooking spray. Toss the cubed sweet potatoes with 2 tbsp. of the olive oil and black pepper until coated. Roast the potatoes within 20 minutes, stirring them once halfway through the process.
2. Meanwhile, toss the apples with the remaining tbsp. of olive oil, cinnamon, and maple syrup until evenly coated. After the sweet potatoes have cooked for 20 minutes, add the apples to the baking sheet and toss the sweet potatoes and apples.
3. Return to the oven, then roast it for 20 more minutes, once again giving it a good stir halfway through. Once the potatoes and apples are caramelized from the maple syrup, remove them from the oven and serve hot.

**Nutrition: Calories:** 100 kcal; **Carbs:** 22 g; **Fat:** 0 g; **Protein:** 2 g; **Sodium:** 38 mg; **Potassium:** 341 mg

### 447. Roasted Turnips

**Preparation time:** 15 minutes
**Cooking time:** 30 minutes
**Servings:** 4
**Ingredients:**
- 2 cups turnips, peels, and cut into ½" cubes
- .25 tsp. black pepper, ground
- .5 tsp. garlic powder
- .5 tsp. onion powder
- 1 tbsp. extra virgin olive oil

**Directions**:
1. Warm the oven to 400°F and prepare a large baking sheet, setting it aside. Begin by trimming the top and bottom edges off of the turnips and peeling them if you wish. Slice them into ½-inch cubes.
2. Toss the turnips with the extra virgin olive oil and seasonings, and then spread them out on the prepared baking sheet.

3. Roast the turnips until tender, stirring them halfway through, about 30 minutes in total.

**Nutrition: Calories:** 50 kcal; **Carbs:** 5 g; **Fat:** 4 g; **Protein:** 1 g; **Sodium:** 44 mg; **Potassium:** 134 mg

### 448. No-Mayo Potato Salad

**Preparation time:** 15 minutes
**Cooking time:** 20 minutes
**Servings:** 8
**Ingredients:**

- 3 lb. red potatoes
- .5 cup extra virgin olive oil
- 5 tbsp. white wine vinegar, divided
- 2 tsp. Dijon mustard
- 1 cup red onion, sliced
- .5 tsp. black pepper, ground
- 2 tbsp. basil, fresh, chopped
- 2 tbsp. dill weed, fresh, chopped
- 2 tbsp. parsley, fresh, chopped

**Directions:**

1. Add the red potatoes to a large pot and cover them with water until the water level is 2 inches above the potatoes. Put the pot on high heat, then boil potatoes until they are tender when poked with a fork, about 15 to 20 minutes. Drain off the water.
2. Let the potatoes to cool until they can easily be handled but are still warm, then cut it in half and put them in a large bowl. Stir in 3 tbsp. of the white wine vinegar, giving the potatoes a good stir so that they can evenly absorb the vinegar.
3. Mix the rest of 2 tbsp. of vinegar, extra virgin olive oil, Dijon mustard, and black pepper in a small bowl. Add this mixture to the potatoes and give them a good toss to thoroughly coat the potatoes.
4. Toss in the red onion and minced herbs. Serve at room temperature or chilled. Serve immediately or store in the fridge for up to 4 days.

**Nutrition: Calories:** 144 kcal; **Carbs:** 19 g; **Fat:** 7 g; **Protein:** 2 g; **Sodium:** 46 mg; **Potassium:** 814 mg

### 449. Zucchini Tomato Bake

**Preparation time:** 15 minutes
**Cooking time:** 30 minutes
**Servings:** 4
**Ingredients:**

- 10 oz. grape tomatoes, cut in half
- 2 zucchini - 5 garlic cloves, minced
- 1 tsp. Italian herb seasoning
- .25 tsp. black pepper, ground
- .33 cup parsley, fresh, chopped
- .5 cup parmesan cheese, low-sodium, grated

**Directions:**

1. Warm the oven to 350°F and coat a large baking sheet with non-stick cooking spray. Mix the tomatoes, zucchini, garlic, Italian herb seasoning, Black pepper, and Parmesan cheese in a bowl.
2. Put the mixture out on the baking sheet and roast until the zucchini for 30 minutes. Remove, and garnish with parsley over the top before serving.

**Nutrition: Calories:** 35 kcal; **Carbs:** 4 g; **Fat:** 2 g; **Protein:** 2 g; **Sodium:** 30 mg; **Potassium:** 649 mg

### 450. Creamy Broccoli Cheddar Rice

**Preparation time:** 15 minutes
**Cooking time:** 40 minutes
**Servings:** 6
**Ingredients:**

- 1 cup brown rice
- 2 cups chicken broth, low-sodium
- 1 onion, minced
- 3 tbsp. extra virgin olive oil, divided
- 2 garlic cloves, minced - .5 cup skim milk
- .25 tsp. black pepper, ground
- 1.5 cups broccoli, chopped
- 1 cup cheddar cheese, low-sodium, shredded

**Directions:**

1. Put 1 tbsp. of the extra virgin olive oil in a large pot and sauté the onion plus garlic over medium heat within 2 minutes.
2. Put the chicken broth in a pot and wait for it to come to a boil before adding in the rice. Simmer the rice over low heat for 25 minutes.
3. Stir the skim milk, black pepper, and remaining 2 tbsp. of olive oil into the rice. Simmer again within 5 more minutes. Stir in the broccoli and cook the rice for 5 more minutes, until the broccoli is tender. Stir in the rice and serve while warm.

**Nutrition: Calories:** 200 kcal; **Carbs:** 33 g; **Fat:** 3 g; **Protein:** 10 g; **Sodium:** 50 mg; **Potassium:** 344 mg

### 451. Smashed Brussels sprouts

**Preparation time:** 15 minutes
**Cooking time:** 40 minutes
**Servings:** 6
**Ingredients:**

- 2 lb. Brussels sprouts

- 3 garlic cloves, minced
- 3 tbsp. balsamic vinegar
- .5 cup extra virgin olive oil
- .5 tsp. black pepper, ground
- 1 leek washed and thinly sliced
- .5 cup parmesan cheese, low-sodium, grated

**Directions:**
1. Warm the oven to 450°F and prepare 2 large baking sheets. Trim the yellow leaves and stems off of the Brussels sprouts and then steam them until tender, about 20 to 25 minutes.
2. Mix the garlic, black pepper, balsamic vinegar, and extra virgin olive oil in a large bowl. Add the steamed Brussels sprouts and leeks to the bowl and toss until evenly coated.
3. Spread the Brussels sprouts and leaks divided onto the prepared baking sheets.
4. Use a fork or a glass and press down on each of the Brussels sprouts to create flat patties. Put the Parmesan cheese on top and place the smashed sprouts in the oven for 15 minutes until crispy. Enjoy hot and fresh from the oven.

**Nutrition: Calories:** 116 kcal; **Carbs:** 11 g; **Fat:** 5 g; **Protein:** 10 g; **Sodium:** 49 mg; **Potassium:** 642 mg

## 452. Cilantro Lime Rice

**Preparation time:** 15 minutes
**Cooking time:** 40 minutes
**Servings:** 6
**Ingredients:**
- 1.5 cups brown rice
- 2 tbsp. lime juice
- 1.5 tsp. lemon juice
- .5 tsp. lime zest
- .25 cup cilantro, chopped
- 1 bay leaf
- 1 tbsp. extra virgin olive oil
- Water

**Directions:**
1. Cook rice and bay leaf in a pot with boiling water. Mix the mixture and allow it to boil for 30 minutes, reducing the heat slightly if need be.
2. Once the rice is tender, drain off the water, and return the rice to the pot. Let it sit off of the heat within 10 minutes. Remove the bay leaf and use a fork to fluff the rice. Stir the rest of the fixing into the rice and then serve immediately.

**Nutrition: Calories:** 94 kcal; **Carbs:** 15 g; **Fat:** 3 g; **Protein:** 2 g; **Sodium:** 184 mg; **Potassium:** 245 mg

# CHAPTER 15:
# Dessert

## 453. Cheesecake Made Easy!

**Preparation time:** 10 minutes
**Cooking time:** 50 minutes
**Servings:** 8–10
**Ingredients:**
- 10 oz. whole-wheat crackers, crushed
- 16 oz. Fat-free cream cheeses
- 2 tsp. vanilla extract
- 5 tbsp. Fat-free butter
- 1 cup coconut sugar
- 2 large eggs
- ¼ cup coconut cream
- 8 oz. sugar-free chocolate, melted
- 2 cups water
- Cooking spray
- 2 tbsp. whole wheat flour

**Directions**:
1. In one bowl, mix crackers with butter and stir, then grease a cooking tin and push crackers into the bottom.
2. Mix the rest of the ingredients into another bowl, and then put it over the crust, then cover the pan with foil.
3. Put it in the instant pot and cook on manual high for 45 minutes.
4. Chill cheesecake in the fridge before you serve it.

**Nutrition: Calories:** 265 kcal; **Fat:** 9 g; **Carbs:** 15 g; **Net Carbs:** 12 g; **Protein:** 4 g; **Fiber:** 3 g

## 454. Grapefruit Compote

**Preparation time:** 5 minutes
**Cooking time:** 8 minutes
**Servings:** 4
**Ingredients:**
- 1 cup palm sugar

- 64 oz. Sugar-free red grapefruit juice
- ½ cup mint, chopped
- 2 grapefruits, peeled and cubed

**Directions:**
1. Take all ingredients and combine them into an instant pot.
2. Cook on low for 8 minutes, then divide into bowls and serve!

**Nutrition: Calories:** 131 kcal; **Fat:** 1 g; **Carbs:** 12 g; **Net Carbs:** 11 g; **Protein:** 2 g; **Fiber:** 2 g

## 455. Instant Pot Applesauce

**Preparation time:** 10 minutes
**Cooking time:** 10 minutes
**Servings:** 8
**Ingredients:**
- 3 lb. apples
- ½ cup water

**Directions:**
1. Core and peel the apples and then put them at the bottom of the instant pot and then secure the lid and seal the vent. Let it cook for 10 minutes, then natural pressure release.
2. From there, when it's safe to remove the lid, take the apples and juices and blend this till smooth.
3. Stores these in jars or serve immediately.

**Nutrition: Calories:** 88 kcal; **Fat:** 0 g; **Carbs:** 23 g; **Net Carbs:** 19 g; **Protein:** 0 g; **Fiber:** 4 g

## 456. Plum Cake

**Preparation time:** 1 hour and 20 minutes
**Cooking time:** 40 minutes
**Servings:** 8
**Ingredients:**
- 7 oz. whole-wheat flour
- 1 tsp. baking powder
- 1-oz. low-fat butter, soft
- 1 egg, whisked
- 5 tbsp. coconut sugar
- 3 oz. warm almond milk
- 1 and ¾ lb. plums, pitted and cut into quarters
- Zest of 1 lemon, grated  - 1-oz. almond flakes

**Directions:**
1. In a bowl, combine the flour with baking powder, butter, egg, sugar, milk, and lemon zest, stir well, transfer the dough to a lined cake pan, spread plums and almond flakes all over, introduce in the oven and bake at 350°F for 40 minutes. Slice and serve cold. Enjoy!

**Nutrition: Calories:** 222 kcal; **Fat:** 4 g; **Fiber:** 2 g; **Carbs:** 7 g; **Protein:** 7 g

## 457. Dates Brownies

**Preparation time:** 10 minutes
**Cooking time:** 15 minutes
**Servings:** 8
**Ingredients:**
- 28 oz. lentils, canned, no-salt-added, rinsed, and drained
- 12 dates
- 1 tbsp. coconut sugar
- 1 banana, peeled and chopped
- ½ tsp. baking soda
- 4 tbsp. almond butter
- 2 tbsp. cocoa powder

**Directions:**
1. Put lentils in your food processor, pulse, add dates, sugar, banana, baking soda, almond butter, and cocoa powder, pulse well, pour into a lined pan, spread, bake in the oven at 375°F for 15 minutes, leave the mix aside to cool down a bit, cut into medium pieces and serve.
2. Enjoy!

**Nutrition: Calories:** 202 kcal; **Fat:** 4 g; **Fiber:** 2 g; **Carbs:** 12 g; **Protein:** 6 g

## 458. Rose Lentils Ice Cream

**Preparation time:** 30 minutes
**Cooking time:** 1 hour and 20 minutes
**Servings:** 4
**Ingredients:**
- ½ cup red lentils, rinsed
- Juice of ½ lemon
- 1 cup coconut sugar
- 1 and ½ cups water
- 3 cups almond milk
- Juice of 2 limes
- 2 tsp. cardamom powder
- 1 tsp. rose water

**Directions:**
1. Heat up a pan over medium-high heat with the water, half of the sugar, and lemon juice, stir, bring to a boil, add lentils, stir, reduce heat to medium-low and cook for 1 hour and 20 minutes.
2. Drain lentils, transfer them to a bowl, add coconut milk, the rest of the sugar, lime juice, cardamom, and rose water, whisk everything, transfer to your ice cream machine, process for 30 minutes and serve. Enjoy!

**Nutrition: Calories:** 184 kcal; **Fat:** 4 g; **Fiber:** 3 g; **Carbs:** 8 g; **Protein:** 5 g

---

### 459. Mandarin Almond Pudding

**Preparation time:** 10 minutes
**Cooking time:** 30 minutes
**Servings:** 8
**Ingredients:**
- 1 mandarin, peeled and sliced
- Juice of 2 mandarins
- 4 oz. low-fat butter, soft
- 2 eggs, whisked
- ¾ cup coconut sugar + 2 tbsp. sugar
- ¾ cup whole wheat flour
- ¾ cup almonds, ground

**Directions:**
1. Grease a loaf pan with some of the butter, sprinkle 2 tbsp. sugar on the bottom, and arrange mandarin slices inside. In a bowl, combine the butter with the rest of the sugar, eggs, almonds, flour, and mandarin juice and whisk using a mixer. Spoon mix over mandarin slices, introduce in the oven, bake at 350°F for 30 minutes, divide into bowls and serve
2. Enjoy!

**Nutrition: Calories:** 202 kcal; **Fat:** 3 g; **Fiber:** 2 g; **Carbs:** 12 g; **Protein:** 6 g

---

### 460. Cherry Stew

**Preparation time:** 10 minutes
**Cooking time:** 10 minutes
**Servings:** 6
**Ingredients:**
- ½ cup cocoa powder
- 1 lb. cherries, pitted
- ¼ cup coconut sugar - 2 cups water

**Directions:**
1. In a pan, combine the cherries with the water, sugar, and cocoa powder, stir, cook over medium heat for 10 minutes, divide into bowls and serve cold.
2. Enjoy!

**Nutrition: Calories:** 207 kcal; **Fat:** 1 g; **Fiber:** 3 g; **Carbs:** 8 g; **Protein:** 6 g

---

### 461. Rice Pudding

**Preparation time:** 10 minutes
**Cooking time:** 45 minutes
**Servings:** 6
**Ingredients:**
- ½ cup basmati rice
- 4 cups almond milk
- ¼ cup raisins
- 3 tbsp. coconut sugar
- ½ tsp. cardamom powder
- ¼ tsp. cinnamon powder
- ¼ cup walnuts, chopped
- 1 tbsp. lemon zest, grated

**Directions:**
1. In a pan, mix sugar with milk, stir, bring to a boil over medium-high heat, add rice, raisins, cardamom, cinnamon, walnuts, and lemon zest, stir, cover the pan, reduce heat to low, cook for 40 minutes, divide into bowls and serve cold.
2. Enjoy!

**Nutrition: Calories:** 200 kcal; **Fat:** 4 g; **Fiber:** 5 g; **Carbs:** 8 g; **Protein:** 3 g

---

### 462. Apple Loaf

**Preparation time:** 10 minutes
**Cooking time:** 35 minutes
**Servings:** 6
**Ingredients:**
- 3 cups apples, cored and cubed
- 1 cup coconut sugar
- 1 tbsp. vanilla
- 2 eggs
- 1 tbsp. apple pie spice
- 2 cups almond flour
- 1 tbsp. baking powder
- 1 tbsp. coconut oil, melted

**Directions:**
1. In a bowl, mix apples with coconut sugar, vanilla, eggs, apple pie spice, almond flour, baking powder, and oil, whisk, pour into a loaf pan, introduce in the oven and bake at 350°F for 35 minutes. Serve cold.
2. Enjoy!

**Nutrition: Calories:** 180 kcal; **Fat:** 6 g; **Fiber:** 5 g; **Carbs:** 12 g; **Protein:** 4 g

## 463. Cauliflower Cinnamon Pudding

**Preparation time:** 10 minutes
**Cooking time:** 20 minutes
**Servings:** 6
**Ingredients:**
- 1 tbsp. coconut oil, melted
- 7 oz. cauliflower rice
- 4 oz. water .- 16 oz. coconut milk
- 3 oz. coconut sugar - 1 egg
- 1 tsp. cinnamon powder
- 1 tsp. vanilla extract

**Directions:**
1. In a pan, combine the oil with the rice, water, milk, sugar, egg, cinnamon, and vanilla, whisk well, bring to a simmer, cook for 20 minutes over medium heat, divide into bowls and serve cold.
2. Enjoy!

**Nutrition: Calories:** 202 kcal; **Fat:** 2 g; **Fiber:** 6 g; **Carbs:** 8 g; **Protein:** 7 g

## 464. Rhubarb Stew

**Preparation time:** 10 minutes
**Cooking time:** 5 minutes
**Servings:** 3
**Ingredients:**
- 1 lemon juice - 1 tsp. lemon zest, grated
- 1 and ½ cup coconut sugar
- 4 and ½ cups rhubarbs, roughly chopped
- 1 and ½ cups water

**Directions:**
1. In a pan, combine the rhubarb with the water, lemon juice, lemon zest, and coconut sugar, toss, bring to a simmer over medium heat, cook for 5 minutes, and divide into bowls and serve cold.
2. Enjoy!

**Nutrition: Calories:** 108 kcal; **Fat:** 1 g; **Fiber:** 4 g; **Carbs:** 8 g; **Protein:** 5 g

## 465. Pumpkin Pudding

**Preparation time:** 1 hour
**Cooking time:** 0 minutes
**Servings:** 4
**Ingredients:**
- 1 and ½ cups almond milk
- ½ cup pumpkin puree
- 2 tbsp. coconut sugar
- ½ tsp. cinnamon powder
- ¼ tsp. ginger, grated
- ¼ cup chia seeds

**Directions:**
1. In a bowl, combine the milk with pumpkin, sugar, cinnamon, ginger, and chia seeds, toss well, divide into small cups and keep them in the fridge for 1 hour before serving.
2. Enjoy!

**Nutrition: Calories:** 145 kcal; **Fat:** 7 g; **Fiber:** 7 g; **Carbs:** 11 g; **Protein:** 9 g

## 466. Cashew Lemon Fudge

**Preparation time:** 2 hours
**Cooking time:** 0 minutes
**Servings:** 4
**Ingredients:**
- ⅓ cup natural cashew butter
- 1 and ½ tbsp. coconut oil, melted
- 2 tbsp. coconut butter
- 5 tbsp. lemon juice
- ½ tsp. lemon zest
- 1 tbsp. coconut sugar

**Directions:**
1. In a bowl, mix cashew butter with coconut butter, oil, lemon juice, lemon zest, and sugar and stir well
2. Line a muffin tray with some parchment paper, scoop 1 tbsp. of lemon fudge, mix in a lined muffin tray, keep in the fridge for 2 hours and serve
3. Enjoy!

**Nutrition: Calories:** 142 kcal; **Fat:** 4 g; **Fiber:** 4 g; **Carbs:** 8 g; **Protein:** 5

## 467. Brown Cake

**Preparation time:** 10 minutes
**Cooking time:** 2 hours and 30 minutes
**Servings:** 8
**Ingredients:**
- 1 cup flour
- 1 and ½ cup stevia
- ½ cup chocolate almond milk
- 2 tsp. baking powder
- 1 and ½ cups hot water
- ¼ cup cocoa powder + 2 tbsp.
- 2 tbsp. canola oil
- 1 tsp. vanilla extract

- Cooking spray

**Directions**:
1. In a bowl, mix flour with ¼-cup cocoa, baking powder, almond milk, oil, and vanilla extract, whisk well, and spread on the bottom of the slow cooker greased with cooking spray.
2. In a separate bowl, mix stevia with the water and the rest of the cocoa, whisk well, spread over the batter, cover, and cook your cake on High for 2 hours and 30 minutes.
3. Leave the cake to cool down, slice, and serve.

**Nutrition: Calories:** 150 kcal; **Fat:** 7.6 g; **Cholesterol:** 1 mg; **Sodium:** 7 mg; **Carbohydrate:** 56.8 g; **Fiber:** 1.8 g; **Sugars:** 4.4 g; **Protein:** 2.9 g; **Potassium:** 185 mg

### 468. Delicious Berry Pie

**Preparation time:** 10 minutes
**Cooking time:** 1 hour
**Servings:** 6
**Ingredients:**
- ½ cup whole wheat flour
- Cooking spray
- ⅓ cup almond milk
- ¼ tsp. baking powder
- ¼ tsp. stevia - ¼ cup blueberries
- 1 tsp. olive oil
- 1 tsp. vanilla extract
- ½ tsp. lemon zest, grated

**Directions**:
1. In a bowl, mix flour with baking powder, stevia, blueberries, milk, oil, lemon zest, and vanilla extract, whisk, pour into your slow cooker lined with parchment paper and greased with the cooking spray, cover, and cook on High for 1 hour.
2. Leave the pie to cool down, slice, and serve.

**Nutrition: Calories:** 82 kcal; **Fat:** 4.2 g; **Cholesterol:** 0 mg; **Sodium:** 3 mg; **Carbohydrate:** 10.1 g; **Fiber:** 0.7 g; **Sugars:** 1.2 g; **Protein:** 1.4 g; **Potassium:** 74 mg

### 469. Cinnamon Peach Cobbler

**Preparation time:** 10 minutes
**Cooking time:** 4 hours
**Servings:** 4
**Ingredients:**
- 4 cups peaches, peeled and sliced
- Cooking spray
- ¼ cup coconut sugar
- 1 and ½ cups whole wheat sweet crackers, crushed
- ½ cup almond milk
- ½ tsp. cinnamon powder
- ¼ cup stevia - 1 tsp. vanilla extract
- ¼ tsp. nutmeg, ground

**Directions**:
1. In a bowl, mix peaches with sugar, cinnamon, and stir. In a separate bowl, mix crackers with stevia, nutmeg, almond milk, and vanilla extract and stir. Spray your slow cooker with cooking spray, spread peaches on the bottom, and add the crackers mix, spread, cover, and cook on Low for 4 hours. Divide into bowls and serve.

**Nutrition:**
**Calories:** 249 kcal; **Fat:** 11.4 g; **Cholesterol:** 0 mg; **Sodium:** 179 mg; **Carbohydrate:** 42.7 g; **Fiber:** 3 g; **Sugars:** 15.2 g; **Protein:** 3.5 g; **Potassium:** 366 mg

### 470. Resilient Chocolate Cream

**Preparation time:** 10 minutes
**Cooking time:** 1 hour and 30 minutes
**Servings:** 4
**Ingredients:**
- 1 cup dark and chocolate, unsweetened, chopped
- ½ lb. cherries, pitted and halved
- 1 tsp. vanilla extract
- ½ cup coconut cream
- 3 tbsp. coconut sugar
- 2 tsp. gelatin

**Directions**:
1. In the slow cooker, combine the chocolate with the cherries and the other ingredients, toss, put the lid on and cook on Low for 1 hour and 30 minutes.
2. Stir the cream well, divide into bowls and serve.

**Nutrition: Calories:** 526 kcal; **Fat:** 39.9 g; **Cholesterol:** 0 mg; **Sodium:** 57 mg; **Carbohydrate:** 47.2 g; **Fiber:** 10.8 g; **Sugars:** 1.1 g; **Protein:** 13.4 g; **Potassium:** 141 mg

### 471. Vanilla Poached Strawberries

**Preparation time:** 10 minutes
**Cooking time:** 3 hours
**Servings:** 10
**Ingredients:**
- 4 cups coconut sugar
- 2 tbsp. lemon juice - 2 lb. strawberries
- 1 cup water - 1 tsp. vanilla extract
- 1 tsp. cinnamon powder

**Directions**:
1. In your slow cooker, mix strawberries with water, coconut sugar, lemon juice, cinnamon, and vanilla, stir, cover, cook on Low for 3 hours, divide into bowls and serve cold.

**Nutrition: Calories:** 69 kcal; **Fat:** 0.3 g; **Cholesterol:** 0 mg; **Sodium:** 18 mg; **Carbohydrate:** 14.7 g; **Fiber:** 1.8 g; **Sugars:** 4.6 g; **Protein:** 1 g; **Potassium:** 143 mg

### 472. Lemon Bananas

**Preparation time:** 10 minutes
**Cooking time:** 2 hours
**Servings:** 4
**Ingredients:**
- 4 bananas, peeled and sliced
- Juice of ½ lemon
- 1 tbsp. coconut oil
- 3 tbsp. stevia
- ½ tsp. cardamom seeds

**Directions**:
1. Arrange bananas in your slow cooker, add stevia, lemon juice, oil, and cardamom, cover, cook on Low for 2 hours, divide everything into bowls and serve with.

**Nutrition: Calories:** 137 kcal; **Fat:** 3.9 g; **Cholesterol:** 0 mg; **Sodium:** 2 mg; **Carbohydrate:** 33.5 g; **Fiber:** 3.2 g; **Sugars** 14.6 g; **Protein:** 1.4 g; **Potassium:** 433 mg

### 473. Pecans Cake

**Preparation time:** 10 minutes
**Cooking time:** 5 hours
**Servings:** 4
**Ingredients:**
- Cooking spray
- 1 cup almond flour
- 1 cup orange juice
- 1 cup coconut sugar
- 3 tbsp. coconut oil, melted
- 1 tsp. baking powder
- ½ tsp. cinnamon powder
- ½ cup almond milk
- ½ cup pecans, chopped
- ¾ cup water
- ½ cup orange peel, grated

**Directions**:
1. In a bowl, mix flour with half of the sugar, baking powder, cinnamon, 2 tbsp. oil, milk, and pecans; stir and pour this in your slow cooker greased with cooking spray.
2. Heat up a small pan over medium heat, add water, orange juice, orange peel, the rest of the oil, and the rest of the sugar, stir, bring to a boil, pour over the mix in the slow cooker, cover, and cook on Low for 5 hours.
3. Divide into bowls and serve cold.

**Nutrition: Calories:** 565 kcal; **Fat:** 48.8 g; **Cholesterol:** 0 mg; **Sodium:** 28 mg; **Carbohydrate:** 26 g; **Fiber:** 7.8 g; **Sugars:** 7.1 g; **Protein:** 10.2 g; **Potassium:** 459 mg

### 474. Coconut Cream and Plums Cake

**Preparation time:** 10 minutes
**Cooking time:** 3 hours
**Servings:** 6
**Ingredients:**
- 2 cups whole-wheat flour
- 1 tsp. vanilla extract
- 1 and ½ cups plums, peeled and chopped
- ½ cup coconut cream
- 1 tsp. baking powder
- ¾ cup coconut sugar
- 4 tbsp. avocado oil

**Directions**:
1. In the slow cooker lined with parchment paper, combine the flour with the plums and the other ingredients and whisk.
2. Put the lid on, cook on High for 3 hours, and leave the cake to cool down, slice, and serve.

**Nutrition: Calories:** 232 kcal; **Fat:** 6.4 g; **Cholesterol:** 0 mg; **Sodium:** 10 mg; **Carbohydrate:** 38.3 g; **Fiber:** 2.2 g; **Sugars:** 2.7 g; **Protein:** 5.1 g; **Potassium:** 238 mg

### 475. Maple Syrup Poached Pears

**Preparation time:** 10 minutes
**Cooking time:** 4 hours
**Servings:** 4
**Ingredients:**
- 2 cups grapefruit juice
- 4 pears, peeled and cored
- ¼ cup maple syrup
- 1 tbsp. ginger, grated
- 2 tsp. cinnamon powder

**Directions**:
1. In your slow cooker, mix pears with grapefruit juice, maple syrup, cinnamon, and ginger, cover, cook on Low for 4 hours, divide everything into bowls and serve.

**Nutrition: Calories:** 214 kcal; **Fat:** 0.5 g; **Cholesterol:** 0 mg; **Sodium:** 5 mg; **Carbohydrate:** 55.3 g; **Fiber:** 7.9 g; **Sugars:** 40.2 g; **Protein:** 1.6 g; **Potassium:** 461 mg

## 476. Ginger and Pumpkin Pie

**Preparation time:** 10 minutes
**Cooking time:** 2 hours
**Servings:** 10
**Ingredients:**
- 2 cups almond flour
- 1 egg, whisked
- 1 cup pumpkin puree
- 1 and ½ tsp. baking powder
- Cooking spray
- 1 tbsp. coconut oil, melted
- 1 tbsp. vanilla extract
- ½ tsp. baking soda
- 1 and ½ tsp. cinnamon powder
- ¼ tsp. ginger, ground
- ⅓ cup maple syrup - 1 tsp. lemon juice

**Directions:**
1. In a bowl, flour with baking powder, baking soda, cinnamon, ginger, egg, oil, vanilla, pumpkin puree, maple syrup, and lemon juice, stir and pour in your slow cooker greased with cooking spray and lined with parchment paper; cover the pot and cook on Low for 2 hours and 20 minutes.
2. Leave the pie to cool down, slice, and serve.

**Nutrition: Calories:** 91 kcal; **Fat:** 4.8 g; **Cholesterol:** 16 mg; **Sodium:** 74 mg; **Carbohydrate:** 10.8 g; **Fiber:** 1.3 g; **Sugars** 7.5 g; **Protein:** 2 g; **Potassium** 157 mg

## 477. Cashew and Carrot Muffins

**Preparation time:** 10 minutes
**Cooking time:** 3 hours
**Servings:** 4
**Ingredients:**
- 4 tbsp. cashew butter, melted
- 4 eggs, whisked
- ½ cup coconut cream
- 1 cup carrots, peeled and grated
- 4 tsp. maple syrup
- ¾ cup coconut flour
- ½ tsp. baking soda

**Directions:**
1. In a bowl, mix the cashew butter with the eggs, cream, and the other ingredients, whisk well and pour into a muffin pan that fits the slow cooker.
2. Put the lid on, cook the muffins on High for 3 hours, cool down, and serve.

**Nutrition: Calories:** 345 kcal; **Fat:** 21.7 g; **Cholesterol:** 164mg, **Sodium:** 247mg, **Carbohydrate:** 28.6 g; **Fiber:** 10.7 g; **Sugars** 6.7 g; **Protein:** 12.3 g; **Potassium:** 327 mg

## 478. Lemon Custard

**Preparation time:** 10 minutes
**Cooking time:** 3 hours
**Servings:** 10
**Ingredients:**
- 2 lb. lemons, washed, peeled, and sliced
- 2 lb. coconut sugar
- 1 tbsp. vinegar

**Directions:**
1. In your slow cooker, mix lemons with coconut sugar and vinegar, stir, cover, cook on High for 3 hours, blend using an immersion blender, divide into small bowls and serve.

**Nutrition: Calories:** 46 kcal; **Fat:** 0.3 g; **Cholesterol:** 0 mg; **Sodium:** 10 mg; **Carbohydrate:** 12.3 g; **Fiber:** 2.5 g; **Sugars** 2.3 g; **Protein:** 1.2 g; **Potassium:** 126 mg

## 479. Rhubarb Dip

**Preparation time:** 10 minutes
**Cooking time:** 3 hours
**Servings:** 8
**Ingredients:**
- 1 cup coconut sugar
- ⅓ cup water
- 4 lb. rhubarb, chopped
- 1 tbsp. mint, chopped

**Directions:**
1. In your slow cooker, mix water with rhubarb, sugar, and mint, stir, cover, cook on High for 3 hours, blend using an immersion blender, divide into cups and serve cold.

**Nutrition: Calories:** 60 kcal; **Fat:** 0.5 g; **Cholesterol:** 0 mg; **Sodium:** 15 mg; **Carbohydrate:** 12.7 g; **Fiber:** 4.1 g; **Sugars:** 2.5 g; **Protein:** 2.2 g; **Potassium:** 657 mg

## 480. Summer Jam

**Preparation time:** 10 minutes
**Cooking time:** 3 hours
**Servings:** 6
**Ingredients:**
- 2 cups coconut sugar
- 4 cups cherries, pitted
- 2 tbsp. lemon juice
- 3 tbsp. gelatin

**Directions:**
1. In your slow cooker, mix lemon juice with gelatin, cherries, and coconut sugar stir, cover, cook on High for 3 hours, divide into bowls and serve cold.

**Nutrition: Calories:** 171 kcal; **Fat:** 0.1 g; **Cholesterol:** 0 mg; **Sodium:** 41 mg; **Carbohydrate:** 37.2 g; **Fiber:** 0.7 g; **Sugars:** 0.1 g; **Protein:** 3.8 g; **Potassium:** 122 mg

## 481. Cinnamon Pudding

**Preparation time:** 10 minutes
**Cooking time:** 5 hours
**Servings:** 4
**Ingredients:**

- 2 cups white rice
- 1 cup coconut sugar
- 2 cinnamon sticks
- 6 and ½ cups water
- ½ cup coconut, shredded

**Directions:**

1. In your slow cooker, mix water with the rice, sugar, cinnamon, and coconut, stir, cover, cook on High for 5 hours, discard cinnamon, divide the pudding into bowls and serve warm.

**Nutrition: Calories:** 400 kcal; **Fat:** 4 g; **Cholesterol:** 0 mg; **Sodium:** 28 mg; **Carbohydrate:** 81.2 g; **Fiber:** 2.7 g; **Sugars:** 0.8 g; **Protein:** 7.2 g; **Potassium:** 151 mg

## 482. Orange Compote

**Preparation time:** 10 minutes
**Cooking time:** 2 hours and 30 minutes
**Servings:** 4
**Ingredients:**

- ½ lb. oranges, peeled and cut into segments
- ½ lb. plums, pitted and halved
- 1 cup orange juice
- 3 tbsp. coconut sugar
- ½ cup water

**Directions:**

1. In the slow cooker, combine the oranges with the plums, orange juice, and the other ingredients, put the lid on, and cook on High for 2 hours and 30 minutes.
2. Stir, divide into bowls, and serve cold.

**Nutrition: Calories:** 130 kcal; **Fat:** 0.2 g; **Cholesterol:** 0 mg; **Sodium:** 31 mg; **Carbohydrate:** 28.4 g; **Fiber:** 1.6 g; **Sugars** 11.4 g; **Protein:** 1.8 g; **Potassium:** 240 mg

## 483. Chocolate Bars

**Preparation time:** 10 minutes
**Cooking time:** 2 hours and 30 minutes
**Servings:** 12
**Ingredients:**

- 1 cup coconut sugar
- ½ cup dark chocolate chips
- 1 egg white
- ¼ cup coconut oil, melted
- ½ tsp. vanilla extract
- 1 tsp. baking powder
- 1 and ½ cups almond meal

**Directions:**

1. In a bowl, mix the oil with sugar, vanilla extract, egg white, baking powder, and almond flour and whisk well
2. Fold in chocolate chips and stir gently.
3. Line your slow cooker with parchment paper, grease it, add cookie mix, press on the bottom, cover and cook on low for 2 hours and 30 minutes.
4. Take the cookie sheet out of the slow cooker, cut into medium bars, and serve.

**Nutrition: Calories:** 141 kcal; **Fat:** 11.8 g; **Cholesterol:** 0 mg; **Sodium:** 7 mg; **Carbohydrate:** 7.7 g; **Fiber:** 1.5 g; **Sugars:** 3.2 g; **Protein:** 3.2 g; **Potassium:** 134 mg

## 484. Lemon Zest Pudding

**Preparation time:** 10 minutes
**Cooking time:** 5 hours
**Servings:** 4
**Ingredients:**

- 1 cup pineapple juice, natural
- Cooking spray
- 1 tsp. baking powder
- 1 cup coconut flour
- 3 tbsp. avocado oil
- 3 tbsp. stevia
- ½ cup pineapple, chopped
- ½ cup lemon zest, grated
- ½ cup coconut milk
- ½ cup pecans, chopped

**Directions:**

1. Spray your slow cooker with cooking spray.
2. In a bowl, mix flour with stevia, baking powder, oil, milk, pecans, pineapple, lemon zest, and pineapple juice, stir well, pour into your slow cooker greased with cooking spray, cover, and cook on Low for 5 hours.
3. Divide into bowls and serve.

**Nutrition: Calories:** 431 kcal; **Fat:** 29.7 g; **Cholesterol:** 0 mg; **Sodium:** 8 mg; **Carbohydrate:** 47.1 g; **Fiber:** 17 g; **Sugars:** 10.9 g; **Protein:** 8.1 g; **Potassium:** 482 mg

## 485. Coconut Figs

**Preparation time:** 6 minutes
**Cooking time:** 5 minutes
**Servings:** 4
**Ingredients:**

- 2 tbsp. coconut butter
- 12 figs, halved
- ¼ cup coconut sugar
- 1 cup almonds, toasted and chopped

**Directions**:
1. Put butter in a pot, heat up over medium heat, add sugar, whisk well, also add almonds and figs, toss, cook for 5 minutes, divide into small cups and serve cold.
2. Enjoy!

**Nutrition**: **Calories**: 150 kcal; **Fat**: 4 g; **Fiber**: 5 g; **Carbs**: 7 g; **Protein**: 4 g

### 486. Lemony Banana Mix

**Preparation time**: 10 minutes
**Cooking time**: 0 minutes
**Servings**: 4
**Ingredients**:
- 4 bananas, peeled and chopped
- 5 strawberries, halved
- Juice of 2 lemons
- 4 tbsp. coconut sugar

**Directions**:
1. In a bowl, combine the bananas with the strawberries, lemon juice, and sugar, toss and serve cold.
2. Enjoy!

**Nutrition**: **Calories**: 172 kcal; **Fat**: 7 g; **Fiber**: 5 g; **Carbs**: 5 g; **Protein**: 5 g

### 487. Cocoa Banana Dessert Smoothie

**Preparation time**: 5 minutes
**Cooking time**: 0 minutes
**Servings**: 2
**Ingredients**:
- 2 medium bananas, peeled
- 2 tsp. cocoa powder
- ½ big avocado, pitted, peeled, and mashed
- ¾ cup almond milk

**Directions**:
1. In your blender, combine the bananas with the cocoa, avocado, and milk, pulse well, divide into 2 glasses and serve.
2. Enjoy!

**Nutrition**: **Calories**: 155 kcal; **Fat**: 3 g; **Fiber**: 4 g; **Carbs**: 6 g; **Protein**: 5 g

### 488. Kiwi Bars

**Preparation time**: 30 minutes
**Cooking time**: 0 minutes
**Servings**: 4
**Ingredients**:
- 1 cup olive oil
- 1 and ½ bananas, peeled and chopped
- ⅓ cup coconut sugar
- ¼ cup lemon juice
- 1 tsp. lemon zest, grated
- 3 kiwis, peeled and chopped

**Directions**:
1. In your food processor, mix bananas with kiwis, almost all the oil, sugar, lemon juice, and lemon zest, and pulse well.
2. Grease a pan with the remaining oil, pour the kiwi mix, spread, keep in the fridge for 30 minutes, slice and serve,
3. Enjoy!

**Nutrition**: **Calories**: 207 kcal; **Fat**: 3 g; **Fiber**: 3 g; **Carbs**: 4 g; **Protein**: 4 g

### 489. Black Tea Bars

**Preparation time**: 10 minutes
**Cooking time**: 35 minutes
**Servings**: 12
**Ingredients**:
- 6 tbsp. black tea powder
- 2 cups almond milk
- ½ cup low-fat butter
- 2 cups coconut sugar
- 4 eggs
- 2 tsp. vanilla extract
- ½ cup olive oil
- 3 and ½ cups whole wheat flour
- 1 tsp. baking soda
- 3 tsp. baking powder

**Directions**:
1. Put the milk in a pot, heat it up over medium heat, add tea, stir, take off the heat and cool down.
2. Add butter, sugar, eggs, vanilla, oil, flour, baking soda, and baking powder, stir well, pour into a square pan, spread, introduce in the oven, bake at 350°F for 35 minutes, cool down, slice, and serve. Enjoy!

**Nutrition**: **Calories**: 220 kcal; **Fat**: 4 g; **Fiber**: 4 g; **Carbs**: 12 g; **Protein**: 7 g

### 490. Green Pudding

**Preparation time**: 2 hours
**Cooking time**: 5 minutes
**Servings**: 6
**Ingredients**:
- 14 oz. almond milk
- 2 tbsp. green tea powder
- 14 oz. coconut cream
- 3 tbsp. coconut sugar
- 1 tsp. gelatin powder

**Directions**:
1. Put the milk in a pan, add sugar, gelatin, coconut cream, and green tea powder, stir, bring to a simmer, cook for 5 minutes, divide into cups and keep in the fridge for 2 hours before serving. Enjoy!

**Nutrition: Calories:** 170 kcal; **Fat:** 3 g; **Fiber:** 3 g; **Carbs:** 7 g; **Protein:** 4 g

## 491. Lemony Plum Cake

**Preparation time:** 1 hour and 20 minutes
**Cooking time:** 40 minutes
**Servings:** 8
**Ingredients:**
- 7 oz. whole-wheat flour
- 1 tsp. baking powder
- 1-oz. low-fat butter, soft
- 1 egg, whisked
- 5 tbsp. coconut sugar
- 3 oz. warm almond milk
- 1 and ¾ lb. plums, pitted and cut into quarters
- Zest of 1 lemon, grated
- 1-oz. almond flakes

**Directions**:
1. In a bowl, combine the flour with baking powder, butter, egg, sugar, milk, and lemon zest, stir well, transfer the dough to a lined cake pan, spread plums and almond flakes all over, introduce in the oven and bake at 350°F for 40 minutes.
2. Slice and serve cold. Enjoy

**Nutrition: Calories:** 222 kcal; **Fat:** 4 g; **Fiber:** 2 g; **Carbs:** 7 g; **Protein:** 7 g

## 492. Lentils Sweet Bars

**Preparation time:** 10 minutes
**Cooking time:** 25 minutes
**Servings:** 14
**Ingredients:**
- 1 cup lentils, cooked, drained, and rinsed
- 1 tsp. cinnamon powder
- 2 cups whole-wheat flour
- 1 tsp. baking powder
- ½ tsp. nutmeg, ground
- 1 cup low-fat butter
- 1 cup coconut sugar
- 1 egg
- 2 tsp. almond extract
- 1 cup raisins
- 2 cups coconut, unsweetened and shredded

**Directions**:
1. Put the lentils in a bowl, mash them well using a fork, add cinnamon, flour, baking powder, nutmeg, butter, sugar, egg, almond extract, raisins, and coconut, stir, spread on a lined baking sheet, introduce in the oven, bake at 350°F for 25 minutes, cut into bars and serve cold. Enjoy!

**Nutrition: Calories:** 214 kcal; **Fat:** 4 g; **Fiber:** 2 g; **Carbs:** 5 g; **Protein:** 7 g

## 493. Lentils and Dates Brownies

**Preparation time:** 10 minutes
**Cooking time:** 15 minutes
**Servings:** 8
**Ingredients:**
- 28 oz. lentils, canned, no-salt-added, rinsed and drained
- 12 dates
- 1 tbsp. coconut sugar
- 1 banana, peeled and chopped
- ½ tsp. baking soda
- 4 tbsp. almond butter
- 2 tbsp. cocoa powder

**Directions**:
1. Put lentils in your food processor, pulse, add dates, sugar, banana, baking soda, almond butter, and cocoa powder, pulse well, pour into a lined pan, spread, bake in the oven at 375°F for 15 minutes, leave the mix aside to cool down a bit, cut into medium pieces and serve.
2. Enjoy!

**Nutrition: Calories:** 202 kcal; **Fat:** 4 g; **Fiber:** 2 g; **Carbs:** 12 g; **Protein:** 6 g

## 494. Mandarin Pudding

**Preparation time:** 10 minutes
**Cooking time:** 30 minutes
**Servings:** 8
**Ingredients:**
- 1 mandarin, peeled and sliced
- Juice of 2 mandarins
- 4 oz. low-fat butter, soft
- 2 eggs, whisked
- ¾ cup coconut sugar+ 2 tbsp.
- ¾ cup whole wheat flour
- ¾ cup almonds, ground

**Directions**:
1. Grease a loaf pan with some of the butter, sprinkle 2 tbsp. sugar on the bottom, and arrange mandarin slices inside.

2. In a bowl, combine the butter with the rest of the sugar, eggs, almonds, flour, and mandarin juice and whisk using a mixer.
3. Spoon mix over mandarin slices, introduce in the oven, bake at 350°F for
4. 30 minutes, divide into bowls, and serve
5. Enjoy!

**Nutrition: Calories:** 202 kcal; **Fat:** 3 g; **Fiber:** 2 g; **Carbs:** 12 g; **Protein:** 6 g

### 495. Walnut Apple Mix

**Preparation time:** 10 minutes
**Cooking time:** 4 hours
**Servings:** 4
**Ingredients:**

- 6 big apples, roughly chopped
- Cooking spray
- ½ cup almond flour
- ½ cup walnuts, chopped
- ¼ cup coconut oil, melted
- 2 tsp. lemon juice
- 3 tbsp. stevia
- ¼ tsp. ginger, grated
- ¼ tsp. cinnamon powder

**Directions:**

1. Spray your slow cooker with cooking spray.
2. In a bowl, mix stevia with lemon juice, ginger, apples, and cinnamon, stir and pour into your slow cooker. In another bowl, mix flour with walnuts and oil, stir, pour into the slow cooker, cover, and cook on Low for 4 hours.
3. Divide into bowls and serve.

**Nutrition: Calories:** 474 kcal; **Fat:** 30.3 g; **Cholesterol:** 0 mg; **Sodium:** 9 mg; **Carbohydrate:** 58.4 g; **Fiber:** 10.7 g; **Sugars:** 35 g; **Protein:** 7.7 g; **Potassium:** 444 mg

### 496. Vanilla and Grapes Compote

**Preparation time:** 10 minutes
**Cooking time:** 2 hours
**Servings:** 4
**Ingredients:**

- 4 tbsp. coconut sugar
- 1 and ½ cups water
- 1 lb. green grapes - 1 tsp. vanilla extract

**Directions:**

1. In your slow cooker, combine the grapes with the sugar and the other ingredients, put the lid on, and cook on High for 2 hours, divide into bowls and serve.

**Nutrition: Calories:** 227 kcal; **Fat:** 1.5 g; **Cholesterol:** 0 mg; **Sodium:** 45 mg; **Carbohydrate:** 47.6 g; **Fiber:** 2.3 g; **Sugars:** 18.8 g; **Protein:** 3.6 g; **Potassium:** 271 mg

### 497. Soft Pudding

**Preparation time:** 6 minutes
**Cooking time:** 1 hour
**Servings:** 4
**Ingredients:**

- ½ cup coconut water
- 2 tsp. lime zest, grated
- 2 tbsp. green tea powder
- 1 and ½ cup avocado, pitted, peeled, and chopped
- 1 tbsp. stevia

**Directions:**

1. In your slow cooker, mix the coconut water with avocado, green tea powder, lime zest, and stevia, stir, cover, cook on Low for 1 hour, divide into bowls and serve.

**Nutrition: Calories:** 120 kcal; **Fat:** 10.7 g; **Cholesterol:** 0 mg; **Sodium:** 35 mg; **Carbohydrate:** 8.5 g; **Fiber:** 4.4 g; **Sugars:** 1.1 g; **Protein:** 1.5 g; **Potassium:** 362 mg

### 498. Ginger and Cinnamon Pudding

**Preparation time:** 10 minutes
**Cooking time:** 1 hour
**Servings:** 4
**Ingredients:**

- ½ cup pumpkin puree
- 2 tbsp. maple syrup
- 1 and ½ cup coconut milk
- ½ cup chia seeds
- ¼ tsp. ginger, grated
- ½ tsp. cinnamon powder

**Directions:**

1. In your slow cooker, mix the milk with the pumpkin puree, maple syrup, chia, cinnamon, and ginger, stir, cover, cook on High for 1 hour, divide into bowls and serve.

**Nutrition: Calories:** 366 kcal; **Fat:** 29.3 g; **Cholesterol:** 0 mg; **Sodium:** 20 mg; **Carbohydrate:** 24.8 g; **Fiber:** 11.5 g; **Sugars:** 10 g; **Protein:** 6.6 g; **Potassium:** 423 mg

### 499. Honey Compote

**Preparation time:** 10 minutes
**Cooking time:** 2 hours
**Servings:** 6
**Ingredients:**

- 64 oz. red grapefruit juice
- 1 cup honey
- ½ cup mint, chopped
- 1 cup water
- 2 grapefruits, peeled and chopped

**Directions**:
1. In your slow cooker, mix grapefruit with water, honey, mint, and grapefruit juice, stir, cover, cook on High for 2 hours, divide into bowls and serve cold.

**Nutrition: Calories:** 364 kcal; **Fat:** 0.1 g; **Cholesterol:** 0 mg; **Sodium:** 52 mg; **Carbohydrate:** 94.9 g; **Fiber:** 1.1 g; **Sugars:** 49.4 g; **Protein:** 0.7 g; **Potassium:** 124 mg

# Conclusion

Dash Diet is easy to follow, and a food guide readily available recipes for people who want to shed some weight to improve their health. It is designed to lower blood pressure and help you lose weight with no need to count calories. This cookbook has no limitations on portions of food. However, it is important to make the right choices. The dash diet follows a healthy approach. It is meant to help you enjoy a long life.

Anyone who wants to lose weight can eat with the dash diet. This diet restricts the intake of salt, fats, and oils. The dash diet is not vegetarian. However, vegetarians can still use this diet. They should avoid dairy and avoid using animal fats. Vegetarians who eat fish should avoid salt and animal fats. The dash diet is very flexible. It shows you how to make great-tasting food that you and your family can enjoy.

The main reason is to help people who have low self-esteem to improve their health and daily life. You will see benefits to your health if you follow this diet and maintain glucose metabolism and avoid obesity.

Exercise and dietary modifications can help in reducing weight and controlling blood pressure. Keeping track of your performance with exercise or physical activity can help you keep motivated for a longer period. Similarly, a dietary record is also helpful in estimating the daily intake and calories consumed per day. The Dash strategy is a new way to eat—for a living. When you slip a few days off the eating plan, don't let it keep you from reaching your health goals.

Ask yourself why you got off-track.

Get on track again. Here's how: Tell yourself why you've gone off track. Was it drinking at a party? Have you experienced tension at home or work? Find out what started your sidetrack, and then begin the Dash plan again.

**Look out for if you tried to do too much at once.**

Anyone starting a new lifestyle sometimes tries to change too much at once. Instead, one or 2 things should be changed at a time. The only way to succeed is, slowly but surely.

Break down the process into small steps.

Not only does this discourage you from having to do too much at once, but it also makes the changes easier. Break complicated objectives into smaller, easier measures, each achievable.

**Write it down.**

Keep a record of what you eat and what you do. That can help you figure out the issue. The record also allows you to ensure that each food group and physical activity are being enough every day.

You will see a lot of changes in your lifestyle. Your meals, blood pressure, and health will improve. This will help you live a better life, and you will be healthier.

The diet also has many health benefits as it helps in reducing hypertension and obesity, lowering osteoporosis, and preventing cancer. This well-balanced diet strengthens metabolism, which further helps in decomposing the fat deposits stored in the body.

**This diet is easy to follow as you get to everything but in a healthier fashion and limited quantity.**

Talking about the DASH diet outside the theory and more in practice reveals more of its efficiency as a diet. Besides excess research and experiments, the true reasons of people looking into this diet are its certain features. It gives the feeling of ease and convenience, which makes the users more comfortable with its rules and regulations.

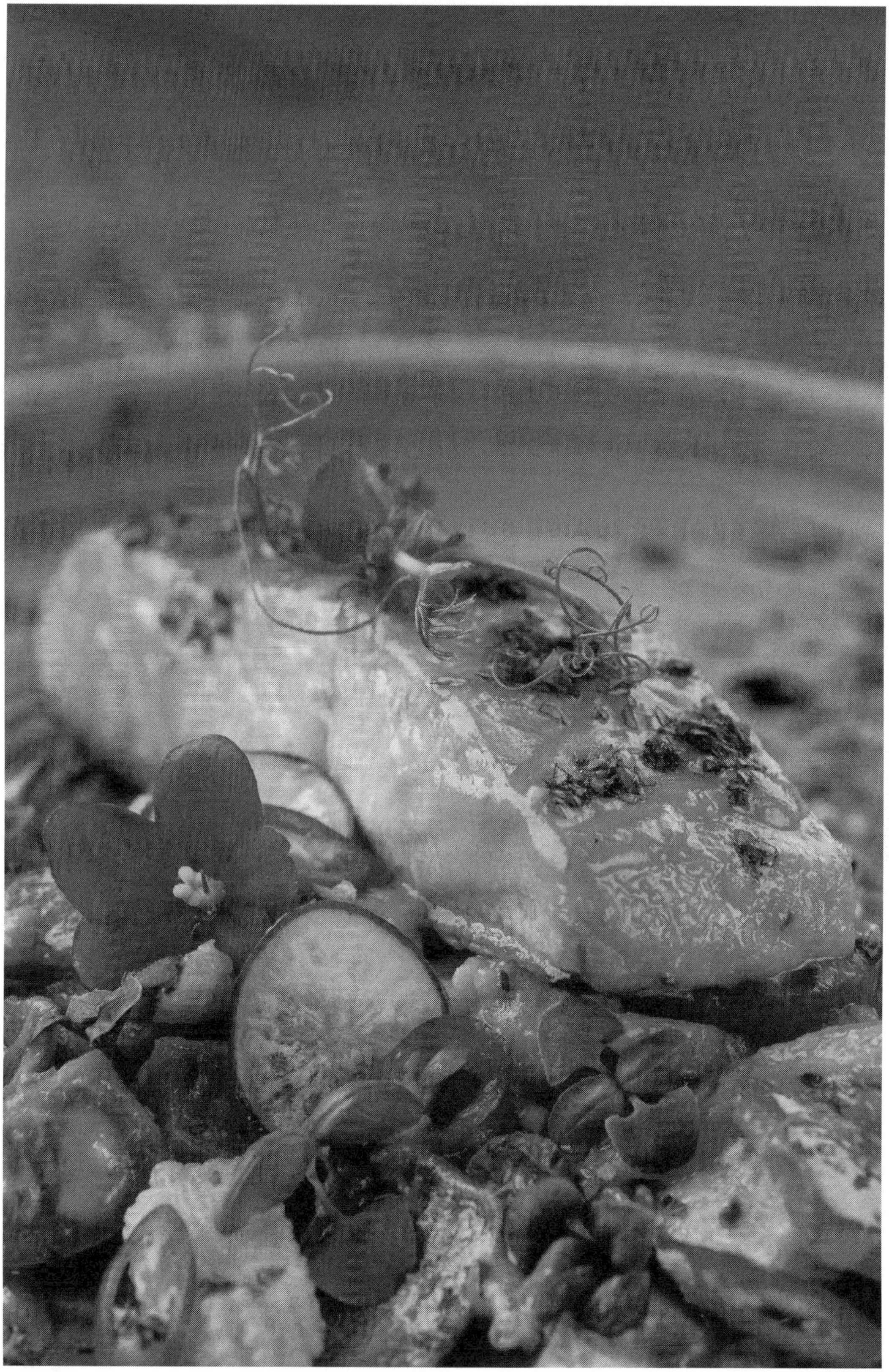

# This my Experience in a Nutshell

### How did I lower my blood pressure?

I did the following:

I followed the DASH diet very closely for 4 ½ months, lost 34 lbs and my cholesterol became normal. Continue to follow the DASH diet. I have lost a total of 44 lbs and now weigh what I weighed when I was 28.

I limited salt and sugar use and increased potassium, ate 2 daily hot meals of mostly whole grains, fresh legumes and vegetables rich in potassium and magnesium. Occasionally lean meats and fish.

I exercised an hour each day, usually in parks or at the beach with some steep trails that forced me to breathe deeply. I practiced deep breathing and meditation whenever my blood pressure tended to rise a bit. I made it a point to lower my blood pressure by 20–30 points.

I practiced staying calm in many situations.

I focused more on helping others and doing other things that brought joy into my life.

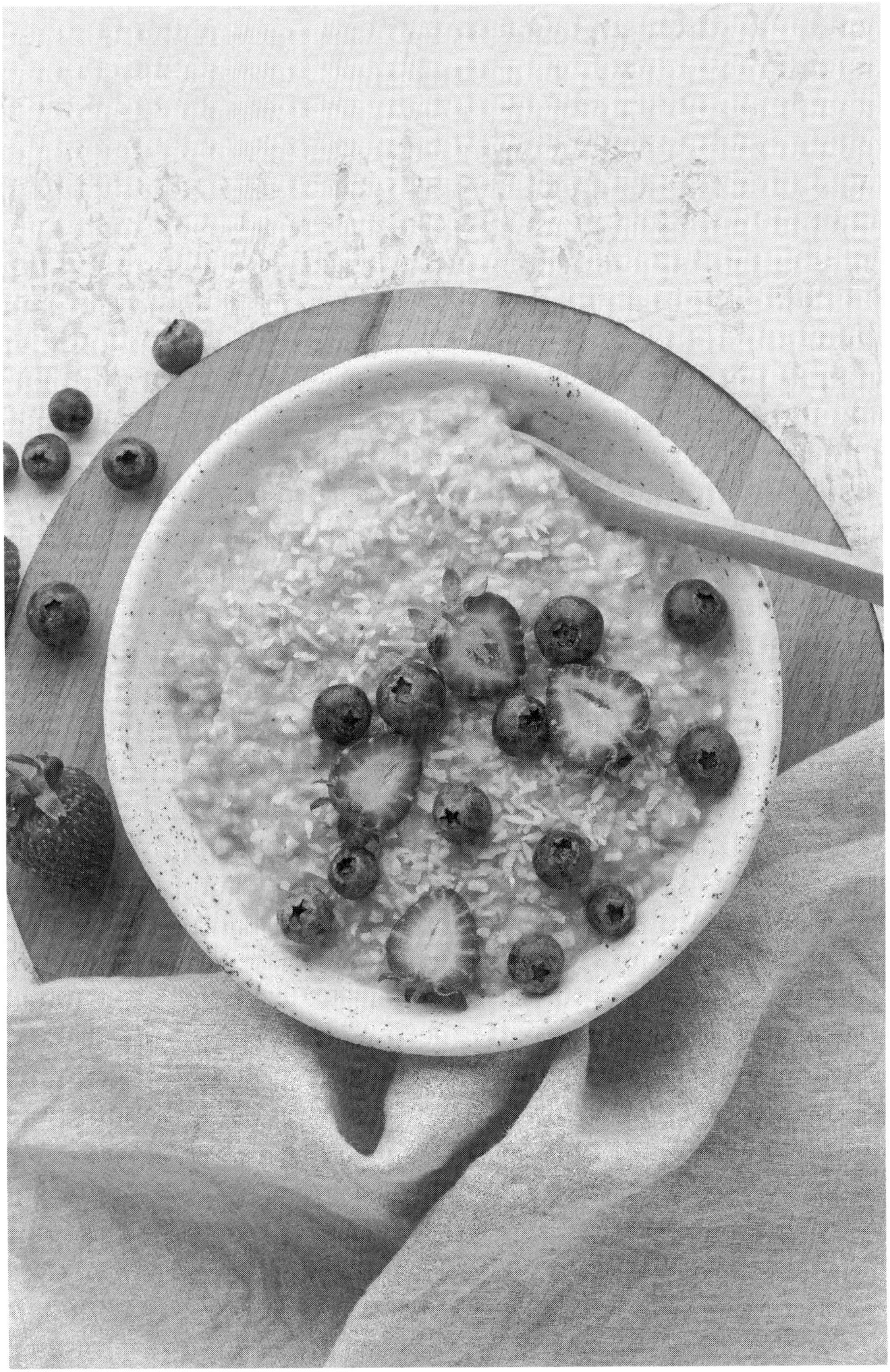

# INDEX

## A

A  136
Air-Fryer Fish Cakes ..................................... 123
Almond butter Pork Chops .............................. 89
Almond Butter-Banana Smoothie ..................... 38
Amazing Grilled Chicken and Blueberry Salad ... 88
Amazing Sesame Breadsticks ........................... 90
And-Rosemary Omelet .................................. 161
Apple Loaf .................................................. 172
Apple Oats ................................................... 47
Apple Pancakes ............................................. 30
Apple Pie Crackers ........................................ 96
Apple Quinoa Muffins .................................... 43
Apple-Apricot Brown Rice Breakfast Porridge ... 35
Apricot Chicken .......................................... 107
Aromatic Salmon with Fennel Seeds ............... 116
Artichoke and Spinach Chicken ..................... 107
Arugula Salad ............................................. 166
Arugula Salad with Figs and Walnuts ............... 54
Asian Pork tenderloin .................................. 138
Asparagus Pasta ............................................ 52
Avocado Cup with Egg ................................... 37
Avocado, Tomato, and Olives Salad ............... 166
Awesome Pasta Salad .................................... 57

## B

Bacon and Chicken Garlic Wrap ...................... 91
Bacon Bits ................................................... 44
Bagels Made Healthy .................................... 37
Baked Chicken ............................................. 99
Baked Eggplant Parmesan ............................ 153
Baked Eggs in Avocado ................................ 158
Baked Enoki and Mini Cabbage ...................... 71
Baked Smoky Broccoli and Garlic ................... 66
Baking Powder Biscuits ................................. 36
Balsamic Cabbage ....................................... 165
Balsamic Chicken and Vegetables ................... 92
Banana and Cinnamon Oatmeal ...................... 36
Banana-Peanut Butter and Greens Smoothie ..... 36
Basil Olives Mix .......................................... 166
Beef and Barley Farmers Soup ...................... 135
Beef and Vegetable Stir-Fry .......................... 134
Beef Heart ................................................. 132
Beef Pot .................................................... 133
Beef Sage Soup .......................................... 148
Beef Soup ................................................... 87
Beef Stew with Fennel and Shallots ............... 139
Beef Stroganoff .......................................... 140
Beef Veggie Pot Meal .................................. 131

Beef with Cucumber Raito ........................... 133
Beef with Mushrooms .................................. 132
Bell Pepper Soup ........................................ 146
Bistro Beef tenderloin ................................. 133
Black Bean Burgers ..................................... 154
Black Bean Stew with Cornbread .................... 77
Black Eyed Peas and Spinach Platter ............... 93
Black Tea Bars ........................................... 178
Black-Bean and Vegetable Burrito ................. 157
Black-Bean Soup ........................................ 159
Black-Eyed Peas and Greens Power Salad ...... 159
Blueberry Waffles ........................................ 30
Blueberry-Vanilla Yogurt Smoothie ................. 33
Braised Beef Shanks ................................... 132
Breakfast Banana Split .................................. 40
Breakfast Fruits Bowls .................................. 41
Breakfast Hash ............................................ 32
Broccoli and Cod Mash ................................ 115
Broccoli Salad ............................................. 58
Brown Butter Duck Breast ............................. 90
Brown Cake ............................................... 173
Brown Rice Casserole with Cottage Cheese ..... 155
Brown Sugar Cinnamon Oatmeal .................... 38
Buckwheat Crepes ........................................ 47
Buckwheat Pancakes with Vanilla Almond Milk ... 38
Buffalo Chicken Salad Wrap ......................... 101
Bulgarian Salad ............................................ 53
Butternut-Squash Macaroni and Cheese ........ 160

## C

Cabbage Borscht ........................................ 148
Cane Wrapped Around In Prosciutto ............. 131
Caramelized Fennel and Sardines with Penne ... 120
Caramelized Pork Chops and Onion ................ 95
Carrot Cake Overnight Oats ........................... 35
Carrot Muffins ............................................. 40
Cashew and Carrot Muffins .......................... 176
Cashew Lemon Fudge ................................. 173
Cauliflower and Tomato Salad ........................ 49
Cauliflower Bread Stick ................................. 91
Cauliflower Cinnamon Pudding ..................... 173
Cauliflower Mashed Potatoes ....................... 162
Cauliflower Salad with Tahini Vinaigrette ........ 55
Cauliflower-Tomato Salad ............................. 61
Cereal with Cranberry-Orange Twist ............... 37
Cheesy and Spiced Pilaf ................................ 61
Cheesy Broccoli Soup ................................. 149
Cheesy Pistachio Salad ................................. 62
Cherry Stew ............................................... 172
Chia Seeds Breakfast Mix .............................. 41

| | |
|---|---|
| Chicken Divan | 105 |
| Chicken Fiesta Salad | 56 |
| Chicken Noodle Soup | 149 |
| Chicken Salad | 58 |
| Chicken Salsa | 89 |
| Chicken Sliders | 101 |
| Chicken Thighs and Apples Mix | 108 |
| Chicken Tikka | 105 |
| Chicken Tortellini Soup | 104 |
| Chicken Tortillas | 110 |
| Chicken with Mushrooms | 98 |
| Chicken with Noodles | 103 |
| Chicken with Potatoes Olives and Sprouts | 110 |
| Chicken, Pasta and Snow Peas | 103 |
| Chicken, Tomato and Green Beans | 110 |
| Chickpea and Zucchini Salad | 53 |
| Chickpea Cauliflower Tikka Masala | 73 |
| Chili Broccoli | 165 |
| Chilled Cucumber-And-Avocado Soup with Dill | 161 |
| Chipotle Lettuce Chicken | 92 |
| Chocolate Bars | 177 |
| Chopped Tuna Salad | 120 |
| Cilantro Lime Rice | 169 |
| Cinnamon Peach Cobbler | 174 |
| Cinnamon Pudding | 177 |
| Citrus Celery Salad | 60 |
| Citrus-Glazed Salmon with Zucchini Noodles | 117 |
| Classic Chicken Soup | 145 |
| Classic Minestrone | 151 |
| Clean Chicken and Mushroom Stew | 88 |
| Clean Parsley and Chicken Breast | 86 |
| Cobb Salad | 58 |
| Cocoa Banana Dessert Smoothie | 178 |
| Coconut Cream and Plums Cake | 175 |
| Coconut Figs | 177 |
| Coconut Turkey Mix | 85 |
| Cod and Cauliflower Chowder | 119 |
| Cod Salad with Mustard | 115 |
| Cool Apple and Carrot Harmony | 93 |
| Coppin | 121 |
| Corn and Black Bean Salad | 56 |
| Crab, Zucchini and Watermelon Soup | 125 |
| Crazy Japanese Potato and Beef Croquettes | 65 |
| Creamy Apple-Avocado Smoothie | 33 |
| Creamy Avocado and Egg Salad Sandwiches | 32 |
| Creamy Broccoli Cheddar Rice | 168 |
| Creamy Cauliflower Mash | 165 |
| Creamy Chicken Fried Rice | 105 |
| Creamy Oats, Greens and Blueberry Smoothie | 36 |
| Creamy Pumpkin Pasta | 76 |
| Creamy Salmon and Asparagus Mix | 114 |
| Crispy Cashew Chicken | 104 |
| Cucumber Chicken Salad with Spicy Peanut Dressing | 55 |
| Cucumber Soup | 145 |
| Curried Pork tenderloin in Apple Cider | 140 |
| Curry Tofu Scramble | 48 |
| Curry Vegetable Noodles with Chicken | 81 |

## D
| | |
|---|---|
| Dates Brownies | 171 |
| Decent Beef and Onion Stew | 86 |
| Delicious Aloo Palak | 94 |
| Delicious Berry Pie | 174 |
| Delicious Lemon Chicken Salad | 111 |

## E
| | |
|---|---|
| Easy Greek Salad | 54 |
| Easy Pork Chops | 137 |
| Easy Shrimp and Mango | 124 |
| Easy Spaghetti Squash | 50 |
| Easy to Understand Mussels | 117 |
| Easy Veggie Muffins | 40 |
| Egg White Breakfast Mix | 42 |
| Eggplant Parmesan Stacks | 74 |
| Elegant Pumpkin Chili Dish | 88 |
| Especial Glazed Salmon | 126 |
| Everyday Vegetable Stock | 95 |
| Exuberant Sweet Potatoes | 92 |

## F
| | |
|---|---|
| Falafel Salad Bowl | 54 |
| Falling | 108 |
| Feisty Chicken Porridge | 109 |
| Feta and Spinach Pita Bake | 52 |
| Feta Beet Salad | 49 |
| Feta Cheese and Beet Salad | 61 |
| Fish Amandine | 123 |
| Fish Stew | 84 |
| Flax Banana Yogurt Muffins | 47 |
| Flounder with Tomatoes and Basil | 118 |
| French toast with Applesauce | 35 |
| Fruit Pizza | 46 |
| Fruit Shrimp Soup | 84 |

## G
| | |
|---|---|
| Garden Salad | 66 |
| Garlic Mushroom Chicken | 110 |
| Garlic Pepper Chicken | 99 |
| Garlic Pork Shoulder | 138 |
| Garlic Potato Pan | 164 |
| Garlic Shrimp Mix | 115 |
| Generous Garlic Bread Stick | 91 |
| Generous Stuffed Salmon Avocado | 126 |
| German Hot Potato Salad | 56 |
| Ginger and Cinnamon Pudding | 180 |
| Ginger and Pumpkin Pie | 176 |
| Gnocchi with Tomato Basil Sauce | 76 |
| Golden Eggplant Fries | 65 |
| Granola Parfait | 48 |
| Grapefruit Compote | 170 |
| Greek Flatbread with Spinach, Tomatoes, and Feta | 156 |

Greek Salmon with Yogurt ............................................. 114
Greek Style Salmon ....................................................... 116
Greek Yogurt Oat Pancakes ............................................. 34
Green Goddess Crab Salad with Endive ....................... 121
Green Pudding .............................................................. 178
Grilled Chicken ............................................................. 111
Grilled Chicken with Lemon and Fennel ....................... 95
Grilled Fennel-Cumin Lamb Chops ............................... 132
Grilled Flank Steak with Lime Vinaigrette ...................... 138
Grilled Mahi-Mahi with Artichoke Caponata .................. 119
Grilled Pork Fajitas ......................................................... 141
Ground Beef Soup ......................................................... 148

## H

Halibut in Parchment with Zucchini, Shallots, and Herbs .. 118
Harissa Bolognese with Vegetable Noodles ...................... 80
Hassel back Eggplant ........................................................ 78
Healthy Carrot Chips ........................................................ 87
Healthy Mediterranean Lamb Chops ................................. 90
Healthy Vegetable Fried Rice .......................................... 160
Hearty Breakfast Casserole ............................................... 33
Hearty Lemon and Pepper Chicken .................................. 87
Hearty Lentil Soup .......................................................... 158
Hearty Pork Belly Casserole .............................................. 96
Herb-Roasted Vegetables .................................................. 62
Honey Compote ............................................................. 180
Honey Crusted Chicken .................................................. 100
Honey Spiced Cajun Chicken ......................................... 106
Hot Brussels sprouts ....................................................... 165
Hot Chicken Wings ........................................................ 104
Humble Mushroom Rice .................................................. 94

## I

Instant Banana Oatmeal ................................................... 38
Instant Pot Applesauce .................................................. 171
Italian Chicken .............................................................. 106
Italian Stuffed Portobello Mushroom Burgers .................. 75

## J

Jack-o-Lantern Pancakes .................................................. 46
Jerk Beef and Plantain Kabobs ....................................... 133

## K

Kale, Quinoa, and Avocado Salad .................................... 58
Kiwi Bars ....................................................................... 178

## L

Lamb Chops with Kale .................................................. 134
Lamb Chops with Rosemary .......................................... 131
Leek, Potato, and Carrot Soup ....................................... 146
Lemon and Garlic Scallops ............................................ 125
Lemon Asparagus ........................................................... 164
Lemon Bananas .............................................................. 175
Lemon Custard .............................................................. 176
Lemon Garlic Shrimp .................................................... 122
Lemon Pepper and Salmon ............................................ 128
Lemon Zest Pudding ..................................................... 177

Lemon-Parsley Chicken Breast ....................................... 106
Lemony Banana Mix ...................................................... 178
Lemony Braised Beef Roast ............................................ 132
Lemony Plum Cake ........................................................ 179
Lemony Salmon and Pomegranate Mix .......................... 113
Lentil Avocado Tacos ....................................................... 75
Lentil Quinoa Gratin with Butternut Squash ................. 155
Lentils and Dates Brownies ............................................ 179
Lentils Sweet Bars .......................................................... 179
Lime Carrots ................................................................. 164
Lime Shrimp and Kale ..................................................... 85
Loaded Baked Sweet Potatoes ....................................... 159
Loaded Tofu Burrito with Black Beans .......................... 157

## M

Mac and Chokes .............................................................. 93
Mackerel and Orange Medley ....................................... 127
Mandarin Almond Pudding ........................................... 172
Mandarin Pudding ........................................................ 179
Maple Syrup Poached Pears ........................................... 175
Mediterranean Lentil Soup ............................................ 150
Mediterranean Potato Salad ............................................. 55
Mediterranean Shrimp Salad ........................................... 63
Mediterranean Toast ........................................................ 38
Mediterranean Turkey Breast .......................................... 98
Melon-Mozzarella Salad ................................................... 60
Mexican Bean Salad ........................................................ 59
Mexican Tortilla Soup ................................................... 149
Mexican-Style Potato Casserole ...................................... 77
Mint Avocado Chilled Soup .......................................... 151
Monkfish with Sautéed Leeks, Fennel, and Tomatoes .... 120
Mushroom Florentine ..................................................... 78
Mushroom Risotto with Peas ........................................ 156
Mushroom Shallot Frittata .............................................. 46
Mushrooms and Cheese Omelet ..................................... 42
Mushrooms and Turkey Breakfast ................................... 42
Mussels and Chickpea Soup ............................................ 84
Mustard Chicken tenders ................................................ 99

## N

New York Strip Steak with Mushroom Sauce ................ 141
No-Bake Breakfast Granola Bars ...................................... 46
No-Cook Overnight Oats ................................................ 37
No-Mayo Potato Salad .................................................. 168

## O

Oatmeal Banana Pancakes with Walnuts ......................... 36
Oaxacan Chicken .......................................................... 102
Olive Capers Chicken ..................................................... 98
Orange and Chili Garlic Sauce ........................................ 94
Orange Compote ........................................................... 177
Oregano Chicken Thighs .............................................. 109
Oven-Fried Chicken Breasts ......................................... 107
Oven-Roasted Broccoli Salad .......................................... 60
Oven-Roasted Vegetable Salad ........................................ 61

## P

| | |
|---|---|
| Paella with Chicken, Leeks, and Tarragon | 100 |
| Pan-Fried Salmon with Salad | 79 |
| Paprika Brussels sprouts | 165 |
| Parmesan and Chicken Spaghetti Squash | 107 |
| Parmesan Baked Chicken | 64 |
| Parmesan Barley Risotto | 62 |
| Parmesan Endives | 163 |
| Parsley Cod Mix | 85 |
| Parsley Seafood Cocktail | 83 |
| Pasta with Tomatoes and Peas | 160 |
| Peanut Butter and Banana Breakfast Smoothie | 45 |
| Peanut Vegetable Pad Thai | 72 |
| Pear Salad with Roquefort Cheese | 59 |
| Pecans Cake | 175 |
| Penne with Tahini Sauce | 51 |
| Pesto Chicken Breasts with Summer Squash | 109 |
| Pesto Omelet | 42 |
| Pesto Shrimp Pasta | 123 |
| Pilaf with Cream Cheese | 50 |
| Pineapple Oatmeal | 40 |
| Plum Cake | 171 |
| Pork and Celery Mix | 136 |
| Pork and Dates Sauce | 136 |
| Pork and Roasted Tomatoes Mix | 137 |
| Pork Chops with Black Currant Jam | 141 |
| Pork Meatballs | 130 |
| Pork Medallion with Herbes de Provence | 141 |
| Pork Medallions with 5 Spice Powder | 140 |
| Pork Roast and Cranberry Roast | 137 |
| Pork tenderloin with Apples and Balsamic Vinegar | 142 |
| Pork tenderloin with Fennel Sauce | 142 |
| Pork with Apples and Blue Cheese | 142 |
| Portobello-Mushroom Cheeseburgers | 161 |
| Provencal Artichoke Salad | 53 |
| Provence Pork Medallions | 137 |
| Pumpkin and Black Beans Chicken | 108 |
| Pumpkin Cookies | 41 |
| Pumpkin Muffins | 39 |
| Pumpkin Pudding | 173 |

## Q

| | |
|---|---|
| Quinoa and Pistachio Salad | 55 |
| Quinoa Bowls | 43 |
| Quinoa-Stuffed Peppers | 156 |

## R

| | |
|---|---|
| Radish and Olives Salad | 166 |
| Red Beans and Rice | 158 |
| Red Velvet Pancakes with Cream Cheese Topping | 45 |
| Resilient Chocolate Cream | 174 |
| Rhubarb Dip | 176 |
| Rhubarb Stew | 173 |
| Rice Pudding | 172 |
| Rich Potato Soup | 150 |
| Roast and Mushrooms | 136 |
| Roasted Broccoli Sweet Potatoes and Bean Sprouts | 70 |
| Roasted Brussels sprouts and Broccoli | 70 |
| Roasted Button Mushrooms and Squash | 69 |
| Roasted Cauliflower and Lima Beans | 67 |
| Roasted Chicken Thighs | 98 |
| Roasted Eggplant Salad | 51 |
| Roasted Kale and Bok Choy Extra | 68 |
| Roasted Lemon Swordfish | 126 |
| Roasted Mini Cabbage and Sweet Potato | 71 |
| Roasted Napa Cabbage and Turnips Extra | 68 |
| Roasted Soy Beans and Winter Squash | 68 |
| Roasted Sweet Potato and Red Beets | 70 |
| Roasted Tomatoes Rutabaga and Kohlrabi Main | 69 |
| Roasted Triple Mushrooms | 71 |
| Roasted Turnips | 167 |
| Roasted Vegetable Enchiladas | 74 |
| Roasted Veggies | 51 |
| Rose Lentils Ice Cream | 171 |
| Rosemary Roasted Chicken | 107 |
| Rustic Beef and Barley Soup | 139 |

## S

| | |
|---|---|
| Saffron Shrimp | 124 |
| Salmon and Beans Mix | 112 |
| Salmon and Beets Mix | 114 |
| Salmon and Brussels sprouts | 114 |
| Salmon and Cabbage Mix | 86 |
| Salmon and Cucumber Platter | 129 |
| Salmon and Egg Scramble | 39 |
| Salmon and Potatoes Mix | 115 |
| Salmon and Veggie Mix | 113 |
| Salmon Cakes with Bell Pepper plus Lemon Yogurt | 118 |
| Salmon with Peas and Parsley Dressing | 127 |
| Salsa Chicken Chili | 99 |
| Sardine Bruschetta with Fennel and Lemon Cream | 119 |
| Sausage Kale Soup with Mushrooms | 150 |
| Savory Yogurt Bowls | 31 |
| Scallions Omelet | 48 |
| Scrambled Egg and Veggie Breakfast Quesadillas | 34 |
| Seafood and Avocado Salad | 62 |
| Seafood Corn Chowder | 148 |
| Seared Scallops with Blood Orange Glaze | 122 |
| Seven-Layer Salad | 57 |
| Shrimp and Broccoli Soup | 85 |
| Shrimp and Onion Ginger Dressing | 83 |
| Shrimp and Orzo | 125 |
| Shrimp Fra Diavolo | 122 |
| Shrimp Quesadillas | 117 |
| Sichuan Style Baked Chioggia Beets and Broccoli Florets | 71 |
| Simple Beef Brisket and Tomato Soup | 138 |
| Simple Cheese and Broccoli Omelets | 32 |
| Simple Mediterranean Chicken | 97 |
| Simple One-Pot Mussels | 128 |
| Simple Pork and Capers | 135 |

Simple Roasted Broccoli and Cauliflower .......................... 67
Simple Roasted Kale Artichoke Heart and Choy Sum Extra 68
Simple Sautéed Garlic and Parsley Scallops ....................... 128
Simple Veal Chops ............................................................. 135
Smashed Brussels sprouts ................................................. 168
Smoked Salmon and Green Beans .................................... 124
Soft Pudding ...................................................................... 180
Southern Potato Salad ........................................................ 57
Southwest Tofu Scramble ................................................. 157
Southwestern Bean-And-Pepper Salad ............................. 162
Southwestern Chicken and Pasta ..................................... 100
South-Western Pork Chops ................................................ 89
Southwestern Posole ......................................................... 147
Spanish Mussels ................................................................ 126
Spanish rice ...................................................................... 167
Spelled Salad ...................................................................... 52
Spicy Beef Curry ............................................................... 143
Spicy Beef Kebabs ............................................................ 143
Spicy Chicken with Minty Couscous ................................ 103
Spicy Chili Salmon ........................................................... 128
Spicy Ginger Sea bass ...................................................... 116
Spicy Tofu Burrito Bowls with Cilantro Avocado Sauce ...... 73
Spinach and Endives Salad ............................................... 166
Spinach Muffins .................................................................. 41
Spinach, Egg, and Cheese Breakfast Quesadillas ............... 31
Spinach, Mushroom, and Feta Cheese Scramble ................ 45
Sporty Baby Carrots ........................................................... 66
Spring Salmon Mix ........................................................... 124
Spring Vegetable Soup ..................................................... 147
Squash and Turmeric Soup ............................................... 145
Squid and Shrimp Salad ..................................................... 82
Steel Cut Oat Blueberry Pancakes ...................................... 44
Steel-Cut Oatmeal with Plums and Pear ............................ 35
Strawberry Sandwich .......................................................... 43
Strawberry Spinach Salad ................................................... 59
Strawberry, Orange, and Beet Smoothie ............................ 33
Stuffed Breakfast Peppers ................................................... 34
Stuffed Chicken Breasts .................................................... 100
Summer Barley Pilaf with Yogurt Dill Sauce .................... 154
Summer Jam ..................................................................... 176
Sun-dried Tomato Salad ..................................................... 60
Super-Simple Granola ......................................................... 31
Sweet and Sour Cabbage and Apples ................................. 94
Sweet Berries Pancake ........................................................ 39
Sweet Potato Cakes with Classic Guacamole .................... 73
Sweet Potato Rice with Spicy Peanut Sauce .................... 153
Sweet Potato Toast Three Ways ......................................... 34
Sweet Potatoes and Apples ............................................... 167
Sweet Potato-Turkey Meatloaf .......................................... 102

**T**

Tahini Spinach .................................................................... 50
Tantalizing Mushroom Gravy ............................................. 94
Tasty Roasted Broccoli ....................................................... 88
Teriyaki Chicken Wings .................................................... 104
Thai Chicken Thighs ........................................................ 108
Thai Roasted Spicy Black Beans and Choy Sum ................ 67
The Almond Breaded Chicken Goodness .......................... 89
The OG Tuna Sandwich ................................................... 117
The Surprising No ............................................................ 134
The Ultimate Faux-Tisserie Chicken ................................ 109
The Vegan Lovers Refried Beans ....................................... 92
Tilapia Broccoli Platter ..................................................... 127
Tofu and Green Bean Stir-Fry ............................................ 72
Tomato and Olive Orecchiette with Basil Pesto ................. 75
Tuna Salad .......................................................................... 57
Turkey Meatball and Ditalini Soup .................................. 151
Turkey Sausage and Mushroom Strata ............................... 44

**V**

Vanilla and Grapes Compote ............................................ 180
Vanilla Poached Strawberries ........................................... 174
Vegetable Noodles with Bolognese .................................... 80
Vegetable Pasta ................................................................... 79
Vegetable Red Curry ........................................................ 154
Vegetarian Kebabs .............................................................. 78
Vegetarian Lasagna ............................................................. 79
Veggie Quiche Muffins ....................................................... 44
Veggie Scramble ................................................................. 41
Veggie Variety .................................................................... 79
Very Berry Muesli ............................................................... 43
Very Wild Mushroom Pilaf ................................................. 65

**W**

Walnut Apple Mix ............................................................ 180
Walnut Encrusted Salmon ................................................ 125
Walnuts and Asparagus Delight ......................................... 87
White Beans Stew ............................................................... 78
White Beans with Spinach and Pan-Roasted Tomatoes ..... 159
White Chicken Chili ......................................................... 101
Whole Grain Pancakes ........................................................ 47

**Y**

Yogurt Shrimps ................................................................ 116
Yucatan Soup ................................................................... 146

**Z**

Zesty Taco Soup ............................................................... 147
Zucchini Beef Sauté with Coriander Greens ...................... 86
Zucchini Pancakes .............................................................. 39
Zucchini Pasta .................................................................... 51
Zucchini Tomato Bake ..................................................... 168

Made in the USA
Columbia, SC
09 May 2022